THE SOCIOLOGY OF EMERGING ADULTHOOD

Studying Youth in the Context of Public Issues

First Edition

Edited by Patricia S. Herzog
University of Arkansas–Fayetteville

Bassim Hamadeh, CEO and Publisher
Kassie Graves, Director of Acquisitions
Jamie Giganti, Senior Managing Editor
Miguel Macias, Senior Graphic Designer
Angela Schultz, Senior Field Acquisitions Editor
Michelle Piehl, Project Editor
Alexa Lucido, Licensing Coordinator
Chelsey Schmid, Associate Editor

Copyright © 2017 by Cognella, Inc. All rights reserved. No part of this publication may be reprinted, reproduced, transmitted, or utilized in any form or by any electronic, mechanical, or other means, now known or hereafter invented, including photocopying, microfilming, and recording, or in any information retrieval system without the written permission of Cognella, Inc.

Trademark Notice: Product or corporate names may be trademarks or registered trademarks, and are used only for identification and explanation without intent to infringe.

Cover image copyright © 2015 iStockphoto LP/Maxiphoto.

Printed in the United States of America

ISBN: 978-1-5165-0359-9 (pbk) / 978-1-5165-0360-5 (br)

CONTENTS

Introduction: The Sociology of Emerging Adulthood — 1
- Overview & Purpose — 1
- Chapter Overview — 2
- References — 3

Chapter 1: The Life Course & Emerging Adulthood — 5
- A New Life Stage—Macro-Structural Changes & The Life Course — 6
- Reading 1.1: Emerging Adulthood: Learning and Development During the First Stage of Adulthood — 9
  By Jennifer L. Tanner, Jeffrey J. Arnett, and Julie A. Leis
- Coming of Age?—Importance of Identity in Subjectively Evaluating Adulthood — 14
- Reading 1.2: Coming of Age in America: The Transition to Adulthood in the Twenty-First Century — 15
  By Mary C. Waters, Patrick J. Carr and Maria J. Kefalas
- Disordered Adulthood—Status Markers, Adulthood Roles, and Sequences in transitioning to Adulthood — 24
- Reading 1.3: Becoming Adult: Meanings and Markers for Young Americans — 27
  By Richard A. Settersten
- Contestable Adulthood—All That Matters is Perception? — 34

Pathways to Adulthood—It Ain't All a Matter of Choice 34

Reading 1.4: Six Paths to Adulthood: Fast Starters, Parents without Careers, Educated Partners, Educated Singles, Working Singles, and Slow Starters 37
By Wayne D. Osgood, Gretchen Ruth, Jacquelynne S. Eccles, Janis E. Jacobs, and Bonnie L. Barber

References 46

Chapter 2: Social Changes & Rising Complexities 49

Generational Changes & Social Differentiation 50

Reading 2.1: Families and the Generations 51
By Glen H. Elder and Rand D. Conger

De-Standardized Life Course 57

Diversity, Complexity, and Multiple Pathways 58

The Age of Insecurity 59

Reading 2.2: One Nation Under Worry 61
By Marianne Cooper

The Life Course Patterns & Consequences 71

Adulthood Markers Still Matter 72

Reading 2.3: Subjective Age Identity and the Transition to Adulthood: Demographic Markers and Personal Attributes 75
By Michael J. Shanahan, Erik Porfeli, Jeylan T. Mortimer, and Lance D. Erickson

References 85

Chapter 3: Inequalities & Invisible Identities 93

Middle-Class Squeeze 93

Reading 3.1: A Vulnerable Middle Class: Bankruptcy and Class Status 95
By Elizabeth Warren and Deborah Thorne

Struggling for Success 110

Reading 3.2: Introduction: Why Focus on the Transition to Adulthood for Vulnerable Populations? 111
By D. Wayne Osgood, E. Michael Foster, Constance Flanagan, and Gretchen R. Ruth

Bifurcating Inequalities & Cumulative Disadvantages 116

Social Classes 117

Reading 3.3: Social Classes and the Struggle for Power 119
By David Swartz

"Invisible" Identities 122

Reading 3.4: Class Differences in Parents' Information and Intervention in the Lives of Young Adults 123
By Annette Lareau

References 132

Chapter 4: Delinquency & Criminal Activities 137

Emerging Adults & Crime 137

Reading 4.1: Emerging Adulthood & Crime 139
By Christopher Salvatore

Disadvantage & Delinquency 146

Predictors of Delinquent Activities 146

Desistance in Adulthood Transitions 147

Persistence of Delinquency 147

Reading 4.2: Young Adults Reentering the Community from the Criminal Justice System 149
By Christopher Uggen and Sara Wakefield

References 160

Chapter 5: Schooling & Higher Education 163

Transition To College 165

Education as Cultural & Relational Capital 165

College Pathways	168
Degrees, Debts, and Disillusions	169
Transitions Out of College	171
Reading 5.1: College and Emerging Adults	173
By Richard Arum and Josipa Roksa	
Reading 5.2: A Way Forward	187
By Richard Arum and Josipa Roksa	
Changes to Higher Education	192
References	192

Chapter 6: Finding Work & Establishing Careers — 197

From College To Careers	197
Disgruntled Employers	198
Generational Values in the Workplace	199
Reading 6.1: Millennials and the World of Work: An Organization and Management Perspective	201
By Andrea Hershatter and Molly Epstein	
References	221
Labor Market Realities	225
Reading 6.2: Low-Skilled Jobs: The Reality Behind the Popular Perceptions	227
By Nan L. Maxwell	
References	241

Chapter 7: Family Formations & Romantic Partnerships — 245

Men, Women, Babies	245
Marital Discords	246

Reading 7.1: What Marriage Means	249
By Katherine Edin, Maria J. Kefalas, and Frank Furstenberg	
Boomerangs & Accordions	255
High-Speed Families	256
References	258

Chapter 8: Connective Friendships & Supportive Communities — 263

Connectivity	263
Belonging	265
Reading 8.1: Why Do They Behave Like That/Fitting In, Standing Out, and Keeping Up	267
By Murray Milner	
Community	279
Contact	281
References	282

Chapter 9: Faith, Meaning-Making, & Religion — 287

Private Faith, Public Worship	287
Reading 9.1: Spiritual Well-Being, Spiritual Intelligence, and Healthy Workplace Policy	289
By Michael R. Leveson, Carolyn M. Aldwin, and Heidi Igarashi	
The Meaning-Making Crisis	293
Religion & Civic Life	296
References	297

Chapter 10: Civic Engagement & Collective Voices — 303

Generation Me or Generation We?	303
A Nation of Individuals	304

Reading 10.1: Individualism	305
By Robert N. Bellah, Richard Madsen, William M. Sullivan, Ann Swidler, and Steven M. Tipton	
Taking Collective Actions	311
Gaining Civic Experiences	312
References	313

Conclusion: Social Changes & Pathways to Adulthood — 317

Troubling Pasts	317
Complex Paths	318
Optimistic Potentials	318

Acknowledgments — 321

Glossary — 325

INTRODUCTION

The Sociology of Emerging Adulthood

OVERVIEW & PURPOSE

This is a book about the sociology of emerging adulthood. Now, you may be wondering what exactly emerging adulthood is. In Chapter 1, we will start to answer that question, beginning with the social changes that led to this new life stage. Next we will look at the coining of the term and its meaning and relevance today. We will also cover what it means to study emerging adulthood from a *sociological approach*, as compared to the *psychological approach* that has tended to be more prevalent in academic studies of emerging adulthood thus far. There is a great deal to know about emerging adulthood sociologically, and this book is the first of its kind in collecting and synthesizing sociological research in this burgeoning area of study.

Since this is a book on the sociology of emerging adulthood, this is likely a book on the sociology of *you*. That is, if you are between the ages of 18 and 35, you are an emerging adult, or you were recently one. Academics define *emerging adulthood* as the life stage that coincides with the third decade of life, the 20s. And some even argue that emerging adulthood should be seen in modern times as extending into the fourth decade, until about 35 years old. On the other side of the age bracket, emerging adulthood is likely to begin a bit before the onset of the 20s, typically closer to high school graduation. What this means, then, is that studying the sociology of emerging adulthood

1

allows you a chance to apply the *sociological imagination* (Mills 2000) to better understand your personal experiences within broader social contexts.

Drawing on an interdisciplinary field, this anthology assembles a diverse range of scholarship to help you understand the research out there on emerging adults. In practical terms, this simply means that not all the readings included or references cited in this text are written by sociologists. With that said, all of the works cited will help us carry out a quality sociological analysis of the *life course*, and especially the relatively newly acknowledged life stage of emerging adulthood.

Even though this text focuses on emerging adulthood, not every one of the studies summarized is specifically about emerging adults. Some are about youth, adolescents. Others are about the life course generally. Still others are about general, structural, and cultural patterns occurring in the contexts surrounding emerging adults. These studies are included because of their direct focus on the life course, youth, or emerging adulthood *or* because of the importance of their findings for understanding emerging adults within social contexts.

Since we are going to be talking a good deal about social contexts and processes, we also note that social science is itself in an evolving *social process*. Over time, diverse voices refine, debunk, discover, rearticulate, and study the ideas that make up social science's body of knowledge. Sometimes we social scientists get it right, and sometimes we get it wrong. Research lets us learn from each other in an ongoing process.

For students coming into this continuously evolving set of discussions, it can be difficult to know how to understand a single study when it is isolated from the context of the ongoing discussions, debates, and refinements that surround it. To help address this challenge, our text brings together numerous findings that provide color and pattern to the broader tapestry of emerging adults in social context. Like any good piece of scholarly research, it is a work in progress, and this is how it looks for now.

CHAPTER OVERVIEW

Chapter 1 focuses on emerging adulthood as a new life stage, situating it within the macro-structural changes that occurred in recent decades to create it. It reviews the importance of the identity construction and subjective experience of oneself as an adult. Also summarized are the disordered processes involved in the timing and sequencing of adulthood roles, and yet their persistence in mattering for subjective adulthood.

Chapter 2 takes a broader, historical perspective on the social changes leading to marked generational shifts via social differentiation processes. The result of these changes was the de-standardization in the pathways to adulthood due to increasing diversity and complexity in social life and rising economic insecurity. The ongoing importance of the life course in shaping long-term consequences is reviewed, as is the importance of adulthood markers.

In Chapter 3, the focus shifts to social inequalities—first through the lens of middle-class squeeze, then through the lens of working class and poor who are struggling for success. Trends over time are reviewed regarding bifurcating social inequalities and cumulative disadvantages, all of which bundle into social classes. Social class dynamics often pattern lives unequally, reproduced through invisible cultural knowledge about how to navigate to adulthood.

Delinquency and criminal activity in emerging adulthood are reviewed in Chapter 4, also focusing on the role of cumulative disadvantage and other predictors of delinquent activities. Desistance and persistence in delinquency during transitions to adulthood are also summarized, showing how emerging adults are further patterned by their legal experiences.

Chapter 5 reviews findings on schooling and higher education, especially pathways into, through, and out of college. Inequalities pattern multiple layers of pathways at each entry and exit point, with marked sorting processes occurring in the pursuit of education. Also reviewed are the cultural and relational capitals of higher education, and their unequal attainment.

In Chapter 6, findings on work and careers are summarized, focusing on moving from college to careers and the labor market realities of struggling to establish viable career trajectories. Also reviewed are voices of employers, including reflections on generational conflicts over changing values, and how those values are shaped by social changes.

Family formation and romantic partnerships are the topic of Chapter 7. Findings are reviewed to situate current trends within their historical context, showing how some of what gets perceived as the preferences of young people are actually responses to prior generations.

Chapter 8 reviews findings on emerging adult friendships, community, and social support. Multiple dimensions of connectivity are reviewed: relational networks, communities of physical proximity or of affinity, belonging, face-to-face contact, and technology-mediated connection.

Chapter 9 summarizes findings on emerging adult faith, religiosity, and meaning-making. Cultural trends in individualist versus collectivist orientations are also summarized, and the role of religion in civic life is explored.

The final chapter, Chapter 10, reviews emerging adult trends in voluntary participation and civic engagement in charitable and political causes, focusing on generational orientations, actions, and experiences.

REFERENCES

Mills, C. Wright. 2000. *The Sociological Imagination.* Oxford University Press.

CHAPTER 1

The Life Course & Emerging Adulthood

This chapter describes the life stage of emerging adulthood, summarizes the macro-structural changes leading to it, highlights the importance of identity and social roles in demarcating adulthood, and contests the notion that all that matters in becoming adults is perceiving oneself to be an adult. To set the intensity of the rapid changes in historical context, two emerging adult scholars state: "There was a time not so long ago when a popular high school graduation gift was a suitcase" (Settersten & Ray 2010, ix), but:

> Parents today play much larger roles in the lives of their young children than ever before. One-half of young adults between eighteen and twenty-five say they see their parents daily, and nearly three-quarters say they see their parents at least once a week. Nearly two-thirds live within an hour of their parents. If they do not see one another, they talk on the phone regularly; nearly eight in ten young adults under age twenty-five talk with their parents by phone daily (p. 120).

Why are parents so involved in the lives of their children today? Emerging adults rely on parents for longer into the life course in order to have help in navigating elongated and complex adult transitions resulting from numerous macro-structural changes.

A NEW LIFE STAGE—MACRO-STRUCTURAL CHANGES & THE LIFE COURSE

Beginning around the 1990s, scholars began to recognize that major social changes over the previous several decades were resulting in marked differences between younger generations and prior generations. In some cases, younger generations were heralded as ushering in positive changes, receiving labels such as "the ambitious generation" (Schneider & Stevenson 2000). However, more often than not younger generations were viewed as lazier or more self-centered, resulting in negative labels and views of younger generations (e.g., Trzesniewski & Donnellan 2014). At a minimum, younger generations were often seen as having a new set of values that placed more emphasis on leisure activities and flexibility, as opposed to the values of duty or loyalty (e.g., Twenge et al. 2010). These are examples of a generational perspective on change.

An important shift began to happen in scholarly understandings of social changes in the early 2000s, primarily with the aid of Jeffrey Arnett, a psychologist acutely attuned to the role of social changes and cultural norms in the lives of young people. Arnett is credited with coining the term *emerging adulthood* (1994, 1997, 2000, 2001, 2003, 2007, 2014, 2015). In so doing, he aided progress in the interdisciplinary study of young people in two important ways. One was to shift the center of the discussion from a focus on generational qualities to instead focus on the development of a new life stage. The other was to coalesce the disparate studies on young people into a singular term—emerging adulthood—which had resonance with people studying this phenomenon and helped to unify efforts to understand this relatively new life stage.

Arnett summarized the social changes leading to this life stage in a presidential address to the Society for the Study of Emerging Adulthood (Arnett 2014, 156–57):

> Thinking about them in historical context, and comparing them to young people of the same age 40 or 50 years previously, it seemed to me that the period from age 18 to 25 had changed so much in how it was experienced that the old developmental model of adolescence, then young adulthood, and then middle adulthood did not fit any more. Longer and more widespread education, the Sexual Revolution, broader opportunities for women, and later ages of entering marriage and parenthood—all of this combined to make the age period from 18 to 25 different than it had ever been before (Arnett 2014). I concluded that what I was really witnessing was the birth of a new life stage.

What Arnett and others (Anon 2005; Bynner 2005; Côté 2009; Hartmann & Swartz 2006) helped identify is that young people were increasingly taking a longer path to adulthood. The extended duration required to launch into *adulthood roles* meant that young people spent years, even a decade or more, in between adolescence and young adulthood (Arnett 2015). They were not yet young adults, having not experienced most or any of the adulthood roles that characterized people of their age in times past. But they were also no longer adolescents. Somewhere in between these two previously identified stages are *emerging adults*, individuals who were no longer as dependent on their parents as they were when they were teenagers, and who were in varying ways "trying on" the adulthood patterns they would more firmly settle into later on in their 30s. Arnett (2000) describes this as a more "volitional" stage of life, when young people have more choices but also remain in an ongoing state of identity crisis (Erikson 1968).

The first reading included in this chapter is from Tanner, Arnett, and Leis (2009), which describes the developmental process that characterizes the life stage of emerging adulthood and describes social changes leading to elongated adult transitions.

READING 1.1

Emerging Adulthood: Learning and Development During the First Stage of Adulthood

By Jennifer L. Tanner, Jeffrey J. Arnett, and Julie A. Leis

Theory of Emerging Adulthood: Ages 18–29

The theory of emerging adulthood was proposed by Arnett (2000, 2004, 2006) to identify a new and distinct period of the life course that came to define the experiences of 18- to 29-year-olds in industrialized societies over the past half-century. Prior to the 1950s, few people obtained higher education, and most young men became employed by the end of their teens, if not sooner. In 1950, only 25% of Americans obtained any higher education, and nearly all of them were young men (Arnett & Taber, 1994). Most young women, as well as many young men, remained in their parents' household until they married in their late teens or very early twenties. The median marriage age in the United States as recently as 1960 was just 20.3 for women and 22.8 for men (Arnett, 2000). The entry to parenthood came about a year later, on average. Thus, most young people went directly from adolescence to a settled young adulthood by their early twenties.

Over the past half century, the changes related to the age period from the late teens through the twenties have been dramatic. Participation in higher education has risen steeply,

Jennifer L. Tanner, Jeffrey J. Arnett, and Julie A. Leis, "Emerging Adulthood: Learning and Development During the First Stage of Adulthood," Handbook of Research on Adult Learning & Development, ed. M. Cecil Smith and Nancy Defrates-Densch, pp. 35-38. Copyright © 2009 by Taylor & Francis Group. Reprinted with permission.

especially among young women. Now over 60% of young persons enter higher education the year after graduating from high school, and among undergraduates in the United States, 57% are women (National Center for Education Statistics, 2005). The median age of first marriage has risen steeply as well, to its current record-high of 26.0 among women and 27.5 among men, with a corresponding rise in the median age of entering parenthood (U.S. Bureau of the Census, 2007). Furthermore, changes in attitudes toward premarital sex have taken place in American society, and the majority of young Americans have sexual intercourse for the first time in their late teens, a decade or more before they enter marriage. About two-thirds cohabit before marriage.

Arnett argues that it no longer makes sense to group 18- to 29-year-olds with "young adults," because—unlike young adults—many emerging adults are not married, do not have children, and have not yet settled into stable full-time work. Nor does it make sense to call them "adolescents," because unlike adolescents they are not going through puberty, they are not in secondary school, and most of them no longer live in their parents' household. Calling them "emerging adults" recognizes that they are distinct in many ways from both adolescents and young adults, and that a new period of the life course has now developed in between these two periods.

So, what is distinctive about emerging adulthood as a period of the life course? Arnett has proposed five features that are prominent in emerging adulthood (Arnett, 2004). Not all emerging adults experience these five features, but these are features that are more prominent during emerging adulthood than during other periods of the life course. According to the theory, emerging adulthood is 1) the age of identity explorations, 2) the age of instability, 3) the self-focused age, 4) the age of feeling in-between, and 5) the age of possibilities.

Identity explorations have been associated in the past with adolescence, because Erikson (1950) proposed in his life-span theory that each period of the life course has a central challenge or crisis, and that adolescents confront an identity crisis. In Erikson's view, adolescents focus on forming an identity, especially with respect to love and work. This may well have been true in the 1940s, when Erikson first formulated his theory. However, today most identity explorations take place in emerging adulthood, according to Arnett. With respect to love, many adolescents experience their first romantic relationships, but it is during emerging adulthood that romantic relationships become more identity focused, as emerging adults ask themselves, "Given what I know about myself, what kind of person would make a good life partner for me?" Similarly, many adolescents have part-time jobs, but it is in emerging adulthood that work becomes more identity-based, as emerging adults seek to find a job that fits well with their sense of what their abilities and interests are.

The identity explorations of emerging adulthood contribute to making it the age of instability because, in the course of their explorations, emerging adults often experience changes in love partners and in educational and occupational paths. They change residences more frequently than in any other part of the life course, for example moving out of their parents' household, living with friends, moving in to cohabit with a partner, moving out again, perhaps moving back home during a transition related to love, education, or work. Although emerging adulthood is largely experienced as positive, and numerous studies have found that median well-being and life satisfaction increase steadily during this age period (e.g., Galambos, Barker, & Krahn, 2006), the instability of the period adds an element of stress and anxiety for many emerging adults.

Emerging adulthood is the self-focused age in the sense that it is the time of life that is the least structured and the least bound by obligations to others. Children and adolescents live with their parents and have to follow the program of daily life laid down by their parents and other adults: living with their parents, going to school, taking part in parent-approved leisure activities. In young adulthood and beyond, obligations to others also structure daily life for most people, in their roles as spouse/partner, parent, and worker. However, emerging adulthood is the time when structure and obligations reach their nadir, and individuals are free to make their own decisions without consulting others and to structure their daily lives as they wish. This does not mean that they are selfish—on the contrary, they tend to be considerably less egocentric than adolescents are—but that they are temporarily relatively free from binding social roles and allowed to live as they wish to a large extent.

Emerging adulthood is the age of feeling in-between adolescence and adulthood. In numerous surveys, in the United States as well as in other industrialized countries, when asked if they have reached adulthood, most emerging adults respond neither yes nor no but "in some ways yes, in some ways no" (Arnett, 2001, 2003; Mayseless & Scharf, 2003; Facio & Micocci, 2003). Their subjective sense of making the transition to adulthood takes place gradually over the course of emerging adulthood. For most, the passage to adulthood is not marked by traditional transition events such as finishing education, marriage, and parenthood, but by more intangible and individualistic criteria, especially these three: accept responsibility for yourself, make independent decisions, and become financially independent. These criteria have been found to rank at the top in a wide range of studies in the United States and other countries, across regions, social classes, ethnic groups, and nationalities.

Finally, emerging adulthood is the age of possibilities in two respects. First, emerging adulthood is a time of high hopes and great expectations. Even if their current lives are stressful and difficult—which is often the case, since many of them are financially strained and are stressfully attempting to balance the demands of education, work, and social relationships—they nevertheless believe almost universally that adulthood will work out well for them in the end. They have high hopes of finding not merely a reliable marriage partner but a "soulmate," and not merely a stable and reasonably well-paying job but a job that is self-fulfilling, an expression of their identity. Second, emerging adulthood is the age of possibilities in the sense that it represents a window of opportunity for people to make dramatic changes in their lives. Children and adolescents are dependent on their parents and cannot leave even if their parents are incompetent or cruel. But emerging adults can leave, and some of them have the freedom to leave a pathogenic family life and make their own decisions which allow them to turn their lives around.

The American college experience and the college environment are well-suited to the developmental features of emerging adulthood. Taking a variety of courses in their first two years of higher education is a form of identity exploration for many emerging adults, as they see what areas resonate most strongly with their own abilities and interests. Explorations in love, too, are facilitated by having so many unattached persons in their age group in the same place. Pursuing a college education is in many ways a self-focused enterprise, because the focus is on building one's own knowledge and credentials, and much of one's time during these years is spent studying and attending classes. The college environment also promotes a sense of feeling in between adolescence and young adulthood, because college students often have more responsibilities than they did as adolescents but fewer than they will in adulthood, especially if they live in a group residential environment such as a dormitory.

Nevertheless, emerging adulthood is not experienced only by college students. Emerging adults who do not pursue higher education also seek satisfying identity-based work, although their explorations may be in different types of jobs rather than different college majors, and they also seek a "soulmate" in marriage. They also experience instability, through frequent job changes in their late teens and early twenties. They are self-focused, as most of them leave their parents' household but wait until at least their late twenties to enter marriage and parenthood. They are as likely as college-attending emerging adults to report the in-between status of feeling adult in some ways but not others (Arnett, 1997). And they have their own dreams, the belief that many doors are still open to them, even though without higher education credentials the attainment of those dreams may be elusive.

Individual Pathways from Adolescence to Young Adulthood

Arnett's theory describes the key population characteristics of the emerging adult age period, pointing to the critical developmental task of gaining self-sufficiency. Subjectively and psychologically, the experience of becoming an adult is a process rather than an event or string of social transitions. Complementing Arnett's characterization of emerging adulthood as a universal stage of development, Tanner (2006) articulated a three-stage process, recentering, that characterizes the individual, developmental process of transitioning from adolescence, through emerging adulthood, into young adulthood.

The developmental process of recentering is formulated utilizing life-span developmental (Baltes, 1997) and life-span developmental systems theories (Lerner, 2002), stressing the relational nature of human development, interactions between individuals and contexts that produce development. Individual pathways of development across emerging adulthood, as with all stages of human development, involve continuities and discontinuities, plasticity, normative and non-normative experiences, and variability in experiences (i.e., individual differences). As individuals move toward greater independence and adult self-sufficiency, as they recenter, development involves both gains and losses.

Recentering is a three-stage process by which individuals shift their primary involvements from the contexts of childhood and adolescence (which promote dependence) to contexts of adulthood (which nourish adult interdependence). Beginning when the individual is embedded in contexts of youth, primarily the family-of-origin, stage 1 is objectively marked by the legal emancipation of individuals from the responsibility of their parents. Despite a concentration of this occurrence at age 18, a small minority of individuals are emancipated legally as adolescents (e.g., financial emancipation from parents, early graduation from high school), some dissociate from institutional care before age 18 (e.g., runaway youth, those who leave high school before graduation), and a subgroup who reverse the dependent role before age 18 (e.g., those who become parents or take on head-of-household responsibilities). By definition, leaving adolescence and entering emerging adulthood is marked by a weakening of institutional ties. The extent to which resources remain available to the emerging adult (i.e., via families and/or institutions) and opportunities available to the individual represent two sources of individual differences predicting the extent to which an individual experiences emerging adulthood proper.

As adolescents age out of traditional contexts of dependence, they enter emerging adulthood proper, stage 2, marked by temporary role commitments that serve the purpose of exploration of adult identities. During this stage, emerging adults progress in identity development by trying out different, albeit temporary commitments, and eliminating those that do not "fit" with their plans and goals. While adolescence is marked by subjective, internalized identity exploration, it is not until emerging adulthood that the active phase of identity exploration begins during which individuals attempt to match their adult senses-of-self with the socially-sanctioned adult roles.

Stage 3 of the recentering process occurs when individuals make enduring commitments to relationships and careers, taking on adult roles and responsibilities. These, in turn, serve to sustain adult self-sufficiency.

COMING OF AGE?—IMPORTANCE OF IDENTITY IN SUBJECTIVELY EVALUATING ADULTHOOD

The previous reading describes a process called *recentering*, in which people often reevaluate the norms of behavior they took for granted during their childhood; they may experience conflict with their parents or other important socializers from their childhood as they consider alternative perspectives. Emerging adults experience a relative degree of autonomy as the direct control by their parents declines, even while they continue to rely upon them for various kinds of support. A key characteristic of this stage of life is that many young people turn inward and rely more upon themselves as the source of authority for what they should be and do, resulting in many emerging adult scholars referring to this life stage as the *age of identity* (Erikson 1968; Waters et al. 2001; Schwartz et al. 2005, 2013; Tanner 2006). The enormous array of identity choices make this a stage of *self-focus*, when young people focus most of their energy on trying to establish who they are and what they want (Schwartz et al. 2005, 2013).

Emerging adults and scholars studying them tend to perceive a high degree of agency during this life stage, seeing young people as freeing themselves from inherited patterns of life from their childhood and not yet fully bound by adulthood commitments. This is the dominant perspective in the *psychological approach* that is most widely available in emerging adulthood scholarship. However, there is an important balance offered by a more sociological approach to understanding the life course, which focuses on the social and structural factors surrounding personal choices. It is true that emerging adults are able to make a variety of choices during this stage of life and experience major changes from previous life stages, including relative freedom. However, many emerging adults also experience constraints in seeking to establish themselves as adults, while others have significant social and economic supports on which to rely as they transition into adulthood. A complete picture of emerging adulthood needs to interpret subjective experiences within their social contexts.

An example of this *sociological approach* to emerging adulthood comes from the second reading included in this chapter (Waters et al. 2011). In this reading, the authors describe the results of a study that collected 437 in-depth interviews with women and men ranging from 21 to 28 years old. The study queried young people directly about their perception of transitioning to adulthood in an America with tremendous diversity and a range of opportunities to navigate. The authors help elucidate the vulnerabilities of emerging adulthood by highlighting complexities in the social context surrounding coming of age in the United States today, and the difficulties in discerning exactly when one has become an adult. They describe a decoupling of transitioning into adulthood from the traditional markers of adulthood, meaning the elongated periods before reaching *adulthood roles* leaves many emerging adults wondering whether they are an adult or not. For some this equates to an experience of freedom to choose; for others this is more of what the authors call a "perilous passage" in which *disconnected youth* do not transition into any adulthood roles.

READING 1.2

Coming of Age in America: The Transition to Adulthood in the Twenty-First Century

By Mary C. Waters, Patrick J. Carr and Maria J. Kefalas

Introduction

What is it like to become an adult in twenty-first-century America?

While there are many answers to that question, one thing is certain. The journey to adulthood that today's twentysomethings make is not the same as the one completed by their parents or grandparents. Becoming an adult in America in the immediate postwar period of the 1950s was envisioned as a remarkably uniform, swift, and unproblematic process: finish school, get a job and get married, set up an in de pen dent house hold, have kids, and settle into a career as a single-earner, two-parent family. But almost as soon as this "Leave It to Beaver" lifestyle became an ideal that young Americans aspired to, subsequent social and economic transformations made it more and more difficult to achieve.[1] Indeed, scholars who study the life course have demonstrated that the transition from adolescence to adulthood has in recent years become more complicated, uncertain, and extended than ever before (Furstenberg et al. 2004; Settersten et al. 2005 [see, especially, chapters by Fussell and Furstenberg; Mouw; and Osgood et al.]). This is not only happening in the United States, but also

Mary C. Waters, Patrick J. Carr and Maria J. Kefalas, "Introduction," Coming of Age in America: The Transition to Adulthood in the Twenty-First Century, pp. 1-5, 17-20. Copyright © 2011 by University of California Press. Reprinted with permission.

characterizes other developed countries in Western Europe and Japan (Brinton 2011; Newman and Aptekar 2007).

The reasons for these changes are complicated—including changes in gender norms that have led women into the workforce in unprecedented numbers, growth in the numbers of people never marrying, and growth in the ability to postpone marriage and yet still have sexual relationships. There have also been increases in the amount of schooling many Americans achieve—with the growth of prolonged schooling, the entry into the labor force has been delayed. In addition, the rise of housing prices in many parts of the nation, along with rising educational expectations, means that many young people find it hard to live independently even if they would like to. So, too, the severe recession that began in 2008 has restricted work opportunities for young people, as well as their ability to live independently, exacerbating many of the long-term trends that had led to delays in independence for young adults. And the rise of nonmarital childbearing means that many young people become parents before marrying or even forming stable long-term relationships.

As the traditional markers of the transition to adulthood become decoupled from each other and the line between adolescence and full-fledged adulthood becomes less sharp, many young people face a period of prolonged transition—with marriage postponed, education prolonged, and full-time employment taking longer to attain. Without these extrinsic markers, how does a young person know when he/she is a grown-up? If norms about independence and the "right" age to leave home or achieve financial independence are changing, how do families know whether their children are "normal" or not? Today's fretful parents of twentysomething offspring would be shocked to learn that half a century ago, experts feared young people were actually *growing up too fast* and losing out on the support and time they needed to acquire the sound psychological footing required for a healthy adulthood.

Indeed the image in popular culture of young adults is that they are a problem, that they refuse to grow up. A 2005 *Time* magazine cover story exhorted the nation to "Meet the Twixters," *twixter* being the term they coined for the twentysomething who just can't seem to grow up (Grossman 2005). The twixter is in her/his mid-20s, has finished college (not always in four years), and doesn't yet have a distinguishable career. Usually, the twixter is living back at home with vexed upper-middle-class parents who had been expecting at this stage of their lives to preside over an empty nest. Other treatments in popular magazines and in the cinema have variously chronicled the new "adultolescent" stage of life where young people have not quite left adolescence behind nor yet fully attained adulthood, or lampooned people who just refuse to grow up and get on with their lives—such as the character played by Matthew McConaughey in the film *Failure to Launch* (Tyre 2002).

As the recognition that young adulthood is now different has seeped into popular consciousness, a mini-industry has arisen to troubleshoot the problems faced by young adults. For instance, the phrase "Thirty is the new twenty" has been elevated to the popular *zeitgeist* courtesy of Dr. Melfi, Tony Soprano's therapist on the HBO series *The Sopranos*, who used it to explain the difficulties that A.J., Tony's ne'er-do-well son, was experiencing in becoming an adult. This new "problem" of twenty-somethings who aren't grown up has spawned a number of self-help books with titles like *The Quarter-Life Crisis*, and *Twenty-Something, Twenty-Everything*. These books offer advice to young people overwhelmed by the freedom and self-exploration that define the postcollege experience.

There has also been an academic discovery of the stage of life known as "young adulthood" or "emerging adulthood." Scholars have begun to ask whether this is a new stage of life, brought about by changes in the economy and social norms that create a long period of quasi-adulthood, and whether it represents a period of "exploration" of adult roles, or "drift." While the full psychological and sociological implications of these changes remain to be fully understood, it is clear that young adults face a less scripted and more individualistic transition from teenager to full adult, and it is clear that many of our societal institutions are only beginning to catch up with these changes. For instance, most young people do not move directly from school into full-time employment at jobs that provide health insurance. Yet most insurance policies used to end when a young person finished school or turned 19, leaving young adults one of the groups in our society least likely to have health insurance. This was addressed with the 2010 Health Care Reform law, which allows young people to remain on their parents' health insurance through age 25.

This book explores this new period of young adulthood, focusing on two important themes—the role of local context in shaping the transition to adulthood, and the subjective experience of young adults themselves as they experience this period of change, possibility, and uncertainty. The interplay between the structural changes in the economy, the housing market, and the educational system, and the cultural changes in norms and expectations about the "normal" course of behavior for young adults, lies at the heart of our analyses. This book reports on young adults we interviewed in four different sites in America—rural Iowa, Minneapolis, San Diego, and New York City. Young people age 18–34 were interviewed about their life histories, the choices they are making about education, work, and relationships, and their subjective understandings of where they are in the life course. In the portrait that emerges, huge regional differences are evident across sites—indeed, national averages obscure some of the ways in which local labor, housing, and education opportunities structure people's lives. The subjective experience of young adulthood is also highlighted here. Young people discuss how they make choices about big life transitions and how that makes them feel. We show in the pages that follow that norms about adulthood have changed—that young people are more aware of how their lives are less scheduled and scripted than their parents' and grandparents' were, and yet we show how young people still manage to make distinctions that mark their passage from child and teenager into full-fledged adults.

In addition to regional diversity, the portrait that emerges in the book also highlights class and ethnic diversity. Much of the popular discussion of the issues of young adulthood focuses on the problems of middle-class young adults. The popular press abounds with stories of people who graduate from college and move back home with mom and dad, sometimes for an indeterminate period of time, or young people who eschew adult responsibilities of job and family in order to travel or explore their artistic side. But the transition to adulthood has also changed for the poor and the working class. While some middle-class kids have the institutional support of residential colleges to support them in a supervised way as they learn to live without their parents, working-class and poor kids do not have those institutional supports. They often struggle to combine education, part-time work, and parenting while remaining in their parents' home.

Because twentysomethings have vastly different resources in terms of human, social, economic, and cultural capital, it is hardly surprising that some young people face far more treacherous journeys than others during this critical time of life. Some young people neglect school to enter the labor force but find that, without training, their opportunities are severely curtailed in a high-tech global economy. A small number, less than 3 percent, will join the military (which provides some of those institutional supports that middle-class kids get from residential colleges), while others seem to drift along bouncing from job to job, school to school, aimlessly. Still others will opt out of school and work and start families during their twentysomething years.

Then there are the vulnerable and disconnected youth, who, some estimates suggest, account for about 14 percent of 18- to 24-year-olds. These youth face a truly "perilous passage" as they come of age (Hagan and McCarthy 2005). Many disconnected youth have aged out of the foster care system, have experienced bouts of homelessness, or have spent time in juvenile detention facilities, and these experiences leave them marginalized and vulnerable. Many disconnected youth do not have high school diplomas, which restricts their employment and earning opportunities in the short and long term. Disconnected youth also disproportionately experience an array of other physical, psychological, and emotional problems, which further degrade their quality of life. Perhaps most disturbingly for a segment of Americans, prison is the site of their transition to adulthood. Sociologist Bruce Western documents that among young male dropouts, 5 percent of whites and of Hispanics are in prison. Among African American young male high school dropouts, 29 percent are in prison. By their mid-thirties, 6 percent of whites and 30 percent of black men who did not attend college will have a criminal record (Western et al. 2004). We interviewed some young men who had been in prison and note how profoundly it has affected their lives and will affect their life chances. To date, no one has studied the subjective experience of young adulthood in prisons in the United States, but the depressing statistics tell us that for far too many young men, it is the institutional context for their coming of age. By including a variety of young people with different socioeconomic and familial resources in this book, we hope to provide a corrective to the media stories of young adulthood, which tend to privilege the stories of the upper-middle class.

This generation of 18- to 34-year-olds is also remarkably ethnically diverse. The large wave of international migration that began in the 1960s and continues unabated adds a million or more immigrants to the United States each year, many of them concentrated in the young adult years. And many people in this age group are the young adult children of immigrants—the second generation. Of the 67.3 million (civilian, noninstitutionalized) young people born between 1971 and 1987, and age 18–34 in 2006, nearly one of every five is an immigrant, and another 10 percent are second generation. Rumbaut and Komaie (2007) report that non-Hispanic whites are only 61 percent of this age group, Hispanics are another 18 percent, blacks are 13 percent, and Asians, 5 percent. We explore how different ethnic groups navigate the transition to adulthood, and how different cultural values about gender roles, living apart from parents, and when to have children interact with local opportunity structures to shape the experience of young adulthood.

We describe an even more complex relationship between structural and cultural change. The contexts within which young people come of age differ a great deal across the sites where we conducted research. In New York and San Diego, children of immigrants with a cultural openness to multigenerational living confront a very expensive labor market and the availability of plentiful low-cost educational institutions. The result is a maintenance of parental subcultural values that define multi-generational living as benign and helpful, along with a large number of young people attending college as nontraditional students combining work, parenthood, and education. In these sites alternative definitions of adulthood are invoked by young people who "feel grown-up," perhaps without the demographic markers to prove it. In Minneapolis, the stable employment of parents and relative affordability of in de pen dent housing allow young people the scaffolding to explore many different adult identities and yet maintain a rather traditional view of what being an adult is. In Iowa, young people are enabled to make quick orderly transitions by the social structure around them—they can finish high school, live on their own, marry early, and become parents at a young age. But many of them find that these markers of adulthood do not bring the subjective experience of maturity they might have imagined. And divorces and job changes mean that some of these milestones come undone over time as cultural expectations of exploration and self-fulfillment from the wider society influence their wants and needs. In the pages that follow, we provide a snapshot of a moving picture—behaviors and meanings are no longer set in stone when it comes to young adulthood, providing a very opportune moment to explore how young people themselves creatively imagine their own passage to full-fledged maturity.

Young Adults Today

Out of the total 291 million noninstitutionalized civilian population measured in the 2005 Current Population Survey, Rumbaut and Komaie (2007) find that about a fourth of our national population is concentrated in the young adult years—there are 67.3 million people age 18–34. Table 1.1 (page 20) provides a profile of young people in 2005, divided into the early, middle, and late transition years.

Table 1.1 Demographic and Socioeconomic Characteristics of Young Adults, 18–34, by Age Groups

Selected Characteristics		Age Groups in Young Adult Transitions			Total
		(18–24 yrs) Early transition	(25–29 yrs) Middle transition	(30–34 yrs) Late transition	(18–34 yrs)
Total young adults:	n	27,972,112	19,498,868	19,808,008	67,278,988
Sex:					
Female	%	49.8	49.6	50.3	49.9
Male	%	50.2	50.4	49.7	50.1
Nativity/generation:					
Foreign-born (1st generation)	%	13.6	21.3	22.8	18.5
U.S.-born, foreign-born parents (2nd gen.)	%	11.0	8.7	6.7	9.0
U.S.-born, U.S.-born parents (3rd+ gen.)	%	75.4	70.0	70.6	72.4
Pan-ethnicity:					
Hispanic:	%	17.1	19.7	18.2	18.2
Non-Hispanic:					
White	%	62.0	59.6	60.8	61.0
Black	%	13.6	12.7	12.2	12.9
Asian	%	3.9	5.3	6.1	4.9
American Indian, Other	%	0.6	0.5	0.7	0.6
Two or more "races"	%	2.7	2.2	2.0	2.3
Not living with parents:	%	50.3	85.5	92.7	73.0
Marital and parental status:					
Never married	%	78.0	40.1	23.2	50.8
Cohabiting	%	7.4	9.9	7.3	8.1
Currently married	%	13.0	44.8	61.2	36.4
Divorced, separated, widowed	%	1.7	5.3	8.3	4.7
Has one or more children	%	11.1	36.9	56.5	31.9

Continued

		Age Groups in Young Adult Transitions			Total
Selected Characteristics		(18–24 yrs) Early transition	(25–29 yrs) Middle transition	(30–34 yrs) Late transition	(18–34 yrs)
Mean number of children		0.17	0.68	1.16	0.61
Educational attainment:					
Less than high school	%	21.8	13.9	12.7	16.8
High school graduate	%	30.0	29.4	28.1	29.3
Some college	%	35.2	19.6	17.9	25.6
Associate's degree	%	4.6	8.5	9.4	7.1
Bachelor's degree	%	8.0	22.4	22.3	16.4
Advanced degree	%	0.4	6.2	9.6	4.8
Economic status:					
Poverty rate (below poverty line)	%	18.1	13.1	11.9	14.9
Personal annual income	$	14,665	28,821	35,238	25,323

Source: Rumbaut et al. 2007, Table 1, calculated from the Current Population Survey, 2005.

In terms of markers of adulthood, just over half of all 18- to 24-year-olds were no longer living with parents or other relatives. The census shows about half of this group having formed their own households, while the remainder were living with nonrelatives such as roommates (Jekielek and Brown 2005). By ages 30–34 93 percent are no longer living with their parents. In terms of educational attainment, 28.6 percent of 25- to 29-year-olds have a bachelor's degree or higher, while 13.9 percent of the same age group have less than a high school degree. By age 30–34 the number with a bachelor's degree or higher has risen to 32 percent (Rumbaut and Komaie 2007).

At the other end of the adulthood experience is the category of so-called "disconnected youth," who are defined as those age 18–24 who are not in school, not working, and have no degree beyond a high school diploma or GED. Disconnected youth make up 14 percent of the total population of 18- to 24-year-olds in 2000, and they are disproportionately likely to be black, Hispanic, or American Indian. Disconnected young people are obviously struggling to navigate the transition to adulthood (Jekielek and Brown 2005).

In terms of the family formation markers of adulthood, 13 percent of 18- to 24-year-olds reported that they were married in 2005, 11 percent had one or more children, and another 1.7 percent were divorced, separated, or widowed. In this age group, young women are more likely than young men to marry and have children, and in terms of ethnicity, Hispanics are the most likely group to marry and have children, with Asian Americans the least likely.

Table 1.2 provides data on the number and types of adult transitions people have undergone by age. Rumbaut and Komaie (2007) find that while only a third of all 30- to 34-year-olds have completed all adult transitions, the majority of the population have completed each of the transitions, ranging from 93 percent of people who are no longer living with their parents to 56 percent who already have one or more children. There is a steady progression of people experiencing adult transitions throughout their 20s and 30s, which underscores the fact that this decade of life does matter—many more people have undergone adult transitions by the end of the age period than at the beginning. (Although it should be kept in mind that many of these transitions are reversible—boomerang kids move out of their parents homes only to return at a later date, marriages occur and then divorces sometimes follow, full-time employment can end, resulting in a return to full-time schooling. Perhaps the only nonreversible transition is having children—and it is also the one that is least prevalent across all individuals.)

Table 1.2 Number and Types of Adult Transitions, by Age

Selected Characteristics		Age Groups in Young Adult Transitions			Total
		(18–24 yrs) Early transition	(25–29 yrs) Middle transition	(30–34 yrs) Late transition	(18–34 yrs)
Total young adults:	n	27,972,112	19,498,868	19,808,008	67,278,988
Number of adult transitions:					
None or one	%	49.2	5.4	2.3	22.7
Two	%	20.5	16.5	8.5	15.8
Three	%	18.7	30.4	20.5	22.6
Four	%	8.4	29.3	35.4	22.4
Five	%	3.1	18.4	33.2	16.4
Mean number of adult transitions		1.69	3.24	3.80	2.76
Types of adult transitions:					
Not living with parents	%	50.3	85.5	92.7	73.0

Not attending school*	%	55.5	85.5	91.2	75.0
Working full-time	%	37.5	65.3	67.7	54.4
Married or ever married	%	15.1	51.8	72.3	42.6
Has one or more children	%	11.1	36.9	56.5	31.9

Source: Rumbaut and Komaie 2007, Table 7, calculated from the Current Population Survey, 2005.

* Percentages for 25- to 34-year-olds are imputed from the 2000 Census 5 percent PUMS, because the CPS only measures school attendance for 18- to 24-year-olds.

One of the key themes of the book is that the transition to adulthood varies based on the local context. It matters whether you grow up in a rural area, a city undergoing massive demographic change due to immigration, a state with high housing prices, or a city with a stable economic base ... San Diego and New York are both very expensive places to come of age, Minneapolis is in the middle, and rural Iowa is dramatically less expensive. This is especially true when it comes to housing costs, which very much affects the age at which young people can leave their parents' homes and establish independent living.

DISORDERED ADULTHOOD—STATUS MARKERS, ADULTHOOD ROLES, AND SEQUENCES IN TRANSITIONING TO ADULTHOOD

The transitional period from the teenage years to young adulthood is what some refer to as a demographically dense time period (e.g., Mouw 2005). Emerging adulthood is typically the life stage during which people earn their most advanced educational degree, establish their career, meet romantic partners they intend to establish long-term relationships with, and often have their first child. It is an exciting time!

One of the most marked differences between younger generations and older generations is that the order in which *adulthood roles* are established has become more variable. People from previous generations tended to think that there was one *normative pathway into adulthood*. This is an expectation that only one sequence of assuming adulthood roles was thought to characterize how most young people became adults—namely, complete education, establish long-term work, get married, and have a baby. It turns out that even for previous generations the majority of young people did not enter adulthood in this exact sequence. For example, in the 1960s around 37 to 40 percent of young people were characterized by this sequence of adulthood roles (Mouw 2005). But this was the largest single group of young people, meaning the normative path was in fact the *modal path for adulthood transitions*. Thus, the normative expectation for growing up resembled the reality of becoming an adult for the largest single majority of young people.

However, emerging adults today are characterized by multiple pathways to adulthood. In fact, in a study by Mouw (2005), 62 different sequences of adulthood transitions were found. In some sequences, emerging adults got married and then finished their college degree. In others, young people had children, and then got married. In others, they finished school, launched careers, and had not yet married or had children well into their 30s. As one way of understanding the intensity of the changes since the 1960s, it is important to note that the order in which these demographic events occur is now so variable that the previously normative sequence of school, job, marriage, kids represents only 3 percent of emerging adults today.

In sum, the modal path of emerging adulthood is non-modal, meaning there is no one clear dominant sequencing pattern that describes the majority of emerging adults. Instead, emerging adulthood is characterized by a *disordered adulthood* process in which variation is the norm. People transition into adulthood by navigating a wide array of options for timing and sequencing in their establishment of adulthood roles. Figure 1.1 visually represents the complexities of what this disordered adulthood process means for understanding risks and advantages in adulthood transitions.

Figure 1.1 represents the complexities involved in understanding adulthood transitions by considering three groups: those who left home at age 23, at age 27, and at age 35. This chapter began with a quote that the normal high school graduation gift used to be a suitcase, meaning most were thought to be on their own by age 18. Given this perspective, we would imagine that staying at home longer could represent a disadvantage. This is the case when comparing Group 3 to Group 1, finding in these charts that those staying at home the longest completed all adulthood markers later. However, a more nuanced story emerges in comparing Group 2 to

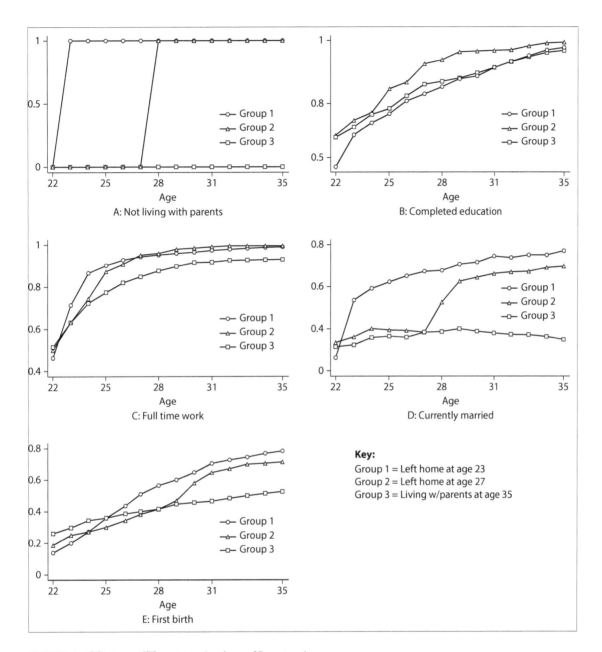

FIGURE 1.1 Timing of Transition by Age of Leaving home

Ted Mouw, "Sequences of Early Adult Transitions: A Look at Variability and Consequences," On the Frontier of Adulthood: Theory, Research, and Public Policy, ed. Richard A. Settersten, Frank F. Furstenberg, and Rubén G. Rumbaut. Copyright © 2005 by University of Chicago Press.

the other two groups. Group 2 appears to be the most advantaged of the three because young people in this path completed their education prior to establishing work and forming families.

In this chapter's third reading, Settersten (2011) explains what it is like to become an adult, given this wide variability in pathways to adulthood, and highlights the remaining import of these adulthood markers, despite disordered sequences.

READING 1.3

Becoming Adult: Meanings and Markers for Young Americans

By Richard A. Settersten

The Significance and Meanings of Age

Age matters for societies, for groups of people in it, and for individuals (Settersten 2003). The meanings and uses of age are often formal. For example, age underlies the organization of families, schools, workplaces, and leisure settings, as well as many legal rights, responsibilities, and entitlements. The meanings and uses of age can also be informal. For example, members of a society may share ideas about behavior that is appropriate or inappropriate at particular ages, or ideas about when or in what order men and women are or are not supposed to assume social roles, such as student, worker, spouse, or parent. Individuals use age-related ideas to make plans and set goals and to judge their own lives and those of others. Age also enters into and shapes everyday social interactions, even in subtle and unconscious ways, affecting how we judge and act toward the people we encounter in our daily rounds. Age has long been a significant social dimension in the United States, yet there is also evidence that its meanings are changing and its significance is declining (Settersten 2007).

Richard A. Settersten, "Becoming Adult: Meanings and Markers for Young Americans," Coming of Age in America: The Transition to Adulthood in the Twenty-First Century, ed. Mary C. Waters, Patrick J. Carr, Maria J. Kefalas and Jennifer Holdaway, pp. 169-176. Copyright © 2011 by University of California Press. Reprinted with permission.

How does chronological age matter for the young people in our study as they describe the process of becoming adult?

Age as an Anchor for Meaningful Experiences

Becoming adult is inherently about age in that it is about growing up and older. It is not surprising, then, that young people associate adulthood with age and easily provide specific ages at which they began to feel adult, almost always between 18 and 26. But there is nothing magic about the ages per se. What matters is what the age indexes—important experiences that happen at those times. Most references to age are quickly followed up with examples of such experiences. For example:

> [I began to think of myself as an adult] maybe when I was like 20. And really, like, got out of my parents' house and started, like, living, I mean working to pay the bills. (Female, age 24–26, from San Diego)

> [I began to think of myself as an adult] um, probably at 21.... I finished school. Finally working. Taking care of myself. And no longer dependent on my parents. (Female, age 24–26, from San Diego)

These examples are typical in that these individuals see themselves as accomplishing key markers of adulthood at or around this time—in the first case, leaving home and working, and in the second case, finishing school and establishing herself as separate from, and no longer financially dependent on, her parents. Age simply anchors the experience; it is a window into a larger process. The exceptions to this rule are the ages of 18 and 21, which are symbolic to many young people because they are explicitly tied to legal age norms.

Legal Age Norms as Starting Points in Becoming Adult

Not surprisingly, 18 and 21 are often given as ages of adulthood because they are embedded in laws and signal the acquisition of significant legal rights and responsibilities, such as when one can vote, drink, marry, have consensual sex, or serve in the military. For example:

> [I began to think of myself as an adult at] 18, I guess.... Because it seemed to be, it was the age at which I was legally able to do a lot of things. And I guess to me that had significance, so that was the age at which I could vote ... [and] have a credit card in my own name. It was also the age at which—or was it 17?—the government informed me that I would have to register for selective service. (Male, age 30–32, from New York)

Young people, however, do not suddenly feel adult upon reaching these landmark legal ages. Instead, they view these ages as representing starting points for adulthood rather than as things that immediately render them adult. They are also quick to point out that these legal rights and responsibilities are given gradually at different ages and in ways that seem inconsistent or arbitrary.

Legal ages are also important to parents and other people in the social worlds of young adults. As youth reach these ages, other people begin to think about them in new ways. These legal markers seem especially important in situations where the young person is viewed as being adrift or as lagging behind expectations:

> When I turned 21 … [my parents said], you know what? You're an adult now. You should start thinking like an adult. You know, you should start setting up for your future as, you know, adult stuff that adults do.… [But it wasn't until] the "Big Two–Five" [25] that I started thinking more as an adult and stuff life that. (Male, age 24–26, from San Diego)

The fact that parents and others send subtle and not-so-subtle cues to young people about their progress, or lack thereof, is consistent with dynamics described in the literature on "age norms," in which age-related expectations are reinforced by positive or negative social sanctions (Settersten 2003). Positive social sanctions come to young people who stay "on track," while negative social sanctions come to young people who stray too far from the expected course. These sanctions may be informal (for example, persuasion, encouragement, reinforcement, ridicule, gossip, ostracism) or formal (for example, political, legal, or economic ramifications).

In some instances, however, young people regard chronological age as meaningless in determining when one becomes adult. That is, age is a poor proxy for an individual's readiness for adult roles and responsibilities:

> [Questions about age can't really be answered] for the simple fact that the individual can be a type of person that's not ready for society. That individual can be between the ages of 15 through 30. If that person isn't quite ready mentally, then obviously that person can't be separate from their parents.… There's people that are older who are still childish. Assuming that the person is somewhat responsible, then I think it's extremely important to be separate from their parents, not to have to rely on their parents for anything. To have to do everything on their own. And understand what it is to be independent. (Male, age 24–26, from San Diego)

This example illustrates a commonly expressed disconnect between the legal assumptions about when adulthood begins and the reality that most young people do not achieve psychological, social, or financial maturity until well after the ages encrypted in law.

Traditional Markers Still Matter

It will surprise some readers to know that traditional markers of adulthood continue to be important in the minds of young people. This includes what we might describe as the "Big Five" traditional markers—leaving home, finishing school, getting a job, getting married, and having children. Yet these traditional markers also bring significant tensions in how young people evaluate their progress toward adulthood. Although many young people think there is at least an ideal order (as listed above) for experiencing these traditional markers, many also acknowledge that their own lives have not gone or will not go in these ways. While the pattern may be viewed as outdated and reflective of the lives of older cohorts, young people may nonetheless see benefits to it.

> I would say that's my belief as well [accomplishing traditional markers in the traditional order] ... even though ... a lot of times it's not realistic because ... it depends on ... your family and your growing up—how you make that a reality. (Female, age 24–26, from San Diego)

> [It's hard] living up to the expectations of being an adult. You should have a good job. You should have your own place. Should have a family.... It's "What's wrong with you?"—what's wrong with you if you don't have a good job, what's wrong with you if you don't have a family. (Male, age 30–32, from New York)

These examples reveal an awareness of an ideal sequence—in the first case, regretting that her family's circumstances did not allow her life to happen in this way, and in the second case, feeling the social repercussions of not being able to meet the social script.

These traditional assumptions about the timing and order of adult transitions also underlie many institutions and policies—especially those related to schooling, work, and family—despite a growing awareness that lives no longer fit this model. This is where new questions about risk come into play, as unusual pathways into adulthood bring new risks, many of which are not known in advance. Atypical timing or sequencing of school, work, or family experiences may leave individuals vulnerable, as they are subject to social policies that are based on outdated models of life (for example, eligibility rules for Social Security and pensions are based on having a continuous full-time work history or on having a long-lived marriage to someone who has such a work history—both of which are questionable today). From the perspectives of young people, when one's own patterns mesh with normative patterns, the process of navigating life is also easier, and when life is easier to navigate, personal growth and development come more easily. Crafting a life of one's own, especially when it goes against the grain, is a difficult enterprise.

Young adults also view these traditional markers as ultimately being connected to more abstract concepts such as "maturity," "responsibility," or "control." These qualities are often viewed as being *facilitated by* traditional markers rather than as necessary conditions for *entering* into them. The view directly contradicts many political and public discussions. Consider marriage or parenting, for example, where it is often argued that individuals should be mature or responsible *before* they marry or become parents, or that the problems with marriage and parenthood today result from individuals who enter these roles before they are ready. Surely, some degree of maturity, responsibility, or control is necessary to assume these roles, or at least to perform them with minimal effectiveness. But our interviews suggest that many young people are now actively postponing marriage and parenthood because they really *want* to be ready for, and do well in, these roles once they get there. For many, their concerns about wanting to be ready for marriage and parenthood are also driven by the prevalence of divorce or fragile relationships among their parents—they do not want this for themselves.

Given the significant delays in marriage and parenting today, it is perhaps no surprise that recent public opinion data show that marriage and parenting are becoming disassociated with conceptions of adulthood (Furstenberg et al. 2004), though it is clear that these roles continue to have a strong presence in the minds of young people. Indeed, once these roles have been assumed, there is the sense that these experiences, especially parenthood, are the very things that crystallize one's sense of self as an adult.

Financial independence from parents is also an important marker in the United States, reflected not just in the opinions of young people, but also the public at large (Furstenberg et al. 2004). At the same time, there is new evidence that large proportions of middle- and upper-class American "children" receive sizable instrumental, and especially financial, assistance well into their 30s (Schoeni and Ross 2005). In addition, in places such as New York or San Diego, where opportunities for housing are limited or costs are prohibitive, living independently is not a possibility for many young people. This draws our attention to the fact that the ability (and even interest) of young people to tackle traditional markers is intimately affected by regional and local conditions.

Given postponements in marriage and parenting, traditional markers related to education and work now seem to be the minimal and earliest set of transitions that young people experience as they navigate the early adult years. Markers related to education and work also seem more in one's control than marriage and parenthood, which rely on others. It is important to recognize, however, that young people from disadvantaged backgrounds have far fewer opportunities in education and work than those from more privileged backgrounds. As the prior chapters illustrate, young people across the sites we have studied are both searching and striving, and their experiences are heavily conditioned by opportunities in local markets, whether those markets are related to jobs, education, housing, or marriage.

Caught Up In The Process Of Becoming

When asked, most young people across our research sites say that they are adults. But when one looks carefully at responses to this question and others, it is clear that almost everyone we interviewed does not yet feel *entirely* adult, even into their late 20s and early 30s. In some ways and in some spheres they feel like adults, and in some ways and in some spheres they do not. Consider the following:

> I'm still a kid ... not in the sense of, you know, my mindset.... I know what I need to do to, you know, bring home money, stuff like that, but I still feel like a kid, meaning I like to have fun ... [and] I haven't gotten married,
>
> I haven't bought a house and all that.... And I don't have kids. I bought a car; that's about as close as I [get] ... [but] I think the fact that I know what to do or when to do it or, you know, basically I'm grown up. I have control of my own life. (Male, age 27–29, from New York)
>
> I still kind of sometimes think to myself, "Oh my God, I'm a grown-up." ... I don't think the adult thing will [completely] hit me until I have kids.... I mean I'm responsible for myself and, yeah, I'm married and, yeah, I'm responsible for making my health payment and my car payment, but you know I'm not really responsible for any other human life or anything like that. So ... I know I'm an adult because I'm 28 years old, but I ... didn't wake up one day when I was 23 and think, oh, I'm an adult now.... I still sometimes don't think of myself [that way]. (Female, age 27–29, from Iowa)

These quotes illustrate common distinctions between thoughts and feelings on the one hand, and actions on the other. They reveal that individuals are able to sort a wide range of possible markers in complex ways, judge their relative importance in determining adult status, and evaluate their own progress with respect to these benchmarks. In the second case, the woman has already married, but she does not yet fully think of herself as an adult—a theme that is echoed in the voices of many young people who have already attained some of these markers. In the first case, we hear another common theme: that adulthood is often equated with letting go of fun, a sense that many of life's joys must be relinquished or diminished when one "grows up" (or is forced to do so), such as no longer being able to hang out with friends, party, or have time for leisure and recreational activities.

Similarly, striving for greater control over life also emerges as a key theme in these interviews. What many young people do not seem to recognize, however, is that this is a challenge they will wrestle with throughout life, not one that will somehow be resolved in early adulthood. What is unique about early adulthood is that individuals are encountering this struggle in a significant way for the first time. This struggle often involves navigating the blurry and evolving spaces between control, autonomy, and independence, and recognizing new kinds of responsibilities and consequences. For example:

> [B]eing 18, I knew that there were different consequences for me ... so in that way I felt like an adult. But I ... recognized it [age] didn't really make me an adult.... I can't say there was any one event [when I suddenly felt like an adult], even after joining the army I ... kind of let other people kind of take care of me in a way.... I'd say 25 is really when I became an adult and kind of

made my own decisions and kind of took control of my own destiny. (Male, age 27–29, from Minneapolis)

This man sees the process starting at 18, though it is not until 25 that he feels more fully settled into adulthood. Even then, his sense of himself as an adult is hedged: he *kind of* made his own decisions, and *kind of* took control of his own destiny. There is tremendous awareness among young people of being caught up in the process of "becoming." The passage above reveals that part of becoming an adult is not just *knowing* when one could or should take control and responsibility but, more importantly, actually *doing* it. There is a grace period where young people may be exempt from not taking (or not taking enough) action, partly from their own perspectives, but especially from the vantage points of others. But that grace period eventually ends:

[Do you think of yourself as an adult now?] Yes and no. I do in the fact that … I'm 29 years old now. If I don't consider myself an adult now, I've got some serious issues. [But] also I look at it from a responsibility standpoint. I don't have the responsibilities of an adult yet. I'll feel like an adult when I have kids or once I'm married. You're taking that next step and moving on. (Male, age 27–29, from Minneapolis)

So, while it is common to not think of oneself as an adult *even if* some traditional markers have been attained, it is also clear that, beyond some age threshold, one simply *is* an adult even if he/she does not feel it. Chronological age eventually becomes a sufficient condition for adult status.

CONTESTABLE ADULTHOOD—ALL THAT MATTERS IS PERCEPTION?

The final paragraph of the previous reading particularly highlights the complex intersection of age, adulthood markers, and subjective experience in demarcating adulthood. The variability of pathways into adulthood means there is no one specific milestone (Suárez-Orozco 2015) or one sequence of milestones that characterizes what it means to be an adult (Trzesniewski & Donnellan 2014). When surveying parents and emerging adults regarding the criteria they use to determine if someone is an adult, Nelson and colleagues (2007) found that even parents and their own children used different criteria. This diversity in criteria employed to determine adulthood status has led some scholars to conclude that all that matters is perceiving oneself to be an adult, and that resulting adulthood could be desirable (e.g., Horowitz & Bromnick 2007).

Such *self-perceived adulthood* is advocated by many of the emerging adult scholars who focus on independence as the central value of adulthood development. For example, Tanner (2006) describes emerging adulthood as a time in life when people are "relatively free from the contextual structures (e.g., family, school) of earlier years" (p. 29). Emerging adults and their parents are thus often guided to allow growing children to break away from parental influence and establish their own choices. This has caused repercussions for "helicopter parents" who maintain regular involvement in their children's lives as they establish adulthood. However, these accounts overly emphasize the individual and negate important social experiences.

PATHWAYS TO ADULTHOOD—IT AIN'T ALL A MATTER OF CHOICE

To be sure, there are many choices available to young people today, and emerging adulthood is often an intense stage of life in which people attempt to sort out all the available options, trying on different potential adulthood lifestyles like they try on pairs of jeans. There is a great deal of individuality and relative autonomy in the process.

In the past, some scholars even interpreted this diversity in approaches to emerging adulthood as evidence that it was not truly a life stage. However, that is similar to saying that adolescence does not exist merely because different people and groups have varied experiences of being a teenager. Perhaps the same sort of misinterpretation occurred when that life stage initially began around the *Industrial Revolution*, but today hardly anyone would deny the existence of adolescence. This sort of change in our understanding occurs repeatedly throughout the historical progression of science and ideas. When paradigm shifts are first introduced, they are often not well accepted. Then evidence begins to mount, until concessions must at least be made to a contingent version of the previous paradigm. Ultimately, the new paradigm becomes the old paradigm, evidenced by it being widely accepted and understood. Then the process begins anew. This is all part of the *social process of science*.

The same sort of process has occurred around understanding emerging adulthood to be a new stage in the life course. We are on the cusp of a paradigm shift, meaning that evidence has been mounting for the existence of a new life stage, but social scientists still have uneven familiarity with the implications of this life stage for understanding social life. The next stage of the process will likely entail more common knowledge of emerging adulthood, which may then be given a colloquial label, as with teens or youth for adolescence. Until then, some may still simply bundle all these social changes when they refer to "twentysomethings" and others may continue to use the term young adults without attention to the subtle but important differences between being an emerging adult versus an adult who is young.

Another approach, often used in popular press, is to refer to the social trends discussed in what follows via reference to a generation, such as *Millennials*. To be sure, there are generational differences, precisely because prior generations—for example, the Baby Boomers—did not grow up during a point in social history when this new life stage existed. They did not go through emerging adulthood, at least not entirely as a generation in a way that affected the culture surrounding adulthood transitions for everyone. This is similar to preindustrial societies not having a life stage of adolescence. Yet many people in that era lived to see a day in which younger generations grew into adulthood by first being adolescents. There are generational differences as each cohort progresses through social conditions at a different point in their life course. Yet to attribute the life stage characteristics to the generation itself is to individualize a social process by describing it as if the generation has its own personality that will progress throughout the life course in the same way. This is a rather limited understanding of a social group and process, whereas a more sociologically informed perspective understands generations to be social groups formed in response to the social contexts present during their life course development. In this case, Millennials are the first generation to transition into adulthood with the life stage of emerging adulthood as part of the dominant life course culture in the United States.

What characterizes this emerging adulthood life stage is the "in-betweeness" as adulthood patterns are established. However, many scholars draw attention to the fact that the life stage is *heterogeneous*, meaning people experience it in different ways. For example, Settersten and Ray (2010) describe two categories of young people transitioning to adulthood: "swimmers," those who are able to keep afloat while making the long swim across to the shore of adulthood, and "treaders," a group that faces more challenges to keeping their head above water. Other scholars have described the experience of disadvantaged emerging adults as "arrested adulthood" (e.g., Côté 2000) or "accelerated adulthood" (e.g., Lee 2012). These scholars point out the risks of not assuming adulthood roles at all and the risks of entering adulthood roles too soon. There are advantages and disadvantages to the multiple trajectories people take into adulthood, and a balance between entering adulthood too soon and too late appears to be best. The fourth reading of this chapter describes six pathways that characterize the majority of emerging adults, revealing life stage inequalities (Osgood et al. 2005).

READING 1.4

Six Paths to Adulthood: Fast Starters, Parents without Careers, Educated Partners, Educated Singles, Working Singles, and Slow Starters

By Wayne D. Osgood, Gretchen Ruth, Jacquelynne S. Eccles, Janis E. Jacobs, and Bonnie L. Barber

It must be remembered, however, that these are not empirical relations in the usual sense. The five measures are not simply related to group membership but, rather, define groups in much the same way that answers to a series of attitude items define scores on the scale that they comprise. This next section of our chapter moves beyond the definition of the latent classes to draw a richer picture of their lives at age twenty-four. In other words, we seek to better understand what it means for individuals to take each of the six paths by describing other aspects of their lives that extend beyond their basic status on these five traditional role domains. To do so we compare the six classes on a number of additional lifestyle variables measured at the same point in time. ... We report only differences between groups that meet the conventional standards of statistical significance (two-tailed $p < .05$), except in a few cases when we note otherwise.

Wayne D. Osgood, Gretchen Ruth, Jacquelynne S. Eccles, Janis E. Jacobs, and Bonnie L. Barber, "Six Paths to Adulthood: Fast Starters, Parents without Careers, Educated Partners, Educated Singles, Working Singles, and Slow Starters," On the Frontier of Adulthood: Theory, Research, and Public Policy, ed. R. A. Settersten, F. F. Furstenberg, and R. G. Rumbaut, pp. 330–339. Copyright © 2008 by University of Chicago Press. Reprinted with permission.

The Fast Starters.

The fast starters are the respondents who had gone the farthest in entering adult roles. As noted above, they had the highest rates of marriage, home ownership, and employment in jobs they saw as long term; most of the fast starters were parents as well.

More detailed information about the fast starters' employment supports the impression that they were the group most firmly established in the world of work. They worked more hours per week than most of the other groups (forty-two hours per week compared to an overall mean of thirty-five), and their average earnings per week were the highest of the six ($674 compared with an overall mean of $471).[1] Yet their employment profile also showed the limits of their education. Only 26% held jobs with prestige ratings above the midpoint of the scale, compared to 42% for the entire sample. Furthermore, few fast starters held professional positions (9% vs. 22% overall), while jobs in skilled and technical trades were especially common (35% vs. 24% overall). Few of the fast starters were taking steps to gain the postsecondary education they had lacked so far. Only 9% were currently enrolled in college-level courses, compared to 23% for the entire sample.

In the realm of romantic or family relationships, there were no reliable differences among the six groups on average levels of satisfaction with marital, cohabiting, or steady dating relationships. There were slight differences across groups, however, with respect to whether they thought the relationship was in trouble or had thought about ending the relationship. Fast starters were less likely to view their romantic relationships negatively. When asked if they had ever felt that their relationship was in trouble, only 55% of this group agreed versus 68% for the full sample. Fast starters were also less likely ever to have suggested ending their relationship, at 23% compared to 34% in the full sample. Yet fast starters were significantly more likely to indicate being involved in physically abusive relationships, reporting the highest number of times their partners had thrown something at them.

The length of time respondents had been married and cohabiting did vary across these six groups, with the fast starters falling near the sample mean for both. At age twenty-four, the average length of their marriages was twenty-six months (vs. twenty-five for the entire sample) and the average length of their cohabitations was twenty-four months (vs. twenty-one). Before marrying, the fast starters had dated their future spouses an average of thirty-five months (also the overall sample mean), while their period of dating before cohabiting was on average twenty-one months (compared to nineteen for the entire sample). This indicates that married and cohabiting fast starters had typically been with the same partner since ages nineteen and twenty, respectively. Thus, the fast starters had entered long-term romantic relationships quite early in the transition to adulthood.

There was considerable variation across the groups in patterns of time use, and this variation corresponded to differences in romantic relationships and patterns of residence. As was typical of the groups that lived with romantic partners and away from parents, the fast starters devoted a great deal of their time to household and family-oriented activities, such as housework, yard work, and child care. Seventy-two percent of the fast starters spent more than twenty hours per week in such activities, compared to only 50% for the sample as a whole. Conversely, while 70% of the entire sample spent more than twenty hours per week in leisure pursuits, this was true for only 58% of the fast starters. The lower level of leisure time for fast starters held across physical activities (e.g., fitness, sports), skill-oriented activities (e.g., hobbies, reading), and hedonistic activities (e.g., hanging out with friends, going to bars and nightclubs, playing games). The fast starters also had low rates of illegal behavior, with only 42% engaging in any of a set of activities including illicit drug use, assault, and vandalism in the past six months, compared to 51% of the entire sample.

We asked respondents how much of the responsibility they took for a set of four adult tasks: earning their own living, paying rent, paying their other bills, and making sure that their household ran smoothly. Interestingly, although the fast starters had made more transitions into adult roles than the other groups, they were no more inclined than the average respondent to indicate that they had taken each of these adult responsibilities. With a few notable exceptions, members of all the six groups felt highly responsible in all of these areas. Only with regard to running the household did the fast starters feel somewhat more responsible than the average respondent (73% reported they did so most of the time, compared to 66% for the total sample).

To summarize, as our label implies, the fast starters had the most adult-like lives at age twenty-four. They were heavily invested in work and family, working full-time at jobs they saw as long term and living in romantic partnerships that they saw as stable and that had already lasted for several years. These commitments also translated to devoting more time to home and family and less time to leisure pursuits. The trade-off for these early transitions was less education, which brought less prestigious employment and weaker prospects for long-term occupational advancement.

Parents Without Careers.

Virtually all of the respondents on this path were parents who lived with romantic partners or spouses and who either did not work or held a job they regarded as short term. A high proportion of the parents without careers were female (71% vs. 58% for the entire sample). Most members of this group were housewives or mothers who worked at jobs in which they were not heavily invested. Even so, more than a quarter of the group were men, typically fathers who held short-term jobs.

The employment of the parents without careers was much more limited than those of the other groups. On average they worked only twenty-three hours per week and earned an average of only $239 per week, both figures the lowest of the six groups. The men in the group averaged many more hours of work per week than the women (forty-two vs. sixteen) and, accordingly, had far higher incomes ($476 per week vs. $154). Compared to other groups, the parents without careers were more likely to have jobs in sales, low-level service, and skilled trades and less likely to have jobs classified as professional or office work. Very few respondents on this pathway held positions with prestige rankings above the midpoint of the scale (18% vs. 42% overall). Furthermore, it is likely that many of the parents without careers will be in a weak position to raise the quality of their employment in the future. Not only did this group have the lowest level of previous education, at age twenty-four they were unlikely to be building on it by taking college-level courses (12% vs. 23% for the entire sample).

The marriages and cohabiting relationships of the parents without careers had lasted longer, and thus had begun at an earlier age, than those of the other groups. The average length of their marriages was thirty-three months, versus twenty-nine for the entire sample, and the average length of their cohabiting relationships was thirty-four months, versus twenty-nine for the entire sample. Parents without careers had a shorter period of dating before marriage (a mean of twenty-nine months vs. thirty-five overall). Thus, the length of their relationships with their spouses was effectively the same as the other groups, but they had married earlier. This pattern did not hold for cohabitation, however, so that the parents without careers had been involved in longer cohabiting relationships than respondents in the other five groups. Some differences appeared, however, with respect to the quality of partnerships, with 77% of this group feeling that their relationship was in trouble, compared to only 68% of the full sample. The parents without careers also reported a high number of times that their partner had thrown something at them compared to other groups (with the exception of fast starters, who had a slightly higher rate of abuse), indicating that their relationships may be more problematic than those in other groups.

The time use of the parents without careers also showed a greater emphasis on home and family: 82% spent more than twenty hours per week on activities in this domain, compared to 50% for the entire sample. Though this figure may be partly due to the high concentration of females in this group, the pattern holds for both sexes: 91% for females versus 59% overall and 74% for males versus 35% overall. Correspondingly, the parents without careers spent less time than all other groups in leisure activities, with only 20% reporting more than twenty hours per week, compared to 70% for the entire sample. They were also the group that spent the least time in the specific leisure domains of physical and hedonistic activities and the second lowest for time in skill-oriented activities. Relatively few committed any of the illegal acts assessed in this study.

Oddly enough, this high investment in home and family was associated with reporting relatively low levels in the assumption of some adult responsibilities. On average, parents without careers were the least likely to report that were responsible for earning their own living (54% vs. 84% for the entire sample) and paying their own bills (64% vs. 85% overall). It seems likely that this reflects a gender division in the household rather than a delayed transition to adulthood. Because many of these primarily female respondents either did not work or held poorly paying short-term jobs, they may have been indicating that their spouses or partners carried these responsibilities. Correspondingly, parents without careers were especially likely to report that they took most of the responsibility for seeing that their households ran smoothly (87% vs. 66% overall).

It is simplest to summarize the situation of parents without careers at age twenty-four by comparing them to the fast starters. These were the two groups with the deepest involvement in adult family roles. With their high rate of parenthood and heavy time investments, family may have been even more prominent in the lives of the partners without careers than in the lives of the fast starters. Yet these two groups are quite distinct when it comes to employment. Many parents without careers do not work, and those who do have jobs work few hours and earn little.

Educated Partners.

The profile of educated partners is quite distinct from those of fast starters and parents without careers. Although all three groups lived with romantic partners, the educated partners had much higher levels of education and none were parents by age twenty-four. Like the parents without careers, females were overrepresented among the educated partners (66% vs. 58% for the sample as a whole). ...

The *employment situation* of the educated partners was quite variable. A more detailed examination of their employment reveals both strengths and weaknesses. Educated partners held jobs with higher average prestige ratings (45% over the scale midpoint) than all other groups except the educated singles. Both of these groups also had the highest proportions of members employed in professional positions (24% for educated partners vs. 8% for all other groups except the educated singles). But other office work, including administrative support positions such as office supervisors, secretaries, typists, and clerks, was also *especially common in* this group. The educated partners worked a few more hours per week than the total sample on average (thirty-eight vs. thirty-five) and earned the same weekly wage ($471). Though the educated partners earned much less than the fast starters at age twenty-four, their future job prospects may have been brighter. Not only did the educated partners have much more previous education, they also were continuing to build their educations at a higher rate than the first two groups, with 27% currently enrolled in college-level courses (compared to 9% and 12%, respectively, for the first two groups).

In contrast to the other groups who lived with romantic partners, the educated partners had lived with their partners for a shorter period and their lifestyles were less distinct from those of respondents who did not live with romantic partners. Not only were the educated partners especially likely to cohabit rather than marry, but their cohabiting relationships were also newer—an average of seventeen months versus twenty-one for the entire sample. Furthermore, the average length of the marriages was only eighteen months, compared to twenty-five months for the entire sample. Nevertheless, they did date longer before marriage, an average of forty-one months versus thirty-five overall. This pattern of relative delay for entering marriage and cohabitation is consistent with the higher education of this group (see Fussell and Furstenberg, this vol., chap. 2; and Sandefur et al., this vol.; chap. 9). Adding an interesting wrinkle to this pattern, those educated partners who were married expressed the greatest satisfaction with their marriages of all six groups. In contrast, the cohabiting educated partners did not differ from the cohabiting members of the other five groups in their level of satisfaction with cohabitation. Finally, the educated partners were less likely than all other groups except the fast starters to feel that their relationship was in trouble (66% compared to 72% of all groups except fast starters).

The educated partners spent less time in household maintenance and family activities than the fast starters and parents without careers did (51% spending more than twenty hours per week, compared to 72% and 88%, respectively), and they spent more time in leisure pursuits (69% spending more than twenty hours per week, compared to 58% and 53%). Yet, like the other groups living with romantic partners, the educated partners spent relatively little time in hedonistic activities (29% spending more than twenty hours per week, compared to 39% in the full sample), and relatively few engaged in any of the illegal behaviors (44% engaging in one or more acts).

Similar to respondents in most of the other groups, the educated partners felt that they took most of the responsibility for earning their own living and paying rent. Like the first two groups, they were especially likely to feel that they were responsible for running their own household (78% vs. 66% overall), but they were somewhat less inclined to report that they bore most of the responsibility for paying their bills (78% vs, 85% overall).

In summary, despite living with a romantic partner, the educated partners in many ways exemplify the notion of emergent adulthood (Arnett 2000), for they appear to have delayed some adult commitments in favor of an extended period of exploration. The educated partners were less deeply involved in adult family roles than the fast starters and parents without careers. Furthermore, they had entered their romantic relationships more recently, they did not have children, and they spent less time in activities at home and with family. In these respects they are more similar to the groups who did not live with romantic partners. The educated partners also differed greatly from the first two groups in their employment trajectory. Their current employment profile is less stable and lower paying than the fast starters, indicating that many have not yet made strong progress in this domain. Yet their greater education and the higher prestige of their jobs suggest strong prospects for long-term success.

Educated Singles.

With their long-term schooling and later entry into family roles, the educated singles also appear to fit the mold of emergent adulthood (Arnett 2000). As defined by the latent class analysis (see fig. 10.1), the primary difference between educated singles and educated partners was that the educated singles did not live with romantic partners, and they were more likely to live with their parents. The educated singles had the highest level of education, with 61% holding bachelor's degrees.

Consistent with this high level of education, the educated singles were most likely to have high-status employment. Fifty-eight percent held jobs with status rankings above the midpoint of the prestige scale, compared to 45% for the educated partners and 31% or less for all other groups. Employment in professional positions was highly concentrated among the educated singles (34% vs. 24% for educated partners and no more than 13% for other groups). Surprisingly, their hours of employment (thirty-six per week) and earnings ($484 per week) were near the mean for the entire sample (thirty-five and $471, respectively), but this is attributable to the portion of the educated singles who were unemployed or in short-term jobs. The educated singles also tended to be on an upward trajectory that would increase their educational advantage: 30% were currently enrolled in college-level courses, the highest among the six groups.

There were few differences in relationship satisfaction among the three groups who were not living with romantic partners. In all three of these groups, however, respondents with steady dating relationships felt very differently about romantic relationships than those without. Respondents who were steadily dating were quite satisfied with their relationships (mean of 6.2 on a seven-point scale), which had lasted an average of twenty-nine months. Fifty-seven percent of those without steady relationships wanted one; and 63% felt it was somewhat to very important to have a committed relationship. Respondents without a steady relationship typically went on dates no more than once per week (72%). On the whole, respondents without a steady romantic relationship were not satisfied with their dating situation (66% responded 1-3 on a seven-point scale).

All three groups of respondents who did not live with romantic partners spent relatively little time in family and household activities. This was especially true of the educated singles, only 33% of whom devoted more than twenty hours per week to these endeavors, compared to 49% for the entire sample. Correspondingly, the educated singles spent the most time in leisure activities (80%, more than twenty hours per week), including high rates of physical activities, skill-oriented activities, and hedonistic activities. Fifty-six percent of the educated singles had engaged in at least one of the illegal behaviors, far more than any of the groups living with romantic partners (44% or less). Among the educated singles, those who lived on their own had even lower rates of family and household activities and higher rates of socializing than did the educated singles who lived with parents or relatives.

Despite their less settled lifestyle, the educated singles were just as likely as members of the other five groups to report bearing adult responsibilities in the areas of earning a living, paying their own bills, and paying rent. They were slightly less likely to report that they took the major responsibility for running their own households (60% vs. 66% overall).

The overall picture for the educated singles is of slower entry into adult roles associated with emergent adulthood. They were neither parents nor living with romantic partners, and they devoted little time to activities with family or at home. They were in the early stages of their careers, holding jobs *they saw as short term or steps in careers*. In accord with their high level of education, however, those jobs were more prestigious. For this group, which is by far the largest of the six (39%), there is clear evidence that the midtwenties are a period of continuing exploration and delayed commitment to adult roles. At the same time, the educated singles had gathered considerable personal capital through education and employment that should prove valuable resources for long-term economic success.

Working Singles.

The combination of living with parents and career-oriented employment distinguished the working singles from the other five groups. ... The working singles were similar to the educated singles in their pattern of romantic relationships and residence, and they were similar to the fast starters in their pattern of employment and education. Males were overrepresented in this group (53% vs. 43% overall)— the only group for which this was true.

A more detailed examination of employment illustrates the similarity of the working singles with the fast starters. The working singles earned relatively high incomes ($593 per week compared to an average of $471) and worked many hours per week (forty-two compared to thirty-five overall). Many of these respondents were employed in skilled and technical trades (33% vs. 24% overall). The average prestige of their positions was somewhat higher than the fast starters, with 31% above the scale midpoint, compared to 26% for the latter. Both of these two groups held jobs with considerably lower prestige than the educated partners and educated singles (45% and 58% above the midpoint, respectively). Thus, the working singles were well established in the world of work, with stable positions and jobs that provide moderate incomes and prestige. Sixteen percent of the working singles were currently taking college-level courses.

Our picture of the romantic relationships of the working singles is essentially the same as the educated singles and slow starters. The working singles' time use fell between that of the educated singles and the groups who lived with romantic partners. Forty-nine percent of the working singles spent more than twenty hours per week in family and household activities (compared to 50% overall), and 66% spent more than twenty hours per week in leisure activities (compared to 70% overall). The working singles spent higher than average amounts of time in physical activities and hedonistic activities but lower than average in skill-oriented activities. Their rate of illegal behavior was comparable to the educated singles (56% committed at least one of the acts). As with the educated singles, the working singles were especially likely to indicate that they were responsible for earning their own living, paying rent, and paying other bills but were less likely than groups living with partners to indicate that they were responsible for running their own households.

In sum, the working singles were *similar to the fast starters* in the world of work and education and similar to the educated singles in their family involvements. They invested more heavily in work than in education, and at twenty-four they had good earnings from long-term jobs that did not carry much prestige. They were less adult-like in their family relations in that they were neither married or cohabiting nor serving as parents, and they were quite likely still to live with their parents.

Slow Starters.

... The slow starters were not well established in the realms of romantic relationships, residence, employment, and education, but a moderate portion had *become parents*. Additional analysis showed that the slow starters worked fewer hours and earned less than all groups other than the parents without careers (thirty hours and $370 per week, respectively). They were especially likely to hold low-level service jobs (23% vs. 17% overall) and office jobs (27% vs. 22% overall); many had jobs in skilled or technical trades as well (28% vs. 24% overall). The prestige ratings of their positions were as low as those of the parents without careers, with only 18% rising above the midpoint of the scale. In contrast, a sizable portion of the slow starters was then taking college-level courses (21%, which was higher than all other groups except the educated partners and educated singles), and that should improve *their future employment prospects*.

It is notable that a particularly large portion of the slow starters was single, without a steady dating relationship (49%), and in all groups, respondents in this situation were those least satisfied with their romantic relationships. If slow starters did have a steady relationship, they were more likely than members of the other groups to report that their relationship was in trouble (78% vs. 68% overall). Unlike the educated singles and working singles, many of the slow starters were already parents. Among nonparents, however, the slow starters were somewhat less likely than other groups to expect that they ever would become parents.

The slow starters' time use was comparable to that of the working singles, falling between the educated singles and the groups living with romantic partners. More than half of the slow starters spent more than twenty hours per week in household and family activities (54% vs. 50% overall), and 68% spent more than twenty hours per week in leisure activities (compared to 70% overall). They devoted higher than average amounts of time to hedonistic activities (43% spending twenty hours per week or more compared to 39% in the full sample). Their rate of illegal behavior was the highest of all groups, with 63% reporting at least one of the acts.

The slow starters were about average for the amount of responsibility they reported taking for earning their own living, paying rent, and paying other bills. As with the educated singles and working singles, they were less likely than average to indicate that they took most of the responsibility for running their households.

As the label implies, the slow starters were the group least advanced in their progression into adult roles. They can be seen as representing another version of emergent adulthood (Arnett 2000), for they have not assumed most of the traditional roles of adulthood, and they are, perhaps, in an extended period of exploration. In contrast to the educated partners and singles, however, they do not seem to be placing themselves in a strong position to succeed when the time comes to enter those roles. Most had reached their midtwenties with little education, they were still living with their parents, had unsatisfactory romantic relations, and were either not working or holding jobs with poor pay and prospects.

REFERENCES

Arnett, Jeffrey Jensen. 1994. "Are College Students Adults? Their Conceptions of the Transition to Adulthood." *Journal of Adult Development* 1(4):213–24.

Arnett, Jeffrey Jensen. 1997. "Young People's Conceptions of the Transition to Adulthood." *Youth & Society* 29(1):3–23.

Arnett, Jeffrey Jensen. 2000. "High Hopes in a Grim World: Emerging Adults' Views of Their Futures and 'Generation X.'" *Youth & Society* 31(3):267–86.

Arnett, Jeffrey Jensen. 2001. "Conceptions of the Transition to Adulthood: Perspectives from Adolescence through Midlife." *Journal of Adult Development* 8(2):133–43.

Arnett, Jeffrey Jensen. 2003. "Conceptions of the Transition to Adulthood among Emerging Adults in American Ethnic Groups." *New Directions for Child and Adolescent Development* 2003(100):63–76.

Arnett, Jeffrey Jensen. 2007. "Emerging Adulthood: What Is It, and What Is It Good For?" *Child Development Perspectives* 1(2):68–73.

Arnett, Jeffrey Jensen. 2014. "Presidential Address: The Emergence of Emerging Adulthood: A Personal History." *Emerging Adulthood* 2(3):155–62.

Arnett, Jeffrey Jensen. 2015. *Emerging Adulthood: The Winding Road from the Late Teens through the Twenties*, 2nd edition. Oxford University Press.

Anon. 2005. *Emerging Adults in America: Coming of Age in the 21st Century*. Washington, DC: American Psychological Association.

Bynner, John. 2005. "Rethinking the Youth Phase of the Life-Course: The Case for Emerging Adulthood?" *Journal of Youth Studies* 8(4):367–84.

Côté, James E. 2000. *Arrested Adulthood: The Changing Nature of Maturity and Identity*. New York University Press.

Côté, James E. 2009. "Identity Formation and Self-Development in Adolescence." In *Handbook of Adolescent Psychology*. John Wiley & Sons, Inc.

Erikson, Erik Homburger. 1968. *Identity: Youth and Crisis*. Faber & Faber.

Hartmann, Douglas and Teresa Toguchi Swartz. 2006. "The New Adulthood? The Transition to Adulthood from the Perspective of Transitioning Young Adults." *Advances in Life Course Research* 11:253–86.

Horowitz, Ava D. and Rachel D. Bromnick. 2007. "'Contestable Adulthood' Variability and Disparity in Markers for Negotiating the Transition to Adulthood." *Youth & Society* 39(2):209–31.

Lee, JoAnn S. 2012. "An Institutional Framework for the Study of the Transition to Adulthood." *Youth & Society* 46(5):706–30.

Mouw, Ted. 2005. "Sequences of Early Adult Transitions: A Look at Variability and Consequences." In *On the Frontier of Adulthood: Theory, Research, and Public Policy*, edited by

Richard A. Settersten, Frank F. Furstenberg, and Rubén G. Rumbaut, 256–91. University of Chicago Press.

Nelson, Larry J., Laura M. Padilla-Walker, Jason S. Carroll, Stephanie D. Madsen, Carolyn McNamara Barry, and Sarah Badger. 2007. "'If You Want Me to Treat You Like an Adult, Start Acting Like One!' Comparing the Criteria That Emerging Adults and Their Parents Have for Adulthood." *Journal of Family Psychology* 21(4): 665–74.

Osgood, Wayne D., Gretchen Ruth, Jacquelynne S. Eccles, Janis E. Jacobs, and Bonnie L. Barber. 2008. "Six Paths to Adulthood: Fast Starters, Parents without Careers, Educated Partners, Educated Singles, Working Singles, and Slow Starters." In *On the Frontier of Adulthood: Theory, Research, and Public Policy*, edited by Richard A. Settersten, Frank F. Furstenberg, and Rubén G. Rumbaut, 320–55. University of Chicago Press.

Schneider, Barbara L. and David Stevenson. 2000. *The Ambitious Generation: America's Teenagers, Motivated but Directionless*. Yale University Press.

Schwartz, Seth J., James E. Côté, and Jeffrey Jensen Arnett. 2005. "Identity and Agency in Emerging Adulthood: Two Developmental Routes in the Individualization Process." *Youth & Society* 37(2):201–29.

Schwartz, Seth J., Byron L. Zamboanga, Koen Luyckx, Alan Meca, and Rachel A. Ritchie. 2013. "Identity in Emerging Adulthood: Reviewing the Field and Looking Forward." *Emerging Adulthood* 1(2):96–113.

Settersten, Richard and Barbara E. Ray. 2010. *Not Quite Adults: Why 20-Somethings Are Choosing a Slower Path to Adulthood, and Why It's Good for Everyone*. New York: Bantam.

Settersten, Richard A. 2011. "Becoming Adult: Meanings and Markers for Young Americans." In *Coming of Age in America: The Transition to Adulthood in the Twenty-First Century*, edited by Mary C. Waters, Patrick J. Carr, Maria J. Kefalas, and Jennifer Holdaway . Berkeley: University of California Press.

Suárez-Orozco, Carola. 2015. "Introduction to the Special Issue on Emerging Adulthood." *Journal of Adolescent Research* 30(5):535–37.

Tanner, Jennifer L., Jeffrey J. Arnett, and Julie A. Leis. 2009. "Emerging Adulthood: Learning and Development during the First Stage of Adulthood." In *Handbook of Research on Adult Learning and Development*, edited by M. Cecil Smith and Nancy Defrates-Densch. Routledge.

Tanner, Jennifer L. 2006. "Recentering during Emerging Adulthood: A Critical Turning Point in Life Span Human Development." In *Emerging Adults in America: Coming of Age in the 21st Century*, edited by Jeffrey J. Arnett and Jennifer L. Tanner, 21–56. American Psychological Association.

Trzesniewski, Kali H. and M. Brent Donnellan. 2014. "'Young People These Days …': Evidence for Negative Perceptions of Emerging Adults." *Emerging Adulthood* 2(3):211–26.

Twenge, Jean M., Stacy M. Campbell, Brian J. Hoffman, and Charles E. Lance. 2010. "Generational Differences in Work Values: Leisure and Extrinsic Values Increasing, Social and Intrinsic Values Decreasing." *Journal of Management* 36(5):1117–42.

Waters, Mary C., Patrick J. Carr, Maria J. Kefalas, and Jennifer Holdaway, eds. 2011. *Coming of Age in America: The Transition to Adulthood in the Twenty-First Century*. Berkeley: University of California Press.

CHAPTER 2

Social Changes & Rising Complexities

Millennials are a hot topic these days, and many popular press publications are written on the topic of Millennials and social change. Based on a selection of popular press publications available for purchase from Amazon.com, Figure 2.1 displays a word count representation of the most commonly used words in the description of these publications. Excluding words such as the, a, and an, the results indicate that how is the most common word in these publications and is written around 230 times. The second most common word is their at about 200 instances, followed by your with about 165 instances. Education is the fourth most common word, with about 150 instances in the descriptions. What is the fifth most common with just under 150, and new is the sixth most common, with about 130 instances. Combined, these word counts provide an initial read of current curiosity regarding Millennials and the social changes they represent. Reading across their modal words, there is an indication that people are wondering how to understand Millennials. The high prevalence of the words their and your give an impression of an "us and them" picture that accurately describes most of these publications. They are largely written for people from the Baby Boom generation who are experiencing some generational disconnects with Millennials and wondering how to work with them, educate them, church them, or in other ways interact.

GENERATIONAL CHANGES & SOCIAL DIFFERENTIATION

Generational disconnects refer to generations representing distinct starting points for understanding society that can result in generational disconnects. To understand these disconnects, it is important to take a historical view on the social changes of the last few decades. Many refer to these as a silent revolution in the ways *industrialization* reconfigured the social landscape and changed social values for family, work, and success from stability, hard work, and connection to the land toward adaptability, flexibility, self-expression, and companionship to navigate a changing society. In the mid-twentieth century, sociologist Ernest Burgess (1948) reported:

> The American family presents an external picture of diversity and winstability. When viewed in the context of the social change from rural to urban conditions of life, a trend is revealed to the companionship type of family, adapted to urbanization and exemplifying the American ideals of democracy, freedom, and self-expression. The seeming instability of the family is largely a symptom of this transition which may be regarded as a vast social experiment in which adaptability becomes more significant for success in marriage and family living than a rigid stability (p. 417).

This is evidenced in the first reading of this chapter, in which Elder and Conger (2000) discuss how changes to the agricultural economy continued to reshape family configurations, intergenerational interdependency, and social values. After the Great Farm Crisis of the 1980s, many farming families in this study based in Iowa had still not recovered from the losses to their agricultural way of life and expressed feeling nostalgic for the past. The losses these farm families described helps to contextualize generational changes in a longer historical perspective, recognizing that Millennials are growing up entirely after these changes to the economy, family, and society occurred.

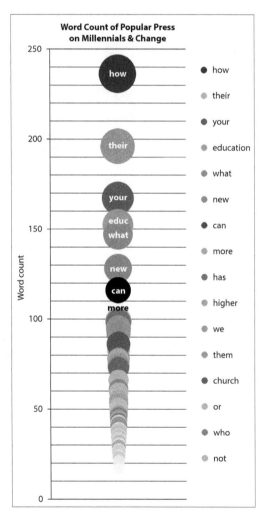

FIGURE 2.1 Millennial popular Press Word Count

READING 2.1

Families and the Generations

By Glen H. Elder and Rand D. Conger

The Great Farm Crisis of the 1980s placed many Iowa families in precarious circumstances. Over a third of the fathers who were farming during the early 1990s still felt that they would not be able to recover financially from their losses, and a fifth made similar claims about their lingering emotional distress. Nevertheless, virtually all remained committed to the belief that "farming was a good way of life," and most of their wives shared this appraisal. In large part, farming was good for family life and for children. The farmstead represented a place where children acquired sound values, where freedom meant responsibility, a place where the generations worked together.

When traced across the generations, belief in the virtues of a farm childhood clearly has elements of a romantic image of the past, a "world in which children can run and play freely, safe from the problems and threats of the city."[1] Yet

---

1   Garkovich, Bokemeier, and Foote, Harvest of Hope, 48. One Kentucky farmer they interviewed concluded that "a farm is the best place in the world for a child to grow up. They have a lot of advantages. They learn the sense of responsibility for one thing. They don't have a lot of idle time with nothing to do; there's always something for them to do" (61). Idealized views of farm life and the rural countryside as a place "to bring up children" are commonplace in the Iowa sample. Gill Valentine

Glen H. Elder and Rand D. Conger, "Families and the Generations," Children of the Land: Adversity and Success in Rural America, pp. 33–35. Copyright © 2000 by University of Chicago Press. Reprinted with permission.

many Iowans in the study embraced this view, ignoring the high accident rate among farm children. Over a fourth of the grandparents stressed the close-knit relations of farm families, while others mentioned a responsible work ethic, the ease of parental supervision and control, the experience of nature, and constructive things for children to do. Their grandchildren shared these sentiments, particularly if they came from farms. For example, over two-thirds of the boys described a farm as the best place for a child, compared to fewer than 13 percent of the boys from nonfarm households.[2]

In theory, some of these virtues of a farm childhood represent qualities that make farm families resourceful pathways to adulthood for children. Three domains have special significance:

- The embeddedness of farm families within the larger community through kin ties and connections to social institutions, especially the school, church, and civic organizations
- The interdependency of farm family life, as expressed in joint work and social activities between the generations, and in collective commitments that subordinate individual interests to family considerations
- Values of responsibility, industry, nonmaterialistic attitudes, and family commitments.

… Each of these domains constitutes potential connections between Iowa families with ties to the land and the behavioral competence of their children. Thus, the first question to answer is, Are families with ties to the land more embedded in the larger rural community when compared to families with no such connections to agriculture? Are these families characterized by more shared activity among grandparents, parents, and child, and by a stronger sense of family? Is the civic engagement of parents also mirrored in the lives of their children, in church functions, school activities, and community associations? And, last, Are families in farming more likely to expose children to values of responsibility, industry, and nonmaterialistic sentiments?

Iowa families, as we have seen in the study sample, vary widely on ties to the land, ranging from the ecologies of full-time and part-time farming to the displaced who lost their farms, the farm-reared parents who grew up on a farm but are not now

---

has investigated the process by which such imaginings are constructed in a rural community in England ("A Safe Place to Grow Up?").

The other side of the safe-haven image of rural farm life is the extraordinarily high accident rate. In general, agriculture is among the most hazardous industries in the United States (Michael D. Schulman, Christian T. Evensen, Carol W. Runyan, Lisa R. Cohen, and Kathleen A. Dunn, "Farm Work Is Dangerous for Teens"). Boys are most likely to have farm jobs in adolescence and were at highest risk of injuries in this North Carolina study.

2   In an open-ended interview during the twelfth grade, Iowa youth from farms were most likely to cite the following advantages of living on a farm and in the rural countryside: the freedom and beauty of the open space, privacy, the appeal of wildlife and nature, and the acquisition of practical skills. Small-town young people cited friendliness and safety as primary advantages of their locale. As disadvantages, youth from the farm and open countryside cited the distance and transportation challenge, while town youth stressed the lack of things to do, the prevalence of gossip, and the disadvantages of a more sheltered life.

farming, and nonfarm households. The parents in nonfarm families have no farming experience, either in childhood or in the adult years. We use this category as our comparison in a series of analyses that estimate the effect of ties to the land. Depending on the outcome, we contrast each ecological group with the nonfarm, adjusting for socioeconomic influences. Though some families changed their ecological niche over the course of the study, we focus on the typical placement of the Iowa families when their study children were in the seventh through tenth grades.

We begin this chapter on the theme of kinship ties and family continuity in agriculture, an intergenerational transition in which farm sons succeed their fathers or are launched by them with newly acquired land. Mark Friedberger tells the story of an Iowa farmer who managed to launch nine of eleven sons in farming between the economically depressed 1930s and the 1960s.[3] He did so by working out low-interest loans for run-down property with the Farmer's Home Administration or Land Bank, and then proceeding to sell the land to his sons on contract well below the market value. Family continuity on the same land and homestead understandably requires opportunity as well as motivation,[4] such as access to an economically successful farm and good relations with father.

Nearly 70 percent of the Iowa parents have fathers who once farmed (the study child's grandfathers), but only a third were engaged in farming at the end of the 1980s. We first identify socioeconomic and family factors that made a difference in the paths followed by young men in the G2 generation (fathers of the study children), and then compare the life histories of farmers in the two generations. This provides a social and cultural context for understanding the social capital of farming generations in the lives of children, the second part of this chapter. Social capital refers to the web of ties between grandparents and parents, and the interdependence of farming parents and children.

Farm families are distinguished by a collective interdependence that relates members to family goals, whether business or other. Children are brought up in farm families to consider family business needs as family needs. Especially in planting and harvest seasons, the farm takes priority over everything. During these periods of family mobilization and the routine cycle of farm life, children experience heightened expectations of interdependency. Salamon points out from her Illinois study of farming communities that "involvement in farm activities conveys to children, from an early age, their importance to the family enterprise."[5]

Kinship ties and the interdependence of farm families are important components of the social embeddedness of farm children. Another component involves the community connections of parents and children. In the second part of this chapter, we turn to the civic, school, and church ties of parents, and to the social activities of their children in school and community. The residential stability of farm life favors social

---

3   Friedberger, *Farm Families and Change*, 133.
4   Thomas A. Lyson, "Pathways into Production Agriculture."
5   Salamon, *Prairie Patrimony*, 52.

investments in local institutions, as does the German farming heritage of most families in the sample. Accordingly, we expect such involvement to be most characteristic of both generations in farm families as compared to more mobile nonfarm households.

Our concluding section centers on values that distinguish family life in farming. These include a sense of responsibility, a work ethic, and nonmaterialistic goals. If Iowa farm youth are more involved in activities with their parents than nonfarm adolescents, as observations suggest, they would rank high on a belief that they are counted on by parents, that they are responsible. Family-based farming has also traditionally subordinated consumption to the priorities of successful farming and its way of life. In her study of family-based farming in Georgia, Barlett interpreted the intrusion of materialistic goals of consumption as a threat to the financial survival of family farms.[6] With these observations in mind, we expect farm parents and youth to be less oriented toward materialistic objectives in life when compared to nonfarm families.

---

6   Barlett, *American Dreams*.

As Elder and Conger (2000) describe, what characterized farm living was heredity across generations and shared family commitments. Farming families all shared in common with each other a feeling of being tied to the land, a place attachment that literally kept people grounded. Whether Baby Boomers grew up on farms or not, this understanding of social life was still the dominant perspective during their childhood. However, this agricultural-based perspective is foreign to most young Americans today, the vast majority of whom grew up in urban areas, or at least have spent most of their adulthood in cities, and often without major ties to land. Even those remaining in rural areas are not immune to the social and cultural changes resulting from the increasing urbanization of the United States as a whole:

> Today, more than 80% of Americans live in urban areas; the largest 10 metropolitan areas alone account for more than 25% of the U.S. population (U.S. Census Bureau 2010a). Whereas the rural share of the U.S. population has declined over time, the number of rural residents remains relatively stable at approximately 50 million, a large population by any measure. Unlike the past, however, the communities and people left behind in rural America are much less isolated from mainstream cultural and economic influences. Paradoxically, rural and small-town America is experiencing a new urbanization and urbanism (Lichter and Brown 2011, 566).

This shift away from an agricultural lifestyle, even in remaining farming communities, has tremendously affected what it means to be an adult in the contemporary United States, including how people experience growing up and transitioning to adulthood. For this reason, sociologists have long been interested in *adulthood transitions* and the ways individual choices interact with social structural patterns to shape life experiences over time. As the following quote exemplifies, the key sociological distinction in studying the life course is that adulthood transitions are not merely a reflection of individual choices but instead represent choices made in reference to changing social contexts:

> Life-course transitions are more than an individual matter; they involve an interplay between the individual and what he or she confronts as society or the social structure. The historical and cross-cultural variability of transitions supplies ample evidence that they are not a simple result of developmental processes but, instead, reflect specific kinds of institutional structures (Foner and Kertzer 1978, 1081).

The changes underway with life course transitions intensified further with the *technological revolution* of the 1980s. Bell (1989) describes four characteristics of these monumental technological changes: the rise of electromechanical electronics, miniaturization ("shrinkage" of units conducting electricity), digitization, and software (as opposed to merely static operating systems). He described their importance as extending beyond advances in technology to affecting every aspect of society:

> The most crucial fact about the new technology is that it is not a separate domain (such as the label "high-tech" implies), but a set of changes that pervade all aspects of society and reorganize all older relationships (p. 445).

Bell continued by explaining that prior generations produced an "age of motors" and that the current times were producing an "age of computers." The resulting society is what he and others termed a postindustrial society. In particular, a postindustrial society is one characterized by the rapid expansion of a service-based economy. Describing the ensuing changes to social life during the postindustrial transition, Bell (1989) stated: "In effect, the world of the postindustrial society requires new modes of social organization, and these are only now being fashioned by entrepreneurs of the new technology" (p. 453).

The outcome was a monumental shift in social life. Browne (1995) described the major economic restructuring that came with the decline in manufacturing jobs and the loss of employment for unskilled workers that resulted in more un/under-employment and increased vulnerability to layoffs and recessions. The increased risks and decreased opportunities across generations led to different processes of aging (Gove et al. 1989), with a decline in intergenerational solidarity (Bengston & Achenbaum 1993; Silverstein & Bengston 1997).

All of these change cumulated into a process called *social differentiation*, referring to a rise in smaller social groups which marked distinctions among people. That is, rather than sharing a common bond as agricultural families, postindustrial society is characterized instead by many more social groups and various options for family, work, and social life without a great deal of shared commonality.

In terms of the impact on social science, a burgeoning body of scholarship investigating the multiplicity of processes led to keen interest in the sociology of the life course, with more survey data becoming available and the development of longitudinal studies that were able to track youth through their teenage years and into early adulthood (e.g., Furstenberg 2000).

Like their psychologist peers described in Chapter 1, sociologists in the 1980s and 1990s also recognized the impact of these *macro-structural changes* on life course transitions (e.g., Kohli 1986; Rindfuss et al. 1987; George 1993; Elder 1994; Hill & Yeung 1999; Furstenberg 2000). They shared a similar interest in the personal results of these social issues for personal optimism and social identity (e.g., Cerulo 1997; Arnett 2000). However, a key distinction in sociological investigations of the life course is attention to social statuses, such as patterns of employment (e.g., Mare et al. 1984; Morgan et al. 1985), timing of marriage (e.g., Modell et al. 1978), effects of divorce on the residential mobility of children (e.g., South et al. 1998), diversity in timing of leaving home and adulthood values by ethnic and religious culture (e.g., Goldscheider & Goldscheider 1988), and the net effect of life experiences in the transition to adulthood for psychological well-being (e.g., Singer et al. 1998).

For example, in tracking social trends from the 1970s into the 1980s, Smith (2005) described several trends characterizing generational changes across time, saying: "In terms of family structure, the young are more likely to have grown up in broken homes, to have gone through a parental divorce, and to have fewer brothers and sisters than previously" (p. 179). He continues: "Young people also display different patterns of family formation. They are less likely to be married than previous cohorts, have had fewer children, and live in smaller households than they used to" (p. 179).

Smith (2005) describes the socioeconomic changes across generations by stating: "In terms of labor force measures, young adults experience less long-term employment and are more likely to be in full- and part-time employment than previous cohorts of young adults" (p. 181). He also describes that younger generations are more racially and ethnically diverse than their predecessors due to changes in population demographics across time. All this, Smith states, results in changes in attitudes, values, and behaviors. Most notably, younger generations feel greater job insecurity than do older generations, coupled with increased cynicism, decreased trust in social institutions, and an overall greater disconnect from social organization among young people. In sum, he states: "the young are more disconnected from society" (p. 194).

To summarize these social and historical changes in the context of generations, bringing a sociological perspective on the history of social changes in recent decades reveals that generational labels mistakenly characterize generations as having different personalities. What *is* distinct across time, however, is the social context in which generational cohorts come of age. Putting all of this together, we can understand generations as mirrors reflecting the social contexts of their formative experiences during childhood. The *Silent Generation* born before 1950 represents the farming and agricultural community described in the nostalgia of the Elder and Conger (2000) study, whereas the *Baby Boomers* born between around 1946 and 1964 represent the first generation to grow up entirely in mostly urbanizing places, but with parents who still had agricultural roots, and since the age of motors described by Bell (1989). Gen Xers, born roughly between 1964 and 1980, represent the first generation to grow up since the age of computers caused personal computers to become commonplace during their adolescence and young adulthood. Those born since around 1980, Millennials, represent the first generation to come of age since the postindustrial changes to a service economy and with widespread availability of the Internet, Wi-Fi, and smart phones. With each set of economic and technological changes came accompanying social changes to the configurations of cities, families, school, work, and organizations. Thus, to sociologists, the life course is itself a social process that changes over time.

DE-STANDARDIZED LIFE COURSE

In the early to mid-2000s, sociologists highlighted the variability in life course pathways (e.g., Shanahan 2000). *Disordered adulthood*: Some called this de-standardization of the life course (e.g., Brückner & Mayer 2005); others referred to it as differentiated adulthood trajectories (e.g., Macmillan 2005); and still others the deinstitutionalization of the life course (e.g., Kohli 2007). In an article section entitled "Heterogeneity and Social Differentiation," Kohil (2007) explained:

> As the life course has become more complex, the assumption of a unified model may be less and less appropriate. Of course, life has always been complex, and it is only in retrospect that we have been able to detect a (fairly) homogenous evolutionary pattern. However, in many respects, there has indeed been a trend toward complexity since the 1960s (p. 261).

What all this means is that age, and generation, have become a marker of social diversity, and often one that relates to major social inequalities. The most substantial changes are the nonchronological processes of establishing adulthood markers, meaning there is greater variability in the timing of adulthood events. Perhaps the root cause of this is that monogamous work—lifelong work to a single organization—is less likely and even obsolete for many young people today (Kohli 2007). Meanwhile, life course patterns are also shaped in different ways based on class, gender, and race (Brückner 2004; Aronson 2008; Lichter 2013; Syed & Mitchell 2013).

Whatever one makes of the larger societal impact of generational changes, there is no mistaking that today emerging selves are more flexible, constructed, multiple, and relational than the fixed and determined selves of previous generations (Thomson 2000, 89). Static social roles evolved into interpersonal relationships, and goals of achieving a stable long-term self-identity evolved to desirability for an ever-changing self in a multiplicity of adulthood options. Thomson (2000) explains the result:

> The new model of self that appears to be emerging in contemporary American society is relational rather than in conflict with society, fluid rather than fixed, constructed rather than determined, and multiple rather than unified. In its fluidity and its constructed and multiple nature, it resembles a variety of contemporary theories of self.... The postmodern self ... is clearly multiple (p. 107).

What all of these social changes and evolving understandings of selves as social beings mean for transitions to adulthood is increased diversity and variability in the process of becoming an adult in a socially differentiated American culture.

DIVERSITY, COMPLEXITY, AND MULTIPLE PATHWAYS

Increased social differentiation and variability in life course pathways mean that emerging adulthood today, and social life more generally, is characterized by diversity and complexity. Arnett (2015) states: "There are likely to be many emerging adulthoods—many forms the experience of this life stage can take—depending on social class, culture, and perhaps other characteristics such as gender and religious group" (p. 265).

When applied to emerging adulthood, diversity means there are many ways in which young people navigate social institutions while seeking to establish adult lives. Some marry and then go to school, others work, then start a family, and then return to school, and so on. While all emerging adult scholars agree on the diversity of adulthood pathways, the key characteristic of sociological approaches to the life course is an understanding that not all paths are created equal.

While *heterogeneity* in institutional arrangements during adulthood transitions make them challenging to study in a unified way (e.g., Settersten 2003), many life course sociologists highlight the importance of investigating the sequencing patterns in establishing markers of adulthood (e.g., Buchmann & Kriesi 2011). For example, the timing of when emerging adults leave home, and when they return—as many do during the extended launch to adulthood self-sufficiency—are important differentiators of life course paths (e.g., South & Lei 2015).

In viewing diversity of adulthood pathways from another angle, we see the importance of different social statuses for conditioning experiences of emerging adulthood. For example, scholars find that the meaning of adulthood markers varies for men and women, in other words gender conditions experiences of emerging into adulthood (e.g., Brückner 2004; Fussel & Gauthier 2005; Wu & Li 2005; Aronson 2008; Widmer & Ritschard 2009). Similarly, race and ethnicity related to different experiences of adulthood transitions (e.g., Arnett 2003; Mollenkopf et al. 2005; Tandon & Solomon 2009; Swisher et al. 2013; Lichter 2013; Syed & Mitchell 2013), as does immigrant status (e.g., Katsiaficas et al. 2015). Even more complex is the fact that race, nativity, and gender intersect in shaping adulthood trajectories (Fussell & Furstenberg 2005). Emerging adulthood is a life stage characterized by some shared characteristics and also experienced in different ways by subgroups of young people.

In summary, emerging adulthood is a life stage that young people experience in different ways, some because of the choices made along the path to adulthood, some because of the circumstances faced, and especially because of the two simultaneously (Côté 2002).

THE AGE OF INSECURITY

With all this diversity and complexity, what then do emerging adults share in common? They are growing up in a diverse and complex social milieu in which age does not necessarily default one into adulthood, or at least not with the same circumstances.

Emerging adults also share in common that they are navigating to adulthood in a less economically secure time than their parents and prior generations did. Pugh (2015) calls America today the "tumbleweed society" and states:

> We live in a tumbleweed society, where job insecurity is both profound personal experience and mundane conventional wisdom, widely seen as inevitable, part of what people consider the inescapable cost of broad social forces that none of us can do anything about, such as the spread of globalization, information technology, privatization, and neoliberalism (p. 197).

Stable and long-term employment has become the anomaly (e.g., Mendenhall et al. 2008), and people who have it are in markedly better circumstances than those who do not. The precariousness of employment means that some young people experience variability not just in the labor market but also in family and marriage configurations—dubbed the "marriage-go-round"(p. 199). Detachment, or a lack of commitment, is often the primary defense mechanism protecting selves from social ambiguity.

In the fourth reading of this chapter, Cooper (2014) describes families as cut adrift on a sea of insecurity and highlights the inequality of security in today's society. The author identifies four strategies for how most Americans cope with and seek to create some security in their lives: downscaling, upscaling, holding on, and turning to God. On downscaling in particular, Cooper states:

This attitude of seeming indifference puzzled me until I realized that it reflected a way of managing economic hardships and the deep tensions they provoked. This downscaling of security involves lowering the bar on requirements for security, resigning oneself to living with these reduced levels, and suppressing anxiety when it arises. It's a form of emotion work in which those who are struggling economically submerge certain emotions and bring forth others in order to control their anxiety over difficult or precarious circumstances (p. 22).

READING 2.2

One Nation Under Worry

By Marianne Cooper

Security Transformations and The Inequality of Security

Since the 1970s, economic, political, and social trends have transformed the way Americans go about creating security in their lives. Americans can no longer expect to work for the same company their whole career. They can no longer assume that a job will offer health benefits or that a pension will provide for them in their old age. Indeed, Americans are increasingly required to provide for their own security—to fund their own health care, retirement, and the ever-increasing costs of higher education—at the same time they are burdened by increases in the cost of living and an uncertain job market. Yale political scientist Jacob Hacker has described this transformation as the "Great Risk Shift," in which "economic risk has been offloaded by government and corporations onto the increasingly fragile balance sheets of workers and their families."[1]

We now live a new American reality: we are on our own, and it is tougher out there than it used to be. But exactly *how* tough it is depends on where one sits in relation to these

---

1 Jacob Hacker, *The Great Risk Shift: The Assault on American Jobs, Families, Health Care, and Retirement and How You Can Fight Back* (New York: Oxford University Press, 2006), ix.

Marianne Cooper, "One Nation Under Worry," Cut Adrift: Families in Insecure Times, pp. 13–24, 251–253. Copyright © 2014 by University of California Press. Reprinted with permission.

transformations. For this shift in risk has been accompanied by an enormous increase in income and wealth inequality. The rich have gotten richer while much of the middle and working classes have stagnated or fallen behind and the ranks of the poor have grown.[2] For example, from 1983 to 2007, the top 20 percent of households accounted for 89 percent of the total growth in wealth, while the bottom 80 percent accounted for just 11 percent.[3] In 2010, the top 20 percent of households in the United States owned almost 90 percent of all privately held wealth. By contrast, the networth of the bottom 40 percent of households was negative.[4]

The shift in risk affects everyone. However, because of the growth in economic inequality, Americans live in vastly different *risk climates* that are shaped by how much they earn, how much they can save, the level of benefits they receive, and their likelihood of experiencing financial hardship.[5] Younger and less-educated workers suffer higher rates of job displacement, while lower-income workers have experienced the largest drop in health insurance coverage and the least growth in retirement benefits.[6] Highly educated professional workers also face a shaky job market, but their benefits have remained more stable. Also, relative to other workers, higher-skilled workers earn more money and have better working conditions.[7] Low-income and middle-class households are more likely to experience financial hardships like bankruptcy or falling behind on payments, and African Americans and Hispanics are more likely to suffer a significant economic loss. In contrast, upper-class households and whites are more shielded from financial trouble.[8] Thus, not only is America highly unequal in terms of income and wealth, it is also unequal in terms of exposure to risk and insecurity.

This layering of inequalities in income, wealth, and risk, one atop the other, leads me to call these disparities in our society the *inequality of security*. It's a serious social and economic problem. Exploring how families grapple with their place within the inequality of security is one of the central themes of this book.

---

2 For a detailed review and explanation of economic inequality in the United States, see Rebecca M. Blank, *Changing Inequality* (Berkeley: University of California Press, 2011).
3 Edward N. Wolff, "Recent Trends in Household Wealth in the United States: Rising Debt and the Middle-Class Squeeze—An Update to 2007" (June 2010), Levy Economics Institute of Bard College, Working Paper No. 589.
4 Edward N. Wolff, "The Asset Price Meltdown and the Wealth of the Middle Class" (November 2012), National Bureau of Economic Research, Working Paper No. 18559.
5 For a review of the distribution of economic risk, see Bruce Western et al., "Economic Insecurity and Social Structure," *Annual Review of Sociology* 38 (2012): 341–59.
6 Neil Fligstein and Taek-Jin Shin, "The Shareholder Value Society: A Review of Changes in Working Conditions and Inequality in the United States," in *Social Inequality*, ed. Kathryn M. Neckerman (New York: Russell Sage Foundation, 2004), 401–32.
7 Ibid., 402–3.
8 Laura McCloud and Rachel Dwyer, "The Fragile American: Hardship and Financial Troubles in the 21st Century," *Sociological Quarterly* 52, no. 1 (2011): 13–35; Jacob S. Hacker et al., "Economic Security at Risk: Findings from the Economic Security Index" (July 2010), The Rockefeller Foundation.

Coping with Insecurity

Hundreds of scholars and researchers have studied the large-scale transformations in security, risk, and inequality and the social forces behind them. I'll summarize their most important findings in the next chapter. Less studied, however, has been the question of how families are responding to these changes. How secure do Americans feel? What do they think about their economic situations and what do they do about them? What problems are they most worried about? How are families managing in such uncertain times?

Even less studied is how a family's place within the inequality of security differentially shapes both what they have to react to and how they respond. In fact, most accounts of the shift in risk and the rise of insecurity are presented in a "top-down" fashion, as if these security transformations affect everyone in the same way and to the same degree.[9] However, the drastic increase in economic inequality and the existence of different risk climates alert us to the variability in how each of us must manage our security. How do the responses of families on different rungs of the inequality-of-security ladder vary depending upon their economic resources and educational attainment?

When I started the research for this book, my plan was to fill this gap in our understanding by exploring the structural and perhaps cultural differences in how a sample of families provided for their own security. Did some families face more insecurity while others faced less? Did some families' skills and resources help them navigate through the new world of risk more easily than other families?

My hypothesis was that the deepening social and economic divisions among Americans would significantly shape a family's level of exposure to insecurity and their ability to plot a steady course. Accordingly, at the start of this project, I imagined that those at the top of the wealth and income ladder would feel great—secure in their jobs, pleased with the luxuries they could afford, happy with the fine schools their children attended, and complacent about the comfortable retirements they planned to enjoy— while those on the lower rungs of the ladder would feel anxious and insecure, worried about their jobs, pressured to stretch their paychecks, resentful of the lower-performing schools their children attended, and despondent over the gloomy futures they foresaw.

As my research unfolded, however, the reality I uncovered was far more complex. I began to suspect that sometimes anxiety was just as palpable at the top of the ladder as it was at the bottom. Thus my initial question, "How secure do Americans feel?," gave way to a series of more probing questions: "What does it take to feel secure?" "How do people define security?" "Where do these definitions come from?" And "What benchmarks and ideologies frame people's understanding of their security—or lack thereof?"

---

9   For a review of how analyses of the risk society fail to take social class and educational differences into consideration, see Marianne Cooper, "The Inequality of Security: Winners and Losers in the Risk Society," *Human Relations* 61, no. 9 (2008): 1229–58.

With an ear attuned to the anxiety in people's lives, my narrow focus on structural and cultural differences among the families in my study started to broaden. I began to see that despite their critical importance, these factors didn't fully convey the kind of differences I saw emerging. In the lives of the families I came to know, feelings—anxieties, worries, perceptions of risk, beliefs about responsibility—and the way these feelings were managed also shaped their approach to maintaining and building security.

For example, as the opening vignettes about the Cliffords, the Chopras, and the Meehans reveal, these families contend with the specific pressures bearing down on them—from job layoffs to globalization to credit card debt—in a variety of ways. Debbie Clifford changed careers in search of greater security; Ditra Chopra travels the globe to network with business colleagues and prepare her children for their globalized future; Owen Meehan works two jobs as a way of attaining both the stability of paid employment and the extra income provided by entrepreneurship.

But their stories also show that forging security isn't simply a practical matter of choices regarding work or school; it's also an extraordinarily emotional process. The way Debbie Clifford compartmentalizes her stress, Ditra Chopra fixates on her children's futures, and Owen Meehan "outsources" financial worries to his wife all point to the complex role feelings and emotions play in how families go about creating stability in their lives.

Having attained this insight, when I met a family struggling with debt, I made an effort to examine not only the practical ways in which they coped with the debt but also the steps they took to manage its emotional weight. When I came across a family that meticulously planned for retirement, I examined not only their financial planning approach but also the feelings that gave rise to the need to plan so carefully.

By drawing attention to the feelings involved in people's responses to staving off insecurity, this book captures the interplay between large-scale macroeconomic changes that have increasingly shifted the job of creating and maintaining security onto individuals and the ways in which people are adapting to and coping with these forces. This kind of lens, which pays attention to the back-and-forth among structure, culture, and feeling, enabled me to see that people were *doing security*—they were developing coping strategies, consciously and unconsciously, that helped them deal with the changing nature of inequality and risk in our time. By illuminating how social factors like class position, education, and gender influence our emotional responses, this book lays bare just how deep our economic inequalities seep.

This exploration into both the strategies families employ to handle an economic situation and the emotions interacting with and shaping that strategy extends our understanding about how individuals and families get by in the new economy. In most other sociological examinations, the emotional component is overlooked in favor of documenting economic struggles with particular attention paid to how families with limited means make ends meet in hard times.[10] In the wake of massive economic restructuring, scholars have been especially concerned with the financial situation of those who have lost the most.

However, our understanding of how new inequalities and the shift in risk impact families is incomplete without a comparative understanding of the security strategies families in different socioeconomic boats pursue and the emotional dynamics involved in those strategies. If the goal is to understand inequality and its consequences, then we must study those who have more, not just those who have less. This is ever more the case when the rise in inequality is a result of the top pulling away from everybody else.

Moreover, people are not simply economic actors; they are also emotional actors, whose feelings are heavily influenced by inequality. As epidemiologists Richard Wilkinson and Kate Pickett have shown, where there are great economic disparities, there are also higher levels of physical and mental illness, violence, and social distrust.[11] Thus, inequality must be measured not just by the amount of money in our wallets, but also by the thoughts in our heads and the feelings in our hearts. Consequently, understanding how families are faring requires an investigation that is about more than just the economic conditions they face and the ways in which they acquire, allocate, and manage their financial resources. It also requires understanding how families manage their feelings, anxieties, and emotional burdens, which is inextricably tied to their financial troubles and their economic provisioning. A focus on feelings provides a "buried" yet illuminating perspective on these issues.[12]

Doing Security and The Emotion Work It Requires

In conceptualizing families' search for stability and reduced risk as "doing security," and in bringing an emotional lens to my study, I am drawing simultaneously on two distinct sociological frameworks. Sociologists use the concept of "doing" as a way to highlight the extent to which things like gender and social class are socially constructed. With regard to gender, for example, sociologists have shown how individuals are not simply born as men or women but *become* men and women through particular kinds of "doings" such as interactions (opening the door for someone) and practices (wearing cosmetics). In this way, gender is performed and enacted all the time. It is something a person does or says rather than something that a person is—an ongoing

---

10 For scholarship that focuses on economic struggles and economic provisioning, see Katherine Porter, ed., *Broke: How Debt Bankrupts the Middle Class* (Stanford, CA: Stanford University Press, 2012); Hacker, *The Great Risk Shift*; Elizabeth Warren and Amelia Warren Tyagi, *The Two-Income Trap: Why Middle-Class Parents Are Going Broke* (New York: Basic Books, 2003); Teresa A. Sullivan, Elizabeth Warren, and Jay Lawrence Westbrook, *The Fragile Middle Class: Americans in Debt* (New Haven, CT: Yale University Press, 2000); Margaret K. Nelson and Joan Smith, *Working Hard and Making Do: Surviving in Small Town America* (Berkeley: University of California Press, 1999).
11 Richard Wilkinson and Kate Pickett, *The Spirit Level: Why Greater Equality Makes Societies Stronger* (New York: Bloomsbury Press, 2010).
12 Arlie Russell Hochschild, *The Managed Heart* (Berkeley: University of California Press, 1983), 85.

activity or a *doing* within daily life.¹³ Furthermore, gender is not fixed but fluid. It is continually reconstituted—socially, psychologically, and institutionally.

The concept of "doing security" draws upon this tradition in that it highlights the work (or ongoing activity) involved in the search for (and achievement of) stability and security. In this sense, security—or insecurity—is created, performed, and worked toward in daily life. The notion of doing security reminds us that people are not simply secure or insecure. They "become" secure or insecure in part through social, psychological, and institutional interactions and practices. By viewing security (or insecurity) as partly a social construction, I'm able to illuminate the work—especially the emotion work—that is involved in creating it and performing it. My approach also reveals the degree to which the state of being secure (or insecure) is a deeply subjective one. Who feels secure and who feels insecure is, in many ways, a matter of perception.

My understanding of the role of feelings in the strategies that families develop is also guided by the sociologist Arlie Russell Hochschild's concepts of *emotion work* and *emotion management*. Hochschild's research reveals that people don't simply have feelings. Rather, social factors influence both what people feel as well as what "people think and do about what they feel." In other words, people actively work on and manage their *emotions*. They monitor, assess, inhibit, evoke, and shape emotions in different ways, often to get their feelings in line with cultural expectations or workplace expectations about how they should feel.¹⁴ Depending on people's sense of what they ought to feel in a given situation, they will "try not to feel guilty," or "try to feel happy," or they will "swallow their pride." In her classic account of emotional labor, Hochschild illustrated how flight attendants must, for example, suppress their anger at a misbehaving passenger, evoke instead an upbeat and pleasant demeanor, and continue to cater to the passenger's needs, all the while smiling.¹⁵

Emotion work is central to how people do security. For example, Debbie Clifford worked on her feelings when she tried to submerge and compartmentalize her anxiety in order to hold her economic unease at bay. By contrast, Ditra Chopra managed her emotions by focusing incessantly on her concern about her daughter's educational pursuits. As the chapters to come will show, how people manage their feelings tells us a lot about where they sit in relation to macroeconomic change.

In analyzing why those I studied hold certain views about and approaches to their security, I connect the concerns people have and the emotion work they do with their class-based standards and expectations about security. For example, Kate Casper, an upper-class white mother I interviewed, not only expected her three children to attend top colleges, but she also believed that she and her husband were the ones responsible for funding this education. This belief gave rise to her concern about the amount of

---

13 Candace West and Don Zimmerman, "Doing Gender," *Gender & Society* 1, no. 2 (1987): 125–51; and Judith Butler, *Gender Trouble: Feminism and the Subversion of Identity* (New York: Routledge, 1990).
14 Arlie Russell Hochschild, "Emotion Work, Feeling Rules, and Social Structure," *American Journal of Sociology* 85, no. 3 (1979): 551–75.
15 Hochschild, *The Managed Heart*.

money they had saved. Despite having about $60,000 saved for their fourteen-year-old, about $45,000 saved for their twelve-year-old, and close to $35,000 saved for their seven-year-old, Kate was worried. "We should have more. I think we need to have a hundred thousand by now… If [our oldest child] had to go to college next year, [$60,000] isn't going to do it. Tuition is $25,000 or $30,000 and that's not including expenses… so we're behind. In my book, we're behind." Kate's belief about what she and her husband ought to provide their children generates a concern that she must manage.

Tactically speaking, when it comes to standards and expectations about security, if you increase or decrease your threshold for security—what you need to have to feel secure—you inflate or reduce the dynamics of your worry. If Kate Casper instead decided that her children should attend a more affordable community college or that they should be the ones to pay for their own college educations, she would have less to worry about. However, because she held fast to the belief that a part of their parental responsibility was funding their children's higher educations at top-tier universities, Kate and her husband were concerned. Consequently, for the Caspers the $140,000 they have set aside feels like too little. For many of the other families I interviewed, and probably for most Americans, that $140,000 would feel like an enormous amount of money.

As we shall see, the kinds of beliefs people possess about security, whether they tend to round up or round down their security thresholds, and the type of related emotion work they do tell us a lot about their social position, and especially about their place within the inequality of security.

The Security Project

The key finding of my research is that, as a result of the inequality of security, the security preoccupations, security strategies, and emotional burdens experienced by families in various economic, social, and class tiers are dramatically different. Thus, the families in my study were engaged in widely divergent "security projects."

A security project, broadly defined, is all the economic and emotion work done by a family to create, maintain, and further their particular notion of security. This work may range from crossing national borders in search of higher pay, to cutting hours at work to better address a child's learning disability, to investing in a 401(k) account for retirement, to putting off paying an insurance premium in order to have enough money to pay the electric bill.

Not all aspects of security projects involve intentionality, planning, or even well-advised actions. Some ways of coping, like turning to drugs or alcohol in the face of difficult economic times, can worsen a family's circumstances—yet these, too, can be considered part of their security project. Moreover, since some families have numerous resources to draw upon while others have more limited options, parents may have multiple ways of coping or very few.

Finally, family members may not be in agreement about all aspects of a security project. There may be debate and disagreement about key aspects. For example, husbands and wives can be at odds about where they are going, *how they will get there, and who is in charge.* In fact, a common source of tension between couples was the security bargains that husbands and wives strike regarding who will be their family's security guard—who it is who will end up taking on the responsibility for worrying about money and security in the first place. A single security project thus may embrace different and even conflicting approaches and coping strategies.

The concept of security projects, then, involves a mix of objective conditions, subjective reactions to and ways of coping with these conditions, deliberate strategies of action, and unwitting coping mechanisms. Security projects are worked on every day, in small and large ways, both consciously and unconsciously. They evolve over time, getting negotiated, renegotiated, refined, and revised as economic and family circumstances change.

All security projects are united by a similar logic—namely, the need to define and attain security for the family and its members. However, a family's position in relation to larger economic forces influences both the objective and subjective dimensions of their security project. These variations are at the heart of my research. For example, middle and low-income families are financially vulnerable to problems like uninsured medical emergencies because of stagnating wages and declines in employer-provided benefits like health care. By contrast, upper-income families whose highly paid jobs provide full benefits are less encumbered by such worries. Also, the security bargains struck by affluent couples in which the husbands were more often their family's security guard looked much different than the bargains struck by less well-off couples in which the wives were usually security guards. Such realities shape the security projects that different families pursue.

What's more, socioeconomic differences among families affect their subjective experiences of security and the design of their security projects. We'll explore how this happens in the chapters to come as we examine security projects among affluent, middle-class, and poor families, each one a different response to the macroeconomic environment surrounding a particular family.

Ways of Doing Security

For the typical family, there will be a primary way they go about doing their security. In my study, I discovered four main approaches to security projects, which I describe as *downscaling, upscaling, holding on,* and *turning to God.* Of course, it is hard to know to what extent these patterns can be generalized from a single study that was conducted in one place at one time. Nonetheless, by examining these four approaches in depth, I hope to shed light on important questions about how families do security in insecure times, tracing how the rise in inequality and the shift in risk have played out in the private lives of people impacted by these forces. Here is a brief introduction to each of these four ways of doing security.

Downscaling.
During my research, I often left interviews with less well-off families with the sense that I was more concerned about their family's well-being than they were. At times it seemed as if the people I spoke to were trying to convince me—and themselves—that they were doing just fine with fewer material and economic resources and that they really had nothing to worry about.

This attitude of seeming indifference puzzled me until I realized that it reflected a way of managing economic hardships and the deep tensions they provoked. This downscaling of security involves lowering the bar on requirements for security, resigning oneself to living with these reduced levels, and suppressing anxiety when it arises. It's a form of emotion work in which those who are struggling economically submerge certain emotions and bring forth others in order to control their anxiety over difficult or precarious circumstances.

Upscaling.
Many of my interviews with affluent families left me with the sense that they were much more concerned about their family's wellbeing than their objective situation seemed to warrant. The surprising anxieties that I discovered among the rich led me to wonder why privileged families seem to yearn for even more than they already had. Why did they ratchet up what they needed to feel secure, feeling the need for millions of dollars in their retirement accounts as well as savings sufficient to allow their children to attend the world's best colleges and graduate schools?

I call this approach to doing security upscaling. As a result of upscaling, those with the most resources in my study were often plagued by the sense that they didn't *quite* have enough. Gender plays an important role in upscaling: it is generally the men in upper-class families who focus on financial concerns while the women focus on family issues. Nonetheless, both upper-class men and women in my study dealt with their anxieties similarly, mainly by thinking about their concerns, financial or otherwise, incessantly. Ironically, the way they managed their woriy was to worry, as if to distill and quantify the exact nature of the problem in order to come up with potential solutions. Paradoxically, however, rather than reducing their fears, this spotlight approach merely heightened their levels of anxiety.

Holding On.
Grappling with layoffs, income declines, debt, and insecurity was common among the middle-class, working-class, and poor families I studied. Yet when I interviewed members of these families about how they managed during these rough times, I often got conflicting his and hers accounts. Why, I wondered, were the women in these families expected to be the family's security guards, the "designated worriers" charged with keeping insecurity at bay, while their husbands were comparatively less burdened?

Eventually I found that the process I call holding on—trying to keep a family's security project on track in the face of economic challenges—is a profoundly gendered one. It is the women in middle-class and working-class families who generally do the worry work, figuring out whether there is enough money to pay the bills, afford the after-school activities, and save for retirement. I link holding on to the improving circumstances of better-educated women and the deteriorating circumstances of less-educated men.

Turning to God.
Many of the families I interviewed were religious, attending a church or synagogue on a regular basis. However, the interviews in which the church, religion, and faith came up most consistently were with working-class and poor respondents who had dealt with extreme economic difficulties. Social services offered by houses of worship enabled many of these families to survive, while their faith in God and their belief that God has a plan provided them with psychic and emotional relief and support. Why, I wondered, was it only these economically vulnerable families that relied so heavily on their churches and their faith to build their security projects? I connect this way of doing security with a growing tendency for government to hand over welfare responsibilities to faith-based organizations. In this book, I'll explore the potential negative consequences of religious institutions playing a central role in providing those in need with social supports.

Table 2.1 Social Class and Security Strategies

	Upper income	**Middle income**	**Low income**
Upscaling	√		
Downscaling		√	√
Holding On		√	√
Turning to God			√

Table 2.1 provides an overview of the relationships between social class and the different ways of doing security.

THE LIFE COURSE PATTERNS & CONSEQUENCES

Sociological approaches also study social changes resulting from globalization and describe contemporary, globalized society as the age of uncertainties (e.g., Jeffrey & McDowell 2004) in which more is unknown than known. People have an increasing amount of choices, which leaves postmodern people with an interesting paradox: too many choices (e.g., Schwartz 2005). The result is that even adulthood is a differentiated process that can be entered through many different paths and with ambiguous outcomes for the choices made. Such ambiguity, uncertainty, and complexity obscures that *patterns* in adulthood trajectories exist and are meaningful, but are also challenging to measure (e.g., Billari 2001; Billari & Piccarreta 2005; Billari & Liefbroer 2010).

For example, Krahn and colleagues (2015) find that annual reporting of employment statuses during emerging adulthood drastically underestimate the variability in education and employment trajectories due to more rapid fluctuations in these statuses during the life stage. In investigating month-to-month snapshots over a six-year period, they find that emerging adults experienced an average of four employment status changes and five educational status changes, with 7 percent of emerging adults reporting ten or more status changes in employment and 15 percent reporting ten or more changes in education in six years.

In fact, fluctuations were the norm. Krahn and colleagues (2015) found that only 13 percent of emerging adult university graduates had the same employer at one, three, and five years post-graduation. Meanwhile, 37 percent had a different employer at each of those times. The trouble with these trends is that emerging adults who had uninterrupted employment earned significantly more six years later than those with interruptions. Even more complicated, however, they found that emerging adults who explored different employment options had greater earnings than those who did not.

How can both of those findings be the case? What the scholars uncovered was an important interaction between educational and employment statuses during the transition to adulthood. Namely, early employment fluctuations, in the context of student status (i.e., enrolled in college) paid off for emerging adults, but later employment fluctuations while not a student hindered income earnings. What this means is there is an important difference between exploring and floundering during emerging adulthood, but one that is subtle and more difficult to detect than in times past due to the rapid churning of employment and education fluctuations today.

Similarly, Berzin and De Marco (2010) find that the timing of leaving parents' home was significantly affected by growing up in poverty, with impoverished emerging adults more likely to leave home early and also less likely to move out of parental homes after the age of 18. This complex and nonlinear relationship in the timing makes it difficult to measure adulthood markers but makes them no less significant in impacting adulthood trajectories. Counter-intuitively, it is emerging adults who assume adult roles too early who are most at-risk of negative long-term outcomes, while emerging adults who are able to have delayed transitions into adulthood roles fare better in the long run. Yet, Chapter 1 also reported findings that emerging adults who perceive themselves to be adults tend to fare better as well. So the multiplicative reality is that emerging adults need to perceive themselves to be relatively "on track" with normative timings of adulthood roles, despite the mostly non-normative timings.

Crosnoe and Johnson (2011) view one of the promising future directions for life course sociology to be a focus on the kinds of social changes described in the first half of this chapter and their implications on the social structure for programs, policies, and parenting practices that best support emerging adults. They state:

> We are only just beginning to address a number of other important questions related to these broad social changes, including what they mean for the achievement of social and financial autonomy and relationships with others, including parents, and what we need to equip adolescents with in order for them to successfully navigate the transition to adulthood (p. 452).

A more comprehensive approach to supporting emerging adults in their transition to adulthood begins by acknowledging the real generational differences in social conditions, and then carefully studying how some social mechanisms facilitate successful adulthood pathways and others do not—or at least do not provide enough support to last the extended duration to adulthood required in a service- and knowledge-based economy.

What is clear is that life course experiences can, and often do, have long-term consequences. The question is how, and in what ways? In a comprehensive review of sociology of the life course, Mayer (2009) highlights the importance of ongoing investigations in this area by identifying rising intra-cohort inequality across life trajectories based on exposure to risks in adulthood pathways. The key issue is better understanding the mechanisms by which early conditions relate to later life outcomes, especially by focusing on interplays between the social and psychological processes of growing up:

> Life course development is analyzed as the outcome of personal characteristics and individual action, as well as of cultural frames and institutional and structural conditions (relating micro, meso, and macro levels of analysis, structure, and agency) (p. 414).

This approach to the life course views a stage such as emerging adulthood as providing a window on how personal selves interact with, respond to, and shape their social contexts. Emerging adults are shaping their lives via personal choices in social contexts.

ADULTHOOD MARKERS STILL MATTER

Chapter 1 reviewed scholarship on subjective adulthood, describing self-perceived adulthood as potentially "in the eye of the beholder," by evidencing the variability in who considers themselves to be an adult and by what criteria. As Figure 2.2 shows, one of the defining characteristics of emerging adulthood is the feeling of being in-between—represented by the "yes and no" response of 60 percent of 18 to 25 year olds when asked "Do you feel that you

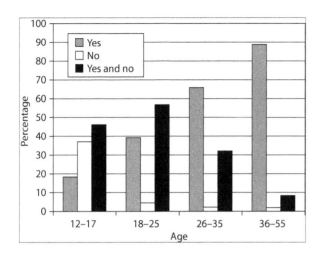

FIGURE 2.2 "Do you Feel That You Have Reached Adulthood?"

Jeffrey Jensen Arnett, "Subjective Adulthood," Emerging Adulthood: The Winding Road from the Late Teens Through the Twenties. Copyright © 2015 by Oxford University Press.

have reached adulthood?" (Arnett 2015, 14).

However, what is equally important to note is that this proportion is dramatically lower among adults ages 36 to 55. What explains the decline? Arnett (2015) lists the top three most stated criteria that people use for defining adulthood: accepting responsibility for oneself, making independent decisions, and becoming financially independent. On the surface, these all seem like personal markers, but they are not. As Settersten (2011) states: "traditional markers still matter" (p. 172). Though the criteria for adulthood are described in individualistic terms, and emerging adults are aware of the wide range of sequencing patterns in adulthood trajectories, they also continue to report the importance of "leaving home, finishing school, getting a job, getting married, and having children" for symbolizing being an adult (e.g., Tilton-Weaver et al. 2001; Ramscher 2011; Sumner et al. 2015; Sharon 2015).

As Settersten explains, no one single marker is absolutely necessary in order to consider oneself an adult, but it is also not the case that most people see themselves as adults in the absence of any of these markers. Adulthood is somewhere between those two poles, having some commonalities across groups and differences (e.g., Spéder et al. 2014). However, the opportunity to establish these markers, especially in the desired ways—which are still described in a highly normative sequence—is unequal. So while the timing of establishing adulthood markers is more variable, the timing and sequencing still matter for predicting positive social and life outcomes (e.g., Shanahan et al. 2005).

The key to understanding the complex interaction between social and personal is that subjective identity as an adult is not purely self-perceived. Life experiences also condition pathways to adulthood (e.g., Suárez-Orozco 2015) and subjective experience of oneself as an adult (e.g., Benson & Furstenberg 2006; Salmela-Aro et al. 2007; Johnson et al. 2007). Emerging adults still have expectations for adulthood, and the roles they will have in it, and these shape the meanings of life course events.

Thus, differences in life course opportunities become internalized as self-perceived adulthood status, with people from disadvantaged backgrounds being more likely, in general, to rate themselves as adults (Johnson et al. 2007). However, arrests and incarcerations diminish self-perceived adulthood (e.g., Massoglia & Uggen 2010), evidencing that socially disadvantaged situations can alternatively diminish potential to rate oneself as an adult. Together, these findings indicate that perceiving oneself to be an adult is influenced by social factors, but this occurs in non-determinative ways with some disadvantaged statuses resulting in greater adulthood self-perception and some resulting in lesser self-perceived adulthood.

The fifth and final reading elucidates how the third criteria for adulthood status—being financially independent—also reflects a social process. For many emerging adults, financial independence from their parents is relatively murky during emerging adulthood. They may have moved out of their parents' house, but their parents may still help them cover the costs of rent. Or they may pay their rent, but their parents cover their medical insurance, hefty cell phone bills, and other costs which still amount to subsidizing their lifestyle. Given such murky independence, adulthood markers such as forming a family and establishing one's own household can remain important as clear demarcations of independence. Shanahan and colleagues (2005) explain this further.

READING 2.3

Subjective Age Identity and the Transition to Adulthood: Demographic Markers and Personal Attributes

By Michael J. Shanahan, Erik Porfeli, Jeylan T. Mortimer, and Lance D. Erickson

At what point in life does a young person become an adult? For many decades, scholars held that five transition markers delineated entry into adulthood: completing school, leaving home, beginning one's career, marrying, and becoming a parent. By assuming these roles, youth were thought to relinquish the hallmarks of adolescence, including dependency on parents, "immature" behaviors that reflect experimentation with roles, and indecision about one's identity. In turn, the newly acquired adult roles brought with them strong expectations for "adult" behaviors. Indeed, most adults at midtwentieth century held expectations about the timing of these transitions and about the inappropriateness of being "off time" (Neugarten, Moore, and Lowe 1965).

Based on these five criteria, however, the percentage of youth in their twenties and thirties who would qualify as adult has decreased significantly in recent decades (Fussell and Furstenberg, this vol., chap. 2; Mortimer and Aronson 2001; Shanahan 2000). For a considerable segment of the population, education has extended into the late twenties and

Michael J. Shanahan, Erik Porfeli, Jeylan T. Mortimer, and Lance D. Erickson, "Subjective Age Identity and the Transition to Adulthood: Demographic Markers and Personal Attributes," On the Frontier of Adulthood: Theory, Research, and Public Policy, ed. R. A. Settersten. Jr, F. F. Furstenberg, and R. G. Rumbaut, pp. 225-226, 240-248. Copyright © 2005 by University of Chicago Press. Reprinted with permission.

early thirties, family formation has been postponed, and many young people plan on remaining single and childless well into their thirties, if not indefinitely (e.g., Casper and Bianchi 2002). Moreover, at century's end, most adults hold expectations about the timing of these markers, but they do not view off-time transitions as deserving of disapprobation (Settersten 2003; Settersten and Hagestad 1996).

In turn, these social changes have prompted new views of what constitutes adulthood. Arnett (2001) argues that "emerging adulthood" now constitutes a phase of the life course that extends between adolescence and adulthood. Emerging adulthood is characterized by relative independence from age-normative tasks, by experimentation with social roles, and by little meaningful commitment to one's relationships and organizational involvements. In the context of emerging adulthood, young people identify individualistic indicators of maturity (e.g., independent decision making) as the new markers of whether one is an adult and, according to this view, the demographic markers are deemed substantially less important by youth. Similarly, Côté (2000) suggests "youthhood" as a new phase of life during which "psychological adulthood" is hopefully attained through personal strivings. Côté likewise maintains that the importance of the traditional markers has declined significantly, largely replaced by emotional and cognitive maturity and an advanced sense of ethics.

The possibility that adulthood is now viewed by young people primarily as a reflection of individualistic criteria is intriguing to life-course sociologists, who have assumed, based on research by Neugarten and her colleagues (1965), that adult identity is founded on the assumption of related social roles. Perhaps with increasing variability in the timing of transition markers, the criteria that define adulthood have become individualized, now resting primarily on subjective self-evaluations. Yet surprisingly little empirical research has examined the extent to which youth view their adult status as a reflection of individualistic criteria and transition markers. In this chapter, we draw on data from the Youth Development Study to examine the importance of the traditional transition markers and personal qualities in predicting whether young people view themselves as adult. We begin by briefly examining the conceptual and empirical basis for claims about the changing nature of adult identity. ...

Transition Markers, Individualistic Criteria, and Adulthood

Table 2.2 shows the bivariate associations among the domains of self-perceived adulthood, on the one hand, and the transition markers and individualistic criteria, on the other. Several patterns emerge from these results.

First, the family transitions are often significantly correlated with dimensions of perceived adulthood. Cohabiting/marriage and parenthood whether ever experienced or presently experienced—are significantly, weakly related to several dimensions of adulthood, particularly feeling entirely like an adult at work, when engaged in sports, at home, with romantic partner, and most of the time. Second, the family dummy variable index—indicating whether the respondent is an independent householder, cohabited or married, and a parent—is significantly related to numerous dimensions

TABLE 2.2 Self-Perceived Adulthood, Transition Markers, and Individualistic Criteria: Bivariate Associations—Youth Development Study

	Self-Perceived Adulthood Dimensions										
	School	Work	Community	Sports	Recreation	Friends	Home	Child	Parents	Partner	Most of The Time
Ever:											
Cohabited/married	.24***	.11**	.09+	.07	.07+	.05	.19***	.04	.03	.11**	.09*
Own home	.02	.06	.06	.02	.08*	-.00	.11**	.10+	.03	.09*	.04
Parent	.13+	.12**	.09+	.09*	.03	.08*	.11**	...	.05	.11**	.12**
School complete	...	.04	-.06	-.03	-.06	-.00	.00	.10+	-.02	.01	.04
Career	.07	.08+	.06	.00	-.00	-.03	.04	.03	-.03	-.11**	.06
Family	.06	.13**	.09+	.12**	.13**	.07+	.11**	...	.08*	.11**	.11**
Attainment	...	.06	-.05	.01	-.02	-.04	.03	.04	-.06	.05	.02
Present:											
Cohabited/married	.15*	.10*	.03	-.02	.08+	.01	.13***	.04	.04	.10*	.05
Own, rent	.03	.03	.02	.02	-.02	-.00	.11**	.06	-.01	.07+	.04
Parent	.09	.10**	.08+	.09*	.03	.10**	.09*	...	.08*	.10**	.12**
Not in school	...	-.03	.01	.00	-.05	.03	-.02	.05	-.19**	-.00	-.00
Full-time work	.01	.06	.04	.03	.01	-.03	.03	.02	.00	-.00	.01
Family	.06	.08*	.05	.07+	.09*	.07+	.12**	...	.07+	.12**	.10**
Attainment	...	-.02	.01	.03	-.02	-.03	-.01	.00	-.05*	-.02	.00
Financial independence	.11+	.10*	.03	.01	.05	-.01	.04	.11+	.11**	.08*	.08*
Personal responsibility	.03	.04	.05	.08+	.07+	.03	-.01	-.04	-.01	-.01	.06
n (range)	206–26	592–652	374–416	561–616	578–634	631–93	615–77	269–97	618–78	575–636	631–92

+*p* < -.10.
*p < .05.
**p < .01.
***p < .001.

of perceived adulthood, and this relationship appears stronger if ever experienced when compared to currently experienced transitions. Third, financial independence is significantly, weakly related to several domains of adulthood, including at work, with romantic partners or parents, and most of the time. Finally, the associations are generally weak in magnitude, suggesting that few, if any, of these variables are important predictors of selfperceived adulthood.

Table 2.3 shows multivariate logistic regression models that interrelate the individualistic criteria and transition markers ever experienced (as predictors) to the dimensions of self-perceived adulthood. Several conclusions can be drawn from this table. First, respondents who have ever cohabited or married are more likely to report feeling entirely like an adult when taking care of their house or apartment (odds ratio = 2.2) and when spending time with their romantic partner (odds ratio = 1.6, marginally significant).

Second, starting a career increases the likelihood of self-perceived adulthood when spending time with a romantic partner (odds ratio = 1.62).

Third, respondents who have ever had a child are more likely to report feeling entirely like an adult when engaged in work (odds ratio = 1.5), when spending time with partner (odds ratio = 1.53), and most of the time (odds ratio = 1.69). Parenthood is also associated with self-perceived adulthood when participating in the community and in sports, and when spending time with friends, but these equations are insignificant in their overall fit. Indeed, no other patterns emerge in table 2.3, suggesting that family transitions—particularly parenthood—are important predictors that are significantly associated with feeling entirely like an adult. Finally, however, the models have very low explanatory value, as indicated by the pseudo-R^2, and indeed many do not have significant overall explanatory value.

In order to examine whether constellations of family and attainment transitions are important, we reestimated the models presented in table 2.3. The family-related transitions (cohabited/married, own home, and become parent) were replaced with a dummy variable that indicates whether the person ever experienced all three transitions. Similarly, the attainment-related transitions (complete school and full-time job) were replaced with a dummy variable indicating whether the person ever experienced both transitions. (The models for school and children are not considered given that the attainment dummy includes school completion and that the family dummy includes becoming a parent.) The results are shown in table 2.4 and confirm the importance of the family transitions. Young people who have cohabited or married, had at least one child, and have owned their home or rented their own apartment are significantly more likely to report feeling entirely like an adult along every dimension of the dependent variable. The magnitude of these odds ratios ranges from 1.5 (with parents) to 2.4 (work, community, home). (Two models, feeling like an adult among friends and with partner, were not statistically significant overall, and two models—community and house—were overall marginally significant, $p < .10$).

TABLE 2.3 Models of Self-Perceived Adulthood, Ever Experienced Adult Roles, And Individualistic Criteria: Youth Development Study

				Self-Perceived Adulthood Dimensions						Most of
Predictors	School	Work	Community	Sports	Recreation	Friends	Home	Child	Parents	Partner	The Time
Financial independence	.39	.33	−.25	−.27	−.19	−.32	−.23	.18	.51	.01	.10
	(.63)	(.31)	(.43)	(.31)	(.30)	(.30)	(.38)	(.63)	(.31)	(.35)	(.29)
Personal responsibility	.13	.11	.20	.24	.27	.15	.16	−.14	.02	−.02	.16
	(.37)	(.17)	(.21)	(.16)	(.16)	(.16)	(.14)	(.27)	(.15)	(.17)	(.15)
Cohabited / married	.79	.32	.09	.17	.36	.29	.79**	.06	.20	.46+	.22
	(.49)	(.23)	(.30)	(.23)	(.22)	(.23)	(.25)	(.71)	(.22)	(.24)	(.22)
Own home	−.26	.15	.18	.11	.24	−.12	.17	.33	.02	.16	.00
	(.56)	(.23)	(.27)	(.20)	(.20)	(.20)	(.25)	(.35)	(.20)	(.22)	(.20)
Become parent	.58	.43+	.66*	.44*	.14	.35+	.37	...	.24	.42+	.52**
	(.56)	(.23)	(.28)	(.20)	(.20)	(.20)	(.24)		(.19)	(.22)	(.20)
Complete school	...	.16	−.29	−.17	−.30	−.19	−.02	.36	−.12	−.18	.00
		(.21)	(.25)	(.19)	(.19)	(.19)	(.22)	(.34)	(.18)	(.21)	(.19)
Start career	.32	.23	.24	.09	−.06	.04	.09	.01	−.15	.48*	.20
	(.42)	(.22)	(.27)	(.20)	(.20)	(.20)	(.24)	(.35)	(.19)	(.22)	(.19)
Constant	−1.07	−.47	−.13	−.90	−.83	−1.07	.23	1.09	−.92	.14	−.72
	(1.39)	(.67)	(.87)	(.66)	(.64)	(.65)	(.75)	(1.37)	(.62)	(.74)	(.62)
n	107	524	332	501	514	557	543	218	546	511	559
X^2, df	7.3, 6	16.3, 7	11.3, 7	11.0, 7	13.2, 7	9.2, 7	21.8, 7	2.9, 6	9.1, 7	18.3, 7	14.3, 7
p	.29	.02	.13	.14	.07	.24	.00	.83	.25	.01	.05
Pseudo R^2	.05	.03	.03	.02	.02	.01	.04	.01	.01	.02	.02

Note. Unstandardized effects, with standard errors in parentheses.
+p < .10.
*p < .05.
**p < .01.

The model also shows that respondents who had ever left school and started their careers were less likely to feel entirely like an adult with parents (b = −.42, $p < .05$, odds ratio = 0.66). This is consistent with the bivariate findings, which showed a negative, significant zero-order relationship between the two variables. Follow-up analyses revealed that the effect is being driven by school completion. Youth who were not in school were less likely to view themselves entirely like an adult. Although this result is unexpected, perhaps youth still in school are acquiring advanced educational degrees and are thus not inclined to think of themselves as only somewhat of an adult; in contrast, youth who have left school may be just starting their occupational careers and inclined to view themselves as not entirely an adult around their parents, who may have well-established professional careers. It could also be that the school dropouts—those who start college but don't finish—feel less like an adult (and because these are very numerous, determine the negative coefficient) than those who complete high school and do not go on further.

The analytic sequence reported in tables 2.3 and 2.4 was repeated for one's present roles in tables 2.5 and 2.6. That is, table 2.5 interrelates the individualistic criteria and presently occupied roles (e.g., presently cohabiting or married) with self-perceived adulthood. Being presently married or cohabiting significantly increases the likelihood of reporting feeling entirely like an adult when taking care of the house or apartment (odds ratio = 1.6); this variable also predicts self-perceived adulthood when engaged in recreation, although the overall model is not significant. Also, consistent with the previous tables, currently being a parent is significantly related to feeling entirely like an adult across a wide range of dimensions, including work (odds ratio = 1.6), when engaged in sports (odds ratio = 1.7; equation is not significant), spending time with friends (odds ratio = 1.5; equation is not significant), interacting with parents (odds ratio = 1.6), and most of the time (odds ratio = 1.7; equation is marginally significant, $p = .09$). Thus, specific family-related roles are significantly associated with self-perceived adulthood.

Also, finishing school is negatively related to feeling like an adult when with parents (odds ratio = 0.60) and when at home (odds ratio = 0.60; marginally significant). This is, once again, likely due to students pursuing advanced degrees thinking of themselves as entirely adult, while new graduates just entering labor markets may view themselves as somewhat adult.

With respect to the individualistic criteria, financial independence is positively associated with self-perceived adulthood when with parents (marginally significant, odds ratio = 1.8, $p = .053$). On the one hand, these results make intuitive sense, particularly since financial independence is largely a function of not relying on one's parents for money. Yet these same variables were unrelated to self-perceived adulthood in tables 2.3 and 2.4, suggesting that the statistical significance of this effect is contingent on the model's specification. Personal responsibility is not significantly related to any dimensions of self-perceived adulthood.

Table 2.4 Models of Self-Perceived Adulthood, Ever Experienced Adult Role Configurations, And Individualistic Criteria: Youth Development Study

Predictors	Self-Perceived Adulthood Dimensions								
	Work	Community	Sports	Recreation	Friends	Home	Parents	Partner	Most of The Time
Financial independence	.45	-.13	-.22	-.10	-.23	-.09	.59+	.18	.24
	(.30)	(.43)	(.30)	(.29)	(.29)	(.36)	(.30)	(.34)	(.28)
Personal responsibility	.10	.17	.24	.27+	.14	.12	.02	.05	.15
	(.17)	(.21)	(.16)	(.16)	(.16)	(.19)	(.15)	(.17)	(.15)
Family sum	.87**	.86**	.75**	.77**	.46*	.86*	.41+	.62*	.67**
	(.30)	(.33)	(.24)	(.25)	(.23)	(.33)	(.23)	(.27)	(.24)
Attainment sum	.16	-.31	.02	-.20	-.30	-.03	-.42*	.10	-.10
	(.20)	(.24)	(.18)	(.18)	(.18)	(.21)	(.18)	(.20)	(.18)
Constant	-.09	.21	-.77	-.76	-.86	.82	-.77	.69	-.40
	(.65)	(.83)	(.64)	(.63)	(.63)	(.73)	(.60)	(.70)	(.59)
n	524	332	501	514	557	543	546	511	559
X^2, df	14.2, 4	9.0, 4	11.5, 4	13.3, 4	7.4, 4	8.1, 4	12.0, 4	6.8, 4	9.8, 4
p	.01	.06	.02	.01	.12	.09	.02	.15	.04
Pseudo R^2	.02	.02	.02	.02	.01	.01	.01	.02	.02

Note. Unstandardized effects, with standard errors in parentheses.
+$p<.10$.
*$p<.05$.
**$p<.01$.

Table 2.5 Models of Self-Perceived Adulthood, Currently Experienced Adult Roles, And Individualistic Criteria: Youth Development Study

Predictors	Self-Perceived Adulthood Dimensions										
	School	Work	Community	Sports	Recreation	Friends	Home	Child	Parents	Partner	Most of The Time
Financial Independence	.32	.49	.00	−.29	−.02	−.12	−.28	.51	.61[+]	.04	.23
	(.71)	(.31)	(.43)	(.31)	(.30)	(.30)	(.36)	(.58)	(.31)	(.34)	(.29)
Personal Responsibility	.26	.15	.23	.23	.25	.09	−.00	−.15	−.03	−.07	.20
	(.37)	(.17)	(.21)	(.16)	(.15)	(.15)	(.18)	(.27)	(.15)	(.16)	(.15)
Cohabited/Married	.63	.23	.04	−.21	.33[+]	−.03	.47*	−.14	.08	.30	−.04
	(.46)	(.21)	(.25)	(.19)	(.19)	(.19)	(.22)	(.37)	(.18)	(.20)	(.18)
Own, Rent	−.65	−.09	−.16	.29	−.22	−.20	.58	.05	−.33	.32	.02
	(.64)	(.32)	(.43)	(.30)	(.29)	(.28)	(.32)	(.68)	(.28)	(.33)	(.28)
Become Parent	.94	.45*	.53	.55**	.23	.41*	.37	...	.46*	.38	.52**
	(.59)	(.22)	(.27)	(.20)	(.19)	(.19)	(.23)		(.19)	(.21)	(.19)
Complete School	...	−.34	−.19	−.17	−.28	−.05	−.53[+]	−.07	−.53*	−.14	−.23
		(.26)	(.29)	(.23)	(.22)	(.22)	(.28)	(.50)	(.22)	(.25)	(.22)
Full-Time Job	.42	.37	.18	.17	.04	−.07	.33	−.02	.07	.07	.09
	(.43)	(.23)	(.28)	(.21)	(.21)	(.20)	(.24)	(.34)	(.20)	(.23)	(.20)
Constant	−.87	−.21	−.10	.84	−.64	−.65	.82	1.34	−.30	.48	−.62
	(1.44)	(.71)	(.88)	(.68)	(.64)	(.64)	(.75)	(1.40)	(.63)	(.73)	(.61)
n	109	559	351	512	547	595	580	223	585	547	596
X^2, df	8.0, 6	14.9, 7	5.4, 7	11.6, 7	9.4, 7	6.2, 7	17.0, 7	1.3, 6	16.9, 7	10.3, 7	11.9, 7
p	.24	.03	.61	.12	.22	.51	.02	.97	.02	.17	.10
Pseudo R^2	.06	.02	.01	.02	.01	.01	.03	.00	.02	.02	.01

Note. Unstandardized effects, with standard errors in parentheses.
[+] $p < .10$.
* $p < .05$.
** $p < .01$.

Table 2.6 Models of Self-Perceived Adulthood, Currently Experienced Adult Role Configurations, And Individualistic Criteria: Youth Development Study

	Self-Perceived Adulthood Dimensions								
Predictors	Work	Community	Sports	Recreation	Friends	Home	Parents	Partner	Most of The Time
Financial Independence	.64*	.04	−.22	.03	−.16	.08	.63*	.21	.30
	(.29)	(.41)	(.29)	(.28)	(.28)	(.34)	(.30)	(.33)	(.27)
Personal Responsibility	.14	.21	.24	.25	.08	−.00	−.02	−.09	.19
	(.16)	(.20)	(.16)	(.15)	(.15)	(.18)	(.14)	(.16)	(.14)
Family Sum	.27	.38	.40+	.51*	.31	.60	.32	.56**	.43*
	(.23)	(.27)	(.20)	(.20)	(.19)	(.25)	(.19)	(.22)	(.20)
Attainment Sum	−.08	−.07	.08	−.09	−.14	−.14	−.28*	−.02	−.02
	(.20)	(.24)	(.18)	(.18)	(.18)	(.21)	(.17)	(.19)	(.17)
Constant	−.11	−.06	−.75	−.85	−.70	1.11	−.74	.81	−.63
	(.64)	(.79)	(.63)	(.59)	(.59)	(.68)	(.57)	(.66)	(.56)
n	559	351	532	547	595	580	585	547	596
X^2, df	7.0, 4	2.98, 4	6.6, 4	9.1, 4	3.8, 4	7.0, 4	10.5, 4	8.2, 4	8.1, 4
P	.13	.56	.16	.06	.43	.13	.03	.08	.09
Pseudo R^2	.01	.01	.01	.01	.00	.01	.01	.01	.01

Note. Unstandardized effects, with standard errors in parentheses.

+$p < .10$.
*$p < .05$.
**$p < .01$.

Table 2.6 shows the results for the models that replace the transition markers with dummy variables indicating whether all of the family or attainment transitions are currently completed. Financial independence is positively associated with self-perceived adulthood while at work (odds ratio = 1.77; equation insignificant) and with parents (odds ratio = 1.90). The family composite is positively associated with feeling like an adult when engaged in sports and recreation, when with a romantic partner, and most of the time. However, these equations are insignificant or marginally insignificant in their overall fit. Like the results shown in table 2.3, the attainment dummy likewise is significantly, negatively predictive of feeling entirely like an adult with parents.

Thus far, the results suggest that the family transitions are positively, significantly related to feeling entirely like an adult, and this pattern may be stronger for the ever experienced than currently experienced transitions. Can the relative importance of the past and present transitions be tested directly? Because of collinearity, all ten past and present demographic markers cannot be entered into one equation. The composite variables, however, are less strongly related and analyses suggest that collinearity is much less of an issue. The models in tables 2.4 and 2.6 were thus combined such that both past and current family and attainment composites predicted each dimension of self-perceived adulthood. The results (not shown) suggest that ever experiencing the family transitions is decisive in many cases: youth are more likely to report feeling completely like an adult if they have ever experienced all three family-related transitions at work (odds ratio = 2.7), participating in community affairs (odds ratio = 2.2), while exercising (odds ratio = 1.9), while engaged in recreation (odds ratio = 1.8), and most of the time (odds ratio = 1.9), controlling presently experienced roles and past and present attainment transitions. Given small cell sizes (i.e., most youth have never experienced all of the transitions in the past or present), the results should be viewed with caution. Nevertheless, they suggest an interesting possibility for future research: that ever experiencing family-related transitions, regardless of one's present status with respect to those roles, may be important predictors of feeling like an adult.

Even though emerging adults may not list adulthood markers as their criteria for self-perceived adulthood, they still seem to use them as demarcations in globally assessing their adulthood status across several markers simultaneously. In concluding, Shanahan and colleagues (2005) report that emerging adults who have established an independent household, have gotten married or are cohabitating with a romantic partner, and who have become a parent are twice as likely to describe themselves as an adult than emerging adults who have not established all of those markers, including those who have established some but not others of those markers (pp. 249–50).

Perhaps most importantly sociologically is that people are more likely to see themselves entirely as adults when they are in situations in which other people confirm their adult status. People interact with others who reinforce their adulthood identity in positive or negative ways, and such reinforcements accumulate and are internalized in self-perceived adulthood, making it a reflection, rather than a cause, of social and personal circumstances. Similarly, *life course* trajectories, especially in educational attainment, relate to a sense of control over one's life, which relates to long-term consequences of adaptability (Mirowsky & Ross 2007).

Combined, sociologists of emerging adulthood highlight the ways *social structures* (e.g., social networks: Easley & Klienberg 2010) and social institutions (e.g., Lee 2012; Gerson 2009) pattern the life course. Precisely what makes emerging adulthood such an interesting area of research, and an exciting life stage, is the dynamic interplay between personal and institutional experiences (Heinz & Krüger 2001; Heinz 2009). Changing opportunity structures condition life course trajectories, and cultural norms and expectations at both the national and subgroup levels interact in shaping life courses, especially transitions into adulthood (Furlong et al. 2011).

Such a structural-cultural interactional perspective is the approach of the remainder of this text, beginning with a structural and cultural review of social class inequalities and how they shape the life course and emerging adulthood. The central takeaway relative to where the chapter began is that it is more socially and historically accurate to focus on the life stage of emerging adulthood than to talk only of the Millennial generation as an isolated group with personality labels—obscuring how generations reflect social changes over time. Instead, it is important to contextualize Millennials in these social changes described in this chapter and view them as the first generation to transition into adulthood with the life stage of emerging adulthood being part of the normal life course progression for young people in the United States.

REFERENCES

Arnett, Jeffrey J. 2000. "High Hopes in a Grim World: Emerging Adults' Views of Their Futures and 'Generation X.'" *Youth & Society* 31(3):267–86.

Arnett, Jeffrey Jensen. 2015. *Emerging Adulthood: The Winding Road from the Late Teens through the Twenties*, 2nd edition. Oxford University Press.

Aronson, Pamela. 2008. "The Markers and Meanings of Growing Up: Contemporary Young Women's Transitions from Adolescence to Adulthood." *Gender & Society* 22(1): 56–82.

Bell, Daniel. 1989. "The Third Technological Revolution and Its Possible Socioeconomic Consequences." *Dissent*, Spring.

Bengston, Vern L. and W. Andrew Achenbaum. 1993. *The Changing Contract across Generations*. Transaction Publishers.

Benson, Janel E. and Frank F. Furstenberg Jr. 2006. "Entry into Adulthood: Are Adult Role Transitions Meaningful Markers of Adult Identity?" *Advances in Life Course Research* 11:199–224.

Berzin, Stephanie Cosner and Allison C. De Marco. 2010. "Understanding the Impact of Poverty on Critical Events in Emerging Adulthood." *Youth & Society* 42(2):278–300.

Billari, Francesco C. 2001. "The Analysis of Early Life Courses: Complex Descriptions of the Transition to Adulthood." *Journal of Population Research* 18(2):119–42.

Billari, Francesco C. and Aart C. Liefbroer. 2010. "Towards a New Pattern of Transition to Adulthood?" *Advances in Life Course Research* 15(2–3):59–75.

Billari, Francesco C. and Raffaella Piccarreta. 2005. "Analyzing Demographic Life Courses through Sequence Analysis." *Mathematical Population Studies* 12(2):81–106.

Browne, Irene. 1995. "The Baby Boom and Trends in Poverty, 1967–1987." *Social Forces* 73(3):1071–95.

Brückner, Hannah. 2004. *Gender Inequality in the Life Course: Social Change and Stability in West Germany 1975–1995*. Walter de Gruyter.

Brückner, Hannah and Karl Ulrich Mayer. 2005. "De-Standardization of the Life Course: What It Might Mean? And If It Means Anything, Whether It Actually Took Place?" *Advances in Life Course Research* 9:27–53.

Buchmann, Marlis C. and Irene Kriesi. 2011. "Transition to Adulthood in Europe." *Annual Review of Sociology* 37(1):481–503.

Burgess, Ernest W. 1948. "The Family in a Changing Society." *American Journal of Sociology* 53(6):417–22.

Cerulo, Karen A. 1997. "Identity Construction: New Issues, New Directions." *Annual Review of Sociology* 23(1):385–409.

Cooper, Marianne. 2014. *Cut Adrift: Families in Insecure Times*. Berkeley: University of California Press.

Côté, James E. 2002. "The Role of Identity Capital in the Transition to Adulthood: The Individualization Thesis Examined." *Journal of Youth Studies* 5(2):117–34.

Crosnoe, Robert and Monica Kirkpatrick Johnson. 2011. "Research on Adolescence in the Twenty-First Century." *Annual Review of Sociology* 37(1):439–60.

Easley, David and Jon Kleinberg. 2010. "Strong and Weak Ties." In *Networks, Crowds, and Markets: Reasoning about a Highly Connected World*, 47–84. Cambridge University Press.

Elder, Glen H. Jr. 1994. "Time, Human Agency, and Social Change: Perspectives on the Life Course." *Social Psychology Quarterly* 57(1):4–15.

Elder, Glen H. Jr. and Rand D. Conger. 2000. "Families and the Generations." In *Children of the Land: Adversity and Success in Rural America*, 33–57. University of Chicago Press.

Foner, Anne and David Kertzer. 1978. "Transitions Over the Life Course: Lessons from Age-Set Societies." *American Journal of Sociology* 83(5):1081–104.

Furlong, Andy, Dan Woodman, and Johanna Wyn. 2011. "Changing Times, Changing Perspectives: Reconciling 'Transition' and 'Cultural' Perspectives on Youth and Young Adulthood." *American Journal of Sociology* 47(4):355–70.

Furstenberg, Frank F. 2000. "The Sociology of Adolescence and Youth in the 1990s: A Critical Commentary." *Journal of Marriage and Family* 62(4):896–910.

Fussel, Elizabeth and Anne H. Gauthier. 2005. "American Women's Transition to Adulthood in Comparative Perspective." In *On the Frontier of Adulthood: Theory, Research, and Public Policy*, edited by Richard A. Settersten, Frank F. Furstenberg, and Rubén G. Rumbaut , 76–109. University of Chicago Press.

George, Linda K. 1993. "Sociological Perspectives on Life Transitions." *Annual Review of Sociology* 19:353–73.

Gerson, Kathleen. 2009. "Changing Lives, Resistant Institutions: A New Generation Negotiates Gender, Work, and Family Change." *Sociological Forum* 24(4):735–53.

Goldscheider, Calvin and Frances K. Goldscheider. 1988. "Ethnicity, Religiosity and Leaving Home: The Structural and Cultural Bases of Traditional Family Values." *Sociological Forum* 3:525–47.

Gove, Walter R., Suzanne T. Ortega, and Carolyn Briggs Style. 1989. "The Maturational and Role Perspectives on Aging and Self through the Adult Years: An Empirical Evaluation." *American Journal of Sociology* 94(5):1117–45.

Heinz, Walter R. 2009. "Structure and Agency in Transition Research." *Journal of Education and Work* 22(5):391–404.

Heinz, Walter R. and Helga Krüger. 2001. "Life Course: Innovations and Challenges for Social Research." *Current Sociology* 49(2):29–45.

Hill, Martha S. and W. Jean Yeung. 1999. "How Have the Changing Structures of Opportunities Affected Transitions to Adulthood?" In *Transitions to Adulthood in a Changing Economy: No Work, No Family, No Future?*, edited by Alan Booth, Ann C. Crouter, and Michael J. Shanahan, 3–39. Greenwood Publishing Group.

Jeffrey, Craig and Linda McDowell. 2004. "Youth in a Comparative Perspective: Global Change, Local Lives." *Youth & Society* 36(2):131–42.

Johnson, Monica Kirkpatrick, Justin Allen Berg, and Toni Sirotzki. 2007. "Differentiation in Self-Perceived Adulthood: Extending the Confluence Model of Subjective Age Identity." *Social Psychology Quarterly* 70(3):243–61.

Katsiaficas, Dalal, Carola Suárez-Orozco, and Sandra Isabel Dias. 2015. "'When Do I Feel Like an Adult?' Latino and Afro-Caribbean Immigrant-Origin Community College Students' Conceptualizations and Experiences of (Emerging) Adulthood." *Emerging Adulthood* 3(2):98–112.

Kohli, Martin. 1986. "The World We Forgot: A Historical Review of the Life Course." In *Later Life: The Social Psychology of Aging*, edited by V. W. Marshall, 271–303. Sage Publications.

Kohli, Martin. 2007. "The Institutionalization of the Life Course: Looking Back to Look Ahead." *Research in Human Development* 4(3-4):253–71.

Krahn, Harvey J., Andrea L. Howard, and Nancy L. Galambos. 2014. "Exploring or Floundering? The Meaning of Employment and Educational Fluctuations in Emerging Adulthood." *Youth & Society* 47(2):245–66.

Lee, JoAnn S. 2012. "An Institutional Framework for the Study of the Transition to Adulthood." *Youth & Society* 46(5):706–30.

Lichter, Daniel T. 2013. "Integration or Fragmentation? Racial Diversity and the American Future." *Demography* 50(2):359–91.

Lichter, Daniel T. and David L. Brown. 2011. "Rural America in an Urban Society: Changing Spatial and Social Boundaries." *Annual Review of Sociology* 37(1):565–92.

Macmillan, Ross. 2005. *The Structure of the Life Course: Standardized? Individualized? Differentiated?* Elsevier.

Mare, Robert D., Christopher Winship, and Warren N. Kubitschek. 1984. "The Transition from Youth to Adult: Understanding the Age Pattern of Employment." *American Journal of Sociology* 90(2):326–58.

Massoglia, Michael and Christopher Uggen. 2010. "Settling down and Aging out: Toward an Interactionist Theory of Desistance and the Transition to Adulthood." *American Journal of Sociology* 116(2):543–82.

Mayer, Karl Ulrich. 2009. "New Directions in Life Course Research." *Annual Review of Sociology* 35(1):413–33.

Mendenhall, Ruby, Ariel Kalil, Laurel J. Spindel, and Cassandra MD Hart. 2008. "Job Loss at Mid-Life: Managers and Executives Face the 'New Risk Economy.'" *Social Forces* 87(1):185–209.

Mirowsky, John and Catherine E. Ross. 2007. "Life Course Trajectories of Perceived Control and Their Relationship to Education." *American Journal of Sociology* 112(5):1339–82.

Modell, John, Frank F. Furstenberg Jr., and Douglas Strong. 1978. "The Timing of Marriage in the Transition to Adulthood: Continuity and Change, 1860–1975." *American Journal of Sociology* 84:S120–50.

Mollenkopf, John, Mary C. Waters, Jennifer Holdaway. 2005. "The Ever-Winding Path: Ethnic and Racial Diversity in the Transition to Adulthood." In *On the Frontier of Adulthood: Theory, Research, and Public Policy*, edited by Richard A. Settersten, Frank F. Furstenberg, and Rubén G. Rumbaut, 454–500. University of Chicago Press.

Morgan, S. Philip and Ronald R. Rindfuss. 1985. "Marital Disruption: Structural and Temporal Dimensions." *American Journal of Sociology* 90(5):1055–77.

Pugh, Allison J. 2015. *The Tumbleweed Society: Working and Caring in an Age of Insecurity*. New York: Oxford University Press. pp. 5–8, 22–4, 96–8, 197–204.

Rauscher, Emily. 2011. "Producing Adulthood: Adolescent Employment, Fertility, and the Life Course." *Social Science Research* 40(2):552–71.

Rindfuss, Ronald R., C. Gray Swicegood, and Rachel A. Rosenfeld. 1987. "Disorder in the Life Course: How Common and Does It Matter?" *American Sociological Review* 52(6):785–801.

Salmela-Aro, Katariina, Kaisa Aunola, and Jari-Erik Nurmi. 2007. "Personal Goals During Emerging Adulthood: A 10-Year Follow-Up." *Journal of Adolescent Research* 22(6):690–715.

Schwartz, Barry. 2005. *The Paradox of Choice: Why More Is Less*. New York, NY: Harper Perennial.

Settersten, Richard A. 2003. "Propositions and Controversies on Life-Course Scholarship." In *Invitation to the Life Course: Toward New Understandings of Later Life*, edited by Richard A. Settersten, 15–48. Baywood Publishing Company.

Settersten, Richard A. 2011. "Becoming Adult: Meanings and Markers for Young Americans." In *Coming of Age in America: The Transition to Adulthood in the Twenty-First Century*, edited by Mary C. Waters, Patrick J. Carr, Maria J. Kefalas, and Jennifer Holdaway, 169–76. Berkeley: University of California Press.

Shanahan, Michael J. 2000. "Pathways to Adulthood in Changing Societies: Variability and Mechanisms in Life Course Perspective." *Annual Review of Sociology* 26(1):667–92.

Shanahan, Michael J., Erik Porfeli, Jeylan T. Mortimer, and Lance D. Erickson. 2005. "Subjective Age Identity and the Transition to Adulthood: Demographic Markers and Personal Attributes." In *On the Frontier of Adulthood: Theory, Research, and Public Policy*, edited by Richard A. Settersten, Frank F. Furstenberg, and Rubén G. Rumbaut, 224–55. University of Chicago Press.

Sharon, Tanya. 2015. "Constructing Adulthood: Markers of Adulthood and Well-Being Among Emerging Adults." *Emerging Adulthood*. doi: 2167696815579826.

Silverstein, Merril and Vern L. Bengston. 1997. "Intergenerational Solidarity and the Structure of Adult Child-Parent Relationships in American Families." *American Journal of Sociology* 103(2):429–60.

Singer, Burton, Carol D. Ryff, Deborah Carr, and William J. Magee. 1998. "Linking Life Histories and Mental Health: A Person-Centered Strategy." *Sociological Methodology* 28(1):1–51.

Smith, Tom W. 2005. "Generation Gaps in Attitudes and Values from the 1970s to the 1990s." In *On the Frontier of Adulthood: Theory, Research, and Public Policy*, edited by Richard A. Settersten, Frank F. Furstenberg, and Rubén G. Rumbaut, 177–224. University of Chicago Press.

South, Scott J., Kyle D. Crowder, and Katherine Trent. 1998. "Children's Residential Mobility and Neighborhood Environment Following Parental Divorce and Remarriage." *Social Forces* 77(2):667–93.

South, Scott J. and Lei Lei. 2015. "Failures-to-Launch and Boomerang Kids: Contemporary Determinants of Leaving and Returning to the Parental Home." *Social Forces* 94(2):863–90.

Suárez-Orozco, Carola. 2015. "Introduction to the Special Issue on Emerging Adulthood." *Journal of Adolescent Research* 30(5):535–37.

Spéder, Zsolt, Lívia Murinkó, and Richard A. Settersten. 2014. "Are Conceptions of Adulthood Universal and Unisex? Ages and Social Markers in 25 European Countries." *Social Forces* 92(3):873–98.

Sumner, Rachel, Anthony L. Burrow, and Patrick L. Hill. 2015. "Identity and Purpose as Predictors of Subjective Well-Being in Emerging Adulthood." *Emerging Adulthood* 3(1):46–54.

Swisher, Raymond R., Danielle C. Kuhl, and Jorge M. Chavez. 2013. "Racial and Ethnic Differences in Neighborhood Attainments in the Transition to Adulthood." *Social Forces* 91(4):1399–428.

Syed, Moin, and Lauren L. Mitchell. 2013. "Race, Ethnicity, and Emerging Adulthood Retrospect and Prospects." *Emerging Adulthood* 1(2):83–95.

Tandon, Darius S., and Barry S. Solomon. 2009. "Risk and Protective Factors for Depressive Symptoms in Urban African American Adolescents." *Youth & Society* 41(1):80–99.

Thomson, Irene Taviss. 2000. *In Conflict No Longer: Self and Society in Contemporary America*. Rowman & Littlefield.

Tilton-Weaver, Lauree C., Erin T. Vitunski, and Nancy L. Galambos. 2001. "Five Images of Maturity in Adolescence: What Does 'Grown Up' Mean?" *Journal of Adolescence* 24(2):143–58.

Widmer, Eric D. and Gilbert Ritschard. 2009. "The De-Standardization of the Life Course: Are Men and Women Equal?" *Advances in Life Course Research* 14(1–2):28–39.

Wu, Lawrence L. and Jui-Chung Allen Li. 2005. "Historical Roots of Diversity: Marital and Childbearing Trajectories of American Women." In *On the Frontier of Adulthood: Theory, Research, and Public Policy*, edited by Richard A. Settersten, Frank F. Furstenberg, and Rubén G. Rumbaut, 110–49. University of Chicago Press.

CHAPTER 3

Inequalities & Invisible Identities

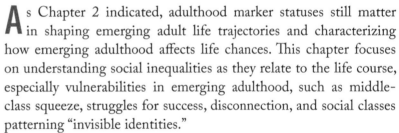

As Chapter 2 indicated, adulthood marker statuses still matter in shaping emerging adult life trajectories and characterizing how emerging adulthood affects life chances. This chapter focuses on understanding social inequalities as they relate to the life course, especially vulnerabilities in emerging adulthood, such as middle-class squeeze, struggles for success, disconnection, and social classes patterning "invisible identities."

To begin, educational attainment is a crucial marker for predicting social status and economic resources. The National Center for Education Statistics (NCES) data on average income earnings from 2000 to 2013 for different levels of educational attainment is listed in Figure 3.1 (page 94). Data covers the following levels of education: less than high school completion, high school degree, associate's degree, bachelor's degree, and master's or higher degree. The chart shows higher earnings for each level of education completion, with the largest difference for earning a bachelor's degree.

MIDDLE-CLASS SQUEEZE

The key demographics demarcating middle-class status are having a college degree and owning a home, yet Porter and colleagues (2012) report that those are statuses for people most likely to be in bankruptcy. The first reading of this chapter explains this.

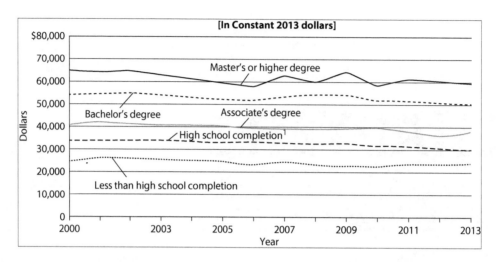

FIGURE 3.1 Annual Earnings of Young Adults

Source: U.S. Department of Education, National Center for Education Statistics, "Annual Earnings of Young Adults.," The Condition of Education.

READING 3.1

A Vulnerable Middle Class: Bankruptcy and Class Status

By Elizabeth Warren and Deborah Thorne

Bankruptcy has become a defining event for millions of families, taking a place alongside college graduation and divorce as a turning point in modern American life. Each month, more than one hundred thousand middle-class families—people who went to college, got respectable jobs, and bought homes—file for bankruptcy. They publicly declare themselves flat broke, losers in the great economic game of life. By the time they file for bankruptcy, unemployment has often decimated their incomes, and their debts are inflated beyond all hope of repayment. But their educations, jobs, and home addresses give some clues about the lives they once lived and the dreams they pursued.

Studies conducted by the Consumer Bankruptcy Project (CBP) in 1991, 2001, and 2007 consistently demonstrate that bankruptcy is a largely middle-class phenomenon.[1] Educational levels, occupational status, and rates of home-

---

[1] The proportion of filers with higher educational accomplishments, more prestigious occupations, or homeownership increased from 1991 to 2001; Warren, "Financial Collapse and Class Status," 115. Using all three criteria to measure class status, we conclude in this chapter that the proportion of filers who would be classified as middle class rose again from 2001 (91.8 percent) to 2007 (95 percent).

Elizabeth Warren and Deborah Thorne; ed. Katherine Porter, "A Vulnerable Middle Class: Bankruptcy and Class Status," Broke: How Debt Bankrupts the Middle Class, pp. 25–39, 249–254. Copyright © 2012 by Stanford University Press. Reprinted with permission.

ownership make it clear that most bankruptcy debtors are squarely in the middle class. These enduring measures of class status indicate that it is ordinary Americans, rather than the marginalized underclass or high-stakes gamblers, who are most apt to experience financial failure.

The only measure that initially seems inconsistent with middle-class status is the income of bankrupt families. Their incomes at the time of filing for bankruptcy situate substantial numbers of them well below the national average for the middle class. But the data also show that shortly before filing, many people lost their jobs or saw their work hours reduced, two economic blows that often are central to part of the crisis that pushes households into bankruptcy. As such, we contend that because income levels often reflect recent declines, income is an unreliable indicator of class status for those in bankruptcy.

Because the families in bankruptcy look so much like the rest of us, their troubles and struggles—job instability, illness and injury, and divorce—can serve as a case study of the economic vulnerabilities of much of middle-class America. The data presented here update studies of bankrupt households from 1991 and 2001. The basic finding remains constant: when measured by enduring criteria, most of the families in bankruptcy are legitimate members of the middle class, even if their incomes are relatively quite low. But the data also reveal two important differences: compared with those earlier bankruptcy filers, debtors since 2001 are more likely to have gone to college and more likely to have bought a home. This suggests that these two traditional strategies for building wealth—college attendance and home-ownership—are increasingly divorced from financial security. In the past, we have assumed that these markers of the middle class strongly protected Americans from the economic instability that often leads to bankruptcy. It appears, however, that the financial tables have turned. Benefits enjoyed by those Americans with some college education or by those who have bought homes have been undermined, so that neither college attendance nor home-ownership seems to correlate with reduced rates of bankruptcy.

It appears that the debts taken on by students and homeowners may turn an otherwise prudent economic move into a high-risk gamble that, for a growing number of people, does not pay off. Now that these time-honored wealth-building strategies fail to provide substantial economic protection, the middle class may face even greater economic instability in coming years. These data suggest that in the modern economy, the path to prosperity may be far more perilous than anyone previously imagined.

The Middle Class Defined

Who holds a place in the middle class? Income has long been a leading measure for identifying middle-class status.[2] Scholars frequently define the middle class as those

---

[2] Many scholars identify middle-class status by reference to income, often with acknowledgement that other measures add additional insight; see Gilbert, *American Class Structure,* 12, 259; Cannon, "On the Absolute or Relative Basis of Perception," 348, 350; and Kolko, "Economic Mobility and Social Stratification," 38.

whose household earnings fall in the three middle quintiles, between the bottom 20 percent and the top 20 percent. This approach is easy to calculate and aligns closely with our collective perception that the American middle class is a large group. Although some researchers amend the cutoff points—for example, expanding the criteria to include the middle 80 percent or 90 percent of the distribution—the dominant metric remains squarely focused on income as a proxy for class status.[3]

Our inquiry into who goes bankrupt indicates that the families who filed for bankruptcy in 2007 had a median gross household income of $32,988.[4] In contrast, the median gross household income for all families in the United States that same year was $50,233.[5] This suggests that in 2007 many of the bankrupt households were trying to make ends meet on considerably less income than the average American household.[6]

Dividing these populations into quintiles highlights the sharp disparity in incomes between bankrupt households and the general U.S. population. At every quintile in the income distribution, the breakpoints for the U.S. population were higher than for the families in bankruptcy. U.S. households and bankrupt households in the bottom quintile had similarly low incomes—$20,300 and $18,240, respectively. However, the gap between those in bankruptcy and those in the general population increased considerably up the income scale. At the top quintiles, the incomes of those in bankruptcy were only about 60 percent that of the population generally. Indeed, the benchmark for the top 20 percent of bankrupt households ($57,228) was not that much greater than the 50 percent benchmark for the U.S. population, with its median income of $50,233.

These data make it clear that, compared with the incomes of all American households, the incomes of those in bankruptcy are visibly concentrated in the lower quartiles. This should come as no surprise. After all, bankruptcy is designed to help

---

3   Cohn includes in the middle class those with an annual income of $50,000-70,000; Cohn, "Middle Class Blues." Gary Burtless of the Brookings Institute defined the middle class as having incomes in the range of $24,000-96,000, while MIT economist Frank Levy explained that the middle class had incomes between $30,000 and $90,000 annually; Vigeland, "What Is the Middle Class."

4   Unless otherwise indicated, all income data for bankrupt respondents are in 2007 dollars. Lawless et al. present more data on the income, debts, and assets of bankrupt households in "Did Bankruptcy Reform Fail?," 404. The income figures in this chapter differ from those reported in Lawless et al. Although both figures come from Schedule I of debtors' bankruptcy court records, this chapter reports a figure that approximates gross income—"combined monthly income" (bottom line figure on Schedule I) plus the households' payroll deductions—whereas Lawless et al. use only "combined monthly income." This chapter uses approximate gross income to increase comparability with the census data on the general population. The choice of Lawless et al. to use an alternate income calculation was to facilitate comparison with bankruptcy data from prior CBP studies in 1981, 1991, and 2001.

5   DeNavas-Walt, Proctor, and Smith, *Income, Poverty, and Health Insurance*, 7, Table 1.

6   In 2007, the year these data were drawn, the U.S. Department of Health and Human Services published the following poverty guidelines: a single person with annual income less than $10,210 is defined as living in poverty; the same is true for a two-person household with annual income of $13,690 or less, a three-person household with annual income of $17,170 or less, and a four-person household with annual income of $20,650 or less; U.S. Department of Health and Human Services, "2007 HHS Poverty Guidelines." And although the majority of the bankruptcy households were not officially "in poverty," their household incomes were low enough that one financial stumble could quickly land them there.

those in financial trouble. Lost income is deeply disruptive to a household's economic security, leaving the family more vulnerable to financial failure.

Although income is a readily available metric for determining class status, it has serious limitations. For example, careers that most Americans would classify as middle or even upper-middle class can have relatively low salaries. For instance, in 2007, mental health counselors, who are required to have either a master's or doctoral degree, earned average pretax incomes of a modest $39,450, or approximately $19.70 an hour.[7] In contrast, some jobs that do not necessarily carry middle-class status and prestige pay relatively high incomes. For example, in 2009, the median annual income for a United Parcel Service tractor-trailer truck driver was $70,550.[8]

Another problem with using income as a sole measure of social class is that over relatively short periods of time, income can fluctuate greatly. For example, a high school math teacher who quits teaching to enroll in a graduate program will immediately experience an income decline that will likely leave her hovering near the poverty level, but her class status will improve as her education increases. Furthermore, income as a measure of social class is uniquely problematic among bankrupt households, as incomes tend to be highly variable shortly before filing. Two-thirds (65 percent) of the households in bankruptcy reported job problems during the two years before they filed for bankruptcy.[9]

The income difficulties faced by families who filed for bankruptcy in 2007 are not the exclusive product of the recession. When our data were collected in the first quarter of 2007, the national unemployment rate was 4.5 percent.[10] Although that rate more than doubled in the following two years, the families filing for bankruptcy in 2007 reported the same concentration of job problems that plagued families who filed for bankruptcy in previous years. In the 1981, 1991, and 2001 CBP studies, bankrupt debtors also reported that their household incomes fluctuated sharply before they filed. When given the chance to explain the reasons behind their bankruptcy filings, a large proportion of bankrupt families in those years also identified job losses and cutbacks in the number of work hours.[11]

---

7   Mental Health Counseling Degree, "Masters Mental Health Counseling Salary."
8   PayScale, "Salary Survey."
9   If a respondent or a respondent's spouse answered yes to any of the following on a written questionnaire administered near the time of their bankruptcy filing, they were defined as having experienced a job problem: (1) they had, during the two years before the bankruptcy, lost two weeks or more of income because they were (a) laid off or fired, (b) ill or injured, (c) took time off to care for a sick family member, or (d) any other reason; OR (2) their employment status at the time of the bankruptcy was (a) not employed, seeking work, or (b) not employed, unable to work for medical reasons; OR (3) they indicated as a reason for filing for bankruptcy any of the following: (a) decline in income, (b) financial problems that resulted from being self-employed, or (c) illness or injury that caused them, or their spouse or partner, to miss two weeks or more of work.
10 Bureau of Labor Statistics, "Employment Status of the Civilian Noninstitutional Population."
11 Scholars have discussed the relationship between loss of income and bankruptcy filings using data from the 1981, 1991, and 2001 CBPs; Sullivan, Warren, and Westbrook, *As We Forgive Our Debtors*, 95–102 (1981 CBP); Sullivan, Warren, and Westbrook, *The Fragile Middle Class*, 15-18 (1991 CBP); Warren and Tyagi, *The Two-Income Trap*, 81, 106 (2001 CBP).

As the examples above illustrate, a meaningful definition of class requires more than income measures. Consequently, social scientists combine other criteria, such as education and occupational prestige, to provide a more accurate indication of social class status, particularly when studying people who experience sharp income fluctuations. Using these well-established variables, Martin Marger concludes that there are three levels of middle class—upper-middle, lower-middle, and working class—and when all three are combined, 68 to 80 percent of Americans are situated, broadly speaking, in the middle class.[12] By merging these criteria, the size of the middle class remains about the same as the rough income comparisons, but the composition shifts somewhat.[13] Sociologists Melvin Oliver and Thomas Shapiro expanded the calculus used to determine social class by adding homeownership—a common proxy for wealth, economic security, and social status.[14]

The critical point for our purposes is that for families in bankruptcy, income is often sharply disrupted near the time of filing, and it is out of synch with other indicia of class status. Because of the problems associated with using income as an indicator of class status for bankrupt households, we believe that the alternate criteria of social class—educational achievement, job status, and homeownership—are more valid measures of middle-class membership. For the remainder of this chapter, we use each criterion to compare the people who file for bankruptcy with the U.S. population. In addition, because we collected similar data from earlier years, we are also able to compare the status of bankrupt debtors today with their counterparts from 1991 and 2001. The data point toward a solidly and consistently middle-class group of households that file for bankruptcy.

Education Matters

The link between education and social class is long established in the social sciences.[15] As Marger notes: "The relationship is quite simple: The higher the number of years of education, the greater the probability of upward mobility."[16] Generally speaking, people with advanced degrees (professional degrees and graduate degrees) enjoy not only higher earnings, but also greater life chances, especially compared with those without a high school diploma.[17] In a nutshell, as a person's level of education increases, so too does his or her social class.

---

12   Marger; *Social Inequality*, 58-61.
13   Marger provides additional discussion of the differences among the three categories of middle class; ibid., 59–61 and 111–114.
14   Oliver and Shapiro, *Black Wealth/White Wealth*, 6, 17-23. Keister describes how for the bottom 80 percent of Americans, 66 percent of their wealth is in their primary residence; Keister, *Wealth in America*, 122. Williams, Nesiba, and Diaz McConnell, "Changing Face of Inequality," 181–208.
15   Featherman and Hauser, *Opportunity and Change*, 266–68, 282.
16   Marge; *Social Inequality, 197.*
17   U.S. Census Bureau, *Statistical Abstract: 2009*, 146, Table 224.

People who file for bankruptcy today are considerably more educated than they were just fifteen years ago ... For example, compared with their 1991 counterparts, those filing for bankruptcy in 2007 were half as likely to have dropped out of high school and were much more likely to have attended some college. Overall, in 1991, the proportion of bankrupt people who had some college coursework, a college diploma, or an advanced degree comprised 46.5 percent of all of those in bankruptcy. By 2007, that proportion increased to 58.9 percent.

Not only are people who filed for bankruptcy in 2007 better educated than those who went bankrupt nearly two decades ago, they continue to be better educated than the general population. For example, between 1991 and 2007, the percentage of the U.S. adult population who had attended college increased from 39.2 percent in 1991 to 53.4 percent in 2007. And although this reflects a positive trend, the total remains notably smaller than the 58.9 percent of bankrupt debtors who had attended college in 2007.

People who file for bankruptcy are also less likely to be represented at either end of the educational spectrum than the U.S. population. ... People in bankruptcy were less likely to drop out of high school, but they were also less likely to have earned advanced degrees from universities. Instead, people in bankruptcy were far more likely to be bunched in the middle—having attended college, but not having graduated.

The spike in "some college" reflects a persistent trend among bankrupt debtors: compared with the general population, they were more likely to have attended college, but less likely to have completed their college degrees. People in bankruptcy were 60 percent more likely than Americans generally to have attended college but to have left without a diploma. When a person attends college but fails to graduate, the benefits that typically accompany the credential are less forthcoming. As Katherine Porter reports, it is not mere college enrollment but a bachelor's degree that dramatically increases income.

Nonetheless, for the purposes of determining class status, college attendance remains a significant event; it signals both aspirations and experiences that are distinctly middle class. When college attendance is used as a measure of social standing, nearly six of ten 2007 bankrupt debtors are in the middle class. As a group, people in bankruptcy appear to have the same or higher educational attainment than the general population, reinforcing the appropriateness of categorizing bankrupt debtors as a middle-class demographic.

The All-Important Job

People often define themselves, and others, by their jobs. Our work shapes our minds, our bodies, and the rhythm of our daily lives. And equally importantly, our work also shapes the prestige others accord to us and our own sense of social standing.[18]

---

18 We recognize that there has been debate over the usefulness of occupational prestige scoring and the meaning of prestige; Goldthorpe and Hope, "Occupational Grading and Occupational Prestige," 23–26, 33–37. The authors

Occupational prestige is a matter of such importance that social science surveys have been used for decades to calibrate, and recalibrate, the status affiliated with virtually every job in the United States. On the basis of results from these surveys, jobs are assigned occupational prestige scores, which range from 0 to 100. For example, the occupation of custodian has been assigned a prestige score of 16; hair stylist, a score of 33; registered nurse, a score of 62; and physician, a score of 84. Not surprisingly, income and educational level are highly correlated with occupational prestige.[19] But there are important exceptions. For example, the occupation of professor is assigned a higher prestige score than a plumber, even though plumbers often earn considerably more money than professors. Because of such divergences, occupational prestige is an important alternative to income for measuring middle-class status.

In 1991, 2001, and 2007, the CBP asked debtors to describe their work and then assigned the corresponding occupational prestige score.[20] The median occupational prestige scores held constant at approximately 36, which is associated with jobs such as clerks, nurses' aides, office administrators, and brick masons. The most prestigious occupations of those in bankruptcy, which included social workers, guidance counselors, and computer programmers, had a score of 51 and were also constant across all three time periods. Most people in bankruptcy had jobs associated with the middle class, which often require some advanced training or specialized job skills beyond a high school diploma.

… In 2007, all workers in the United States and workers who filed for bankruptcy shared a similar occupational prestige score distribution. Figure[s] plot the break points for occupational prestige scores for each decile of the two populations and shows how the bankruptcy scores trail the U.S. population by only a few points at each interval.

---

assert that prestige is primarily an indication of one's ability to demand and receive deference and opportunities over the life course, and as such one's occupation is key to the lived experience of social class.

19 Donald Treiman's classic work concludes that as occupational prestige scores increase, so too do the authority, autonomy, and power that employees enjoy at their jobs; Treiman, "Standard Occupational Prestige Scale," 285–290.

20 As with previous CBP studies, occupations were coded using the 1970 Occupational Classification codes available from the Interuniversity Consortium for Political and Social Research. The 1970 codes are still widely in use as the last "pure" occupational codes used by the U.S. Census Bureau and have been used in major studies such as the General Social Survey. Since the 1970 Census, the bureau has moved to sets of codes that incorporate industry as well as occupation, but there are available several "walkovers" that permit correspondence from one set of codes to another.

In the 2007 CBP study, occupational descriptions of homemaker, housewife, and stay-at-home parent were scored at 51; Dworkin, "Prestige Ranking," 59–63. In 1991 and 2001 CBPs, however, homemakers were not assigned a score. When the 2007 occupation data were scored both ways-with and without a score for homemakers-there was no significant difference in outcomes. For consistency with our earlier studies, the data reported in this chapter do not reflect a score for homemakers. Respondents who indicated that they were retired, disabled, unemployed, or students were not assigned a score. Occupations that were otherwise unclassifiable were also not coded. If respondents listed more than one occupation, the occupation listed first was coded. If they wrote that they were currently unemployed but indicated that they used to work in a specific occupation, that occupation was coded.

Bankrupt debtors are moderately concentrated in lower prestige jobs and are underrepresented at the upper end of the distribution in the higher prestige occupations, such as doctors, lawyers, and engineers. As a group, the individuals in bankruptcy in 2007 had somewhat less prestigious jobs than their counterparts in the population generally, but the magnitude of the difference was modest at most. People who file for bankruptcy are typically working right alongside other Americans.

The pattern of occupational prestige scores for people who filed for bankruptcy in 2007 is virtually identical to those patterns in the 1991 and 2001 CBP studies. Data from 1991 and 2001 also reveal similar patterns of occupational prestige scores between bankrupt individuals and the U.S. population: there is generally a proportional representation among the middle class, a small overrepresentation among the lowest class, and a more noticeable underrepresentation among the highest class.[21]

As our data illustrate, the occupational status of households that file for bankruptcy has remained relatively constant. Likewise, the distribution of occupational prestige scores for all Americans changed very modestly between 1991 and 2007. Nationally, median occupational prestige scores rose only slightly from 1991 to 2001 and then flattened out from 2001 to 2007. The similarity of the patterns reinforces an important and enduring trend: bankrupt Americans tend to have jobs similar to their nonbankrupt counterparts in the general population.

If occupational prestige scores are a marker of class status, then it is possible to demarcate points on the scale that reflect membership in the middle class. For purposes of locating the bankrupt debtors within the larger population, we suggest that the upper 80 percent of 2007 occupational prestige scores nationwide represent people who made it to the middle class. This criterion translates into an occupational score of 32 or higher. By this definition, people with occupational scores of 31 or lower (people working in retail or as delivery drivers, factory and assembly line workers, cooks and waiters, and landscapers) are excluded from the middle class. Because of the concentration of bankrupt debtors near the middle of the national occupational prestige scores, 77 percent of people in bankruptcy exceeded this threshold with an occupational score greater than 31 and therefore have a claim to middle-class status.[22]

For those who might draw the boundaries of middle-class membership more generously, including assembly line workers and others with scores of 30 or 31, for example, then the proportion of bankrupt debtors with middle-class occupations rises to 80.2 percent. For those who might draw a boundary at the other end of the spectrum, declaring those with occupational prestige scores in the top decile (occupational scores of 51 or higher) to be upper class rather than middle class, then the proportion of debtors with middle-class jobs shrinks by 5.4 percentage points. In the latter case,

---

21 Consumer Bankruptcy Project, 1991 and 2001.
22 This analysis represents the scores for each individual debtor who filed for bankruptcy, including husbands and wives separately if they filed joint petitions. In the summary section ("Adding the Ways to the Middle Class"), we recombine the joint debtors to determine the class status of the household as a whole.

however, it is noticeable that much of the discussion of consumer bankruptcy centers around the issue of whether the people filing have achieved middle-class status—not whether they have exceeded it.

Owning A Home

During the housing boom that peaked in 2007, the government-sponsored mortgage agency Fannie Mae ran a series of advertisements depicting itself as being in the "American Dream business." That campaign tapped into the long-held belief that people who could purchase a home, who could put down roots and secure their financial futures, surely had accomplished the American Dream—even if they had borrowed every dollar needed to get there. While real estate agents and mortgage brokers were eager to point out the financial benefits of homeownership, sociologists Oliver and Shapiro stressed that owning a home has traditionally been an enduring, as well as a highly visible, symbol of middle-class achievement.[23]

For whatever combination of economic and social motives, families across the country have acquired homes in ever-growing numbers. From 1991 to 2007, homeownership in the United States expanded from 64.1 percent to 68.4 percent. For families in bankruptcy, the rise in homeownership was far more remarkable. The proportion of bankrupt families who were, or had recently been, homeowners jumped from 43.9 percent in 1991, to 50 percent in 2001, to 66.3 percent in 2007.[24] These data suggest that the housing bubble that began to inflate in the early 2000s included a growing number of homeowners who found themselves in bankruptcy even before the housing bubble burst.

Unlike the education and occupation statistics, the housing numbers are not directly comparable between all Americans and the bankrupt population. For the U.S. population generally, the proportion of homeowners is a measurement taken at a cross section in time, for example, during the month of March in 2007. But families in bankruptcy are in economic turmoil, and part of that turmoil may include losing a home through foreclosure, short sale, or surrender to a lender. A measure of homeownership that extends over a period of time is more likely to accurately capture a household's enduring living situation and class status. For this reason, families in bankruptcy were asked whether they owned a home at the time of filing for bankruptcy *or* had owned a home, but had lost it for financial reasons, in the five years before bankruptcy.

Looking at 2007 homeownership rates of the U.S. population and people in bankruptcy: Slightly more than half (51.2 percent) of the families owned their homes at the time of bankruptcy, while a sizeable fraction, another 15.1 percent, had lost their homes for financial reasons within the five years preceding their bankruptcy

---

23   Oliver and Shapiro, *Black Wealth/White Wealth*, passim.
24   The 43.9 percent reported in 1991 may be artificially low, an artifact of sampling that inadvertently produced a disproportionately high response rate among those receiving legal advice from Community Legal Service in Philadelphia—a group that was unlikely to own homes; Warren, "Financial Collapse and Class Status," 137–38. Even so, the jump from 2001 to 2007 is remarkable.

filings. There is no comparable number for how many families in the general population lost their homes during the five years before 2007. The foreclosure rates in those years remained less than 1 percent, suggesting a small effect, but there is no accurate measure of the number of short sales or other arrangements that occurred outside the formal legal system to end homeownership. As a result, direct comparability about past homeownership is not possible.

If we limit our comparison strictly to current homeownership at a single point in time, the bankrupt population is substantially behind their counter-parts in the general population. Homeownership rates among those in bankruptcy were about 25 percent lower than in the population generally. Even so, the fact that 66.3 percent of the households in bankruptcy either were current homeowners or had been homeowners in the past five years suggests middle-class aspirations and accomplishments—much like those who went to college but did not graduate. The tangible accomplishment of buying a home suggests middle-class status, even for those who were unable to hang on to their houses.

We pause to consider the relationship between our findings and the mortgage boom and bust of the late 2000s. The bankrupt sample was drawn in the first quarter of 2007, just before housing values crashed and home mortgage foreclosures skyrocketed. In the first quarter of 2007, at about the time our data were collected, the number of foreclosures was estimated at 437,000, considerably fewer than the 799,064 posted in the fourth quarter of 2010.[25] Consequently, our data were drawn at the tail end of the housing bubble, when the maximum number of families had been offered easy credit to buy homes, but before they began to lose those houses in large numbers. This means that the "lost home" category, which had already hit 15.1 percent in early 2007 for families in bankruptcy, is likely to have grown substantially during the subsequent years, as the housing market plummeted and mortgage credit evaporated. Put another way, the number of "lost homes" among families in bankruptcy in 2007 is likely an underestimate of the effect of dangerous mortgage practices because these homes were lost well before the housing market crashed.

Before the housing bubble of the 2000s, it would have been plausible to use homeownership as an indicator of families' economic security. Back in the 1970s and 1980s—when average first-time buyers put up 18 percent of a home's purchase price to get a mortgage,[26] and when applications for home mortgages required detailed inquiries about income, length of employment, and credit history—homeownership signaled that people had passed considerable economic scrutiny.[27] By 2005, however, with the median down payment at zero and rampant use of so-called liar's loans (loans

---

25 Realty-Trac, "More than 430,000 Foreclosure Filings Reported." RealtyTrac, "Record 2.9 Million U.S. Properties Receive Foreclosure Filings in 2010."
26 U.S. Census Bureau, *Statistical Abstract:* 1993, 734, Table 1247.
27 Sullivan, Warren, and Westbrook, *The Fragile Middle Class*, 208-09. Warren and Tyagi, *The Two-Income Trap*, 127. These scholars discuss in more detail the extensive financial scrutiny that homeowners once had to endure in order to qualify for a mortgage.

in which there was no verification of borrower's income, often leading to inflated income and higher loan amounts), teaser rate mortgages, and other exotic devices, buying a home might have actually become an unreliable indicator of the buyer's financial stability.

In his acceptance speech to the Republican National Convention in 2004, George W. Bush announced: "Another priority for a new term is to build an ownership society, because ownership brings security and dignity and independence. Thanks to our policies, home ownership in America is at an all-time high. Tonight we set a new goal: seven million more affordable homes in the next ten years, so more American families will be able to open the door and say, 'Welcome to my home.'"[28] The data make it clear that families in bankruptcy, much like most American families, embraced the dream of homeownership. By 2007, two-thirds of all those filing for bankruptcy had punched their admission ticket for the middle class by buying a home. Unfortunately, some people's homeownership dream proved fleeting and elusive; the bankruptcy data show that financial problems led to many families losing their homes even before the housing bubble burst.

Adding The Ways to The Middle Class

There are multiple paths to the middle class. Income is a frequent proxy for class status, but it fails to capture the complexities of the class status of people in financial trouble, particularly of those whose income has recently dropped. Enduring criteria of class—education, occupation, and homeownership—offer a clearer sense of the lives that bankrupt debtors once lived and the lives to which they will again aspire. We use these enduring criteria to determine what proportion of the *households* in bankruptcy might reasonably claim membership in the middle class.

Couples who file joint bankruptcies present a particular statistical challenge when the number of middle-class bankruptcies is being calculated. Couples living together share a home; thus they share class status based on homeownership. But education and occupation are individual accomplishments. To describe accurately the class status of households in bankruptcy—and to avoid overcounting results from married couples—we rely on household, rather than individual, data. We follow the convention that the highest status associated with either spouse of a married couple living together applies to the household.[29] This means, for example, that if a married couple files for bankruptcy and one spouse is a college graduate and the other has earned high school diploma, the household is assigned the higher status of the college graduate. Similarly, if one spouse is a corporate manager and the other is a substitute teacher, the

---

28 "Text: President Bush's Acceptance Speech."
29 Hughes, Jr., and Perry-Jenkins, "Social Class Issues," 175–82. Hughes and Perry-Jenkins discuss the situations in which household class status is best determined by the characteristics of a single adult in the household (individual as unit of analysis) or adults' combined characteristics (household as unit of analysis). They stress that ultimately both measures have their strengths and that the "research question and the family outcomes of interest" should dictate the choice of whether to use data from one or both adults (176).

household is assigned the higher occupational prestige score of the manager. Because of this, *households* had somewhat higher occupational prestige scores and higher proportions in which someone had gone to college than the proportion of *individuals* evidencing those same criteria.

With the household as the unit of analysis, homeownership and education each qualify about two-thirds of the households in bankruptcy as middle class. Occupational prestige sweeps in a larger group, with 82.9 percent of bankrupt households composed of at least one family member whose occupation is among the top 80 percent of occupational scores in the United States.

With these criteria, more than nineteen of twenty households in bankruptcy could be classified as middle class: 95 percent reported at least one measure of middle-class status. This is an increase from 2001, when similar calculations revealed that 91.8 percent showed at least one indication of middle-class status. The data suggest that families in bankruptcy have been drawn largely from the middle at least since 1991, and the proportion with middle-class credentials continues to rise.

The strength of the claim these families might make on middle-class status can be further tested. Of the households that had at least one indicator of middle-class status, 38.7 percent met two of the criteria and 41 percent met all three criteria.

These three indicia of middle-class status are highly correlated, with no single criterion dominating. Homeownership and occupational status combined would classify 90.6 percent of all the filers as middle class. Home-ownership and some college would identify 87.2 percent as middle class. Some college and occupational status would peg 88.4 percent as middle class. These recombinations demonstrate the tight correlation among the variables. Of course, the correlations are expected because these class identifiers tend to reinforce each other, as people with better educations often end up in better jobs, and those with better jobs are more likely to buy houses.

There are no data that combine the indicia of middle-class status for the general U.S. population, making it impossible to carry out a direct, cumulative comparison between the bankruptcy population and the general population. Despite this limitation, the bankruptcy numbers are useful in themselves. They reveal that people who file for bankruptcy graduated from high school and went on to college. They got good jobs. They bought homes. They may trail other Americans at the margins, with fewer bachelor's and graduate degrees and fewer very-high-status occupations, but collectively they have enduring indicia of middle-class achievement. People in bankruptcy accomplished a great deal before their financial collapse, and they reflect a class status that is much like their counterparts around the country.

Implications of The Data

The headline finding is unmistakable: bankruptcy is used primarily by middle-class families in financial distress. With more than nine in ten of all households in bankruptcy achieving middle-class status by virtue of education, occupational status, or homeownership, bankruptcy cannot be dismissed as one more tragedy in lives beset by chronic poverty and limited choices. Bankruptcy has become a clear marker of how far middle-class people are falling from a once-solid economic rung on the American class ladder.[30]

The most disturbing finding in these data may be the trend lines. To the extent that a trend is discernible from the three studies in 1991, 2001, and 2007, the data suggest that the proportion of middle-class families turning to bankruptcy is increasing. The most notable increases were in two areas: the proportion of respondents with "some college," and the proportion who were, or had recently been, homeowners. Compared with the number of bankruptcy filers in 1991, by 2007 the number of filers who owned homes had increased 20 percentage points, and the number who had "some college" had increased 10 percentage points.

The irony is inescapable. To an earlier generation, more education and homeownership spelled economic security. But these traditional paths have become far more treacherous. With more students than ever before taking out student loans, the stretch for an advanced education is considerably riskier. For those who are unsuccessful in their efforts to earn a bachelor's degree, the lack of a credential combined with higher student loan debt and years of deferred earnings from delayed job market entry may spell financial disaster later in life. Furthermore, the financial risks of higher education may be exacerbated by the increased presence of private student loan lenders—who charge higher interest rates and fees than federally backed loans—and by the increasing need for students to rely on credit cards to cover college expenses.

The data also suggest that the economic implications of homeownership are changing. The homeownership rates of bankrupt households showed a marked increase, approaching that of the general population. The housing bubble was inflated by easy money, which meant that down payments vanished; loans became highly leveraged; and borrowers absorbed even more risk by taking on mortgages with adjustable rates, interest-only payments, and teaser rates that reset in two or three years. At the same time, the country saw an expansion of unscrupulous lending practices, with many homeowners deceived about the costs and risks associated with buying a home. The bankruptcy data offer a crucial warning that, absent proper regulation of the mortgage industry, homeownership may actually undermine a family's social class rather than elevate it.

Most Americans will never seek protection from their creditors through bankruptcy.[31] For example, in 2007, the year of this study, there were 112 million households in the United States.[32] That same year, 827,000 bankruptcies were filed—most by households rather than by large corporations. Translated, this means that only seven-tenths of 1 percent (which is less than one in one hundred) of the households in the

---

30   Cf. Ramsay and Sim, "Personal Insolvency in Australia," 12–18.
31   Data for 2000-2008 was from the U.S. Courts, "Bankruptcy Statistics." 254 Numbers of bankruptcy filings for 2009 came from Lawless, "Guesstimate of 2010 Bankruptcy Filings."
32   Kreider and Elliott, *America's Families*, 2.

United States filed for bankruptcy in 2007.[33] Because the percentage numbers are small in any given year, we might expect a sharp deviance from the general population. However, the fact that these data show a strong similarity between bankrupt debtors and the middle class reveals important aspects of the economic and social health of American families. Bankruptcy data are a barometer of financial failure. Knowing that middle-class America is at risk suggests problems that run to the very heart of the American economy.

The findings in this chapter warn of a United States in which "middle class" is no longer synonymous with "financial security,".... Instead, the bankruptcy data reveal an increasingly vulnerable middle class that plays by all the rules—going to college, finding decent jobs, buying homes—and whose members still find themselves in economic collapse.

---

[33] Rates of bankruptcy filings in 2007 were abnormally low as they continued to rebound from the amendments to bankruptcy law in 2005. To put this in context, over the preceding decade, the United States averaged 1.37 million filings annually, or almost double the number that were filed in 2007. Thus, if the number of filings in 2007 had been typical, the percentage of households filing for bankruptcy would have instead been 1.2 percent, rather than 0.7 percent. In 2010, as families struggled with an economy that had not yet emerged from a severe recession, the number of families filing for bankruptcy was approximately 1.56 million, which was nearly double the number in 2007.

In summary, obtaining both these statuses without adequate resources put people more at risk of having economic difficulties than those who do neither (Warren & Thorne 2012). Going to college and buying a home both involve debt, often lots of it. If money is paid and debt incurred in order to go to college, but the degree is not obtained, then economic vulnerability is even more likely. But even for those who graduate with a degree, earning potential may not increase merely as a result of having obtained the credential. They must also have acquired the skills, experience, and networks that a degree is meant to symbolize. So while it is still the case that a college degree is associated with greater earning potential, this is only true of the aggregate, meaning it is an average trend. There are many people to whom this does not apply.

Figure 3.2 represents a peak of increased risk of filing bankruptcy for Americans with some college (but not the degree). Porter reports: "People in bankruptcy were 60 percent more likely than Americans generally to have attended college but to have left without a diploma. When a person attends college but fails to graduate, the benefits that typically accompany the credential are less forthcoming" (p. 30).

However, Warren and Thorne (2012) note the complexity of life chances and college:

> Nonetheless, for the purposes of determining class status, college attendance remains a significant event; it signals both aspirations and experiences that are distinctly middle class. When college attendance is used as a measure of social standing, nearly six of ten 2007 bankrupt debtors are in the middle class. As a group, people in bankruptcy appear to have the same or higher educational attainment than the general population, reinforcing the appropriateness of categorizing bankrupt debtors as a middle-class demographic (p. 31).

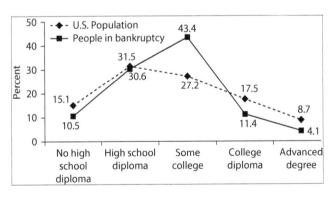

FIGURE 3.2 Educational Attainment of U.S. Population People in Bankruptcy, 2007

Source: ed. Katherine Porter, "Some College Bankruptcy," Broke: How Debt Bankrupts the Middle Class. Copyright © 2012 by Stanford University Press.

What does all this mean? Going to college is important and presents the opportunity to invest heavily in a successful, or at least relatively stable, future. However, it is not determinative, meaning it does not have a 100% success return rate. Instead, it is best to think of a college degree as often *necessary but not sufficient* for higher earnings.

Likewise, people who buy a house before they have the adequate savings and socioeconomic resources to do so may incur more costs through interest than they would have paid out of pocket to rent instead (Warren

& Thorne 2012). These two middle-class statuses are important, and not to be avoided. At the same time, they are not to be taken lightly or entered into without careful thought and sufficient resources. Cumulatively, the increased opportunities *and* potential for greater risks can culminate in what is often called "*middle-class anxiety*" (e.g., Ochs & Kremer-Sadlik 2013), the fear of losing ground or becoming squeezed out of the middle class.

In response to the pressures and difficulties to succeed in the precarious middle, many middle-class families live a fast-paced life that involves sending children to many organized activities to gain necessary skills, a phenomenon Ochs & Kremer-Sadlik (2013) term "fast-forward families." After following several families around for weeks and having all family members recording time diaries that include noting where they were located in the family household, the authors report that the majority of middle-class families spend more time alone than together *while at home*. The times that families did spend together were most often taking care of responsibilities, such as homework and chores, as well as eating. Most recreational activities involved watching TV alone, or in each other's presence but with little communication. In sum, overworked and stressed middle-class families tended to respond to economic squeeze by living a fast-paced lifestyle with little downtime to interact at leisure with one another.

STRUGGLING FOR SUCCESS

Paralleling the middle-class experience, working-class and poor families face increased vulnerabilities attempting to make ends meet in an age of insecurity, often with consequences for mental health (e.g., Miech et al. 1999). As a result of the challenges that working-class emerging adults face in transitioning to adulthood, Silva (2012; 2013) finds that young people from limited means have to do extra "emotional management" to protect themselves from ongoing vulnerabilities. Working-class emerging adults are even more likely to espouse a form of American individualism discussed in the final chapter. Numerous scholars find that poverty-related events have critical impacts on childhood and emerging adulthood trajectories (Berzin & De Marco 2009; Macomber et al. 2009).

The second reading of this chapter describes the particular vulnerabilities that emerging adults can face in making the transition to adulthood with limited social and economic support. Osgood et al. (2005) describe how the extended duration in between adolescence and adulthood roles is a heavy burden for resource-constrained families.

READING 3.2

Introduction: Why Focus on the Transition to Adulthood for Vulnerable Populations?

By D. Wayne Osgood, E. Michael Foster, Constance Flanagan, and Gretchen R. Ruth

Family Support during the Transition to Adulthood

Becoming an adult does not happen all at once, but rather it involves an extended period of semiautonomy during which youth move away from full dependence on their families (Arnett 2000; Goldscheider and Goldscheider 1:999). Indeed, for this reason it is important to recognize the transition to adulthood as a special period in life when people face unique challenges. Although they leave behind the restrictions of childhood and adolescence, their financial resources are limited, as are the experiences and connections that would land them jobs with good pay. Thus, only gradually can they take on adult responsibilities. Typically, they remain at least partially dependent on others, especially their parents, for various kinds of assistance. For some, families provide partial support as they remain at home for a period after high school; for others parents pay a large share of college expenses. Furthermore, steps toward independence are often reversed. For instance, during their late teens and twenties, 40 percent of American

D. Wayne Osgood, E. Michael Foster, Constance Flanagan, and Gretchen R. Ruth , "Introduction: Why Focus on the Transition to Adulthod for Vulnerable Populations?," On Your Own Without a Net: The Transition to Adulthood for Vulnerable Population, pp. 6–9. Copyright © 2005 by University of Chicago Press. Reprinted with permission.

youth move back to their parents' home at least once after leaving (Goldscheider and Goldscheider 1994).

Families provide assistance to their children during the transition to adulthood in many ways. Parents often continue to provide food and shelter; they may give their children money to assist with bills or major expenses like the down payment for a house; and they may help their children by giving their time for tasks such as child care. Families also may provide social or emotional support and the motivation crucial to achieving success during the transition. Attachment to parents, indicating positive parental support, is associated with higher academic achievement (Cutrona et al. 1994) and higher perceptions of scholastic competence during college (Fass and Tubman 2002). Parents can also be a key source of guidance for their young adult offspring, providing advice about topics such as careers, money management, housing, and health care. At the same time, the character of the parent-child relationship changes significantly during this period and one of the important tasks for young adults and their parents is to develop a more peerlike relationship.

During childhood and adolescence, governmental programs have played a major role in augmenting family resources for meeting the needs of the vulnerable populations, but those program services typically end early in the transition period. How problematic is this termination? It is useful to consider this in light of the amount of assistance that families provide to youth in the general population during the transition to adulthood.

In *On the Frontier of Adulthood*, Schoeni and Ross (2005) estimated the amount of money and time that parents provide to their children from age eighteen through thirty-four. They concluded that the average value of parental support (in 2001 dollars) across this age period was $2,200 annually, and the total across these years represents roughly one-third of the amount provided during the years of childhood. On top of this financial assistance, parents continue to give their children a great deal of their time. The average time assistance was 367 hours per year, which is roughly the hours of work in nine weeks of fulltime employment. Schoeni and Ross also concluded that the amount of assistance has increased considerably over the last thirty years due to longer schooling, later age of marriage, and the increase in single parenting.

The amount of assistance that families provide during the transition clearly depends a great deal on the family's resources. For instance, youth receive less assistance if their families have less income, if the parents have less education, or if there are more siblings in the family (Amato and Booth 1997; Jayakody 1998; Steelman and Powell 1991). Schoeni and Ross calculated that the quarter of U.S. households with the highest incomes provide at least 70 percent more assistance to their children from age eighteen through thirty-four than do the quarter with the lowest incomes. Thus, assistance during this age period contributes to a dynamic of diverging pathways (Kerckhoff 1993) in which parents' educational and economic resources contribute to growing advantages for some youth over others. It seems likely that these vulnerable populations, who face a combination of larger challenges and reduced family support, will be at the greatest disadvantage in negotiating the transition to adulthood.

Why These Vulnerable Populations Deserve Our Attention

In this section we make the case for special attention to these particular vulnerable populations in terms of the greater challenges they face in making the transition to adulthood and in terms of the ending of their eligibility for governmental programs as they enter this critical age period.

Sources of Greater Challenge during the Transition to Adulthood

These vulnerable populations require our attention because they face great challenges in several areas during the transition to adulthood. First, some populations must accomplish additional tasks that most people in this age period do not face. For instance, runaway and homeless youth begin the transition in need of housing, rather than having the security of their family's home. Youth with physical disabilities often need to arrange for medical services or devices to assist them with daily tasks. Youth involved in the juvenile or adult justice systems often owe restitution in the form of money or labor, and their freedom may depend on following conditions of probation or parole that restrict their activities. Such burdens may well reduce the chance of obtaining the additional education that would improve future job prospects or of finding an appealing partner and nurturing that relationship into a satisfying marriage.

Many of the vulnerable populations also confront greater challenges in the form of limitations on their skills, and these limitations may directly preclude their receiving opportunities available to others. For instance, reduced strength and range of movement (for youth with physical disabilities) or learning disabilities and cognitive impairments (for youth in special education) would rule out some appealing occupations. Indeed, members of many of these vulnerable populations have very limited skills at dealing with ordinary tasks of daily living for the transition to adulthood, such as managing money, obtaining housing, or even (for a substantial proportion of youth in special education) looking up telephone numbers (Foster and Gifford 2005).

Another type of limitation is learning disabilities, which are quite common not only among children and adolescents in special education, but in several of the other vulnerable populations as well. In the juvenile justice system, for example, 30 to 50 percent of all confined youth have identified learning disabilities (Foster and Gifford 2005). Other limitations include mental illness (for youth involved in the mental health system) or behavioral difficulties (for youth involved in the justice system and many runaway and homeless youth, or youth in foster care). Though these limitations would not preclude the physical and intellectual tasks required by a job, they could reduce the probability of successfully coping with requirements such as punctuality, reliability, and maintaining positive relationships with coworkers.

A third source of challenge for many of the vulnerable populations is the lack of family support. As we discussed above, youth in the general population typically receive a great deal of assistance from their families, and this support often appears critical for overcoming difficulties like becoming a single parent or losing a job. Furthermore, the greater financial resources of middle-class families allow them to continue to elevate their children's prospects of success above those of working-class and poor families. In contrast, youths in these vulnerable populations often come from families whose economic resources are limited. In other instances the quality of the relationships in their families is degraded, poor, or entirely absent. For example, children from poor, single-parent families are overrepresented among youth in the juvenile justice system, and delinquent youth are especially likely to have poor relationships with their parents or care givers. Similarly, children from poor, single-parent families are overrepresented in special education; 68 percent of those in special education come from families with incomes of less than $25,000 compared with only 40 percent of students in the general population. We should be especially concerned about those vulnerable populations that have no families to which they can turn, such as youth leaving foster care and runaway and homeless youth.

We hasten to add that in many cases parents and extended family of vulnerable youth strive to be supportive, and thus it is often not a lack of motivation that hinders their support. As noted, for some families the financial burdens outweigh resources. Yet even committed families with good resources have a difficult task in helping young adults in these vulnerable populations succeed in confronting the challenges detailed in this volume.

Unfortunately, many youth do not have adequate resources to navigate to adulthood as successfully as some of their peers. Instead, Wight et al. (2010) find that the proportion of disconnected youth has risen markedly in the past ten years—nearly 15 percent of youth are disconnected from mainstream educational and occupational institutions. Disconnected youth have lower educational attainment rates, greater unemployment, and are more likely to be "discouraged workers"—defined as people who are available for work, want a job, but are not currently in the labor force—and are significantly more likely to be poor (Wight et al. 2010).

The central issue is that characteristics of emerging adulthood obscure important vulnerabilities. The wide diversity of options for transitioning into adulthood make it appear that no marker is important for constructing adult lives. While no one marker may be singularly important, not acquiring any adulthood role is problematic. Figure 3.3 represents a combination of disconnected status with income and living arrangements (Wight et al. 2010). The two bars on the left represent emerging adults who live with their parents or relatives, while the two on the right represent emerging adults who live alone. Within each of those groupings, disconnected is shown on the left and connected on the right. The percentages within the bars represent the key at the top that is a breakdown of income as a percentage of the federal poverty level (FPL).

What this figure shows is that within both sets of living arrangements there are two groups: those who are well-resourced and launching successful patterns of adulthood, and those who are currently disconnected from mainstream social institutions, experiencing a more precarious pathway through emerging adulthood. This means that living situation alone does not reveal differences in vulnerability, nor does income alone show the full range of differences in adulthood transitions. Instead, vulnerability is better understood as the complex set of statuses of living with parents while being disconnected and having below poverty income (far left), which equates to 55 percent of disconnected youth who are living with parents. Even more vulnerable are youths represented in the third bar who are living alone,

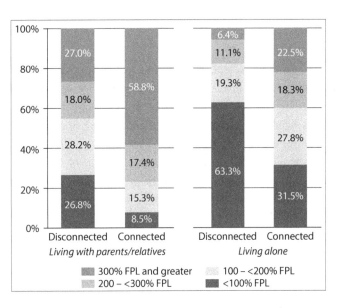

FIGURE 3.3 Income by Disconnected Status and Living Arrangements, 2010

Source: Vanessa R. Wight, Michelle Chau, Yumiko Aratani, Susan Wile Schwarz, and Kalyani Thampi, "Disconnected EA," A Profile of Disconnected Young Adults in 2010. Copyright © 2010 by National Center for Children in Poverty (NCCP).

are disconnected, and have poverty income, which equates to 83 percent of youths who are disconnected and living alone.

In sum, emerging adulthood is not experienced equally. For some, it is not a time of subsidized exploration of educational pursuits and potential career paths. Instead, in the midst of what appear to be normal, average life stage fluctuations are disconnected and vulnerable youth.

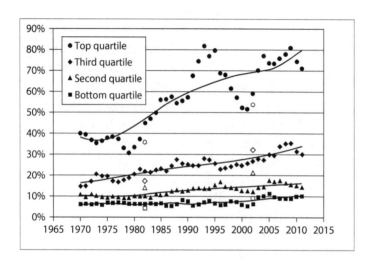

FIGURE 3.4 Growing Gap in Gaining a College Degree, by Family Income, 1970–2011

Source: Robert D. Putnam, "Education Gap," Our Kids: The American Dream in Crisis. Copyright © 2015 by Simon & Schuster, Inc.

BIFURCATING INEQUALITIES & CUMULATIVE DISADVANTAGES

In his book *Our Kids: The American Dream in Crisis*, Robert Putnam (2015) reports trends for the past fifty years as showing significant growth in relative income for those with the highest incomes, compared to stagnation across time for those with lowest incomes. Income earnings significantly associate with educational attainment, and educational opportunities have become increasingly associated with family income levels. As one example of the trends reported by Putnam, Figure 3.4 represents a scissor chart—referring to the marked gap between lines forming half a set of scissors—that evidences the educational opportunity gap by family income level, net of standardized test scores. The trend is a widening in this gap from the 1960s to the present time.

Such divergences in life chances result over time in what scholars refer to as cumulative disadvantage—advantages or disadvantages that accrue at each level of the life course as people encounter social institutions that are more or less equipped to support them in successful transitions into adulthood (DiPrete & Eirich 2006; Giudici & Pallas 2014; Willson et al. 2007; Wodtke et al. 2011). Put another way, scholars find that family income alone does not result in disadvantaged adulthood situations. Rather lower income relates to the likelihood of growing up in impoverished neighborhoods, with more exposure to violence, less quality education, greater health risks, and less regular access to Internet needed to participate in the information-based economy (e.g., DiMaggio & Bonikowski 2008).

SOCIAL CLASSES

The diverging destinies that result from some Americans continually encountering advantages and others accumulating disadvantages across the life course bundle into very different life chances. These bundles of social outcomes have long been thought of in sociology as *social classes*—groups who share similar socioeconomic standing and political power (e.g., Swartz 1997). However, rising intra-occupational inequalities (e.g., Kim & Sakamota 2008) have caused some scholars to question whether social classes exist (e.g., Lareau & Conley 2010) or to debate exactly how many social classes there are (e.g., Weeden & Grusky 2012). Yet, most sociologists agree class competition exists in some form, meaning that different social groups compete with each other for social status, economic resources, and political power (e.g., Alon 2009; Wagmiller et al. 2006) and that social class dynamics are typically reproduced across generations through family socialization patterns (e.g., Liefbroer & Elzingan 2012).

In the third reading of this chapter, Swartz (1997) describes a theory by Pierre Bourdieu that focuses on social classes and struggles for power. As Swartz describes, one of Bourdieu's central goals was to show the relationship between social class, struggles for power, and culture. He does this centrally through a concept called habitus—cultural tastes that operate in the background, below conscious awareness, as patterned cultural habits. What Bourdieu means is that social class competition occurs through symbolic exchanges around *lifestyle* choices and consumption patterns. Some people have a *taste* for luxury, while others have a taste for necessity. People with a taste for luxury look down their noses at generic, cheaply made goods. But likewise, people with a taste for necessity scorn splurging on nonessential, luxurious goods. This class competition plays out in the ways people purchase, and the ways they judge others for their purchases. This kind of competition is a subtle but powerful force in social life. So while most Americans would say that social classes do not exist, they would also abhor buying certain kinds of goods—perhaps a yacht if they are working class or fried food if they are upper-middle class. In this reading, the focus is on explaining the reproduction of social class dynamics through everyday lifestyle choices.

READING 3.3

Social Classes and the Struggle for Power

By David Swartz

Class Conflict and Social Reproduction

We next examine how Bourdieu understands the dynamics of stratification processes in advanced societies. He sees competitive struggle as representing the fundamental dynamic of all social life. Individuals, families, and groups struggle to maintain or improve their relative market positions within the stratified social order. Competition occurs (1) over valued forms of capital, and (2) over definitions of what is legitimate capital. I will first explore Bourdieu's understanding of conflict over types of capital and then examine his view of class struggle as a classification struggle.

Capital Reproduction Strategies

Bourdieu thinks of class struggle in terms of actors pursuing, consciously and unconsciously, social reproduction strategies that maintain or improve their positions in the stratification order. These strategies involve ways of investing various types of capital to maintain or enhance positions in fields (Bourdieu 1984a: 125-68). To illustrate, class fractions richest in cultural capital, such as secondary school teachers and university professors, invest heavily in the education and general cultural enrichment of their children. In contrast, class

David Swartz, "Social Classes and the Struggle for Power," Culture and Power: The Sociology of Pierre Bourdieu, pp. 180–181. Copyright © 1997 by University of Chicago Press. Reprinted with permission.

fractions richest in economic capital, such as industrial and commercial employers, downplay educational and cultural investments for their children in favor of direct transfers of economic wealth.¹ And the economically and culturally well-endowed liberal professions, such as law and medicine, invest heavily in education and especially in those cultural activities that provide a social capital of connections, reputation, and respect that are useful for professional careers (120-22). Thus, reproduction strategies depend largely on the total volume and composition of capital to be maintained.

They also depend on the "state of the instruments of reproduction (inheritance law and custom, the labor market, the educational system etc.)" (125). Bourdieu devotes particular attention to "reconversion strategies" where groups restructure their capital holdings by exchanging one currency for another in order to maintain or improve their relative positions in the class structure.² He argues that study of how individuals and groups convert one type of capital into another and at what rate of exchange provide important insight into the character of class relations (Bourdieu 1980c:57). Reconversion strategies are necessitated by changes in the economy, the growth of bureaucracy, and, most significantly for Bourdieu, the growth of cultural markets. Educational credential markets, in particular, he argues, have become a new important source of stratification in industrial society by providing vital resources for status distinctions among segments within upper- and middle-class groups (Bourdieu and Boltanski 1977).³ Bourdieu contends that economic, political, and legal changes have precipitated a shift in upper-class inheritance practices from one of direct transfer of property to reliance upon the cultural transmission of economic privilege: investment in education gives upper-class offspring the chance to appropriate family privilege and wealth through access to the more powerful and remunerative institutional positions.

---

1 Bourdieu (120) observes, however, that upper-level managers in the private business sector favor investing in the cultural as well as economic futures of their children.
2 See in particular his discussion in *Distinction* (125–68).
3 Here Bourdieu joins the "credential society" theories that developed in the 1970s (Collins 1979, Miller 1976).

What Bourdieu, as recounted by Swartz, draws attention to in this reading is the way social class competition occurs through investment in cultural capital, which allows for the reproduction of social class standing across generations. Specifically, parents spending money on educational credentials is one way of ensuring that their children learn the symbolic rules of fitting in among those with advanced social standing, ensuring that they will remain among the middle class.

We see the trends that Bourdieu theorizes whenever we see lifestyle patterns that relate to social class background. For example, Carlson and England (2011) find that family patterns are correlated with educational attainment and other measures of social class background. Specifically, married people are more likely to have high education levels, while people with lower education levels are more likely to have children without being married or to be divorced. Having children with more than one partner, which is called multi-partnered fertility, is also more common among people with lower education and income levels. Likewise, children of parents with lower education and income levels are more likely to have fathers who live outside their primary household, with intermittent involvement in their development.

As Chapter 2 found, adulthood markers still matter, and coupled with the findings reported in this chapter, the problem is that adulthood markers are patterned by social class backgrounds. Carlson and England (2011) describe these inequalities as related to *socioeconomic status (SES)*— the social and economic position that people hold within the social stratification system:

> The patterns by which individuals enter adulthood are profoundly shaped by socioeconomic status. ... Those raised in high-SES families typically first leave home to enter a four-year college, and upon graduation will likely get a job, get an apartment, and begin to establish a career before "settling down" to get married and have children. Parental transfers along the way help pay tuition and connect youth to a career job, thereby leaving such graduates with limited college debt and connected to a high-paying job. By contrast, those from low-SES backgrounds may or may not finish high school, and if they do finish and go on to college, they are more likely to incur significant debt and to combine work and college-going, thereby prolonging the amount of time they take to earn a degree (pp. 8–9).

These patterns bundle into different lifestyle configurations with more opportunities or greater obstacles, amounting to what many sociologists refer to as social class orientations.

In a book entitled *Social Class: How Does it Work?* edited Annette Lareau and Dalton Conley (2010), numerous scholars debate the exact parameters by which to define social class. What this volume makes clear is that there is no consensus on a precise definition of class boundaries. At the same time, Michael Hout in that volume remarkably finds that Americans identify accurately with the social class that bundles their income, occupation, and education. While it is not easy to view social class through any one of those status indicators alone, the typical American is quite good, it turns out, at assessing all of those indicators together and globally marking themselves in the social class background that best fits them. In fact, averaged across nearly fifty years of data, 68 percent of Americans reported that they identify with a specific social class, namely working class or middle class. Hout reports: "Americans, for the most part, express identities that are quite congruent with their objective circumstances" (p. 11).

But if subjective sense of social class standing relates so well with objective class demarcations, why is that most Americans readily deny the existence of social class and competition for status? The next section addresses this question.

"INVISIBLE" IDENTITIES

The reason that social class continues to pervade the "fabric of social life," as Lareau (2002) describes it, is that it is virtually invisible. Hidden beyond plain sight is what scholars call *cultural knowledge*—which is information regarding how to "play the game" or the rules of engagement that pertain to different social roles, statuses, and positions. Savvy Americans know what it takes to succeed in different contexts and navigate bureaucratic social institutions toward better outcomes for themselves and others whom they help, while disenfranchised Americans tend instead to get frustrated by institutions and overwhelmed by bureaucratic procedures (Lareau 2015).

In the fourth and final reading of this chapter, Lareau (2011) describes how social class affects differences in the kinds of information and interventions that parents have in the lives of their children as they navigate through emerging adulthood. Lareau draws particular attention to the kinds of strategies that parents use to guide their children through higher education toward credentials for competing in the labor market. While parents generally want to provide their children with the best possible advice, it is also the case that the kinds of information they have available to them are patterned by their own social class standing, as well as the kinds of information that was passed on to them by their parents given their social class backgrounds. What happens in this transfer of information is that parents can often unknowingly and unintentionally perpetuate the reproduction of social class, passing on their own background.

READING 3.4

Class Differences in Parents' Information and Intervention in the Lives of Young Adults

By Annette Lareau

The Importance of Class-Based Cultural Repertoires

Does social class matter in American society? Let us assume, for the sake of argument, that it does not. If that is so, then young people's educational and work outcomes should be the result of their own aspirations, abilities, efforts, perseverance, and imagination.[1] If class position is of little importance, then as the members of each new generation reach young adulthood, they should be poised for a fresh start at the race for success, all facing the same opportunity to "find their way" toward a comfortable and fulfilling life, based on their own innate talents. This is the American dream. The American

---

1 The literature is filled with debates on the genetic contribution to intelligence, the role of "nature and nurture" in development, the proper definition and measurement of intelligence, and the contribution of schools and families to outcomes. A discussion of these factors is beyond the scope of this chapter. See Judith Rich Harris, *Nurture Assumption*.

Annette Lareau, "Class Differences in Parents' Information and Intervention in the Lives of Young Adults," Unequal Childhoods: Class, Race, and Family Life, 2nd ed., pp. 305–311. Copyright © 2011 by University of California Press. Reprinted with permission.
Annette Lareau, "End Notes to Class Differences in Parents' Information and Intervention in the Lives of Young Adults," Unequal Childhoods: Class, Race, and Family Life, 2nd ed., pp. 414–416. Copyright © 2011 by University of California Press. Reprinted with permission.

reality is different. A key finding of *Unequal Childhoods* is that class does matter. In real life, the educational and work outcomes of young people are closely tied to the class position of their parents. Because social class *is* a significant force, existing social inequality gets reproduced over time, regardless of each new generation's aspirations, talent, effort, and imagination.[2]

Unequal Childhoods used qualitative methods to study the rituals of daily life that families experience and the influence of these rituals on the development of youths' life chances. The results of the follow-up study provide further support for the argument that a pattern of social inequality is being reproduced. Parents' cultural practices play a role.[3] The commitment to concerted cultivation, whereby parents actively fostered and developed children's talents and skills did not, it turns out, wane over time. Even as children became autonomous adolescents with driver's licenses, jobs, and dorm rooms, the middle-class parents closely monitored and intervened in their lives. A few decades ago many similarly aged young people would have been married, with children of their own. But the middle-class youth in this study, now nineteen to twenty-one years old, appeared to be needy and, in crucial ways, still under the wing of their mothers and fathers. By contrast, although similarly aged, the working-class and poor young adults appeared to be more independent. They were very grateful for the love and support their parents had given them in the face of scarce resources. But they were, in Wendy's words, "grown." For their part, working-class and poor parents generally accepted that their children had become autonomous adults. They offered help when that seemed possible, and they ached with disappointment when the dreams they had held for their children's futures grew increasingly unattainable.

What are the implications of this evidence of persisting patterns? For research on social stratification, the follow-up study results suggest a need to broaden and reconceptualize our analysis of how social class does, and does not, matter in daily life. Researchers need to pay more attention to the crucial role of middle-class parents' informal knowledge of how institutions work; the educational, economic, and social resources they bring to bear in order to realize their goals; and the countless individually insignificant but cumulatively advantageous interventions on behalf of their children these parents make over time.[4]

For example, beyond an aspiration or a desire to see Stacey succeed, Ms. Marshall drew on many different class resources as she sought to prepare her daughter for college. Recall Ms. Marshall's insistence that her daughter enroll in a summer algebra course. In taking this action, Ms. Marshall defined herself as capable of assessing

---

2 See Kathryn M. Neckerman, *Social Inequality;* Grusky and Szelényi, *The Inequality Reader;* Aaron M. Pallas and Jennifer L. Jennings, "Cumulative Knowledge about Cumulative Advantage"; Lareau and Conley, *Social Class;* Bill Keller and the *New York Times, Class Matters;* Future of Children, *Opportunity in America.*

3 See, for example, the influential work of Michèle Lamont, *Money, Morals, and Manners; Dignity of Working Men;* Lamont and Marcel Fournier, eds., *Cultivating Differences;* David J. Harding, Lamont, and Mario Luis Small, eds., *Reconsidering Culture and Poverty.* See also Pierre Bourdieu, *Distinction.*

4 See Pallas and Jennings, "Cumulative Knowledge about Cumulative Advantage."

her daughter's educational needs; unlike Ms. Yanelli, she did not need to depend on someone "educated" to tell her what to do. Ms. Marshall also determined a customized plan of action to shore up the weakness she perceived in Stacey's school performance. Unlike Ms. Driver, she did not accept the generic academic plan offered to her daughter. Instead, she devised an approach that would strengthen Stacey's math skills *before* any serious problems developed. In so doing, Ms. Marshall drew on a formidable amount of informal knowledge about how educational institutions function. This informal knowledge was linked to her own educational and occupational experiences; it was not routinely available to all parents. In addition, Ms. Marshall's plan of action was molded to match her daughter's temperament and needs. The impact of parental interventions that have this level of complexity—involving both customized action and long-term planning—is very difficult for researchers to isolate and measure. Indeed, in studies based on surveys, Stacey's strong math performance in high school would likely be interpreted as a matter of her own ability or her level of educational attainment. The role this middle-class mother played in "boosting" and managing her daughter's math skills vanishes. It is hidden beneath unexamined assumptions regarding the effects of students' natural ability or hard work.[5]

Another area that deserves greater attention from social scientists is the drawbacks of middle-class family life. (Likewise, there should be more studies of the potential advantages of the cultural repertoires of working-class and poor families.) For example, high-achieving middle-class high school students often juggle demanding academic work and multiple extracurricular activities, leaving them with little or no free time. While many enjoy the fast pace and pressures, others are left joyless and alienated by the constant quest to succeed.[6] There are other costs too. Parents complain of spending hundreds of hours helping their children through the college search process. Applying and getting into college has become a family affair. Since some youths resent parents' "interference," the often intense and prolonged focus on college-related matters can produce considerable family conflict.[7] Some middle-class parents, such as Ms.

---

[5] Stacey's success also could be associated with her family background, but the concrete actions her parents took would remain unclear. There are methodological constraints associated with using fixed-response surveys to study the type and timing of interventions middle-class parents undertake. These constraints account for why social scientists so often try to understand a variety of social outcomes by conducting studies of grade point averages, verbal test scores, hours watching television, time parents spend reading to a child, and parents' attendance at parent-teacher conferences. The problem, however, as we have seen, is that many of the things that middle-class parents do are difficult to capture on surveys.

[6] See pictures of art work in Peter Demerath's *Producing Success*, which provide haunting images of alienation. Some elite high schools have been shaken by suicides, including in Palo Alto, Calif., where five high-achieving students committed suicide in six months. See Christina Farr, "After Five Suicides, Palo Alto High School Students Change Culture," www.sfgate.com/cgi-bin/blogs/inthepeninsula/detail?entry_id=80342; accessed March 22, 2011. *College Un-ranked*, edited by Lloyd Thacker, discusses the "arms race" of preparation for college applications. See also Nelson, *Parenting Out of Control*; Suniya Luthar, "The Culture of Affluence."

[7] See Wills, "Parent Trap"; Jacobson, "Help Not Wanted."

Handlon, also experience shame and humiliation when their children do not succeed academically. Parents feel responsible for their children's mistakes.[8]

The emergence and popularity of such trade books as *Not Everyone Gets a Trophy* signal a growing dissatisfaction over the sense of entitlement displayed by middle-class youth.[9] Similarly, working-class parents, such as Ms. Brindle, often do not mince words when describing middle-class youth:

> The people … who I clean for have some really spoiled kids. I never in my life seen kids that have everything you could possibly think of—yet be the biggest slobs in the world and disrespectful to their mothers and fathers.

Yet scholarly inquiry remains focused on searching out deficits in the child rearing of working-class and poor families, rather than probing the limits of middle-class cultural practices.[10] The logic and legitimacy of working-class and poor parents' dependence on educators also need systematic attention. Many middle-class parents feel comfortable supervising teachers and intervening in the educational process. But if these same parents' children needed surgery, they would be likely to turn over responsibility to the attending surgeon.[11] Working-class and poor parents generally look up the status hierarchy to all "educated people." Teachers and surgeons appear to be in the same category—both are experts in their respective fields. From this perspective, depending fully on such professionals to do what they have been trained to do is both logical and sensible. And, when working-class and poor parents accord educators and surgeons a similar status, teachers reap vastly more respect and deference than they frequently receive from middle-class parents. The latter routinely intervene in schooling, requesting that teachers "round up" their children's grades or demanding that their children, despite failing to meet the qualifying criteria, be placed in a gifted

---

8 As Katherine McClelland noted, the "concerted cultivation metaphor itself suggests an explanation of middle-class parents' shame at their children's failures: if cultivation is what we're engaged in, then I am a poor gardener if your flowers bloom while mine do not" (personal communication, September 17, 2010). There are many other drawbacks to middle-class life that draw only limited scholarly attention. For instance, middle-class families, including the Tallingers, often must relocate (sometimes moving great distances) in order to meet one or both parents' career demands. Middle-class parents, including Mr. and Ms. Williams, also work very long hours and spend a great deal of time in airports and hotels, away from home, for their careers. Numerous studies have studied the number of hours spent at work, but the implications for the social class differences in the quality of family life have been harder to unpack (but see Marianne Cooper, "Being the 'Go-To Guy'"; Pamela Stone, *Opting Out*; Mary Blair-Loy, *Competing Devotions* for studies of middle-class families). For discussions of the class divide in time spent at work, see Jerry A. Jacobs and Kathleen Gerson, *The Time Divide*.

9 Bruce Tulgan's *Not Everyone Gets a Trophy* was published in 2009. There is an older popular literature on the downside of what I term concerted cultivation, including David Elkind's 1981 book *The Hurried Child*. See also Suniya Luthar, "The Culture of Affluence."

10 See chapter 8, "The Dark Side of Parent Involvement," in Lareau, *Home Advantage*.

11 It is likely that middle-class parents would try to manage as many elements of a surgical intervention as possible, e.g., learning the names and side effects of the medications, asking about alternative courses of treatment, and researching their child's medical condition enough to formulate informed questions. But they would turn over responsibility for the surgery itself to the surgeon, just as working-class and poor parents turn over responsibility for teaching to educators.

program, or threatening legal action if educators appear hesitant to comply with these or other demands.

Class differences in how parents manage youths' institutional lives are a crucial, understudied piece in the larger puzzle of unequal life outcomes. But, as many studies have shown, there are other important factors as well. The youth I studied were embedded in multiple social contexts. Different aspects of these contexts loomed large as the children traveled the path to adulthood. The interviews revealed some of the ways in which race has impacted their lives as they have grown older. For example, as others have shown, friendship patterns and dating choices were often racially stratified.[12] Racial profiling was common. Alexander's Ivy League admission and high SAT scores did not protect him from being monitored by store clerks as he shopped. And, although their families differed greatly, he and Harold shared very similar levels of deep resignation that race-based harassment was inevitable. White working-class and poor young men also reported being harassed by the police but, strikingly, middle-class white youth did not, a pattern echoed in national data. Given the racially stratified nature of American society, it is not surprising that the young adults reported racial dynamics surfacing in many of their rituals of daily life. Nevertheless, I did *not* observe race-based patterns in parents' institutional knowledge or in their management of their children's experiences within institutions.[13] In these realms, the patterns that emerged fell along lines of social class, not race.[14]

Much as when they were youngsters, class position shaped the young adults' relationships with their extended families. Among the working-class and poor young adults, there were palpably deep connections and tight interweavings of kinship and family life that were not apparent among the middle-class youths. To be sure, the latter were close to their families—in fact, growing older seemed to have improved the relationship among siblings. Both Garret and Stacey reported that they got along "better" with their siblings than they had when they were younger. Still, middle-class young adults seemed comfortable maintaining more physical and emotional distance

---

12   Peggy C. Giordano, "Relationships in Adolescence"; Jennifer Lee and Frank D. Bean, "America's Changing Color Lines."
13   For a review, see Kathleen V. Hoover-Dempsey and Howard M. Sandler, "Why Do Parents Become Involved in Their Children's Education?" See also John B. Diamond and Kimberly Williams Gomez, "African-American Parents' Educational Orientations."
14   I have a very small sample. In the working-class and poor families, all the parents were interviewed. But, among the middle-class, Alexander Williams's parents declined to be interviewed. This limits the conclusions that can be drawn. I looked closely across the sample for signs of racial differences in the character, frequency, and type of interventions parents made in institutions. Class differences were quite striking, but racial differences did not emerge. For discussions of the power of race in family life, see Linda Burton et al., "Critical Race Theories, Colorism, and the Decade's Research on Families of Color." Of course, there are countless studies of race and ethnicity, and there is compelling evidence of continued discrimination in daily life against African Americans. For discussion of race and employment, see Pager, *Marked*. For race and incarceration, see Western, *Punishment*. For a review of race and residential segregation, see Douglas Massey, *Categorically Unequal*. For wealth gaps, see Melvin L. Oliver and Thomas M. Shapiro, *Black Wealth/White Wealth*. For race and public space, see Joseph Feagin and Melvin P. Sikes, *Living with Racism*. See also, among others, the work by Michèle Lamont, Elijah Anderson, Alford Young, and Mica Pollock.

from their families than was common among their working-class and poor counterparts. Harold shared an apartment with his older brother and his family. Katie left her daughter in her older sister Jenna's care while she sorted things out. Katie's relationship with her mother was more openly troubled than it had been when she was in elementary school (in part because Ms. Brindle's drinking had escalated, as had her tendency to be verbally abusive when drunk). Still, Katie continued to see her mother regularly, socializing with her as well as with Jenna and Jenna's family. Wendy also came home often in order to socialize with her family. Regularly interacting with family members provided bonds of support that were particularly valuable in helping working-class and poor youths meet child care needs and cope with other life challenges.

However, class-based cultural repertoires, interwoven with economic resources, continued to matter. Even as the youth grew into adulthood and became more autonomous, class remained important. Middle-class parents and their children had much deeper and more detailed knowledge of the inner workings of key institutional structures, such as high school curricula, college admission processes, and professional job opportunities, than did working-class and poor parents and their children. Middle-class parents and kids also had more knowledge about and detailed understanding of the strengths and weaknesses of their specific "case," and of the options available, given their individual situation. While all parents helped their children in many ways, middle-class parents adopted a concerted cultivation stance that included close monitoring of their young adults' circumstances as well as many interventions. Some of the working-class and poor parents also sought to intervene, but these efforts were less frequent and less successful.

Section 5. Summing Up: Class and the Transition to Adulthood

When they were ten years old, the middle-class youth seemed worldly, blasé, and hard to impress. For them, pizza parties were very common and thus no special treat. Spring concerts drew shrugs. Kids readily complained to their parents about being bored when they were not occupied by an organized activity. Although the working-class and poor children were the same age as the middle-class children, they seemed younger, bouncier, and more childlike. They smiled broadly while on stage for the spring concert, were ecstatic over a pizza party, and entertained themselves for hours on weekends and evenings. Ten years later, the pattern had reversed: it was the middle-class youth who seemed younger. Now college students, they were excited about the way the world was opening up for them. They had dreams of traveling and visions of many different possible pathways. To be sure, most had experienced setbacks. Garrett had his heart broken by a girl, Stacey was told that she would never compete in collegiate gymnastics, and Melanie was disappointed when a plan to live with a friend fell through. Still, the middle-class youth seemed young and upbeat. By contrast, the working-class and poor youth were generally working full-time in jobs they did not like, and they had various pressing responsibilities such as raising children, paying for food and board, and making monthly car payments. Unlike the middle-class kids, who tended to have worked only at summer jobs, youths who had dropped out of school, such as Harold, had already spent many years in the labor force. There were many wonderful features about the lives of working-class and poor youth. Wendy loved being a mother. Billy was very excited about owning a car. Harold enjoyed hanging out with his brother and watching sports on their large-screen television. The working-class and poor youth remained optimistic—they still had hopes and dreams—but they had struggled in a way that the middle-class youth had not.

Moreover, as the children moved from fourth grade into adulthood, the power of class pushed their lives in such different directions that I could not pose the same interview questions to the group as a whole. Middle-class youths' interviews were filled with questions about their college preparation classes, college searches, college choice, and college adjustment. As these young people told their stories, additional probing revealed that their parents had been an integral part of their transition to college. Working-class and poor youths' interviews were filled with discussions of their difficulties in high school, challenges at work, and uncertain future goals. Some working-class and poor youth had undertaken college searches and enrolled in community college courses, but they had done so mainly on their own or with heavy involvement by teachers. Their parents had more circumscribed roles. The follow-up study suggests that over time the gap that existed between the families when the children were ten widened rather than narrowed.

Of course, there is significant variation among the members of all social classes. Some middle-class youth, like Melanie, have learning disabilities or other issues that lead them to not attend college. This in turn may limit their career chances and result in downward mobility—meaning that these individuals wind up in jobs that have lower prestige and lower pay than the ones held by their parents.[15] Some working-class and poor youth, often with the assistance of an influential teacher, become first-generation college students. Armed with college degrees, they are able to defy the odds and become upwardly mobile. What is crucial to keep in mind, however, is that these are examples of *variations*. They tell us about what sometimes happens, not about the norm. As the lives of the families in *Unequal Childhoods* show, social class origins have effects that are powerful and long lasting. Middle-class families' cultural practices, including their approach to child rearing, are closely aligned with the standards and expectations—the rules of the game—of key institutions in society. By contrast, relying on professionals to manage their children's careers is an eminently reasonable decision for working-class and poor parents who have never been to college. But a reasonable decision is not necessarily an advantageous one. In schools especially, today's institutional rules of the game require parents to be actively involved in order to maximize opportunities for their children. Despite their love for their children, it is harder for working-class and poor families, whose

---

15   See Emily Beller and Michael Hout, "Intergenerational Social Mobility."

cultural practices and approaches to child rearing are not fully in sync with the institutional standards of schools, to comply with those standards. Finally, it is important to recognize that in American society, people who are blessed with class advantages tend to be unaware of these benefits and privileges. Instead, drawing on the American belief in individualism, they stress their own hard work and talent. They downplay, or do not even notice, the social class benefits bestowed upon them. Americans have, haltingly, developed a rudimentary language that allows us to "see" and discuss racial and ethnic inequalities. But with respect to social class inequalities, which are equally powerful, we remain largely blind and nearly mute.[16]

---

[16] I am grateful to Katherine Mooney for suggesting this phrase.

The trouble with social class dynamics is that they are durable and hard to see. The differences in information and intervention strategies that Lareau describes often become internalized by emerging adults, and children and teens beforehand. In fact, studies find that educational expectations relate strongly to parental social class backgrounds and are set early (e.g., Andres et al. 2007; Bozick et al. 2010). Likewise, the changing economic patterns of the decline in agricultural industry to an information-based service economy (e.g., Cox et al. 2014) means that parents who earned their living in outmoded industries are less equipped to provide relevant information for existing positions, and the knowledge and experiences needed for them.

While real, structural positions in socially stratified systems leave some emerging adults with fewer resources upon which to draw as they transition to adulthood, the invisibility of inequalities in American culture result in most emerging adults comparing themselves to their peers, sometimes resulting in esteem issues (e.g., Dwyer et al. 2011). When having cross-class interactions, often on college campuses, emerging adults from poor and working-class backgrounds typically take one of two approaches—disassociating from their social class backgrounds by attempting to conceal their differences by fitting in with their upper-class peers or internalizing negative class-based stereotypes by attempting to demean people in their social class as lower than themselves (Radmacher & Azmitia 2013).

The role that parents play in the social reproduction process is often indirect, socializing children into particular value orientations, which shape who they are friends with, reinforce their parental upbringing, and ultimately accumulate into different career aspirations (e.g., Hitlin 2006). During emerging adulthood, these social class differences tend to present as what some call *life course capital*—which is knowledge about how to minimize exposure to risks, navigate challenges, and receive the best possible outcomes from social systems (O'Rand 2006). The social reproduction of social class occurs then through the "invisible" processes of lifestyle choices (e.g., Petev 2013), as well as through the social psychological effects of socioeconomic position on happiness and well-being (e.g., Schnittker 2008).

Cumulatively, social class reproduction amounts to unseen differences in cultural practices that can present in daily life as marital conflicts over parenting (Streib 2015), educational struggles (Terriquez & Gurantz 2015), preferences for independent versus collaborative work (e.g., Stephens et al. 2012), personality differences (Shanahan et al. 2014), and disadvantaged or privileged identities (Seider 2010). This means that what we often perceive to be individual choices are in fact acts of meaning which are deeply patterned by social class backgrounds, and which often unintentionally reproduce social dynamics in the process (Stephens et al. 2007).

Applied to emerging adulthood, a sociological understanding of social inequality dynamics helps reveal that life course choices are not simply a matter of individual preferences. Instead, people shape their life course in reference to the kinds of social and economic resources available to them and by using engrained habits of interaction, and cultural understandings for what is important to be and do as a near adult.

REFERENCES

Alon, Sigal. 2009. "The Evolution of Class Inequality in Higher Education Competition, Exclusion, and Adaptation." *American Sociological Review* 74(5):731–55.

Andres, Lesley, Maria Adamuti-Trache, Ee-Seul Yoon, Michelle Pidgeon, and Jens Peter Thomsen. 2007. "Educational Expectations, Parental Social Class, Gender, & Postsecondary Attainment: A 10-Year Perspective." *Youth & Society* 39(2):135–63.

Berzin, Stephanie Cosner and Allison C. De Marco. 2010. "Understanding the Impact of Poverty on Critical Events in Emerging Adulthood." *Youth & Society* 42(2):278–300.

Bozick, Robert, Karl Alexander, Doris Entwisle, Susan Dauber, and Kerri Kerr. 2010. "Framing the Future: Revisiting the Place of Educational Expectations in Status Attainment." *Social Forces* 88(5):2027–52.

Carlson, Marcia, and Paula England, eds. 2011. *Social Class and Changing Families in an Unequal America*. Stanford, California: Stanford University Press.

Cox, Genevieve R., Corinna Jenkins Tucker, Erin Hiley Sharp, Karen T. Van Gundy, and Cesar J. Rebellon. 2014. "Practical Considerations: Community Context in a Declining Rural Economy and Emerging Adults' Educational and Occupational Aspirations." *Emerging Adulthood* 2(3):173–83.

DiPrete, Thomas A. and Gregory M. Eirich. 2006. "Cumulative Advantage as a Mechanism for Inequality: A Review of Theoretical and Empirical Developments." *Annual Review of Sociology* 32:271–97.

DiMaggio, Paul and Bart Bonikowski. 2008. "Make Money Surfing the Web? The Impact of Internet Use on the Earnings of U.S. Workers." *American Sociological Review* 73(2):227–50.

Dwyer, Rachel E., Laura McCloud, and Randy Hodson. 2011. "Youth Debt, Mastery, and Self-Esteem: Class-Stratified Effects of Indebtedness on Self-Concept." *Social Science Research* 40(3):727–41.

Giudici, Francesco and Aaron M. Pallas. 2014. "Social Origins and Post-High School Institutional Pathways: A Cumulative Dis/advantage Approach." *Social Science Research* 44:103–13.

Hitlin, Steven. 2006. "Parental Influences on Children's Values and Aspirations: Bridging Two Theories of Social Class and Socialization." *Sociological Perspectives* 49(1):25–46.

Kim, ChangHwan and Arthur Sakamoto. 2008. "The Rise of Intra-Occupational Wage Inequality in the United States, 1983 to 2002." *American Sociological Review* 73(1):129–57.

Lareau, Annette. 2002. Invisible Inequality: Childrearing in Black Families and White Families. *American Sociological Review* 67(5):747–76.

Lareau, Annette. 2011. *Unequal Childhoods: Class, Race, and Family Life*, 2nd Edition. University of California Press.

Lareau, Annette. 2015. "Cultural Knowledge and Social Inequality." *American Sociological Review* 80(1):1–27.

Lareau, Annette and Dalton Conley, eds. 2010. *Social Class: How Does It Work?* Reprint edition. Russell Sage Foundation Publications.

Liefbroer, Aart C. and Cees H. Elzinga. 2012. "Intergenerational Transmission of Behavioural Patterns: How Similar Are Parents' and Children's Demographic Trajectories?" *Advances in Life Course Research* 17(1):1–10.

Macomber, Jennifer Ehrle, Mike Pergamit, Tracy Vericker, Daniel Kuehn, Marla McDaniel, Erica H. Zielewski, Adam Kent, and Heidi Johnson. 2009. *Vulnerable Youth and the Transition to Adulthood*. The Urban Institute.

Miech, Richard A., Avshalom Caspi, Terrie E. Moffitt, Bradley E. Wright, and Phil A. Silva. 1999. "Low Socioeconomic Status and Mental Disorders: A Longitudinal Study of Selection and Causation during Young Adulthood." *American Journal of Sociology* 104(4):1096–1131.

O'Rand, Angela M. 2006. "Stratification and the Life Course: Life Course Capital, Life Course Risks, and Social Inequality." In *Handbook of Aging and the Social Sciences*, edited by Robert H. Binstock and Linda K. George, 145–62. Elsevier.

Ochs, Elinor, and Tamar Kremer-Sadlik, eds. 2013. *Fast-Forward Family: Home, Work, and Relationships in Middle-Class America*. University of California Press.

Osgood, D. Wayne, E. Michael Foster, Constance Flanagan, Gretchen R. Ruth, eds. 2005. *On Your Own Without a Net: The Transition to Adulthood for Vulnerable Populations*. University of Chicago Press.

Petev, Ivaylo D. 2013. "The Association of Social Class and Lifestyles Persistence in American Sociability, 1974 to 2010." *American Sociological Review* 78(4):633–61.

Porter, Katherine, ed. 2012. *Broke: How Debt Bankrupts the Middle Class*. Stanford University Press.

Putnam, Robert D. 2015. *Our Kids: The American Dream in Crisis*. Simon & Schuster.

Radmacher, Kimberley and Margarita Azmitia. 2013. "Unmasking Class: How Upwardly Mobile Poor and Working-Class Emerging Adults Negotiate an 'Invisible' Identity." *Emerging Adulthood* 1(4):314–29.

Schafer, Markus H., Kenneth F. Ferraro, and Sarah A. Mustillo. 2011. "Children of Misfortune: Early Adversity and Cumulative Inequality in Perceived Life Trajectories." *American Journal of Sociology* 116(4):1053–91.

Schnittker, Jason. 2008. "Happiness and Success: Genes, Families, and the Psychological Effects of Socioeconomic Position and Social Support." *American Journal of Sociology* 114(S1):233–59.

Seider, Scott. 2010. "The Role of Privilege as Identity in Adolescents' Beliefs about Homelessness, Opportunity, and Inequality." *Youth & Society* 43(1):3333–64.

Shanahan, Michael J., Shawn Bauldry, Brent W. Roberts, Ross Macmillan, and Rosemary Russo. 2014. "Personality and the Reproduction of Social Class." *Social Forces* 93(1):209–40.

Silva, Jennifer M. 2012. "Constructing Adulthood in an Age of Uncertainty." *American Sociological Review* 77(4):505–22.

Silva, Jennifer M. 2013. *Coming Up Short: Working-Class Adulthood in an Age of Uncertainty*. New York: Oxford University Press.

Stephens, Nicole M., Hazel Rose Markus, and Sarah S. M. Townsend. 2007. "Choice as an Act of Meaning: The Case of Social Class." *Journal of Personality and Social Psychology* 93(5):814–30.

Stephens, Nicole M., Stephanie A. Fryberg, Hazel Rose Markus, Camille S. Johnson, and Rebecca Covarrubias. 2012. "Unseen Disadvantage: How American Universities' Focus on Independence Undermines the Academic Performance of First-Generation College Students." *Journal of Personality and Social Psychology* 102(6):1178–97.

Streib, Jessi. 2015. *The Power of the Past: Understanding Cross-Class Marriages.* Oxford University Press.

Swartz, David. 1997. "Social Classes and the Struggle for Power." In *Culture and Power: The Sociology of Pierre Bourdieu.* University of Chicago Press.

Terriquez, Veronica and Oded Gurantz. 2015. "Financial Challenges in Emerging Adulthood and Students' Decisions to Stop Out of College." *Emerging Adulthood* 3(3):204–14.

U.S. Department of Education, National Center for Education Statistics. (2015). *The Condition of Education 2015* (NCES 2015-144), Annual Earnings of Young Adults.

Wagmiller, Robert L., Mary Clare Lennon, Li Kuang, Philip M. Alberti, and J. Lawrence Aber. 2006. "The Dynamics of Economic Disadvantage and Children's Life Chances." *American Sociological Review* 71(5):847–66.

Warren, Elizabeth and Deborah Thorne. 2012. "A Vulnerable Middle Class: Bankruptcy and Class Status." In *Broke: How Debt Bankrupts the Middle Class*, edited by Katherine Porter, 25–39. Stanford University Press.

Weeden, Kim A. and David B. Grusky. 2012. "The Three Worlds of Inequality." *American Journal of Sociology* 117(6):1723–85.

Wight, Vanessa R., Michelle Chau, Yumiko Aratani, Susan Wile Schwarz, and Kalyani Thampi. 2010. *A Profile of Disconnected Young Adults in 2010.* National Center for Children in Poverty.

Willson, Andrea E., Kim M. Shuey, and Glen H. Elder Jr. 2007. "Cumulative Advantage Processes as Mechanisms of Inequality in Life Course Health." *American Journal of Sociology* 112(6):1886–924.

Wodtke, Geoffrey T., David J. Harding, and Felix Elwert. 2011. "Neighborhood Effects in Temporal Perspective: The Impact of Long-Term Exposure to Concentrated Disadvantage on High School Graduation." *American Sociological Review* 76(5):713–36.

CHAPTER 4

Delinquency & Criminal Activities

Emerging adulthood is often characterized as a life stage that is relatively free from societal constraint, full of individual explorations of different lifestyle choices (e.g., Tanner 2006). However, the previous chapters present a variety of findings, which challenge this understanding of emerging adulthood, showing instead that the life stage is characterized by diverse experiences that remain deeply patterned by social class, race-ethnicity, and gender dynamics. Of note is that markers of adulthood remain important in differentiating adulthood trajectories, especially the timing and sequencing of them. Despite a nonhomogeneous normative pathway to adulthood, it is not the case that "anything goes." Instead, there remain age-appropriate transitions, which still normatively label people as on time or deviant in their adulthood transitions.

EMERGING ADULTS & CRIME

Though emerging adulthood is characterized by a delay in the onset of adulthood roles and trajectories, the legal age of adulthood remains 18 years old. This means that emerging adults who continue criminal activities after their eighteenth birthday can be charged as an adult for the same behavior that previously would have sent them into the juvenile court system. This results in an age structuration to crime in the life course (Salvatore 2013). The trouble is that age structuration remains despite declines in other normative structures.

In the first reading of this chapter, Salvatore (2013) discusses the implications of emerging adulthood on crime. The author notes in particular that marriage and parenthood are two key *socializing institutions* which typically require desistance from or avoidance of deviance—stopping or never starting risky behaviors that could result in criminal activity or reducing and/or eliminating participating in formerly deviant behaviors. Another key institution in the decline of deviant behaviors in adulthood transitions of the past was military service.

Scholars found that in the past military service provided a "knifing off" effect that allowed people with criminal records to basically start over in their reentry to society. Military service also provided highly structured routines that regulated supervision, support, and acted to curtail former deviance (Laub & Sampson 1993). However, participation in structuring institutions has declined with the rise of emerging adulthood, meaning there are fewer social factors encouraging desistance from deviance in adulthood transitions. In the first reading, Salvatore (2013) describes the specifics of these increased freedoms and decreased controls.

READING 4.1

Emerging Adulthood & Crime

By Christopher Salvatore

Most research dealing with emerging adulthood has focused mainly on risky behaviors, such as reckless driving, substance use, and dangerous sexual behaviors (Arnett, 1998; Arnett, 2005; Chasin, Pitts, & Prost, 2002; Rohrbach, Sussmann, Dent, & Sun, 2005; Tucker, Ellickson, Orlando, Martino, & Klein, 2005; White, Labouvie, & Papadaratsakis, 2005), but little has been done to explore the genesis of crime during emergent adulthood (Piquero, Brame, Mazerolle, & Haapanen, 2002).

The term "arrested adolescent offender" is intended to describe a person who has failed to make "on-time" life course transitions (normatively defined as "age appropriate" transitions) or meet turning points in trajectories that mark the entrance into adulthood (Thornberry, 1997; Benson, 2002). Life course research has shown for the first half of the twentieth century in Western culture, transitions into adulthood included completion of formal education, getting a job, marrying, and having a family, and this typically occurred during one's late teens and early twenties (Arnett, 2000; Cote, 2000; Okimoto & Stegall, 1987).

More recently, however, changes in social and cultural structures of industrialized nations have contributed to a delay in the timing of many traditional turning points. These changes have

Christopher Salvatore, "Emerging Adulthood & Crime," Arrested Adolescent Offenders: A Study of Delayed Transitions to Adulthood, pp. 9–10, 13–18. Copyright © 2013 by LFB Scholarly Publishing. Reprinted with permission.

included the decline of well paying manufacturing jobs, increases in low paying service positions, a shift to a credential-based employment market, and a rise in the number of people earning post-high school education (Cote & Allahar, 1995). Prior generations had access to a wide variety of employment opportunities that offered the prospect of a comfortable life with only a high school diploma. No longer having access to these positions, more recent generations have been forced to secure greater levels of education and experience to achieve employment that is typically of lower prestige and lower pay than prior generations (Cote & Allahar, 1995, pp. 45-47). Those who make these transitions (e.g., completing education) between the ages of 18-25 are considered *on time* (Cote, 2000; Elder, 1985), and those made either before or after are considered *off time* (Thornberry, 1997). Those who make *on time* transitions meet normatively defined turning points (e.g., marriage, college, children, and full-time employment)[1] symbolizing successful entry into adulthood. Those who fail or delay these turning points often take several additional years to reach them and fully assimilate into adulthood (Cote, 2000).

In the pages that follow, the origin of emerging adulthood as a distinct stage of the life course with be examined, the role of risky behaviors and crime in emerging adulthood will be discussed, the justification for identifying a new category of offender, the arrested adolescent offender (AAO), will be presented, and existing research in the life course perspective will be used as the basis to propose a core hypothesis namely that those who fail to successfully transition to adult roles continue offending as AAOs participating in low level offenses.

As noted above, marriage is considered one of the key transitions to adulthood, acting as a socializing institution that requires conformity to conventional social norms and lessens deviant behaviors such as drug and alcohol use (Arnett, 1998; Cote, 2000; Laub & Sampson, 2003). Prior research examined family role transitions (marriage and parenthood) in relation to risky behaviors (risky driving, substance abuse, and dangerous sexual behavior), finding that being married and having a child were related to reduced participation in these risky behaviors (Arnett, 1998). Moreover, many studies have found that those not married by their early twenties have a greater likelihood of engaging in criminal and dangerous behaviors (Chassin et al., 2002; Laub & Sampson, 2003; & White et al., 2005).

Like marriage, parenthood acts as a socializing institution, requiring avoidance of behaviors that endanger the lives of self or others (Arnett, 2001; Laub & Sampson, 2003). Laub and Sampson (2003) found that a significant number of the males they studied felt being a parent called for taking on adult responsibilities and allowed for less recreational time with peers. Previous research found that along with marriage, parenthood acts as a role transition causing an inverse correlation with deviant

---

1 It is possible that divorce could also act as a negative turning point towards offending as the sample ages. Future studies may want to include hypotheses examining the role of divorce as a turning point. It should also be noted that Moffitt (1993) and Moffitt et al. (2001) stated that early parenthood could act as a 'snare' and act as a risk factor for young people. However, early parenthood would most likely be a risk factor when individuals are in early/mid adolescence (at waves 1 and 2 in this sample).

behaviors. Those who do not have children have a greater likelihood of engaging in criminal and delinquent behaviors (Arnett, 1998; Chassin et al., 2002; Laub & Sampson, 2003; Tucker et al., 2005; White et al., 2005).

In addition to marriage and parenthood, military service also has been identified as a life course turning point away from crime (Laub & Sampson, 1993, 2003). Laub and Sampson found that such service affected life course trajectories through three distinct processes. First, the military re-socializes, nullifying past failures and accomplishments alike, "knifing off" past experiences and reorganizing social roles. Next, the military provided training and educational opportunities, both in-and post-service through the G.I. Bill, increasing social capital which acts to increase attachments to employment and marriage. Finally, the military alters routine activities, and provides a structured environment with direct supervision and support (Laub & Sampson, 2003, pp. 48-51). This provided many of the men in their sample with an opportunity to reshape their social identities. The role of the military as a turning point can have negative consequences as well, as Wright, Carter, & Cullen (2005) found that most research studying the effectiveness of the military as a turning point away from crime mainly focused on veterans of World War II. Their study, in contrast to Laub and Sampson's (2003), used Vietnam veterans and found that service in Vietnam increased drug use. Thus, the inclusion of military service in the present study may provide clarification on how military service operates as a turning point in more recent cohorts.

The final area of cultural change discussed by Arnett is the economy. Starting in the 1970's the United States experienced a substantial increase in overall earnings inequality and in educational salary differentials. As a result, those with lower levels of education experienced large declines in earnings (Katz, 1994). For example, the William T. Grant Foundation (1988) reported that from 1973 through 1986 young males across all races and education levels experienced an average decline in economic prospects of 26 percent. For college graduates, salaries decreased only 6 percent between 1973 and 1986, relative to those with less than high school, who faced a decrease of 42 percent (William T. Grant Foundation, 1988). The cost of living in the United States increased significantly between the late 1960s and the early 1980s as reflected in the cost of tuition, apartment rents, homes, automobiles, and general household expenses (Okimoto & Stegall, 1987). For example, the consumer price index, a measure of money paid by urban residents for basic goods and services, showed a marked series of increases from 1960 through the 1980s (e.g., 1.6% in 1965, 5.7% in 1970, 9.1% in 1975, 13.5% in 1980, and 3.6% in 1985) (Bureau of Labor Statistics, 2008). Higher cost of living led many young people to postpone leaving home or resulted in a return home after living independently because of the inability to be financially independent.

Goldscheider & Goldscheider (1994) found that from the 1920s to the 1980s the rate of young adults returning home increased from 22 percent to almost 40 percent because of the difficulty in keeping an independent residence, a trend that continues to the present (Arnett, 2000; Cote, 2000). Leaving home is one of the key criteria for the transition to adulthood (Arnett, 2000). Living with either parent into ones' mid-twenties represents a delay in reaching adult status. The increased cost of living and education has forced more young people to postpone the customary turning points of leaving home, marriage, completion of education, and having children until they are financially independent (Cote & Allahar, 1995).

Historically, the average age of leaving home had declined from World War II until the 1960s, with white males leaving home at age 23.4 in 1950 and age 18.5 in 1960 (Gutman, Pinonm, & Pullum, 2002). By 1970 through the 1990s, the average age of leaving home rose, with white males leaving home at age 20.4 in 1970, and age 21.7 in 1990 (Gutman, Pinon, & Pullman, 2002). In addition to leaving home at earlier ages, emerging adults have also had the highest rate of residential changes of any group. Goldscheider & Goldscheider (1994) found that almost 40 percent of emerging adults return to and leave their parents' home at least once during emerging adulthood. These lifestyle changes reflect the exploratory nature of emerging adulthood, usually coinciding with the beginning or end of a relationship, entering or leaving college, and starting or quitting a new

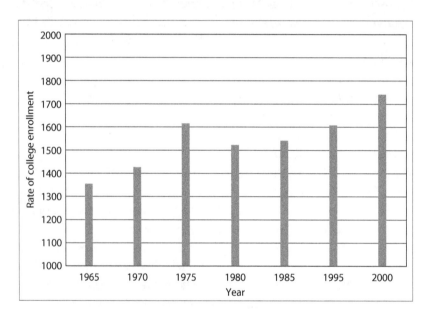

FIGURE 4.1 Rate of college enrollment of recent high school completers 1960-2000 (numbers in thousands)
Source: National Center for Education Statistics, http://nces.ed.gov/programs/digest/d05/tables/dt05_181.asp

job (Arnett, 2000, pp. 473-475). Likewise, higher education is pursued in a nonlinear fashion, with many working full or part-time jobs while in college (Arnett, 2000).

In sum, emerging adulthood has been identified as a new stage of the life course resulting from the intersection of several socio-demographic and economic changes over the past 50 years, including the timing of marriage and parenthood, an overall increase in the cost of living, decreases in wages, education inflation, and an increase in the age at which individuals live independently. Many of those who have experienced emerging adulthood delay various turning points that would usually decrease deviant and criminal behavior. As a result, many in emerging adulthood are caught in a period of "arrested adolescence" in which low-level offending, typically seen in teenagers, continues.

Risky Behaviors, Crime, & Deviance In Emerging Adulthood

One of the defining characteristics of being in emerging adulthood is a greater likelihood of engaging in high rates of risky and delinquent behaviors usually seen in adolescence. Prior research has found that dangerous behaviors (e.g., smoking, risky driving, binge drinking, drug use, and unsafe sexual behaviors) are highly prevalent during emerging adulthood (Arnett, 1998; Tucker et al., 2005; White, McMorris, Catalano, Fleming, Haggerty, & Abott, 2006; White & Jackson, 2004). Transitions (or lack thereof) during emerging adulthood have been found to influence participation in risky and dangerous behaviors (White et al., 2006). For example, White & Jackson (2005) examined the effects of the transition from adolescence to adulthood on drinking behaviors, finding that moving away from the controls of high school and leaving the parental home was related to higher rates of heavy drinking and alcohol-related problems in emerging adults.

Research in the area of risk behavior has traditionally focused on exploring these problems in adolescent populations (Hirschi, 1969; Bell & Bell, 1991; Jessor, Donovan, & Costa, 1991; Moffitt et al., 2001). More recently, studies have started to focus on increased risk behaviors during the period from adolescence to emerging adulthood (Chassin et al., 2002; Chen & Kandel, 1995; Rorhbach et al., 2005), and the period marking the onset and end of emerging adulthood (Shifren, Furnham, & Bauserman, 2003; White & Jackson, 2005). For example, Rohrbach et al., (2005) studied rates of tobacco, alcohol, and other drug use in a sample of alternative high school students for a five-year period from adolescence to emerging adulthood, finding that those who met traditional turning points (e.g., being married at the five year follow up) were less likely to use tobacco, alcohol, and marijuana. In another study, White & Jackson (2005) argued that the instability of emerging adulthood in the areas of education, residence, romantic relationships, and employment, accompanied by decreased levels of parental monitoring leads to increased alcohol use.

Arnett (2005) argued that increased substance abuse and risky behaviors during emerging adulthood are the result of increased freedom and reduced social controls. During the period of emerging adulthood, increasing instability and stress influence increases in rates of alcohol and drug use (Arnett, 2005). Without the informal social controls and attachments built through *on-time* transitions to marriage, family, and employment, those in emerging adulthood have fewer social bonds which act to inhibit risky, deviant, and criminal behaviors.

The motivation most often found in various forms of risky behavior is sensation seeking, the need for new and intense sensory experiences (Arnett, 1994). Those who are high in sensation seeking want to experience a high degree of novel and intense experiences, finding them pleasurable. Dangerous behaviors provide the novelty and stimulation that people who are high in sensation seeking desire. Arnett (1998) provides several examples of such sensation seeking behaviors, including driving a car at high speeds and sexual experimentation with multiple partners. Other factors that influence risky and criminal behaviors in emerging adults include an optimistic attitude, identity exploration, peer influence, and decreased parental monitoring (Arnett, 2005; White & Jackson, 2005).

Arnett (2005) states that an optimistic attitude is a common trait in emerging adults, and because of this attitude many persons in emerging adulthood do not view themselves as vulnerable to the potential dangers association with risky behaviors. Thus, emerging adults are more likely than others to drink excessively or engage in risky behaviors (Arnett, 2005). For example, emerging adults only see the benefits of alcohol consumption (i.e., having fun), but fail to see the negative effects (i.e., being arrested for drunk driving, developing alcoholism).

Another area identified by Arnett (2005) is identity exploration in the areas of love and work that largely occur in emerging adulthood rather than in adolescence (Arnett, 2005). Adolescence is when many have their first relationships and sexual experiences, but it is during emerging adulthood that people start to explore themselves on a deeper level to discover what type of qualities they are looking for in a romantic partner, as well as what type of long term employment they want to pursue (Arnett, 2005).

Identity exploration may relate to substance abuse and other dangerous behaviors in two specific ways. First, many emerging adults want to have various life experiences before they "settle down" into adult life; this can include experimentation with substance abuse (Arnett, 2005). Second, the process of developing an adult identity can be stressful and challenging (Arnett, 2005). Many in emerging adulthood may resort to substance abuse as a coping mechanism to deal with this stress (Arnett, 2005).

As emerging adults enter college or join the workforce, they may be vulnerable to peer influence because of their need to make new friendships (White & Jackson, 2005). Drinking lowers social inhibitions and promotes interacting with new peers (White & Jackson, 2005). Several studies have found that college students may drink more because of perceived attitudes than their own and norms on campus, with many students believing that campus attitudes are more permissive and that other students drink more than they actually do (Borsari & Carey, 2001, 2003).

The final area identified by Arnett (2005) is the role of parental monitoring. As individuals transition from adolescence to emerging adulthood parental monitoring decreases, and parents have less influence on dangerous and risky behaviors (White & Jackson, 2005). The relationship between parental oversight and substance abuse was examined systematically by Kypri, McCarthy, Coe, & Brown (2004). They found that rates of substance abuse increase in the year after high school as adolescents transitioned to emerging adulthood and moved out of their parent's home and levels of parental monitoring decreased. In the following year as many emerging adults left college dormitories and moved away from the monitoring of college residency, rates of substance abuse increased (Kypri et al., 2004). Thus, as emerging adults move away from parental and/or college dormitory monitoring they are subjected to fewer social controls and rates of substance abuse increase.

Turning to the role of crime in emerging adulthood, Piquero et al., (2002) examined the impact of emergent adulthood on criminal activity of male parolees released from the California Youth Authority between the ages of 21 and 28. Piquero and his colleagues found that arrest rates for both nonviolent and violent offenses peak in the early 20s during the period of emergent adulthood. The results of this study are in contrast to other researchers (viz., Gottfredson & Hirschi, 1990) who have argued the peak period to be in the mid to late teens.

What Salvatore points out is that emerging adulthood may actually exacerbate the potential for criminal activity among disadvantaged young people. Crosnoe and Johnson (2011) express this complexity by stating: "A hallmark of adolescence is that maturation can occur at different velocities in different domains of development, so that youth may look or feel like adults in some ways but not in others" (p. 441). Thus, the peak of crime in adolescence could be extending along with adulthood transitions, especially when economic prospects delay the incentives and social control mechanisms delinquency inhibiting workplaces. Likewise, emotional maturity—which is also more scarce in emerging adulthood—has been found to be a key factor in explaining desistance from crime over the life course (e.g., Giordano et al. 2007).

DISADVANTAGE & DELINQUENCY

More generally, the life course has consistently been found to be a major component of understanding criminal behavior, especially as it relates to disadvantage. Sampson and Laub (1997) outlined developmental theories of crime and delinquency by describing development as a dynamic unfolding of systemic influences on social and psychological outcomes. The central aspect of developmental conditioning on crime is the role of cumulative disadvantage discussed in the previous chapter. In focusing on social control over the life course, these authors report numerous findings evidencing that disadvantages accrue across family, school, and peer interactions.

Not only do disadvantages accumulate across developmental stages, but their link to delinquency increases the likelihood of criminal activities earlier in the life course than youth without cumulative disadvantages. Imprisonment early in the life course relates to long-term negative life course outcomes, especially as it intersects with race and ethnicity (e.g., Pettit & Western 2004) and gender (e.g., Hagan & Foster 2003). As with the social class dynamics of previous chapters, this occurs both through structural barriers and through internalization of disadvantages expressed via lower self-esteem in comparison to more advantaged peers. Studies find that low self-esteem early in the life course is itself a predictor of crime (Eitle et al. 2010).

PREDICTORS OF DELINQUENT ACTIVITIES

While sociological understandings of the life course and emerging adulthood recognize the individualization of life course biographies (Kohli 2007), the distinction from psychological approaches is that—rather than promoting this as a developmental necessity—sociologists view this as a social process that burdens some and advantages others. For example, institutional frameworks for adulthood transitions do not view social institutions as disappearing during emerging adulthood but instead see that the alignment between individuals and institutions is variable (e.g., Lee 2012). This means it is possible for people to be "out of whack" with institutional expectations, increasing their likelihood of being delinquent. In addition to institutional alignment, other predictors of delinquent activities in emerging adulthood are peer influences and organizational participation (e.g., Kraeger 2007), alcohol use (e.g., Blokland 2014), and disconnects in adulthood transitions (e.g., Terriquez & Gurantz 2015).

DESISTANCE IN ADULTHOOD TRANSITIONS

Despite the increased variability in the timing and sequencing of transitions to adulthood roles, Massoglia and Uggen (2010) find that "remarkably persistent" is the notion that young people will at some point settle down—meaning they will desist from the delinquent behaviors that were potentially tolerated during youth but have become unacceptable in adulthood. Exactly when the same behaviors tip from tolerable to delinquent is unclear, however.

Studies find that there are trajectories of delinquency—such that delinquent activity peaks and declines across the life course (Powell et al. 2009). However, participating in criminal activity during youth has long-term consequences on adulthood patterns. Given the importance of subjective, self-perceived adulthood status discussed in Chapter 1, it is especially notable that "arrest reduces the probability of feeling like an adult by approximately 78 percent" (Massoglia & Uggen 2010, 14), and that emerging adults who evaluate themselves as desisting from crime have double the likelihood of viewing themselves as adults than those who see themselves as persisting.

PERSISTENCE OF DELINQUENCY

Given the difficulties of emerging into adulthood for the general population, what difficulties do formerly incarcerated young people face? This is the question that Uggen and Wakefield (2005) address, to which they succinctly state:

> Criminal sentences disrupt employment, family arrangements, and civic engagement. While probationers are allowed to complete their sentences in the community, prisoners are removed from most important social contacts for the duration of their sentences. In some case this may be a positive development, such as when inmates are removed from criminal peer networks or volatile family situations. At the same time, incarceration also cuts inmates off from active participation as parents, community members, and employees (p. 126).

In the second reading, Uggen and Wakefield (2005) describe the challenges faced by formerly incarcerated emerging adults reentering the community.

READING 4.2

Young Adults Reentering the Community from the Criminal Justice System

By Christopher Uggen and Sara Wakefield

Adult Status Markers: Work, School, and Family Formation

Given the prevalence of early childhood disadvantage, substance abuse, and disability among prison inmates, it is perhaps unsurprising that this group would also lag behind their age cohort in educational and occupational attainment immediately prior to entering prison. Figure 4.2 compares the school, work, and family statuses of young prison inmates with those of males aged eighteen through twenty-four in the general population (U.S. Bureau of Labor Statistics 2003). Most strikingly, the educational attainment of young inmates lags far behind that of their counterparts in the general population. Almost 75 percent of U.S. males aged eighteen to twenty-four have attained at least a high school diploma; less than 20 percent of inmates have done so. At the time of their most recent arrest, inmates were also more likely to have been unemployed than noninmates, and much less likely to be working full-time. The two groups are roughly comparable in terms of marital status, with the vast majority of both populations unmarried in this age range. Some 48 percent of the

Christopher Uggen and Sara Wakefield, "Young Adults Reentering the Community from the Criminal Justice System," On Your Own Without a Net: The Transition to Adulthood for Vulnerable Population, ed. D. Wayne Osgood, E. Michel Foster, Constance Flanagan, and Gretchen R. Ruth, pp. 125–136. Copyright © 2005 by University of Chicago Press. Reprinted with permission.

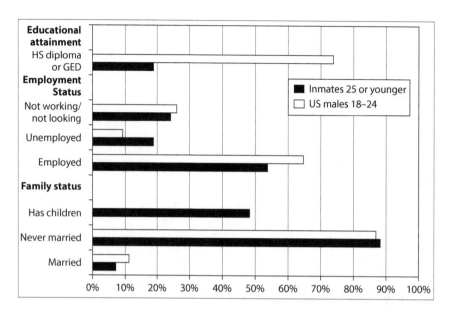

FIGURE 4.2 Comparison of inmates age twenty-five or younger and U.S. males age eighteen to twenty-four by adult status markers, 1997.

inmate group, however, reported having at least one child. (Unfortunately, no directly comparable data are available for the general male population.)

All in all, offenders enter prison with a multitude of problems across most domains of adult adjustment. Young offenders, particularly those with juvenile criminal histories, are more likely to have been raised in adverse economic and familial circumstances. A substantial portion have physical health problems, mental health and substance abuse issues, or learning disabilities. When arrested, many young inmates were homeless, unemployed, or undereducated. To what extent can prisons address these deficits? Below, we explore the opportunities and challenges to improving the health, education, and occupational attainment of young offenders while they are serving their sentences.

Serving A Sentence: Opportunities For Development Behind Bars?

Criminal sentences disrupt employment, family arrangements, and civic engagement. While probationers are allowed to complete their sentences in the community, prisoners are removed from most important social contacts for the duration of their sentences. In some cases this may be a positive development, such as when inmates are removed from criminal peer networks or volatile family situations. At the same time, incarceration also cuts inmates off from active participation as parents, community members, and employees. Additionally, inmates may also be subject to serious injury or sexual assault while behind bars (Bell et al. 1999). The Bureau of Justice Statistics reports that in 1997 roughly 20 percent of state prisoners younger than twenty-five were injured in prison; of these, about 10 percent were injured in fights with other inmates (U.S. Department of Justice 2001c).

Current and former inmates now face substantial difficulty entering programs and receiving services that are likely to improve their employment prospects. Many convicted felons are prohibited from receiving financial aid for higher education. Felons on probation or parole are often barred from public assistance programs and access to public housing (Rubenstein and Mukamal 2002). Larry, a thirty-year-old prisoner, expressed displeasure about recent restrictions on inmate access to higher education.

> I think education is underrated. There's not enough of it. They keep taking it away. You know, I was going to [university] through their program and they took the program away. About a year later they brought a smaller version of it back, but still it's not the same as it was.

Larry also doubts the utility of GED-only educational programs for prisoners.

> Well, the G.E.D.'s not gonna do anything. You know, there's all kind of guys in here that have a G.E.D. and they're still running around committin crime, you know. They need to go to some higher education. A G.E.D. is not going to change anybody's intelligence level. All you got's this little piece of paper saying, "Yeah, I'm *almost like* a high school student."

Offenders also increasingly face the termination of their parental rights as a result of incarceration. For those who retain parental rights, maintaining consistent contact with children is extremely difficult (Travis and Visher, chapter 6). Currently, incarceration rates among women are rising, yielding greater family disruption, since women are more likely to be living with their children prior to incarceration (Hagan and Dinovitzer 1999). Mary, a forty-year-old prisoner, described the difficulties of physical separation from children and the uncertainty of resuming parental duties upon release from prison.

> And it crushes a lot of women. I mean their whole world gets totally shattered in here because they don't have their children nearby. Or their children are in different homes and things like that. There's a lady here who has four children, and they're each in a different foster home. When she gets out is she going to be able to collect her children back? I don't know.

Given the substantial costs associated with removing inmates from community, work, and family life, can prisons release inmates who are better off than when they entered? Whereas prisons generally provide inmates with some degree of education and work experience, jails are much less likely to provide such programming, and jail conditions vary dramatically across jurisdictions. Moreover, though most prisons offer education programs, substance abuse treatment, or vocational training opportunities for inmates, participation in such programs is low and has been declining (Travis and Visher, chapter 6). Inmates are also subject to the long-term trend in U.S. correctional policy emphasizing a punitive rather than a rehabilitative ideology (Altschuler, chapter 4). Our qualitative interviews suggest that inmates are aware of this emphasis as well. Craig, a twenty-two-year-old prisoner, was one of many who felt that the dominance of punitive programs is a direct reflection of the wishes of community members, as opposed to policies imposed by politicians or correctional authorities.

> The general attitude is that, at least with the prison system, is more things are just being taken away. It's getting where it's not so much for politicians, but it's actually the whole community, the whole society is saying, "We want more punishment." "We don't think treatment works. It's not worth it." They just wanna punish. It's real frustrating, it seems like there's not a lot of understanding maybe from the public, or maybe an attempt to work with each other. It seems like a lot of guys in here become angry at the public.

A number of popular biographies have described prison as a transformative experience. For example, *The Autobiography of Malcolm X* and Nathan McCall's *Makes Me Wanna Holler* describe incarceration as a time in which reflection, rest, and growth are possible. Also, despite public skepticism and political resistance, a growing research literature has shown that rehabilitation programs are capable of lowering recidivism rates for those who participate (see Cullen and Gendreau 2000 for a review). Without such programs, the life course perspective, our qualitative interviews, and research on criminal desistance suggest that prison will fail to transform the majority of inmates from immature or disadvantaged offenders into active community members, responsible parents, and stable employees upon release.

Reentering The Community: Consequences of Punishment

Perhaps the most important first step to community reengagement and criminal desistance is the adoption of a noncriminal identity. Viewing oneself as a *former* offender is likely to impact an inmate's desire for legitimate employment (and persistence during the job search), chances of successful family reintegration, and resistance to attractive criminal opportunities. Though such a process may begin prior to prison release (e.g., cognitive behavioral treatment programs), the society outside the prison walls will heavily influence how former inmates perceive opportunities for legitimate success and the fate of their developing prosocial identity (Maruna 2001).

Matsueda and Heimer (1997, 167) offer a social-psychological perspective on crime that is useful for understanding the barriers ex-prisoners face in adopting prosocial identities. In this model, self-concept, identity, and the adoption of some roles ("gang member") over others ("computer programmer") are a function of social interaction. The most salient roles are those played repeatedly over time and those that are reinforced in social relationships. This approach suggests that prison reentry programs may be successful only insofar as the social relationships and environment outside of prison reinforces earlier principles learned in prison.

Life course research helps to explain how young adults make their way into the criminal justice system as well as identify the sorts of barriers they are likely to face when returning to their communities (Edin, Nelson, and Paranal 2004; Pettit and Western 2004). Those with early disadvantages are likely to become embedded in problematic life course trajectories with the attendant barriers to work, family, and civic reintegration. Yet it is often the effects of *punishment* rather than offending that disrupt or delay life course transitions. Thus far, we have shown the substantial disadvantages of probationers, inmates, and parolees prior to entering the criminal justice system and discussed the challenges to development while serving their sentences. We next describe the barriers to a successful transition to adulthood that arise from criminal punishment.

Work

Obtaining legitimate and quality employment may powerfully assist in the adoption of a durable noncriminal identity. There is ample evidence that work may be important for explaining both the onset of crime in childhood and adolescence and desistance from crime in adulthood. Although the transition from school to full-time work is a clear marker of adult status in the United States, the effects of employment on crime are likely to be age graded. For example, Uggen (2000) finds that a basic employment opportunity reduces criminal involvement for offenders age twenty-seven and older, a group that is noticeably delayed with respect to adult work transitions. Though evidence suggests that the simple provision of employment is unlikely to impact the criminal behavior of young offenders (Paternoster et al. 2003; Uggen 2000), job quality and earnings are both tied to reductions in crime among offenders (Crutchfield and Pitchford 1997; Uggen 1999; Uggen and Thompson 2003). In contrast, adolescents who work more than twenty hours per week (Bachman and Schulenberg 1993) or in more adultlike work settings (Staff and Uggen 2003) tend to be more involved in delinquency than those who work less or not at all. Such findings may indicate that a precocious transition to adulthood or a "hurried adolescence" (Safron, Schulenberg, and Bachman 2001) is associated with delinquency, substance use, and other risky behaviors. Thus, early as well as late transitions to adult work roles tend to increase criminal involvement because the meaning of work and other important life course transitions is age dependent.

Beyond the impact of work on crime and criminal desistance, a burgeoning research literature is demonstrating strong punishment effects on employment and earnings, showing that imprisonment affects both the quantity and quality of work available to former prisoners (Pager 2003; Western 2002). This pattern of decreased earnings and fewer job opportunities for ex-prisoners has had an especially strong impact on younger workers and African Americans (Pager 2003; Western and Pettit 2000). In our own interviews, several inmates expressed frustration over their inability to get a good job when their criminal record is known to employers. As Karen, a white inmate in her thirties, put it:

> What is it, the fourth question of every job interview? "Have you ever been convicted of a crime?" They ask you that before they ask for your prior work history or education. All that's on the second page, so they read "felon" before they ever read that side.

Similarly, Rita, another female inmate in her forties, had little work experience and few concrete plans for employment. She described a rich network of associates available to assist her in disposing of stolen merchandise, or trading it for drugs that she could sell at a high profit. Her opportunities for legitimate employment, however, paled in comparison:

> I don't know what I'm going to be able to do to make money unless I go out and sell drugs again … I mean, I'm gonna get a job that probably, if I'm lucky, makes $8 or $9 an hour, which I can go make a drug deal in a half-hour and make $300, you know?

Michael, a probationer, describes himself as "stuck in streetlife" and explained how his criminal justice experiences have affected his work prospects:

> I'm glad I'm gonna get off probation, and drop my felony. For real. I want a good paying job, 'cause I had a job at [a casino] in '97, I was going to get that job, too. That same day I caught that robbery case … that job was gonna pay me like $11 an hour, I had experience as a cook, I went through cooking classes up in the workhouse and got a certificate for like six weeks … I was going to be a top chef out at [the casino]. Couldn't do it though, caught that felony, couldn't even do it, can't work at a casino, you can't get a government job, neither, if you got a felony.

Family

In addition to employment, strong family ties may reduce recidivism and aid in community reintegration of former inmates. Marriage, for example, may reduce crime because spouses provide informal social control for offenders and tend to reduce associations with criminal peers (Laub, Nagin, and Sampson 1998; Warr 1998). As in research on employment, marital quality and commitment, rather than the mere presence of a marital or stable cohabiting union, appears to be critical to inhibiting subsequent crime. Horney, Osgood, and Marshall (1995) report that cohabitation, in the absence of marriage, may even increase offending. Additionally, the presence or even the quality of marriage is less important to future offending when the spouse is also an offender (Giordano, Cernkovich, and Rudolph 2002). Returning prisoners whose spouses are involved in crime may be even *more* likely to continue in crime than unmarried offenders.

Prison inmates increasingly face the formal termination of their parental rights (Braman 2002) and informal barriers to assuming adult family roles. Since 1991, the number of children with an incarcerated parent has increased from about 900,000 to almost 1.5 million (about 2.1 percent of all children under age eighteen). A majority of prison inmates have at least one child under eighteen and almost 50 percent of incarcerated parents were living with their children prior to entering prison. Incarceration also has an impact on a substantial number of very young children—roughly 22 percent of children with an incarcerated parent were under the age of five (U.S. Department of Justice 2000).

Our qualitative interviews suggest that children can have a powerful impact on their parents' offending patterns. For example, Scott, a twenty-six-year-old African-American father on probation, discussed how becoming a "family man" made legitimate work more attractive to him.

> I think being a family man has changed me in that [career] way. To want to be—To get my money right because I don't want to look like a piece of nothing in front of my kids. So stuff like that has to do with pride, too. That helps, man. That helps to have a family.

In contrast, Lori, a thirty-seven-year-old prisoner, describes how losing her parental rights while incarcerated had a dramatic effect on her behavior.

> I remember when they took my son from me. Let me tell you something—I was literally nuts for two years. I didn't give a shit. I did as I pleased when I pleased, and I didn't give a shit about the consequences.

Unfortunately, sociological research on the impact of children on their parents' criminality and the potentially harmful consequences of reuniting children with criminal parents has only begun to emerge (Hagan and Dinovitzer 1999). Several theories of crime, however, suggest ways in which the presence of children may impact the criminal offending of their parents. Children may reduce parental crime if their presence helps to strengthen family attachments and reinforce a prosocial identity. Alternatively, children may increase the criminal involvement of parents by adding stress and financial strain to an already heavy burden of disadvantages. While more young adults are involved with the criminal justice system, we know very little about the impact the experience may have on the transition to parenthood, parenting skills, and parental attachment (Nurse 2004).

Civic Life

As with parenting, barriers to civic engagement and political participation of ex-inmates have been relatively neglected areas of study (Uggen, Manza, and Behrens 2003a). Civic barriers such as the loss of voting rights and restrictions on community life compound the labor market, educational, and early childhood disadvantages experienced by ex-prisoners, powerfully reinforcing their social isolation. In a recent study of felon disenfranchisement, Uggen and Manza (2002) report that nearly 4.7 million felons and ex-felons are legally disenfranchised in the United States. While this group appears to be more alienated from mainstream politics and community life than the rest of the population (Uggen, Manza, and Behrens 2003a; Uggen and Manza 2002), they have valuable political views to contribute, and their civic inclusion may facilitate their successful adjustment when they return to the community (Uggen and Manza forthcoming).

Regardless of whether felons would exercise the right to vote if given the opportunity, those we interviewed generally viewed voting as fundamental to citizenship. As Lynn, a prisoner in her thirties, put it, voting is a "part of being a citizen and being an adult. Once you reach the age of eighteen, that's something you get to do." Correspondingly, they viewed disenfranchisement as a clear indicator that they were unwanted or unaccepted as full citizens in their communities. This sentiment is clearly expressed by Paul, a male in his thirties who describes himself as "exiled" from his community:

> Giving back voting rights is another way to make a person feel part of that community. How can you feel that you're giving back to a community that you're a part of when you're exiled from it by not being able to vote and have a voice in it?

This feeling of exile is especially troubling in light of Matsueda and Heimer's (1997) argument that role adoption is in part a function of the reactions of others and conditioned by social context. Of central concern, then, is Paul's reaction to the denial of voting rights and restrictions placed upon him because of his sex offender status:

> When they say, "What are you going to give back to the community for this and for that?" Well, hey, community doesn't want a damn thing to do with me, why should I go back and give anything?

Paul's viewpoint suggests that civil restrictions may inhibit the assumption of other adult roles and undermine the reintegrative goal of encouraging offenders to empathize or identify with other citizens as a strategy for reducing crime (see, e.g., Bazemore 2001; Braithwaite 1989). Moreover, voting at age eighteen may be the first opportunity for civic engagement for many young offenders. When this opportunity is lost, they may be less likely to exercise this right when and if it is regained.

Social Stigma

In addition to substantial disadvantages in the labor market, barriers to family reintegration and educational attainment, and civil penalties, offenders also face heightened stigmatization once they leave prison. Sex offenders, perhaps the most stigmatized group of offenders returning to the community, face especially severe barriers to community reintegration. In the words of Alan, a Minnesota sex offender in his thirties, "We're a step below murderers. People would rather have a murderer living next door than me."

Alan's comments seem to reflect the sentiments of the general public, for a far greater stigma appears to be associated with sex offenses than even violent crimes. In a nationally representative Harris poll conducted in July 2002, about 80 percent of Americans expressed support for the extension of voting rights to convicted felons who have completed their sentences. In a survey experiment in which the offense category was varied, however, sex offenders received a far lower level of support, with only 52 percent for reenfranchisement upon completion of sentence (Manza, Brooks, and Uggen 2004). The increased use of community notification procedures and sex offender registration requirements may increase public safety. Nevertheless, such requirements may also have the unintended effect of increasing sex offender recidivism by removing virtually all routes to the adoption of adult roles, prosocial community involvement, and occupational or educational advancement.

Cumulative Disadvantage and Multiple Barriers

One of the most important findings of life course research on the causes and correlates of criminal offending concerns the interactions among early life disadvantage, later disadvantages, and criminal outcomes. Early life disadvantages such as poverty, criminal parents, and neuropsychological deficits combine to lower later educational and occupational attainment, thereby increasing the likelihood of criminal involvement (Hagan and Palloni 1990; Laub and Sampson 2003; Moffitt 1993). Earlier disadvantages and delayed transitions are magnified over time, resulting in problematic transitions to adulthood and increased criminal offending.

Also, irrespective of gender, race, conviction offense, or correctional status, the felon label acts as a substantial barrier to returning to normal work, family, and civic roles. (See Lyons and Melton's argument about stigma and mental illness in chapter 11). Our respondents suggested important interactions across these domains as well (Uggen, Manza, and Behrens 2003a). For example, barriers to educational attainment or employment impede family reintegration and the assumption of positive parenting roles. Similarly, restrictions on voting, civic participation, and housing limit the ability of offenders to become active citizens. Those ex-inmates who return to their communities will do so with additional challenges, beyond the difficulties that may have brought them to prison. Yet many were optimistic about the prospects for assuming or resuming roles as active citizens. Lynn, whose drug use and criminal activities were widely discussed in her small town, said that "people seen that I changed." She was eager to rejoin that community and establish a new role as a volunteer.

> When I get out I'll be home in time to do whatever I can to help out with [my hometown] centennial. The last two years I've been on house arrest so I couldn't be involved. I had to sit at home. So this will be my first year not [on

house arrest], and I plan on, you know, whatever day if they need me to clean up the streets, whatever, I plan on doing it.

In contrast, the young probationer Michael described his trepidation upon returning to a high-crime urban neighborhood after a period of incarceration.

You don't really see progress. I mean people work, they get in stuff, volunteer and stuff, but it's, it's the same cycle … Day in, day out, people go to jail, get married, people born, same thing, people get drunk, people get high, it never stops.

Despite these misgivings, Michael also wanted his neighbors to witness his assumption of adult roles:

I want to be there [in my old neighborhood] so people would know, "hey, man, [Mike's] doing something, going to work everyday, family going to church. He was out there wild, look at him now, he's changed" … I'd be right there, but, all in all, when you do that, you still have people who might be mad at you, that you made the change, people you used to run with, you know, might not like that.

Although Michael spoke at length about his desire to someday leave crime behind, become involved in his community, and "raise a family like middle-class people," these roles seem to lack salience for him. In particular, he discussed his difficulties making the most of the employment opportunities available to him.

They gave me a chance, you know, working at [a company] making $8 an hour, [it] was a cool job, you know, I was always by myself, can't complain about that. They gave me a chance. It was a white guy, too. They gave me a chance, because I was looking sincere, you know I came to work on time … I worked there about six months. Then, I don't know, man, I just stopped going. I don't know why.

In contrast, when asked about where he will live after leaving prison, Dylan references the education he received in prison, describing his work plans in terms of a "career" rather than merely getting a "job."

I don't think I'll live there [my hometown] because of the career I've chosen in prison, I'm a computer programmer. I'm from a small town so I won't be able to have a career necessarily. So I'll probably have to live in the city.

A noticeable difference between Dylan and Michael is in their descriptions of themselves and their work goals. Michael is merely "looking sincere" while expressing doubt about his ability to maintain a legal job, whereas Dylan—who has yet to leave prison and put his plans to a test—describes himself as a computer programmer. Michael, at twenty-three a world-weary probationer, has experienced life on the outside as a felon while Dylan has yet to confront the stigma experienced by those with a criminal history. Combating the reactions and expectations of others when coworkers, neighbors, and friends discover his criminal record is a difficulty Dylan has not yet faced.

Karen, a female inmate, echoed the beliefs of other respondents when she described the labor market consequences of her criminal history. She also argued that her status as a felon would interfere with her ability to remain an involved parent once she returned to her community.

> Even to go into the school, to work with my child's class—and I'm not a sex offender—but all I need is one parent who says, "Isn't she a felon? I don't want her with my child."

Frustration over the inability to be viewed as anything other than a felon was a consistent theme throughout our qualitative interviews. As Karen put it:

> I am more than a felon. I am educated. I am intelligent. I'm hard working, I'm a good mother, I'm dependable, all of those things. I don't have to worry about parole telling me I'm a felon because there's gonna be a ton of other people that are going to say, "You're a felon."

Finally, the barriers described in this chapter impact a historically unprecedented rate and number of young adults in the United States (U.S. Department of Justice 2001b). We conclude by placing the United States in an international context and describing differences in the impact of punishment on the transition to adulthood for various groups within this country.

Like these authors, Fader (2014) finds that incarceration during transitions to adulthood is consistently predictive of recidivism to criminal activity during later adulthood. Combined, they highlight that the challenges of successfully navigating to adulthood have increased, while understandings of adulthood pathways have remained constant, perhaps even declined, among formerly incarcerated emerging adults. Add to the mix a criminal record, and an individual's chances to successfully transition into adulthood after an incarceration are bleak.

In summary, emerging adults who enter adulthood roles early are more likely to have aggressive behaviors that can result in criminal records (e.g., Roche et al. 2006). But at the same time, emerging adults who perceive themselves to be adults are more likely to desist from risky behaviors such as drinking (e.g., Rinker et al. 2015). Somewhere in between, then, is a delicate balance between enough delay in structural transition coupled with enough social support to have a perceptual experience of oneself as on track to adulthood. References to peers are key to discerning what "on track" is supposed to look like in this diverse social milieu, and a prior criminal record is all too clear in communicating to emerging adults that they are off track. As with previous chapters, this chapter on delinquency and crime during and preceding emerging adulthood reveals important complexities in understanding life course risks.

REFERENCES

Blokland, Arjan. 2014. "School, Intensive Work, Excessive Alcohol Use and Delinquency during Emerging Adulthood." In *Criminal Behavior from School to the Workplace: Untangling the Complex Relations between Employment, Education, and Crime*, edited by Frank Weerman and Caltrien Bijeveld, 87–107. Routledge.

Crosnoe, Robert and Monica Kirkpatrick Johnson. 2011. "Research on Adolescence in the Twenty-First Century." *Annual Review of Sociology* 37(1):439–60.

Eitle, David, John Taylor, and Kay Kei-ho Pih. 2010. "Extending the Life-Course Interdependence Model: Life Transitions and the Enduring Consequences of Early Self-Derogation for Young Adult Crime." *Youth & Society* 41(4):519–45.

Fader, Jamie. 2013. *Falling Back: Incarceration and Transitions to Adulthood among Urban Youth*. Rutgers University Press.

Giordano, Peggy C., Ryan D. Schroeder, and Stephen A. Cernkovich. 2007. "Emotions and Crime over the Life Course: A Neo-Meadian Perspective on Criminal Continuity and Change." *American Journal of Sociology* 112(6):1603–61.

Hagan, John and Holly Foster. 2003. "S/he's a Rebel: Toward a Sequential Stress Theory of Delinquency and Gendered Pathways to Disadvantage in Emerging Adulthood." *Social Forces* 82(1):53–86.

Kohli, Martin. 2007. "The Institutionalization of the Life Course: Looking Back to Look Ahead." *Research in Human Development* 4(3-4):253–71.

Kraeger, Derek A. 2007. "Unnecessary Roughness? School Sports, Peer Networks, and Male Adolescent Violence." *American Sociological Review* 72(5):705–24.

Laub, John H. and Robert J. Sampson. 1993. "Turning Points in the Life Course: Why Change Matters to the Study of Crime." *Criminology* 31:301.

Lee, JoAnn S. 2012. "An Institutional Framework for the Study of the Transition to Adulthood." *Youth & Society* 46(5):706–30.

Massoglia, Michael and Christopher Uggen. 2010. "Settling down and Aging out: Toward an Interactionist Theory of Desistance and the Transition to Adulthood." *American Journal of Sociology* 116(2):543–82.

Pettit, Becky and Bruce Western. 2004. "Mass Imprisonment and the Life Course: Race and Class Inequality in U.S. Incarceration." *American Sociological Review* 69(2):151–69.

Powell, Darci, Krista M. Perreira, and Kathleen Mullan Harris. 2009. "Trajectories of Delinquency from Adolescence to Adulthood." *Youth & Society* 41(4):475–502.

Rinker, Dipali Venkataraman, Scott T. Walters, Todd M. Wyatt, and William DeJong. 2015. "Do Incoming First-Year College Students Who Think of Themselves as Adults Drink More Responsibly After Starting College?" *Emerging Adulthood* 3(5):359–63.

Roche, Kathleen M., Margaret E. Ensminger, Nicholas Ialongo, Jeanne M. Poduska, and Sheppard G. Kellam. 2006. "Early Entries into Adult Roles Associations with Aggressive Behavior from Early Adolescence into Young Adulthood." *Youth & Society* 38(2):236–61.

Salvatore, Christopher. 2013. "Emerging Adulthood & Crime." In *Arrested Adolescent Offenders: A Study of Delayed Transitions to Adulthood*, 9–29. LFB Scholarly Publishing.

Sampson, Robert J. and John H. Laub. 1997. "A Life Course Theory of Cumulative Disadvantage and the Stability of Delinquency." In *Developmental Theories Of Crime And Delinquency*, edited by Terence B. Thornberry, 133–61. Transaction Publishers.

Tanner, Jennifer L. 2006. "Recentering during Emerging Adulthood: A Critical Turning Point in Life Span Human Development." In *Emerging Adults in America: Coming of Age in the 21st Century*, edited by Jeffrey J. Arnett and Jennifer L. Tanner, 21–56. American Psychological Association.

Terriquez, Veronica and Oded Gurantz. 2015. "Financial Challenges in Emerging Adulthood and Students' Decisions to Stop Out of College." *Emerging Adulthood* 3(3):204–14.

Uggen, Christopher and Sara Wakefield. 2005. In *On Your Own Without a Net: The Transition to Adulthood for Vulnerable Populations*, edited by D. Wayne Osgood, E. Michael Foster, Constance Flanagan, and Gretchen R. Ruth. University of Chicago Press.

CHAPTER 5

Schooling & Higher Education

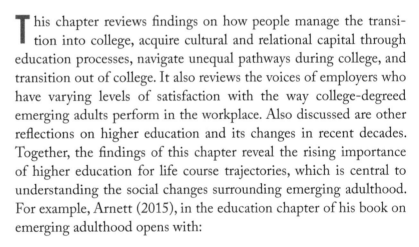

This chapter reviews findings on how people manage the transition into college, acquire cultural and relational capital through education processes, navigate unequal pathways during college, and transition out of college. It also reviews the voices of employers who have varying levels of satisfaction with the way college-degreed emerging adults perform in the workplace. Also discussed are other reflections on higher education and its changes in recent decades. Together, the findings of this chapter reveal the rising importance of higher education for life course trajectories, which is central to understanding the social changes surrounding emerging adulthood. For example, Arnett (2015), in the education chapter of his book on emerging adulthood opens with:

> These days, it is widely recognized that you have to have a college education in order to get a good job in American society. As numerous studies have shown, number of years of college education is positively related to a variety of good things in adulthood, such as higher income and occupational status. Emerging adults may not know the studies or the statistics, but they know, from what they have seen friends, neighbors, and family members experience, that a college education opens up a wide range of job possibilities and that those who don't have one face more limited, less promising employment options (p. 142).

Expectations—for education, for careers, even for life in general—of youth and their parents have risen dramatically, while positions accommodating such expectations have not (Settersten & Ray 2010). College enrollment rates have dramatically increased, but college-degree-required positions have not risen equivalently. In fact, if anything, employers have begun to question the need for a bachelor's degree over occupation-specific certificates or on-the-job training (e.g., Arum & Roksa 2014). The result is that many emerging adults feel let down after years of education leads them toward the same level or lower occupational status than their parents had, usually with a great deal less education (e.g., Reynolds & Baird 2010).

What findings show, then, is that having a college degree correlates with having a higher income than is earned by Americans with less than a college degree. As shown in Chapter 3, Figure 3.1, the median level of income earned in 2013 for Americans with a bachelor's degree was about $50,000, compared to nearly $40,000 median for an associate's degree, $30,000 for high school only, and $25,000 for less than a high school degree (NCES 2015). However, as discussed in the methods caveat above, this means that half of Americans with a bachelor's degree make more than $50,000, while half make less. Thus, some college-degreed Americans make the same as or even less than, the average American with lower education. But, on average, college degrees equate to more incoming earnings, especially when averaged across the life span.

Methods Caveat. That being said, all average trends are a reduction to the mean. As I often say in discussing social science methods of inquiry in class, "reporting only the mean is just that, mean." It is true that measures of central tendency, such as the mean—more commonly known as an average—do tell us something about overall patterns for average Americans. Yet it is also true that average trends can vary tremendously for particular subgroups, such as by gender, race-ethnicity, and social class. What this "means" (pun intended) is that both the average and subgroup trends need to be investigated. It also highlights the importance of investigating central tendency through a variety of angles. Very high or very low numbers can throw off, or skew, the mean significantly, making it a biased indicator of the true center. Instead, the median is more often relied upon by social scientists to describe the true middle, since it literally reflects the number for which half the data are above and half the data are below. Yet, in modeling statistical relationships, it is the means that are investigated. This relationship is called a correlation—an indicator that, on average, there is a relationship between one measure and another (e.g., one trend is higher when the other is higher, or lower when the other is higher, or lower when the other is lower). For example, there is a positive correlation between income earnings and education level, meaning income is higher—on average—when education level is higher.

In summary, earning a college degree still matters a great deal, on average, for long-term economic well-being, in addition to a number of other social and life outcomes. At the same time, it is not the case that all who wind up with "*the piece of paper*"—meaning a college diploma—have the same outcomes just by having earned the degree. Factoring this backwards, the message is that there are pathways into, through, and out of college that matter for differentiating for whom college has the best "returns" and for whom it does not. Not all pathways through college wind up with equal results (e.g., Torche 2011).

TRANSITION TO COLLEGE

Many emerging adulthood scholars find extended time to experiment with roles and experiences (e.g., Arnett 2015; Settersten & Ray 2010) to be of central importance in the role of higher education in adulthood transition. Arnett refers to this positive use of time in college as "exploring." Yet, he also describes a process of "floundering," or what Settersten and Ray describe as "treaders," those who are constantly swimming just to attempt to keep their head above water. Arnett reviews some current critiques of the higher education system and cautions that it does not pay off the same for everyone. He then concludes by saying: "Could the college experience offered to emerging adults be improved? Certainly. But despite these limitations, going to college pays off in multiple ways for emerging adults" (Arnett 2015, 161).

However, Arnett (2015, 147) and other scholars also indicate that the transition into college does not happen as ubiquitously as does the aspiration to, and even enrollment in, college. Arnett reports that about two-thirds of Americans enter college after high school, but then about one-fourth do not return for the second year of college. Plus, in a snapshot of emerging adults ages 25 to 29, only about one-third have obtained their bachelor's degree.

What explains who makes the transition into college and stays the course? There are a variety of investigations and explanations into this question, and more are needed. As one example, Johnson and colleagues (2010) find that managing the transition to college is highly related to a variety of emotional management skills. Contrary to some preconceived notions, it is students who keep their emotions to themselves who tend not to fare as well as students who are more expressive about and regularly name their emotions. As the numerous studies reviewed in Chapter 3 indicated, the kind of cultural knowledge bundled into emotional management and expressive styles are a reflection of the parenting styles children were raised with, coupled with their experiences along the path to emerging adulthood traversing social institutions with different lifestyle patterning. Stephens and colleagues (2007) referred to these kinds of choices as meaningful acts that amount to the invisible identities that reproduce social class dynamics (e.g., Radmacher & Azmitia 2013; Silva 2013).

EDUCATION AS CULTURAL & RELATIONAL CAPITAL

When it "works," higher education also becomes one of the social institutions that patterns expressive styles, emotional management, attitudes, expectations, and behaviors in ways that comport with middle-class ideals (e.g., Swartz 1997; Mirowsky & Ross 2007; Mickelson 2003). More than simply a credential, piece of paper, or diploma, a college degree is a *symbol* of a set of desirable middle-class life and communication styles. Education, if internalized, imprints students with a set of unconscious modes of operating (e.g., Swartz 1997). In America, we tend to attribute behaviors and attitudes to individuals and often see these modes of operating as personality traits, dispositions, internal character. If instead we acknowledge that education is meant to change a person, we have to view changes as internalized teachings, a process of *socialization*.

With the enormous number of applicants available for a smaller pool of employment opportunities, employers need shorthand ways to assess qualifications of people they do not often know. College degrees serve as a benchmark representing a set of desirable qualities, which are difficult and expensive for employers to measure. Universities spend years assessing these qualities and reward emerging adults with the presentation of desired qualities by assigning higher grades, accumulating into a degree earned and higher grade point averages.

The trouble is that students are sometimes resistant to educational strategies. For example, Côté and Levine (2000) find that aptitude, the net of having a positive achievement attitude, negatively predicts learning in college, while an achievement attitude positively predicts learning outcomes. In other words, success in college may be better predicted by desire to achieve than smarts alone.

However, even more complicated is that students are not born into college. They enter with nearly two decades of experiences that are conditioned by their parental resources, social supports, and all their other personal and social experiences. The kinds of expectations and understandings of social life that emerging adults have when they enter college can profoundly shape their experiences of college and likelihood of graduating (e.g., Andres et al. 2007). One explanation for this is what Mirowsky and Ross (2007) find regarding the education and sense of control:

> In some ways a sense of control is to successful action as wealth is to profitable investment—an accumulated product returning subsequent advantage. In theory, perceptions of control grow out of the interaction between intention and outcome. The occurrence of something desired, planned, or attempted reinforces a sense that one's choices and actions have consequences. This in turn encourages attention to setting goals, directing actions toward the goals, evaluating apparent consequences, and revising efforts. The sense of control is more than seeing things occurring as one wants. It is seeing oneself as the author and editor of the choices and actions that link preference to occurrence. Within contexts that support its success, self-direction sharpens ability and encourages effort. The resulting effectiveness and resilience strengthen the sense of control in a beneficial developmental spiral (Mirowsky & Ross 2007, 1341).

Put another way, education imparts people with the patterns of behavior that are accepted by mainstream society. The more education someone has, the more of this patterning they have received, and the more equipped they are to navigate social norms to their advantage. Making social events happen the way someone wants them to is going to reinforce their sense that they have some control over their life. So, people with more education feel they have more control.

Scholars of cultural capital find that people are taught their whole lives to hold certain beliefs about the value of education and the role it plays in social life. This begins with parenting views of childhood, and it patterns how people interact with each other as couples and how they experience authority figures in schools (e.g., Streib 2015; Lareau 2015). The educational expectations patterned in childhood social contexts turn out to be quite durable. Andres and colleagues (2007) find that:

> Students in the current study who earned the highest academic credentials were likely to be those with high SES parents. Consistent with the reproduction theory, it can be surmised that these parents possessed timely information, actively nurtured high expectations, and provided the social capital necessary to wade through postsecondary opportunities and requirements, hence ensuring that expectations were matched with postsecondary participation and eventual outcomes. In addition, higher SES parents possess the cultural skills to communicate with teachers and counselors as partners rather than experts (p. 155).

Likewise, Reynolds and Reynolds (2011; Johnson & Reynolds 2013) found that the educational expectations emerging adults had at the beginning of college remained largely unchanged ten years later. Part of the explanation for who achieves in college depends on what can be called relational capital. After conducting a year-long ethnography as an enrolled college student, Nathan (2000) said: "It is hard to create community when the sheer number of options in college life generate a system in which no one is in the same place at the same time" (p. 38). What Nathan is explaining is that the university is full of numerous options to connect with others, but the options are so numerous, so available, and yet so diversely scheduled that just meeting up with a group of friends or study mates at a set time can be a monumental task. Nathan describes this as the over-optioned university and found that experiences of community were often elusive and unreliable. As with navigating the system of education, this means that part of doing well in college is knowing how to navigate relationships in a complex social milieu. Andres et al. (2007) state:

> High-achieving college students are "more likely to have 'multiplex' (Gluckman 1967) social networks in which linkages among people occur in more than one context (e.g., school personnel, professionals, family friends with knowledge about the postsecondary system)" (p. 155). This could be part of what explains women's achievement anomaly, which is that women have had marked gains in recent decades in their educational performances (e.g., Mickelson 2003).

However, coupled with the findings summarized above, it is important to keep in mind the intersection of different social statuses in their relationship to educational outcomes. Namely, social class, gender, and race-ethnicity all combine in shaping the kinds of social, cultural, and relational capital with which emerging adults enter college. Mickelson (2003) finds that:

> Disadvantaged minority males are the most vulnerable to school failures, while Asian females' and males' achievements in science and mathematics are barely distinguishable. Working-class white male and female college graduates are more likely than their upper middle-class counterparts to major in engineering, accounting, and teaching, rather than in less-applied fields like philosophy, comparative literature, and art history.

And the achievement and attainment edge that women enjoy is the largest among African Americans (p. 373).

In summary, emerging adults enter college with different sorts of experiences and patterned ways of relating, communicating, and understanding.

COLLEGE PATHWAYS

Differences in the ways students enter college play out in their pathways through it. In addition to the long-term effects of childhood disadvantage, neighborhood educational quality, and low-income and marginalized social statuses on education outcomes (e.g., Crowder & South 2011; Wodtke et al. 2011), education itself serves as a sorting mechanism (e.g., Elman & O'Rand 2007). Swartz (1997) explains Bourdieu's theories about educational inequalities by stating: "the educational system—more than the family, church, or business firm—has become the institution most responsible for the transmission of social inequality in modern societies" (p. 190). Unequal pathways through college occur at the front end, the middle, and the back end.

For *non-enrollees*—emerging adults not enrolling in college—Bozick and DeLuca (2011) find that there were two groups in this population. One group is people who said the economic barriers were high, had low test scores, and limited family resources. The other group is people who had high academic performance and family resources but who said they preferred to work and earn instead of pursuing a college degree.

In terms of enrollment in college, studies find that there are important differences in college outcomes for students who enroll immediately after high school and those with a delayed start (e.g., Roksa & Velez 2012; Bozick & DeLuca 2005). *Delayers* often come from families with limited resources, have performed lower on standardized tests, and may have dropped out of high school to earn a GED. These students, on average, do not do as well as students who start immediately, and they are less likely to graduate. However, given the differences in their resources, this finding should not be taken to mean that the solution is to start college right away.

Beyond just enrolling, completing college is also dependent upon returning after the first year. The most marked difference is between the first and second year of college (Bozick 2007). Second year return enrollees are less likely to have worked during the first year of college to pay for school-related expenses. They are also more likely to have been able to live on campus, while students who enroll the first year but do not return are more likely to live at home to save money. Thus, the combination of employment and living arrangements predicts who is likely to return for their second year of college, both of which are related to family socioeconomic resources.

But the sorting is not even done yet, among college enrollees there are additional pathways through college that further sort emerging adults and their adulthood trajectories. Armstrong and Hamilton (2013) find that there are at least three visible pathways of college experiences. One is what they call the "Professional Pathway," which is what many faculty and parents seem to think is the only pathway. This group of students is composed of emerging adults who are focused on college as a means for obtaining professional career knowledge and experiences. At the Midwestern public university they studied, the authors estimate this group is about 38 percent of the students, nearly all of whom come from upper-class background. The third group, representing about 28 percent of students, is what they call the "Mobility Pathway" and is composed of students who are striving to have their college experience help them become upwardly mobile, meaning they come from working-class backgrounds and want to have a higher social class than that of their upbringing.

Between these two bookends, Armstrong and Hamilton (2013) find a large (about 34 percent) and visible group of students on campus who they describe as being in the "Party Pathway." Students in the party pathway are those who tend to treat college as an opportunity to socialize and have fun. The authors state that: "the party pathway is built around an implicit agreement between the university and the students to demand little of each other" (p. 15), even subsidized by the university providing land for fraternizing, social organizations.

What is perhaps surprising to many well-meaning faculty and parents is that there are successful socioeconomic outcomes for each of these groups, relative to the distinct occupations for which they are preparing. As would be expected, many of the professional pathway students land high-paying careers in medicine, law, and other high-status professions, and many of the mobility pathway students are drawn to vocational, skills-based majors that prepare them to become nurses, technicians, and teachers. The perhaps counterintuitive outcome for the party pathway students is that they too gain valuable capital in college, just not typically as much of the knowledge-based kind. Instead, party pathway students build massive and strong network ties through their investment in their friendships that translate to successful outcomes in network-based occupations such as marketing and personal relations.

For each pathway, there are also less positive outcomes. Some students in each of the three groups struggle with college or have difficulty gaining returns on the kinds of investments they made in their college experiences. Often these struggles occur by trying to fit in with more than one group simultaneously and having trouble keeping up with either. For example, some professional pathway students get caught up in the social scene—without switching to the majors that group is preparing for—and wind up having difficulties getting into medical or legal schools. Or some mobility pathway students attempt to join one of the two more advantaged groups and either find their school work slips from too much socializing or they face challenges grappling with professional expectations that they were not exposed to during childhood. Likewise, some students in the party pathway find that socializing is expensive, and they are not able to keep up with the alcohol, fashion, or organizational expenses required to maintain ongoing participation. For each of these groups of students, negative outcomes can occur over time by participating in but not having full access to one or the other pathway. These kinds of mismatches help to explain why non-averaged educational outcomes are diverse, even for emerging adults with the same degree.

DEGREES, DEBTS, AND DISILLUSIONS

Goldrick-Rab (2006) finds that there are marked social class differences in how emerging adults navigate the array of college opportunities and make everyday choices that affect which college pathway they are on and what kinds of rewards they will have from it. Likewise, Terriquez and

Gurantz (2015) find that financial challenges can affect whether or not students take what they call *stop outs*—which are periods of time during which previously enrolled students are not enrolled in college, though they have also not technically dropped out given their strong intentions to return to college within a semester or two. Of course, college experiences are also significantly patterned by the amount of student loan debt that emerging adults incur, and the size of these debts are significantly related to the parental socioeconomic resources available to students (Houle 2013; Hamilton 2013).

Studies also find that there are inequalities in educational outcomes based on the combination of age, period, and cohort effects, making it a challenge for universities to well-serve non-traditional students and straight-from-high-school students simultaneously (e.g., Wilson et al. 2011). Stephens and colleagues (2012) find that universities tend to underserve first-generation students—people who are the first in their family to attend college. While numerous studies find that first-generation students tend to perform less well than their peers whose parents went to college, this study finds that part of the explanation for this is that universities heavily stress independence as a middle-class ideal, while many students from working-class backgrounds were raised in families that were more interdependent, relying on each other for help.

All that being said, it is not that only students from disadvantaged backgrounds experience trouble progressing through college. Mangino (2014) finds that increasingly it is white, male students from wealthy backgrounds who complete four-year college degrees at a lower rate than do women, nonwhites, and average-income students. In fact, the study finds that "rich white men as a single category are shown to complete college less than everyone else" (p. 760). However, the author concludes by clarifying that the reason for this is that: "the super-rich simply do not need a college degree to assume privileged status" (p. 780). When parents have non-income-based wealth, it is easier for them to transfer wealth to their offspring through inheritance and other means. Thus, college is especially important for the middle class.

In summary, college acts as a sorting mechanism in several ways, with more and less successful results for students. Some emerging adults want to go to college but do not get in or cannot afford to go. Other students prefer not to attend. Some students get in to college but then do not continue on past the first year, or do return but take intermittent stop outs, primarily due to financial reasons. Of those who do attend, some students live at home to save money, and others live on campus. Many come straight from high school, but some are nontraditional. The majority come from families whose parents attended college, but some are the first in their family to attend. Other students come from such advantaged backgrounds that they do not need a college degree to maintain their resourced positions.

Within the disadvantaged and advantaged ends of the spectrum is a broad array of middle-class students—some aim to experience college as professional preparation, others as vocational training, and still others as an opportunity to socialize and have fun. For every variety of student, there are positive and negative outcomes.

Thus, there is no singular homogenous claim about the role of higher education in the lives of emerging adults, other than that the complex processes involved in college result in students—perhaps unbeknownst to them or their parents—sorting themselves into distinct adulthood trajectories, which persist long into adulthood (e.g., Alexander et al. 2008).

Such inequalities in the pathways through higher education institutions is what led scholars such as Torche (2011) to ask: "Is a college degree still the great equalizer that it was once thought to be?" Political and cultural critics such as Bennett (2013) question the investment returns of a college degree, highlighting the growing and cumbersome expense of student loan debt relative to less-than-clear payoffs on the degree. Additionally, Hanson (1994) finds that nearly a third of emerging adults reduce their expectations for themselves below the signs of talent they evidence, a category which is significantly associated with social class background. Likewise, Hällsten (2010) finds that class differences pattern *educational decision-making*, resulting in class- and education-based differences in perceived *job security*, and leading to what Mullen (2010) calls *degrees of inequality*.

TRANSITIONS OUT OF COLLEGE

In an important book that challenges the higher education system to rethink itself and its role in society, Arum and Roksa (2014) find in a national study that many college graduates are not successfully transitioning into employment that requires or utilizes their college degree. Instead, they recount story after story of college graduates who are back at home living with their parents and struggling to pay back student loans while working in restaurants, as grocery store cashiers, or returning to school to pursue more vocationally oriented courses and degrees, such as nursing. At the same time, some college students made the transition out of college just fine and are now pursuing advanced degrees in science and medicine or working as engineers and teachers. The authors summarize their central focus in this book is to "emphasize the high level of variability in graduates' employment outcomes, living arrangements, relationships, and levels of civic engagement, as well as to illuminate how this variation was associated with different components of undergraduate education" (p. 5). In sum, they say they "describe how colleges and universities were implicated in shaping the lives of these young adults" (p. 5).

As the reading for this chapter highlights, what Arum and Roksa (2014) find is "aspiring adults adrift." While the emerging adults espouse the same optimism that most scholars find in studying young people, they are in the midst of quite complicated lives without a great deal of social support as to how to launch successfully into adulthood. Unlike the popular press, who blame emerging adults for having non-ideal generational characteristics, as if they choose not to grow up, the authors help illuminate how limited opportunities with complex and confused social institutions result in many emerging adults—and their parents—simply not knowing what to do.

READING 5.1

College and Emerging Adults

By Richard Arum and Josipa Roksa

"I can definitely do better," Nathan reported to us in an interview two years after finishing college: "I feel like I'm not using my degree at all."[1] On the surface, it was hard to disagree with him. Although he had majored in business administration, Nathan was living back at home with his parents, had significant college loans to repay, and—like many of his peers—felt lucky to have any job at all. He found his on Craigslist. Nathan was a delivery driver for a national retail chain. He picked up and dropped off items from the warehouse, shuttling materials to local branch outlets throughout the state. He had been working this job for the last six months and had annual earnings of less than $20,000. Nathan also reported to us that his employer had recently cut back his hours and that as a result he was spending five hours per week looking for other employment.

As far as college was concerned, however, Nathan apparently was considered an ideal student. He had graduated on time with a 3.9 GPA. Even so, when we asked Nathan about

---

1 Names of students reported … are pseudonyms used to protect individual confidentiality.

Richard Arum and Josipa Roksa, "College and Emerging Adults," Aspiring Adults Adrift: Tentative Transitions of College Graduates, pp. 1–6, 14–21, 207, 209–211. Copyright © 2014 by University of Chicago Press. Reprinted with permission.

the experiences, events, or occasions at college when he had learned the most academically, he could initially think of nothing to report. After some prompting, he began to tell us about a final project for his business policy class that took "weeks and weeks and weeks of a lot of research." Nathan noted, "Each group was assigned a business and there [were] problems with the business and we had to come out with three different solutions and basically we had to look in every single aspect of this business and prove why our reasons would work." Nathan added that it was in "one of the toughest classes that I actually learned the most."

Nathan, similar to almost all of the graduates we interviewed, was socially engaged in college. "I went to a lot of events and parties and all that stuff," he reported. When we asked what he learned socially in college, he commented, "Not too much actually from college, I guess just hanging out with my friends." He readily admitted that he was what we have previously referred to as *academically adrift* while at college: "Like, when I first started, I really had no idea what I wanted to do. That is why I kind of took business—it was kind of a general thing that could help me with anything. I wish I would have put more thought in what I actually wanted to do with my life." He reported to us that he spent half his time studying at college with friends, and studied alone less than five hours per week. He also reported that he wished he had joined more clubs while in college.

As a college graduate, however, Nathan appeared to be no more engaged in voluntary associations than he had been at college. Aside from voting in the most recent national election, he did little that could be associated with civic awareness or participation. Although he spent his days crisscrossing the state's roadways, he seldom listened to the news. When we asked him how he kept up with current events, he reported, "Basically just the evening news. I read the Sunday newspaper and look at the string on the Internet that interests me." While his engagement with the news and public affairs was limited, apparently it was sufficient—coupled, perhaps, with his lived experiences—for him to conclude that the country was "kind of towards the bottom."

Given that he was struggling with college loan debts, living at home with his parents, and unable to find a job using his college-level education, one would think Nathan and his peers who were suffering similar fates since graduating college would be depressed, angry, or in general despair about the direction in which their lives were heading. However, this was far from the case. While Nathan reported that the country was "kind of towards the bottom," he quickly added that he thought "we're starting to improve." While he was frustrated by his post-college transition, he was hardly embittered. With respect to his college education, he noted that "I put a lot of money on this thing and I feel like I'm not getting much out of it at the moment, *but I think I will in the future*" (our emphasis).

In spite of current difficulties, Nathan and most of his peers believed that their lives would ultimately be better than those of their parents. "Just because I have had more opportunities," Nathan assured us. "That's the way the world is right now." College might not have delivered on all its promises, but one thing Nathan and his peers appeared to have acquired was a sense of social membership and entitlement. They were college graduates, and rewards would surely follow.

Other recent college graduates who were experiencing difficult transitions shared similar sentiments. For example, since graduating from a selective public university with a degree in public health, Sonya was back living at home with her mother. After struggling to find work, she had become a full-time babysitter. Two years after graduating, she was going back to school to become a nurse like her mother. Far from embittered, however, she was upbeat about how her life was going. "I'm very excited about the direction of my life," Sonya told us. "A year ago, I was depressed; I thought the world was going to end because I couldn't figure out what I was doing with my life." She went on to explain, "I guess it's just like my friends who graduated before me always say, that you go through that period of confusion and then you come out knowing, okay, 'This is what I want to do and this is where I'm going.'" Like Nathan, she told us she believed her life would be better than those of her parents.

And consider Alice, who was back living at home after graduating from an elite residential liberal arts college with a humanities degree. She worked as a grocery store cashier. But when asked about the direction of her life, she replied, "I feel generally confident in it." She continued with a statement that trailed off: "I wish I had a little more direction but...." Or consider Lucy, who had been unemployed for months, was deferring payment on her college loans, and was back living at home with her mother. Lucy perhaps captured this sense of undaunted optimism best for the struggling members of her cohort: "I'm feeling OK about the way my life is going. It would be cool if I had a job. I don't know—I'm like, I tend to look on the bright side because I do what I can to change the things I dislike in my life, but I'm not going to hate things that I can't change, because they're going to stay, so I might as well accept them." She, too, expected her life to be better than her parents' lives had been, "in the emotional sense and more likely than not in the financial sense." While almost one-quarter of the college graduates we studied were living back at home with their families two years after finishing college, a stunning 95 percent reported that their lives would be the same or better than those of their parents.

While some graduates in our study experienced struggles in postgraduation transitions, others were flourishing. Consider, for example, Julie, who majored in biology at a highly selective college and found work as a research associate in environmental sciences at a flagship public research university. When asked about aspects of her college education that she was using in her job, she noted that "they run the gamut from specific information that I learned about ecology" to "theories, and ideas, and papers, and research methods." Julie in particular emphasized that at college she had "learned how to think critically about information, what is useful to me and what is not, how to be selective, and I also learned how to manage my time really well." She was living in a house with her boyfriend, whom she had met in college, and a second bedroom in the house was being rented out to bring in additional income. She kept up with the daily news by reading the *New York Times* online and listening to National Public Radio. She reported that she had voted most recently in a local election held a few months prior in the spring.

Or take the case of Michael, who was already married to a woman he reported having met in college, "the first semester I was there, during exam week." Michael and his wife, "now with the housing market as it is," were considering buying a house. Michael had majored in engineering and technology at a selective public research university. Two years after graduating from college, he had already earned a master's degree in engineering and had landed a job in his field of choice. He believed that his undergraduate education had taught him not only specific skills, but how to think. "I can take on any problem now," Michael noted. "Even if I don't know the answer, I know I can figure it out." Michael also credited college with promoting his active involvement with the American Society of Mechanical Engineers (ASME), an activity which connected him to employers and had led to a highly productive professional internship experience. Michael had voted in the most recent presidential election and occasionally kept up with current events by watching Fox News, because he was comfortable with "their more conservative approach."

We also have individuals such as Mindy, who found work as a fifth-grade math and reading teacher after attending a less selective public university and majoring in education. Mindy reported to us that she "spent probably all of my free time doing homework, and when I wasn't doing homework, I was either working or I was in like four or five clubs. All of them having to do with my major as well as a sorority." Mindy had recently broken up with her boyfriend and was living in a rental apartment with a friend. She could not remember the last time she voted, and she kept up with the news a few times a week by "looking on AOL news or like the local paper online."

C. Wright Mills, in *The Sociological Imagination*, argued that sociological research should work to illuminate how social and historical contexts shape individual life trajectories.[2] We will attempt to fulfill that disciplinary mandate by documenting how recent college graduates in our study attempted to make post-college transitions from the spring of 2009 through the summer of 2011, during a particularly difficult period for the US economy. Throughout this book we will take care to emphasize the high level of variability in graduates' employment outcomes, living arrangements, relationships, and levels of civic engagement, as well as to illuminate how this variation was associated with different components of undergraduate education. We will describe how colleges and universities were implicated in shaping the lives of these young adults. Given the character of our data, while we will not be able to identify the effects of college per se, we will be able to provide a rich description of how students' lives varied during and after college—as well as how these patterns corresponded with the majors those individuals chose, the institutions they attended, and the general collegiate skills with which they left college.

---

2 C. Wright Mills, *The Sociological Imagination* (New York: Oxford University Press, 1959).

This book is based on research that tracks more than 1,600 students through their senior year at twenty-five diverse four-year colleges and universities, and then approximately one thousand college graduates from this sample for two years following their graduation in the spring of 2009.[3] The study does not include community colleges, a critically important part of US higher education, because of constraints on the original research design. Given that limitation, we focus our analysis and broader discussion in this book on four-year colleges and universities. We surveyed graduates each spring after college and conducted in-depth interviews with a subset of eighty graduates in the summer of 2011, not just to document their successes and hardships, but also to try to understand the extent to which their post-college outcomes were associated with collegiate experiences and academic performance. To what extent did it matter that students had performed well on an assessment of their general collegiate skills—that is, the Collegiate Learning Assessment (CLA), a measure of critical thinking, complex reasoning, and written communication—around the time they graduated? Was post-college success associated with college majors and the selectivity of institutions attended? And what about the social networks they had spent so much time cultivating and investing in while enrolled in college? Were these social networks helpful, detrimental, or inconsequential in terms of supporting post-college transitions?

Before documenting the different post-college trajectories of the graduates in our study and examining factors associated with variation in these outcomes, we find it useful to first sketch the broad features of the historical context that provides the backdrop for the variation we observed. As a cohort, the individuals in our study enrolled in four-year colleges and universities at a particular time in US history, one in which they faced high tuition, heavy debt loads, and relative institutional inattention to academic learning (as opposed to social engagement and personal development): a historic period when US colleges and universities as a whole, and many of the students enrolled in them, were academically adrift. Many of today's college students graduate, but then transition only partially into traditional adult roles. While the state considers them legal adults, social scientists have come to refer to them with a more open-ended term: "emerging adults."[4] The students in our study also graduated into a particularly difficult and unforgiving economic climate, where often they had little more than their own optimism and a diploma to sustain them in a quest to realize their expectations. In addition to discussing this larger historical and social context, we will provide readers with a brief outline of the ground covered in this volume.

---

3   Eighty-six percent of our sample graduated on time in 2009. For a full description of our methodology, sample, and data, see appendix A in this volume.
4   Jeffrey J. Arnett, *Emerging Adulthood: The Winding Road from the Late Teens through the Twenties* (New York: Oxford University Press, 2004).

Emerging Adulthood and an Unforgiving Economic Environment

How these college graduates truly are and how their life course conditions and outcomes should be assessed is, however, subject to empirical investigation and general debate. One way to assess graduates' life outcomes is to ask whether colleges support their movement towards adulthood. In general, there is agreement from scholars and the larger public on the definition of what constitutes traditional markers of adult status. For example, sociologist Mary Waters and her colleagues have asserted, "In the United States, becoming an adult is achieved when a person takes on a set of socially valued roles associated with finishing schooling, leaving home, starting work, entering into serious relationships, and having children."[5] Transitions to adulthood do not require the accomplishment of all of these conditions, although it is generally assumed (given prevailing social norms) that the majority of them should be satisfied.

Social, economic, and cultural changes in society have led in recent decades to increasing numbers of individuals, including college graduates, not making traditional adult transitions either in their twenties or beyond. Indeed, researchers studying contemporary transitions to adulthood have noted that "much of the pertinent action occurs in the early thirties."[6] Social scientists have documented that "the transition from adolescence to adulthood has in recent years become more complicated, uncertain, and extended than ever before."[7] The likelihood of young adults living at home has increased significantly from the 1970s to today. In addition, the age of marriage has been delayed six years, from an average of age twenty in 1960 to older than twenty-six today.[8]

The reasons for these changes in life course development are complex. For example, some scholars have emphasized the importance of structural factors, such as changes in the economy. In a recent book, sociologist Katherine Newman has argued that "globalization has ensured that the economic conditions that underwrote the earlier, more traditional, road to adulthood no longer hold," and that "new entrants fall back into the family home because—unless they are willing to take a significant cut in their standard of living, the last resort these days—they have no other way to manage the life to which they are accustomed."[9] Other sociologists have emphasized cultural factors that underlie these changes. Christian Smith writes, "The adult world is teaching its youth all too well. But what it has to teach too often fails to convey what any good

---

5 Mary C. Waters, Patrick J. Carr, and Maria J. Kefalas, introduction to *Coming of Age in America: The Transition to Adulthood*, eds. Mary C. Waters, Patrick J. Carr, Maria J. Kefalas, and Jennifer Holdaway (Berkeley: University of California Press, 2011), 9.
6 Frank F. Furstenberg, Rubén G. Rumbaut, and Richard A. Settersten, "On the Frontier of Adulthood: Emerging Themes and New Directions," in *On the Frontier of Adulthood: Theory, Research, and Public Policy*, ed. Richard A. Settersten, Frank F. Furstenberg, and Rubén G. Rumbaut (Chicago: University of Chicago Press, 2008), 18.
7 Waters et al., introduction to *Coming of Age*, 1.
8 Richard Settersten and Barbara E. Ray, *Not Quite Adults: Why 20-Somethings Are Choosing a Slower Path to Adulthood, and Why It's Good for Everyone* (New York: Bantam Books, 2010), 83.
9 Katherine S. Newman, *The Accordion Family: Boomerang Kids, Anxious Parents, and the Private Toll of Global Competition* (Boston: Beacon, 2012), xix–xx.

society needs to pass onto its children." Pointing to the rise of moral individualism, relativism, and consumerism, Smith asserts that "American culture itself seems to be depleted of some important cultural resources that it would pass onto youth if it had them."[10]

While a range of structural and cultural factors have been responsible for changes in the timing of adulthood in our society, one interesting institutional feature that has received less attention is the extent to which individuals, particularly from middle-class social backgrounds, have been spending more and more time in colleges and universities. The extent to which higher education is therefore implicated, not at the periphery but at the core of these changing patterns, is worth emphasizing. As a set of interdisciplinary scholars organized by the MacArthur Foundation and focused on transitions to adulthood succinctly noted, "The hope for and necessity, if not always the reality, of obtaining post-secondary education (or additional training through the military or an apprenticeship) has created the growing gap between the end of adolescence and achievement of adult statuses."[11]

What is accomplished and what fails to be accomplished at college is thus central to the transitions of many emerging adults. This is true for a number of reasons. As an increasing percentage of individuals are going to college and taking longer to complete undergraduate degrees, large numbers of individuals are living for longer periods of time in relatively unsupervised residential halls or independently, as opposed to living under the auspices of parental authority and commuting from home. National studies of college freshmen show a significant decline in the percentage of students living with parents or relatives, from 21.3 percent in 1973 to 14.3 percent in 2006.[12] With the exception of a handful of Scandinavian countries (Sweden, Norway, Denmark, and Finland), undergraduate students in European countries are much more likely to live at home with their parents and commute to college. For example, 75 percent of Italian college students, 55 percent of Spanish, 48 percent of French, and 22 percent of English and Welsh students live at home with parents during their college years.[13] In the United States, students are not only going to college but are increasingly *going away* to college, and are spending longer and longer periods of time there.

Consequently, large numbers of students—for increasing amounts of time—are deeply immersed in collegiate social life; they are embedded in peer climates that sociologists have characterized as "adolescent societies"—or perhaps, given the age of

---

10   Smith, *Lost in Transition*, 238.
11   Furstenberg, Rumbaut, and Settersten, "On the Frontier," 17.
12   John H. Pryor et al., *The American Freshman: Forty Year Trends, 1966–2006*, report of the Cooperative Institutional Research Program at the UCLA Higher Education Research Institute (Los Angeles: UCLA Higher Education Research Institute, 2007), 70–71.
13   Eurostudent IV 2008–11 data series "Form of Housing by Gender and Study Programme," in Dominic Orr, Christoph Gwosc, and Nicolai Netz, *Social and Economic Conditions of Student Life in Europe: Synopsis of Indicators, Final Report, Eurostudent IV 2008–2011*, report of Eurostudent (Hannover, Germany: Eurostudent, 2011).

the students in these settings, what we might call "emerging adult societies."[14] As we have described above, the power of these young adult peer subcultures is enhanced by school authorities, as social engagement with peers is not discouraged but, rather, is institutionally advocated, endorsed, and subsidized. For many undergraduates, college is understood and experienced primarily in terms of social interaction with their peers. Sociologist Michael Rosenfeld observed that "by the 1970s, coeducational college dorms were common, curfews were a thing of the past, and the college campus had become an important site of social and sexual experimentation."[15] For many individuals from middle- and upper-class social origins, the college years begin a period of independence that allows for the exploration of a wide range of life-course pathways. This period of individual exploration and experimentation can last well beyond college as young adults attempt to "find themselves." Researchers studying transitions to adulthood have observed that "growing numbers of young people give themselves an early sabbatical to travel and experience life or engage in a community service project before deciding what they are going to do with their lives."[16]

While overall trends provide useful contours for understanding the transition to adulthood, as well as how colleges are implicated in this process, individual trajectories vary with respect to different components of undergraduate education—including development of general collegiate skills, college majors, and selectivity of the institutions attended—that are potentially associated with students' post-college trajectories. Individual lives also unfold and are profoundly shaped by social background and historic circumstances. In his classic work *Children of the Great Depression*, Glen Elder demonstrated that the cohort of people who had been children during the Great Depression experienced long-term consequences with respect to their subsequent adult careers, marital formation, health, and worldviews. Interestingly, Elder found that while working-class youth suffered long-term negative outcomes from the economic hardships in their lives, middle-class children who experienced economic deprivation but had familial resources as a buffer often assumed greater responsibility for taking care of others, and had largely positive adult outcomes. The consequences of delayed transition to adulthood in general, as well as the difficulties that recent college graduates experienced specifically as a result of the economic downturn, likely vary on the basis of social origins. As Frank Furstenberg and his colleagues have noted about emerging adulthood, "The ability of families to manage this long and complex period clearly varies greatly by the resources they possess or those they can access through formal or informal ties."[17] Whether delayed transitions to adulthood are a cause for concern is thus partially dependent on the extent to which emerging adults have resources that

---

14 See James S. Coleman, *The Adolescent Society: The Social Life of the Teenager and Its Impact on Education* (Westport, CT: Greenwood Publishing Group, 1981).
15 Michael J. Rosenfeld, *The Age of Independence: Interracial Unions, Same-Sex Unions, and the Changing American Family* (Cambridge, MA: Harvard University Press, 2007), 59.
16 Furstenberg, Rumbaut, and Settersten, "On the Frontier," 17.
17 Furstenberg, Rumbaut, and Settersten, "On The Frontier," 20.

allow them to be adrift for a while, before they "find themselves" to lead more directed and purposeful lives.

The college students we followed in our study, who largely graduated in 2009, faced particularly difficult economic conditions associated with the 2007 recession. While they faced dismal economic circumstances that contributed to the labor market difficulties observed in our study, their conditions were perhaps not as dire as some social commentators have argued. Claims in the popular media, for example, featured unemployed and indebted college students joining Occupy Wall Street and suing their colleges for malpractice.[18] Increasingly, commentators were asking whether college was worth it, and often explicitly invoked our prior work to question the value of undergraduate education.[19] In spite of this sometimes shrill commentary, social scientific research on how college graduates fared during the recent economic downturn demonstrated that college-educated young adults continued to experience significant advantages in finding desirable employment, relative to those young adults without a degree. Sociologist David Grusky and colleagues write, "The deteriorating market situation of recent college graduates, while real and troubling, is nonetheless less extreme than that experienced by less-educated groups."[20]

Significance and Measurement of General Collegiate Skills

Our project is unique in that it includes an objective measure of student performance in critical thinking, complex reasoning, and writing as students move through college and then transition into the labor market as well as other aspects of adulthood following graduation. While we are unable to explore the extent to which other, subject-specific, competencies make independent contributions to improving graduate outcomes, our focus on a measure of general collegiate competencies is particularly relevant now, for multiple reasons.

---

18 See, for example, Geraldine Baum, "Student Loans Add to Angst at Occupy Wall Street," *Los Angeles Times*, October 25, 2011, http://articles.latimes.com/2011/oct/25/nation/la-na-occupy-student-loans-20111026; Tamar Lewin, "Official Calls for Urgency on College Costs," *New York Times*, November 11, 2011, http://www.nytimes.com/2011/11/30/education/duncan-calls-for-urgency-in-lowering-college-costs.html?smid=pl-share; and Samantha Stainburn, "Promises, Promises," *New York Times*, October 26, 2009, http://www.nytimes.com/2009/11/01/education/edlife/01forprofit-t.html.

19 See Arum, "Stakeholder and Public Responses," 234: "Since the release of *Academically Adrift* in January 2011, coverage of our work has increasingly come to focus on the issue of college costs and value. A search of news references of *Academically Adrift* in Lexis-Nexis Academic Universe clearly demonstrates this trend. In the first three months following publication, the book received 115 references in indexed sources with 43 percent of these references also including the search terms 'cost!' or 'value.' Over the next six months, the book received 93 news references with 55 percent utilizing these terms; the next six months had 61 references with 64 percent mentioning these terms; and the last six months ending on October 15, 2012, included 54 news references with 74 percent invoking these items."

20 David B. Grusky et al., *How Much Protection Does a College Degree Afford? The Impact of the Recession on Recent College Graduates*, report of Pew Charitable Trusts, Economic Mobility Project (Washington: Pew Charitable Trusts, 2013).

First, there is increasing evidence that generic skills, such as analytical ability, have significant and growing consequences for labor market success. Recent research by sociologists Yujia Liu and David Grusky is particularly compelling in this regard. Analyzing data from several million respondents in Current Population Surveys (CPS) from 1979 through 2010, Liu and Grusky identify different skill requirements required for occupations by applying ratings developed by independent analysts at the Department of Labor as well as by representative individuals in those occupations who were surveyed about this issue. As the CPS data also include earnings reports, Liu and Grusky were able to track changes in the relative payoffs for different types of occupational skills over this time period. These returns can be thought of as the "revealed demand" for various skills, although changes in occupational earnings are also influenced by other institutional factors (such as the decline of unions).[21]

Liu and Grusky demonstrate increases over the past three decades both in the skill requirements of occupations—particularly for computer, creative, managerial, and nurturing skills—and in economic returns for analytic, computer, managerial, and nurturing skills. Some skills, such as creative competencies, which were rising in prevalence across occupations, had negative returns associated with them in general, and were actually experiencing rapidly deteriorating returns over the last three decades, indicating an oversupply of workers with skills suited for "dancers, journalists, poets, sculptors, creative writers, artists, and all manners of associated creative types."[22] On the other hand, increases in returns for analytical skills were particularly striking. According to Liu and Grusky, "Demand for analytic skills may be increasing because (1) they require intuitive problem solving skills that cannot easily be substituted with computer programming or software (unlike quantitative and verbal skills), and (2) the accelerating 'creative destruction' of modern capitalism places a growing premium on innovation, problem solving, and rapid response to changing market conditions."[23] A standard deviation increase in analytical skills was associated with 10.4 percent greater wages in 1980 and 17.5 percent greater wages in 2010. Analytical skills not only had the greatest increase in returns over this time period, but also had high returns overall. Liu and Grusky note, "The defining feature ... of the last 30 years has been a precipitous increase in the wage payoff to jobs requiring synthesis, critical thinking, and deductive and inductive reasoning."[24]

Second, these generic competencies have broad applications; and multiple stakeholders, from colleges to employers, repeatedly assert that they represent core student learning outcomes. While students are expected to develop subject-specific skills and experience affective growth, the development of generic competencies in college has been argued to be increasingly important in the twenty-first-century knowledge

---

21   Yujia Liu and David B. Grusky, "The Payoff to Skill in the Third Industrial Revolution," *American Journal of Sociology* 118 (2013): 1330–74.
22   Liu and Grusky, "The Payoff to Skill in the Third Industrial Revolution," 1359.
23   Liu and Grusky, "The Payoff to Skill in the Third Industrial Revolution," 1357.
24   Liu and Grusky, "The Payoff to Skill in the Third Industrial Revolution," 1332.

economy.²⁵ Generic competencies—such as critical thinking, complex reading, and writing—are transferable across jobs, occupations, firms, and industry; given the broad character of these skills, they likely also have relevance for other aspects of individuals' lives, including citizenship. The potential broad relevance of these skills for individuals and society has led to extensive support for developing these competencies in college. Commitment to these competencies is found in institutional mission statements and faculty surveys, as well as in employer surveys of desirable skills sought in job candidates.²⁶

Third, there is growing concern that the US higher education system is failing to adequately develop generic collegiate skills in its graduates. For example, recent surveys of employers have highlighted dissatisfaction with the preparation of college graduates, noting that only approximately a quarter of college graduates entering the labor market have excellent skills in critical thinking and problem solving, and only 16 percent have excellent written communication.²⁷ "Woefully unprepared" is how one employer described college graduates in a 2012 survey conducted by the *Chronicle of Higher Education* and American Public Media's radio show *Marketplace*. According to this survey, employers tended to "ding bachelor's-degree holders for lacking basic workplace proficiencies, like adaptability, communication skills, and the ability to solve complex problems."²⁸

More troubling still are the recent results of the Programme for the International Assessment of Adult Competencies, a study of adult skills in twenty-three developed countries conducted by the Organisation for Economic Cooperation and Development (OECD). The study measures individuals' ability to understand and use information from written tests; to use, apply, interpret, and communicate mathematical information and ideas; and to use technology to solve problems and accomplish complex tasks. The OECD disaggregated the results by education level, so that it is possible to compare US college graduates to individuals in other countries with similar levels of education. The results for US college graduates on these assessments were not impressive: on most measures they scored below the average of college graduates in

---

25 David H. Autor, Frank Levy, and Richard J. Murnane, "The Skill Content of Recent Technological Change: An Empirical Investigation," *Quarterly Journal of Economics* 118 (2003): 1279–1333; W. Norton Grubb and Marvin Lazerson, "Vocationalism in Higher Education: The Triumph of the Education Gospel," *Journal of Higher Education* 76 (2005):1–25.

26 Derek Bok, *Our Underachieving Colleges: A Candid Look at How Much Students Learn and Why They Should Be Learning More* (Princeton, NJ: Princeton University Press, 2006); Association of American Colleges and Universities (AAC&U), *How Should Colleges Assess and Improve Student Learning? Employers' Views on the Accountability Challenge* (Washington: AAC&U, 2008); National Research Council, *Education for Life and Work: Developing Transferable Knowledge and Skills in the 21st Century*, (Washington: National Academies Press, 2012).

27 Jill Casner-Lotto, Linda Barrington, and Mary Wright, *Are They Really Ready to Work? Employers' Perspectives on the Basic Knowledge and Applied Skills of New Entrants to the 21st Century U.S. Workplace*, report of the Conference Board (Washington: Conference Board, 2006).

28 Karin Fischer, "A College Degree Sorts Job Applicants, but Employers Wish It Meant More," *Chronicle of Higher Education*, March 12, 2013, http://chronicle.com/article/The-Employment-Mismatch/137625/#id=overview.

other countries.[29] In addition, the results were discouraging when considering change for the population as a whole over recent decades. The OECD states that in spite of increasing percentages of adults in the US having gone to college, "there are few signs of improvement. Today, adults in the U.S. have similar or weaker literacy skills to their counterparts in the mid-90s, and the average basic skills of young adults are not very different from older adults."[30]

In addition to new cross-national research on adult competencies, an important development in efforts to measure general collegiate skills in the United States was also undertaken by the Council for Aid to Education (CAE). The CAE brought together leading assessment experts to design an instrument, the Collegiate Learning Assessment (CLA), that required students to perform a task akin to what they might be asked to complete by an employer following college graduation. Students were given a prompt that required them to analyze and think critically about a set of documents, synthesize information across these documents, and then write a logical response that used evidence from the documents to support the arguments being made. Although all instruments that attempt to measure student competencies are by definition limited and imperfect, the CLA was adopted as a reasonable proxy for students' general collegiate skills by a large number of organizations and higher-education institutions. For example, the OECD used a modified version of the CLA for its cross-national institutional Assessment of Higher Education Learning Outcome (AHELO) project, and the Association of Public and Land-Grant Universities (APLU) and the American Association of State Colleges and Universities (AASCU) promoted use of the instrument through the Voluntary System of Accountability project. Other measures which rely on multiple choice questions, such as the Collegiate Assessment of Academic Proficiency (CAAP) and the Proficiency Profile (formerly known as the Measurement of Academic Progress and Proficiency or MAPP), yield similar findings at the institutional or aggregate level.[31]

Additional Motivations and an Outline of the Book

In exploring graduates' life-course transitions after college, and particularly the extent to which different components of undergraduate education facilitate successful transitions, this book seeks to extend our prior research. In *Academically Adrift: Limited Learning on College Campuses*, we joined an existing longitudinal study of several dozen colleges and universities that was being fielded by the CAE and

---

29 The Organisation of Economic Co-operation and Development, *OECD Skills Outlook 2013: First Results from the Survey of Adult Skills* (Paris: OECD Publishing, 2013), see figures 3.9, 3.10, 5.5.
30 Organisation of Economic Co-operation and Development, *Time for the U.S. to Reskill? What the Survey of Adult Skills Says* (Paris: OECD Publishing, 2013), 11.
31 See Stephen Klein, Ou Lydia Liu, and James Sconing, *Test Validity Study Report* (Washington: Fund for the Improvement of Postsecondary Education, 2009), http://cae.org/images/uploads/pdf/13_Test_Validity_Study_Report.pdf; and Ernest T. Pascarella et al., "How Robust are the Findings of Academically Adrift?" *Change: The Magazine of Higher Learning*, May/June 2011, 20–24.

documented the limited learning and lack of academic rigor that large numbers of students experienced during their first two years of college. Specifically, during the fall of their sophomore year, 50 percent of students had no single class which required more than twenty pages of writing over the course of the semester, 32 percent had no class that required more than forty pages of reading per week, and 36 percent studied alone five or fewer hours per week—less than an hour per day. Given this limited educational "treatment," student gains on the CLA were modest. The average student only improved by 0.18 standard deviations, after two years of college—meaning that if, after two years of college, he or she were to take the assessment with a new cohort of freshmen, he or she would move up only from the 50th percentile to the 57th. If the assessment was scored on a scale from 0 to 100, 45 percent of the students would not have demonstrated an improvement of even one point on this measure at the end of their sophomore year. These findings were not likely an artifact of the assessment instrument or the sample in our study, as researchers using data from the Wabash National Study (WNS), which used a different measure of general collegiate skills and followed several thousand students in a different set of schools, found similar results in a replication study.[32]

---

32 Ernerst Pascarella et al., "How Robust are the Findings of *Academically Adrift?*"

READING 5.2

A Way Forward

By Richard Arum and Josipa Roksa

Aspiring Adults Adrift

Our research documents that many emerging adults are adrift, but so too are the societal institutions designed to support and guide their development, including the colleges and universities they attend. The graduates we studied uniformly had developed confidence and optimism in their future. What was often missing, however, was a sense of what it took to realize their goals, as well as the skills necessary for such achievement. Rather than engaging in purposeful exploration, many students as undergraduates, and then later as graduates, were adrift. While prolonged periods of late adolescent meandering perhaps might have few long-term consequences for individuals from privileged origins, the costs for others are likely great.

In this book we have highlighted the many ways in which colleges structure life-course outcomes and are implicated in broader patterns of increasingly delayed individual transitions to adulthood. We have shown how the selectivity of the college attended is associated with a broad range of outcomes, including civic participation and relationship formation.

Richard Arum and Josipa Roksa, "A Way Forward," *Aspiring Adults Adrift: Tentative Transitions of College Graduates,* pp. 133–136, 224–228. Copyright © 2014 by University of Chicago Press. Reprinted with permission.

College majors also matter for life-course outcomes. Perhaps most importantly, however, given our data and original motivation for the study, we have demonstrated that critical thinking, complex reasoning, and writing skills—a set of generic competencies that colleges aspire to cultivate, and which undergraduates are able to develop under the right conditions—have consequences for individuals. Better performance on the CLA assessment, an instrument designed to measure these generic competencies at the end of college, is associated with a lower likelihood of early-career unemployment, unskilled employment, and job loss. These labor market outcomes, in turn, are associated with other transitions, such as living arrangements and financial independence.

Colleges and universities that hope to improve their graduates' early labor market outcomes might embrace a set of different institutional strategies. One approach would be simply to increase the proportion of graduates who major in fields of study that have early-career payoffs, even though some of those curricular tracks have limited academic rigor associated with them, relatively low levels of student development of general collegiate skills (as measured by gains in CLA performance), and possibly inconsistent long-term career trajectories. We believe that such an approach would be cynical, and not in the general interest of students, schools, or society. A second institutional approach would be limited in character, but consistent with our findings. Specifically, colleges could expand career resources and opportunities for students to gain labor market experience through apprenticeships and internships. Cultivating relationships with a wider range of employers and offering more internships and job opportunities would likely serve to improve many graduates' early labor-market outcomes incrementally.[1] However, this focus on enhancing school-to-work institutional supports is not enough, nor is it consistent with our full set of empirical results.

Our findings, overall, suggest the importance of embracing a third institutional approach: enhancing academic rigor and improving student learning not only of subject-specific skills, but also of generic competencies (such as critical thinking, complex reasoning, and written communication). While those committed to traditional models of liberal arts education have long argued that the development of generic competencies is useful for citizenship and for graduates' capacity to live full and meaningful individual lives, we have shown that these skills also have labor market payoffs over and above the specific fields of study chosen. Colleges and universities thus have a responsibility to address the lack of academic rigor and limited learning we have reported. To prevent graduates from continuing to be adrift in the labor market following college, higher-education institutions could do more than simply shift the composition of graduates' fields of study or enhance career support services; they should ensure academic rigor and the engagement of all students, regardless of field of study, to promote positive outcomes in multiple and important domains in

---

1 In light of the fact that funding for colleges' career services offices was cut by an average of 16 percent in 2012, this may be a challenging task. See Andy Chan and Tommy Derry, eds., "A Roadmap for Transforming the College-to-Career Experience" (Winston-Salem, NC: Wake Forest University, 2013), http://rethinkingsuccess.wfu.edu/files/2013/05/A-Roadmap-for-Transforming-The-College-to-Career-Experience.pdf.

their lives. While a student's CLA performance at the point of graduation reflects not just his or her college curriculum, but twenty-plus years of human development, we have demonstrated that colleges indeed can contribute to a student's performance on these measures.

Colleges also could do more to help students develop the attitudes and dispositions they need to reach their aspirations. In chapter 1 we explicitly raised the issue of whether colleges should be concerned with students taking on extensive debt to socialize rather than study in college, only to find themselves underemployed after graduation, living at home with their parents while reporting high levels of individual satisfaction and well-being. As educators, we think they should be concerned. Consumer satisfaction is not a worthy aim for colleges and universities. A century ago, John Dewey wrote: "What the best and wisest parent wants for his own child, that must the community want for all of its children."[2] Colleges and universities need to attend to that vision—not to make schools narrower, but instead to align educational experiences more closely with adult success. Graduating large numbers of students who have attained high grades with little effort and achieved limited improvement in competencies such as critical thinking, complex reasoning, and writing is a disservice to the students who enroll in these schools, the families who put trust in these institutions, and the larger society that will be dependent on the productivity and citizenship of these graduates in the future.

Since the average four-year college student today studies alone a little more than an hour per day, and since a significant proportion of undergraduates do not have courses with either substantial reading or writing requirements, educators need to come together to agree on rigorous academic standards designed to promote both the development of generic competencies and subject-specific content mastery in occupationally related majors, disciplines, or interdisciplinary fields of study. Student exposure to rigorous coursework and high standards might also produce positive changes in the affective domain. College students today are often exposed to institutional settings that reward minimal effort with high grades (students who reported studying alone less than five hours per week had a 3.2 grade point average), and academic dishonesty is rampant and goes largely unpunished. For example, one recent study of students' self-reported cheating on exams at nine colleges and universities found that cheating increased from 26 percent in 1963 to 52 percent in 1993.[3] Given the lack of standards and rigor, it is hard to imagine that a student with limited academic engagement would greatly develop in affective areas such as civic engagement, moral development, leadership skills, and multicultural tolerance, regardless of whether his or her courses focused on Jacques Derrida or John Rawls.[4] Formal courses focused specifically on

---

2   John Dewey, *The School and Society* (Chicago: University of Chicago Press, 1915), 3.
3   Donald L. McCabe, Linda Klebe Treviño, and Kenneth D. Butterfield, "Cheating in Academic Institutions: A Decade of Research," *Ethics & Behavior* 11 (2001): 219–32.
4   Indeed, when researchers in the Wabash National Study of Liberal Arts Education attempted to document longitudinal growth on a number of indicators reflecting components of affective growth and personal

virtues, morality, and ethics are likely to be less effective at promoting desired dispositions, attitudes, and values than are the larger lessons learned and internalized through student experiences with school structure, relationships with educators, and interaction with adult authorities.[5]

Colleges and universities, not just students, have too often been academically adrift in recent decades. As we have attempted to highlight throughout this book, both students and the schools they attend exist in larger structural and cultural contexts that have created the conditions under which the observed learning outcomes occur. Widespread cultural commitment to consumer choice and individual rights, self-fulfillment and sociability, and well-being and a broader therapeutic ethic leave little room for students or schools to embrace programs that promote academic rigor. The serious promotion of student learning, let alone systematic use of assessments to improve academic outcomes, can be seen as a thankless task— especially when students as clients demand, and government resources subsidize and enable, a focus on a different and more easily delivered model of higher education which emphasizes the social aspects of college.

The hard work required to make these improvements will require courage and determination. Many stakeholders, however, have already begun the arduous task of collaborating to define desired competencies, align curricula, develop improved assessments, and commit their institutions to programs to improve student learning. They have taken this path not because it is easy, but because they believe the work will yield valuable individual, institutional, and societal dividends. Their efforts and investments serve as an example to students of how one embarks on purposeful paths of self-improvement.

---

development, little evidence of gains over four years of college were evident. The Wabash Study included well-known measures of moral reasoning (the Defining Issues Test, DIT-2), leadership (the Socially Responsible Leadership Scale, SRLS-R2), and attitudes, cognitions, and behaviors regarding diversity (Miville-Guzman Universality-Diversity Scale, M-GUDS-S). By collecting longitudinal data on students from entry into college through their senior year, researchers using the Wabash data have been able to report value-added measures of these different indicators. The Wabash Study found that most of the affective and personal development indicators showed smaller gains over time than did measures of generic higher-order skills, such as critical thinking. See Charles Blaich and Kathleen Wise, *From Gathering to Using Assessment Results: Lessons from the Wabash National Study*, report of the National Institute for Learning Outcomes Assessment (NILOA) (Urbana: University of Illinois and Indiana University, NILOA, 2011), http://www.learningoutcomeassessment.org/documents/Wabash_001.pdf.

5   James Davison Hunter, *The Death of Character: Moral Education in an Age without Good or Evil* (New York: Basic Books, 2008).

What all this means is that college degrees remain an important aspect of successful adult transitions, often necessary but not sufficient. In addition to college degrees, it is increasingly important that students have *career directedness*—which refers to the combination of aligned ambitions, planfulness, and planful competence (Hamilton & Hamilton 2008). In a book entitled *The Purposeful Graduate: Why Colleges Must Talk to Students about Vocation*, Clydesdale (2015) challenges the notion that talking about vocation has fallen of style:

> What limits students' genuine learning and authentic citizenship is not inefficiencies in colleges' or universities' organizational structure (about which most students are oblivious), but students' dominant orientation to their education. When students view college education as a means to an economic end and not as an opportunity to learn, explore, and investigate the world, even the most efficient college or university will not foster genuine learning or engaged citizenship (p. 203).

Instead, Clydesdale says that universities need to help students figure out their career paths and be planful about preparing for them.

Likewise, Zimmer-Gembeck and Mortimer (2006) find that students today need a better integration across contexts. While it may have been the case in previous generations that students could leave home with a suitcase, arrive at college with careers in mind, and navigate to jobs with long-term employability, promotion, and security (and even that is debatable), that is not the case today. Given the complex social and economic changes that have occurred as the United States and similar countries have mostly moved past an industrial-based economy, emerging adults today need the opportunity to explore a variety of career paths within the protective college context, but without long and expensive years spent in between. The authors conclude that "by forging stronger links between the contexts of work, school, and family, it may be possible to diminish negative influences of work on

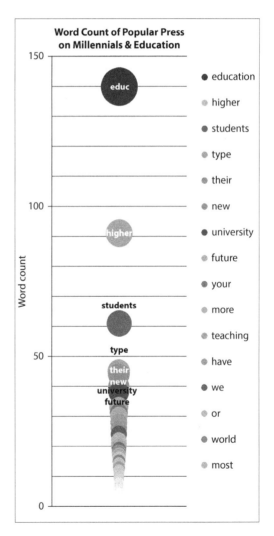

FIGURE 5.1 Millennial Popular Press Word Count

educational achievement, family relationships, and long-term attainment and to promote the positive potentials of employment" (p. 556).

CHANGES TO HIGHER EDUCATION

As with the word count figure described in Chapter 2, Figure 5.1 compiles descriptions of 34 different popular press books on Millennials and their changes to different social settings, in this case, changes in higher education. Not surprisingly, higher, education, and students are the top three most common words. The next three most common words combined as a readable phrase is: "their new university." What is the new university?

Akin to popular press, academic scholarship also reflects a curiosity about the role of higher education in a changing American culture. For example, Selingo (2013) refers to what he calls "the online revolution" and the way it has dramatically altered how emerging (and established) adults navigate their educational experiences. He predicts that massive open online courses (MOOCs) are and will continue to disperse the lecture hall. While academics were initially skeptical about the role of online education, and many still are, Selingo describes results of studies finding that learning is just as good, if not better, in online and hybrid—some classroom time face-to-face and some online—classes. Simultaneously, studies also find that student academic and social involvement is key to retention and promotes meaningful and intensive faculty engagement with students as central to rethinking higher education (e.g., Tinto 2012). All these changes and more lay ahead as the higher education system reinvents itself to better serve emerging adults and their changing social and economic needs.

REFERENCES

Alexander, Karl, Robert Bozick, and Doris Entwisle. 2008. "Warming Up, Cooling Out, or Holding Steady? Persistence and Change in Educational Expectations After High School." *Sociology of Education* 81(4):371–96.

Andres, Lesley, Maria Adamuti-Trache, Ee-Seul Yoon, Michelle Pidgeon, and Jens Peter Thomsen. 2007. "Educational Expectations, Parental Social Class, Gender, and Postsecondary Attainment: A 10-Year Perspective." *Youth & Society* 39(2):135–63.

Armstrong, Elizabeth A. and Laura T. Hamilton. 2013. *Paying for the Party: How College Maintains Inequality*. Cambridge, MA: Harvard University Press.

Arnett, Jeffrey Jensen. 2015. *Emerging Adulthood: The Winding Road from the Late Teens through the Twenties*. 2nd edition. Oxford University Press.

Arum, Richard and Josipa Roksa. 2014. *Aspiring Adults Adrift: Tentative Transitions of College Graduates*. Chicago: University Of Chicago Press.

Bennett, William J. 2013. *Is College Worth It?: A Former United States Secretary of Education and a Liberal Arts Graduate Expose the Broken Promise of Higher Education*. Thomas Nelson.

Bozick, Robert and Stefanie DeLuca. 2005. "Better Late than Never? Delayed Enrollment in the High School to College Transition." *Social Forces* 84(1):531–54.

Bozick, Robert and Stefanie DeLuca. 2011. "Not Making the Transition to College: School, Work, and Opportunities in the Lives of American Youth." *Social Science Research* 40:1249–62.

Bozick, Robert. 2007. "Making It through the First Year of College: The Role of Students' Economic Resources, Employment, and Living Arrangements." *Sociology of Education* 80(3):261–85.

Clydesdale, Tim. 2015. *The Purposeful Graduate: Why Colleges Must Talk to Students about Vocation*. University of Chicago Press.

Côté, James E. and Charles G. Levine. 2000. "Attitude versus Aptitude: Is Intelligence or Motivation More Important for Positive Higher-Educational Outcomes?" *Journal of Adolescent Research* 15(1):58–80.

Crowder, Kyle and Scott J. South. 2011. "Spatial and Temporal Dimensions of Neighborhood Effects on High School Graduation." *Social Science Research* 40(1):87–106.

Elman, Cheryl and Angela M. O'Rand. 2007. "The Effects of Social Origins, Life Events, and Institutional Sorting on Adults' School Transitions." *Social Science Research* 36(3):1276–99.

Gluckman, Max. 1967. *The Judicial Process among the Barotse of Northern Rhodesia*. Manchester, UK: Manchester Press.

Goldrick-Rab, Sara. 2006. "Following Their Every Move: An Investigation of Social-Class Differences in College Pathways." *Sociology of Education* 79(1):67–79.

Hällsten, Martin. 2010. "The Structure of Educational Decision Making and Consequences for Inequality: A Swedish Test Case." *American Journal of Sociology* 116(3):806–54.

Hamilton, Laura T. 2013. "More Is More or More Is Less? Parental Financial Investments during College." *American Sociological Review* 78(1):70–95.

Hamilton, Stephen F. and Mary A. Hamilton. 2008. "The Transition to Adulthood: Challenges of Poverty and Structural Lag." *Handbook of Adolescent Psychology* 2: II: 14.

Hanson, Sandra L. 1994. "Lost Talent: Unrealized Educational Aspirations and Expectations among U.S. Youths." *Sociology of Education* 67(3):159–83.

Houle, Jason N. 2013. "Disparities in Debt: Parents' Socioeconomic Resources and Young Adult Student Loan Debt." *Sociology of Education* 87(1):53–69.

Johnson, Monica Kirkpatrick and John R. Reynolds. 2013. "Educational Expectation Trajectories and Attainment in the Transition to Adulthood." *Social Science Research* 42(3):818–35.

Johnson, Vanessa K., Susan E. Gans, Sandra Kerr, and William LaValle. 2010. "Managing the Transition to College: Family Functioning, Emotion Coping, and Adjustment in Emerging Adulthood." *Journal of College Student Development* 51(6):607–21.

Lareau, Annette. 2015. "Cultural Knowledge and Social Inequality." *American Sociological Review* 80(1):1–27.

Mangino, William. 2014. "The Negative Effects of Privilege on Educational Attainment: Gender, Race, Class, and the Bachelor's Degree." *Social Science Quarterly* 95(3):760–84.

Mickelson, Roslyn Arlin. 2003. "Gender, Bourdieu, and the Anomaly of Women's Achievement Redux." *Sociology of Education* 76(4):373–75.

Mirowsky, John and Catherine E. Ross. 2007. "Life Course Trajectories of Perceived Control and Their Relationship to Education." *American Journal of Sociology* 112(5):1339–82.

Mullen, Ann L. 2010. *Degrees of Inequality*. Johns Hopkins University Press.

Nathan, Rebekah. 2000. *My Freshmen Year: What a Professor Learned by Becoming a Student.* Penguin Books.

Radmacher, Kimberley and Margarita Azmitia. 2013. "Unmasking Class: How Upwardly Mobile Poor and Working-Class Emerging Adults Negotiate an 'Invisible' Identity." *Emerging Adulthood* 1(4):314–29.

Reynolds, John R. and Chardie L. Baird. 2010. "Is There a Downside to Shooting for the Stars? Unrealized Educational Expectations and Symptoms of Depression." *American Sociological Review* 75(1):151–72.

Reynolds, John R. and Monica Kirkpatrick Johnson. 2011. "Change in the Stratification of Educational Expectations and Their Realization." *Social Forces* 90(1):85–109.

Roksa, Josipa and Melissa Velez. 2012. "A Late Start: Delayed Entry, Life Course Transitions and Bachelor's Degree Completion." *Social Forces* 90(3):769–94.

Selingo, Jeffrey J. 2013. "The Online Revolution." In *College (Un)bound: The Future of Higher Education and What It Means for Students*, 86–101. Boston: New Harvest.

Settersten, Richard and Barbara E. Ray. 2010. *Not Quite Adults: Why 20-Somethings Are Choosing a Slower Path to Adulthood, and Why It's Good for Everyone.* New York: Bantam.

Silva, Jennifer M. 2013. *Coming Up Short: Working-Class Adulthood in an Age of Uncertainty.* New York: Oxford University Press.

Stephens, Nicole M., Stephanie A. Fryberg, Hazel Rose Markus, Camille S. Johnson, and Rebecca Covarrubias. 2012. "Unseen Disadvantage: How American Universities' Focus on Independence Undermines the Academic Performance of First-Generation College Students." *Journal of Personality and Social Psychology* 102(6):1178–97.

Stephens, Nicole M., Hazel Rose Markus, and Sarah S. M. Townsend. 2007. "Choice as an Act of Meaning: The Case of Social Class." *Journal of Personality and Social Psychology* 93(5):814–30.

Streib, Jessi. 2015. *The Power of the Past: Understanding Cross-Class Marriages.* Oxford University Press.

Swartz, David. 1997. "Education, Culture, and Social Inequality." In *Culture and Power: The Sociology of Pierre Bourdieu*, 189–217. University of Chicago Press.

Terriquez, Veronica and Oded Gurantz. 2015. "Financial Challenges in Emerging Adulthood and Students' Decisions to Stop Out of College." *Emerging Adulthood* 1–11.

Tinto, Vincent. 2012. *Completing College: Rethinking Institutional Action.* University of Chicago Press.

Torche, Florencia. 2011. "Is a College Degree Still the Great Equalizer? Intergenerational Mobility across Levels of Schooling in the United States." *American Journal of Sociology* 117(3):763–807.

U.S. Department of Education, National Center for Education Statistics. 2015. *The Condition of Education 2015* (NCES 2015-144), Annual Earnings of Young Adults.

Wilson, James A., Christine Zozula, and Walter R. Gove. 2011. "Age, Period, Cohort and Educational Attainment: The Importance of Considering Gender." *Social Science Research* 40(1):136–49.

Wodtke, Geoffrey T., David J. Harding, and Felix Elwert. 2011. "Neighborhood Effects in Temporal Perspective: The Impact of Long-Term Exposure to Concentrated Disadvantage on High School Graduation." *American Sociological Review* 76(5):713–36.

Zimmer-Gembeck, Melanie J. and Jeylan T. Mortimer. 2006. "Adolescent Work, Vocational Development, and Education." *Review of Educational Research* 76(4):537–66.

CHAPTER 6

Finding Work & Establishing Careers

This chapter describes emerging adulthood as it relates to changes to finding work and establishing work in a postindustrial, service and knowledge economy. Many emerging adults do not easily make the transition to stable employment immediately following graduation. In fact, some stay in limbo for a considerable time, often needing to move back in with parents intermittently to make ends meet in the meantime. The studies in this chapter focus on the college-to-career transition for most emerging adults, as well as hearing from employers about what it is like to hire Millennials as emerging adults. Also summarized are the changing values and priorities across generations; explanations for these trends are situated within the conditions of labor markets.

FROM COLLEGE TO CAREERS

The previous chapter discussed the rising expectations of emerging adults and their parents, and how those expectations are often mismatched with job opportunities, leaving many young people disappointed and disillusioned after the long-term investment in education. Murphy and colleagues (2010) interviewed young people about their transitions from college to careers and report the following response from one of the interviewees:

Life in general, I feel almost like I'm in the same place that I was when I graduated, like I haven't really gone anywhere. I've been kind of plugging away at a job, and I guess gaining some experience, but at the same time it's not really applicable to a lot of other industries. I feel that I don't know where I'm supposed to be; I ask myself, Is this how everyone feels? Does everyone kind of go through a lull? I've done a lot of stuff, but I don't really feel like I've gone anywhere (p. 178).

While emerging adults remain optimistic about their futures, they are also beginning to experience some disillusionment—employment experiences often do not live up to their expectations—while facing increasing financial obligations.

What is remarkable is that even at the average age of 25, not even the majority of emerging adults (only 45 percent) have expectations for their occupation at 30 years old that actually align with what they are doing merely five years later (e.g., Rindfuss et al. 1999). Krahn and colleagues (2014) find that "only 13 percent of university graduates had the same employer 1, 3, and 5 years after graduation while 37 percent had a different employer each time" (p.249). At the turn of this century, Csikszentmihalhi and Schneider (2000) found that:

> One of the main differences between growing up at the end of the twentieth century and growing up in generations past is that young people now have less concrete experience with adult occupations. Moreover, the occupations to which they are likely to be most exposed—those of their parents—are probably not the ones they will have (p. 44).

The authors discuss what little access and preparation young people today receive to the kinds of careers they are likely to have. Zimmer-Gembeck and Mortimer (2006) highlight the delicate balance that is needed for young people to gain real experiences while not being overburdened with so much high-intensity work that their educational pursuits are hindered. It seems the ideal is enough exposure to engender *work-driven youth* who have more realistic expectations regarding available employment opportunities and educational options to pursue them. In addition, Clydesdale (2015) urges universities to talk with emerging adults regarding their intended vocations, not in an anti-intellectual, vocational way, but rather by inviting young people to think about the callings that exist and to which they are best suited.

DISGRUNTLED EMPLOYERS

Employers, on the other hand, may prefer a good deal more specific forms of vocational training occur on college campuses. Certainly, a good deal of popular press books and newspaper articles convey the curiosity and concern that employers have about the ways workplaces are affected by Millennial emerging adults. As with the word count figures I have included in previous chapters, Figure 6.1 displays the top words existing in descriptions of popular press books on workplaces and Millennials. Combining the words into a more readable phrase, I gather something along the lines of: "How will they, the workforce of future generations, work with you in the workplace?" This graphic again evidences the curiosity of employers as they grapple with changes ushered

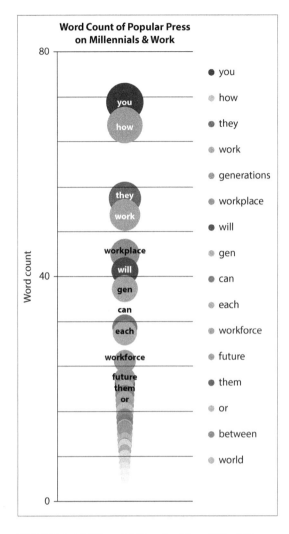

FIGURE 6.1 Millennial Popular Press Word Count

in by Millennials and raise questions regarding the changing workplace as it responds to and is shaped by emerging adulthood patterns.

Sentiments along these lines are conveyed through the voices of 30 different employers interviewed by Konstam (2015). The sectors represented include medicine, education, engineering, law, advertising, nursing, marketing, retailing, psychical therapy, and social services. Managers in these workplaces all talked of issues, even overt conflicts, related to generational diversity in their workforces. As the author states: "management of emerging and young adults has become a popular topic in management training seminars" (p. 161). The author explains: "In a work environment where the rules of engagement are in flux and certitude in short supply, differences in perspective between employer and younger employee bring new tensions to the surface and create possibilities for misunderstanding and resentment" (p. 161).

The kinds of generational differences referred to are typically linked to perceived differences in workplace and life values. Millennials are often labeled as entitled, self-absorbed, self-focused, and having a lack of loyalty whereas Baby Boomers are often viewed as having more organization loyalty, a willingness to put in long hours, and a central part of their identity that focuses on commitment to work (e.g., Konstam 2015). In having these generational misconceptions, employees from different generations can misinterpret each other.

GENERATIONAL VALUES IN THE WORKPLACE

What are the generational values held by Millennials in the workplace? As early as the 1970s, Kalleberg (1977) found trends toward increasing desire for "enriching" and intrinsically meaningful work (e.g., Johnson & Mortimer 2011). Johnson (2002) found that people from higher social class positions tend to place greater value on intrinsic work rewards, which—coupled with the educational trends described in the previous chapter—implies that rising occupational expectations may be part of what explains generational trends in workplace values. Another explanation is a general increase in individualist, as opposed to collectivist, orientations (e.g., Husted & Allen 2008).

While finding a meaningful life has always been a developmental task of establishing adulthood (e.g., Mayseless & Karen 2014), many scholars agree that younger generations place greater emphasis on meaning in the workplace and expect a higher degree of work–life balance (e.g., Schullery 2013; Wray-Lake et al. 2011; Twenge et al. 2010, 2013; Gerson 2009; Grant et al. 2009; Verschoor 2013). Many studies find that Millennials place more emphasis on leisure (e.g., Wray-Lake et al. 2011) and consumptive activities (e.g., Twenge & Kasser 2013). Employers also find Millennials to be more desiring of, or in need of, greater engagement within the workplace (e.g., Schullery 2013) and more inclined to express emotions in their workplace dynamics (Grant et al. 2009).

In the first reading of this chapter, Hershatter and Epstein (2010) summarize:

> The first Millennial college graduates entered the workforce in the summer of 2004. They will continue to do so, in large numbers, until around 2022. To some, they are the next "Greatest Generation," armed with the tools and inclination to drive toward a better future in a world facing economic, geo-political, and environmental crises. To others, they are "Generation Whine," young people who have been so over-indulged and protected that they are incapable of handling the most mundane task without guidance or handholding" (p. 209).

The reading describes a number of generational changes in work values and contextualizes the desires of Millennials entering the workforce within organizational and management perspectives. For example, a *positive atmosphere* was one of the top desires in the workplace for Millennials. They are often willing to accept a job that offers less remuneration if they believe in the non-monetary value of their work (Konstam 2015). This is important to understand from a management perspective, not only because of the cost implications, but also for curbing the incorrect entitlement label Millennials often receive in popular press.

READING 6.1

Millennials and the World of Work: An Organization and Management Perspective

By Andrea Hershatter and Molly Epstein

Abstract

Purpose The purpose of this article is to provide a contextual overview that illustrates and illuminates some of the defining characteristics of the Millennial generation. This study offers a framework for understanding the most compelling issues organizations face in their efforts to effectively incorporate the generation currently entering the workforce.

Design/Methodology/Approach This is a review and commentary that links together current research on Millennials in the workplace into a cohesive narrative, supplemented by several short business case studies and the authors' own research, insights, and experiences working with Millennials in a university.

Findings This article explores the ways in which college-educated members of the Millennial generation approach the world of work, especially in the context of their particular relationships with technology and institutions. Drawing on our experience as educators, we share our observations, along with those of others, highlighting organizational best practices

Andrea Hershatter and Molly Epstein, "Millennials and the World of Work: An Organization and Management Perspective," Journal of Business Psychology, pp. 211–223. Copyright © 2010 by Springer Basel AG. Reprinted with permission.

when we have encountered them. We have grounded our thinking in the context of research and surveys about this population, including our own work, and examined the particular behaviors that seem to be most relevant to the tasks of recruiting, managing, and developing the generation now entering the workforce.

Implications While cross-generational workplace tensions are neither new nor likely to dissipate, we believe that additional insights gained by exploring this complex and sometimes paradoxical generation will facilitate the ability to tap into their many abilities and talents. Additionally, as the tail end of this generation comes of age and a "next generation" population begins to infiltrate the workplace, additional insights regarding likely millennial management styles will be particularly relevant to the talent pipeline.

Originality/Value This article sets aside the question of whether there are genuine differences in values across generations and instead examines two compelling factors that differentiate Millennial behaviors in the workplace. The first is their incorporation of technology as a "sixth sense" and as a fully integrated means of interacting with the world. The second is their expectation of organizational accommodation, stemming from their prior experiences and the degree to which institutions have made themselves malleable to the needs and desires of this cohort. Although much has been written about Millennials in the workforce, this approach provides a unique and nuanced understanding of the genesis of certain sets of behaviors and expectations.

The first Millennial college graduates entered the workforce in the summer of 2004. They will continue to do so, in large numbers, until around 2022. To some, they are the next "Greatest Generation," armed with the tools and inclination to drive toward a better future in a world facing economic, geopolitical, and environmental crises. To others, they are "Generation Whine," young people who have been so over-indulged and protected that they are incapable of handling the most mundane task without guidance or handholding. Still others wonder if they are really very different from other generations, or if the generational moniker and all the media hype it has generated have simply created a self-fulfilling prophecy. As has every generation before them, Millennials have pushed back against type-casting and argue, often convincingly, that they are simply individuals who possess their own agency and personhood and cannot be categorized together by anything more significant than the happenstance of birth-year.

There is no shortage of data regarding the Millennial generation and their values and beliefs. Over the last 10 years, hundreds of surveys have been conducted that have detailed the attitudes, aspirations, and societal and organizational impressions of hundreds of thousands of young people. Depending on the subset of questions considered and the type of survey, it is perhaps not surprising that these data can either support the theory that Millennials are fundamentally unique as compared with other generations, or, alternately, can be read to prove that their perspectives fall nicely along a continuum, marking them as more alike than different from their generational predecessors.

After much study, reflection, and discussion, our strong impression is that this cohort behaves in ways that are readily identifiable, often predictable, and frequently unique to the generation. It does not necessarily follow, nor does the data show that their belief system or values are very different. Despite conventional wisdom, they do not appear to be any more altruistic, family-oriented, or motivated to succeed than those who have preceded them, nor are they any less concerned with making money. However, two over-arching phenomenon typify and define their ways of interaction. First, their relationship with technology has changed the way they know the world, and consequently, how they retrieve, make meaning of, and disseminate information. Second, their deeply-interactive and usually positive experience inside organizations and institutions during their school years and beyond has changed the way they interact with them. For these reasons, managing, directing, and motivating Millennials is a challenge, an opportunity, and a learnable skill. This article explores the ways in which college-educated members of the Millennial generation approach the world of work, especially in the context of their particular relationships with technology and institutions. Drawing on our experience educating and advising this population for well over a decade in the undergraduate business program at Emory University, one as a professor in business communication and the other as faculty member and academic dean, we share our observations, along with those of some of the many professionals with whom we have discussed this topic, highlighting organizational best practices, when we have encountered them. We have grounded our thinking in the context of research and surveys about this population, including our own work, and examined the particular behaviors that seem to be most relevant to the tasks of recruiting, managing, and developing the generation now entering the workforce. While cross-generational workplace tensions are neither new nor likely to dissipate, we firmly believe that additional insights gained by exploring this complex and sometimes-paradoxical generation will greatly facilitate the ability to tap into their many abilities and talents.

Millennials and Technology: Digital Immersion, Content Creation and Engaged Interaction

Perhaps the most apparent difference between Millennials and other generations in the workplace is their distinctive relationship with technology. This should not be surprising. By birth year, the Internet itself is a member of the Millennial generation. The TCP/IP suite that enables the Internet as we know it was established in 1982—the same year the first Millennials were born. AOL, complete with parental controls, emerged when they were seven and served as a first portal for most of them, even though there were fewer than 500 sites on the World Wide Web at the time. These first Millennials were in high school in 1997 when the number of sites reached a million.

Two icons of the millennial lifestyle, cell phones and online social networks, also grew up alongside the generation. The world's first commercial cellular phone, weighing almost two pounds, was introduced when members of the high school Class of 2000 were celebrating their first birthdays: the iPhone emerged as they celebrated their 25th. MySpace was developed in 2003 and Facebook, created by then-Harvard student and millennial Mark Zuckerberg and originally designed for only his Ivy league peers, was launched in 2004, as the first Millennial class prepared to graduate from college. In the current era, members of this generation have emerged as industry disrupters who are not only first-adopters, but also frequently creators of applications that leverage the immediacy of increasingly-visual mobile tech.

Digital Immersion

Since most of these foundational technologies are indigenous to Millennials, they are often referred to as "digital natives," while some of the rest of us, who lived at least part of our lives prior to the development of the Internet and its peripheral devices, feel like digital immigrants. It is interesting to contemplate what value this native familiarity might add to companies as they hire Millennials. Don Tapscott, author of *Grown up Digital*, has interviewed tens of thousands of members of what he calls the "Net Generation" and believes that digital immersion has, quite literally, caused this age group to be wired differently (2009). UCLA neuroscientist Gary Small has mapped actual changes in neural circuitry that develop with the acquisition and repetition of technological skills. Small's research shows significant difference in brain functions among generations, a difference he defines as the "brain gap." For example, digital natives are more effective in some arenas, like multitasking, responding to visual stimulation, and filtering information, but less adept in terms of face-to-face interaction and deciphering nonverbal cues (2008). While these pathways can be developed later in life, and there are clearly many extraordinarily proficient developers and users of the latest technologies in every generation, a marked neurological difference exists between embracing it and embodying it. A brain that developed prior to the emergence of word processing, email, the Web, or social networks must adapt to new technologies in order to use them effectively. On the other hand, Millennials who have been hard wired by technology and for whom it is integral to their academic, social, business and personal lives, don't think about adaptation at all; technology for them is a sixth sense that serves as an indispensable way of knowing and interacting with the world.

Based on their own experiences, Millennials have every reason to assume that all necessary information can be gathered with the touch of a button, or now, a pressure-sensitive screen, on a 24/7/365 basis. If Millennials are asked to investigate a topic, they will turn first to Google and Wikipedia. If they need raw market data, they are able to instantly access extended social networks and obtain immediate feedback. If they want to learn something new, they will find anything from full courses to YouTube videos in bite-sized tutorials. Most who are College-educated are seasoned veterans of ABI/

Inform and can retrieve massive amounts of data on almost any topic in amazingly condensed time periods. Because of the extraordinary investment most universities have made in procuring and licensing electronic resources, Millennials have become accustomed to accessing every scholarly or academic article ever written, instantly and without cost, and they have shown little tolerance for claims of ownership or demands for rent. They present the information they gather in smart classrooms where they move seamlessly from PowerPoint to embedded web sites to user-generated multimedia content. Extraordinarily comfortable with widgets and gadgets, they have not had much experience delivering cohesive, engaging presentations without the benefit of technologically enhanced visual cues.

A workplace filled with young employees who are typical of the Net Generation information gurus described above remains a mixed blessing. While they are often hired to be analysts, there is no particular reason to believe that Millennials are any more adept consumers of the data they retrieve than anyone else and in fact, one can probably assume that their novice status makes them less discriminating than their more experienced co-workers. They often seem to be blissfully unaware that most online sources rarely adhere to any standards of accuracy and validity. When a quick answer is readily available, Millennials sometimes lack the motivation to seek a more in-depth one, and by failing to diligently follow a path of inquiry, they miss perspectives that would enable them to evaluate the analysis of others. They do not worry about response bias when they survey a sample population of their closest friends, nor do they necessarily contextualize the information, charts, and graphs that they so proficiently gather.

While it is true that in most classrooms Millennials are taught to understand the difference between reliable, verifiable data and editorialized content, daily search-and-retrieve behaviors may be too ingrained to overcome. They have been profoundly shaped by a new literacy, complete with different vocabularies and patterns of communication. Mark Bauerlein, professor and author of *The Dumbest Generation: How the Digital Age Stupefies Young Americans and Jeopardizes Our Future*, believes that screen time has eclipsed "great books and powerful ideas and momentous happenings," rendering the younger population incapable of intellectual contribution (2008, p. 234). His is an extreme view, but research clearly shows that this generation reads far fewer books and many faculty members would agree that student research and writing has suffered as the result of a disregard for reading as well as the tendency to trust peer opinion and public consensus over original thought.

On the other hand, David Feldman, a millennial who works in media technology and debated Bauerlein on CNN, shared his thoughts with us.

> My generation started the trend of communicating through blogs and social networks. In turn, every Fortune 500 company has jumped on our bandwagon in order to stay fresh and pertinent in the minds of their audience by creating corporate Facebook pages, Twitter feeds, and regularly updated blogs.

Millennials are so closely watched because of our visual thinking and ability to process information in a much more streamlined and efficient fashion than any previous generation. (Personal communication, September, 2009)

Tapscott agrees, pointing out that Millennials have developed unique abilities as fluent visual thinkers who are extraordinarily gifted at scanning and multi-tasking, but who also have retained, and even honed, the ability to engage in serial focusing (2009, pp. 97–119).

These two viewpoints about generational competencies present an interesting dilemma. Our fast-paced business arena often requires immediacy, including the ability to efficiently retrieve and communicate concise, simplified information. Yet, the complexity of organizations and the environments in which they operate demands a more nuanced, informed framework for analysis and understanding. In order for Millennials to become valued analysts and knowledge workers, they must learn not only what information to gather, but also how to verify and understand it in context. In order to analyze, synthesize, and represent that information in a way that is relevant to the problem at hand, they will need to know more than how to scan; they need to learn to read deeply and between the lines. To do so, they will have to draw on history, books, education, and the theoretical grounding and experience base that older generations can provide.

Content Creation and Engaged Interaction

Perhaps a more intriguing Millennial capacity, particularly among the more educated and economically advantaged members of the population, has to do with the time and inclination they have to create and disseminate content. According to Pew Research Center's measures of social media usage, while 65% of all adults make use of social networking sites, rates of use vary widely by generation. In 2015, 90% of Millennials were on social media, compared to 77% of people age 30-49, and 51% of age 50-64 (Perrin, 2015). In thinking about Millennials' desire to publicly express their opinions, it is noteworthy that one-third of all entering college freshmen have a blog (Pryor et al. 2009). Whether or not they are likely to continue to be prevalent bloggers as they age is still unknown. However, this tendency toward wide-spread dissemination of opinion may be consistent with a population that psychologist Jean Twenge, who refers to them as "Generation Me," has found to be more ambitious, assertive, and even narcissistic than previous generations (2009). Blogging is just one example among the many pieces of evidence that Millennials show strong preferences preferences for using technology to capture, organize, and broadcast their thoughts, opinions, and experiences.

The Millennial on-line experience is also predominantly mobile and increasingly more visual, with 18-24 year olds spending an average of 125 hours a month on smart phone and tablet apps. While Facebook is still the top mobile app for all users, including its rank Millennials who devote 26 hours a month to the mobile site, Instagram and Snapchat now account for 13 monthly hours of Millennial usage (Leila et al.

2015). In spite of many workplace policies governing these personal online activities in the workplace, it is reasonable to assume that at least some Millennials are spending part of their work week using personal mobile apps. Because smartphones serve to provide the technological access that is a natural extension of their sensory experience, to expect them not to use them at work is to ask them to compromise their engagement with the world.

There is growing adoption of workplace applications that attempt to replicate the user-centric experience of personal social networks. Employers encourage new hires to populate and utilize internal networks for a variety of purposes. Studies suggest that use of enterprise-based social media not only facilitates collaborative completion of tasks but also enhances expertise-sharing and strengthens organizational relationships (Subramaniam et al. 2013). There are also many organizations that have successfully used Millennials' proclivities for creating online content to their advantage. Companies that see Millennials as co-developers in marketing and design hold contests inviting young consumers to generate and post commercials or ideas for innovative product use, which are then electronically judged by peers. Millennial customers participate in the creation of consumer goods by designing, rating, and recommending products. In this arena, information, advertising, and entertainment meld together in a millennial style crowd-sourced mashup that perfectly suits the generation's media preferences.

In early 2009, the Walt Disney Company launched Take180.com, a pioneering experiment in collaborative story telling that created episodes of its featured shows based on audience submissions. One show, entitled My Date, invited viewers to kiss and tell by submitting their best and worst date stories. The show co-starred actor Brian Ames as love interest Ben. Brian, who has also starred as a video-game action hero, is very comfortable acting on an interactive stage. "It was a pleasure working in a medium that facilitated customer interaction," he told us. He continued,

> It provided our team with a consensus of how viewers perceived our characters and insight as to where they wanted the story to go. As part of that creative team I found it appealing to tailor a piece for our audiences' expectations. From a business perspective, the interaction/collaboration with the customer ensured we were fulfilling their needs. (Personal communication, September, 2009)

Take180 lasted approximately three years and generated over 100 million video views. Studies suggest that these early efforts were on the right track. A survey conducted as a partnership between Barkley and the Boston Consulting Group found that Millennials were twice as likely to upload content to the web and four times more likely to have a blog than non-Millennials (Fromm et al. 2011). In recent times, Millennial vloggers have emerged as celebrity taste-makers who not only influence consumers but also shape product offerings in categories ranging from food to fashion to travel. While the time and the desire to fully embrace creative digital outlets might be a function of age, at the moment, companies wishing to build loyalty among

Millennials may find that experiential co-creation is a particularly effective means of doing so.

Engaging Millennial employees and consumers through the media they prefer, and with content they will appreciate, raises the same challenges as any other organizational attempt to reach a specific target audience with an appropriate message. In the case of Millennials, because they are so likely to use a wide variety of media on a frequent basis, matching the format to the message becomes particularly important. Younger workers obviously use traditional email to communicate when it is the norm in their workplaces. In fact, there is no real difference between the 91% of Millennials online who use email as compared with the 93% of Gen Xers and the 90% of adults age 50-64 who do so (Zickuhr & Smith 2012). However, Millennials are by far the most likely of any age cohort to embrace texting as a regular mode of communication, with 75% of teens texting (Lenhart 2012). To more effectively reach this elusive generation, organizations ranging from high school teams to fraternities to global businesses are experimenting with group text messaging services like Tatango, founded in 2007 by 22 year old Derek Johnson as a way to help his friend communicate with her sorority sisters ("Interview with Derek Johnson" 2009). By 2016, the organization was growing along with texting's popularity, serving 1000 brands and agencies. Text has the advantage of being simple and timely, and falls nicely into the spectrum between phone calls and emails as a means of interactive, relatively immediate, but not necessarily intrusive, communication.

Beyond text and email, companies wishing to engage this generation should also rethink use of the web in terms of interactivity, visually appealing interfaces, and opportunities for personalized interaction and co-creation. The web, by definition, is non-linear, and Millennial navigation will naturally follow neural, rather than sequential, patterns (Tapscott 2009, pp. 104–109). Circuitous routes with collaborative touch points and ample use of multi-media—all aspects that might distract or annoy members of other generations–are intriguing and comfortable to Millennials. As technological devices, web-based search capacities, and web enabled mash-ups continue to evolve, Millennials, as early adapters of emerging technologies, may have an advantage in instinctively understanding and building upon their potential applications. Just as members of GenX created Google, Amazon, and Wikipedia, Millennials are next in line to develop the organizations that capitalize on the power of emerging technologies and applications. In addition to Mark Zuckerberg, founders Evan Spiegel, of Snapchat, Pete Cashmore of Mashable and David Karp of Tumblr are all Millennials.

Like many other Millennial propensities, major challenges come with these opportunities. Currently, Millennials use blogs, reviews, social networks, and created content to endorse, recommend, and share, but also to reposition, vent, and complain. Companies should be forewarned that content co-creation is an anarchistic process that cannot be controlled at the corporate level. This format yields an interesting paradox; some of the companies that have most aggressively attempted to create experiential technological interactions for this generation are also those that most vigilantly protect the use and placement of their company names and products. It is a little like handing the keys to a Porsche to a 17-year-old boy and then telling him he can only drive on carefully designated roads, and within speed limits.

Millennials and Organizations: Millennial Meritocracy and Supporting Structures

While technological developments have played a primary role in shaping the ways Millennials learn, interact, and communicate, changes in the ways societal institutions think about and treat the youngest demographic group have had a no less profound impact on the Millennial mindset. Starting in their earliest years, U.S. Millennials were revered, sheltered, and protected by a nation with Boomers at the helm, who seemed suddenly aware that home and school had failed Generation X.

In 1983, four years before the first Millennials entered kindergarten, a national commission report on education, also positioned as "an open letter to the American people," described an educational system in crisis and a "nation at risk." The seminal report detailed widespread illiteracy, declines in standardized test scores, diluted curricula, and a severe shortage of qualified teachers, and then advocated for broad academic reform, standardized measures, and increased fiscal support (National Commission for Excellence in Education 1983). The report's recommendations and the effectiveness of their implementation continue to be the subject of debate. Nevertheless, there is no question that "A Nation at Risk," thrust educational policy into the national spotlight, legitimized a heightened role for the federal government in school systems, and spawned two and a half decades of reforms, ranging from the accountability movement to the No Child Left Behind Act.

Similarly, since the first Millennials could walk, the Federal government has played the role of an over-protective Uncle Sam, activating federal agencies to assure that cars, products, homes, schools, and airwaves were safe zones for them (Howe and Strauss 2000, pp. 112–113). As a consequence, Millennials have an inherent trust in organizations and a strong preference for the structures and systems that support them. Research shows that they are more confident in businesses, financial institutions, and government than other age cohorts and than other generations were at the same age (Levine et al. 2008). Longitudinal data gathered across more than 800 students attending four universities confirm these findings. Sixty percent of Millennials enrolled as business students agreed with the statement, "I trust authority figures to act in my best interest," while only forty percent of Gen Xers agreed with this statement when they were in business school (Epstein, n.d.).

Millennial Meritocracy

Millennials' trust in institutions assumes and relies upon an equitable system, one that assures that industriousness and accomplishment will be rewarded with acknowledgment, encouragement, and access. They have always felt loved and wanted by their doting parents, guided and cared for by teachers whose training included the importance of building self-esteem, and desired by corporate recruiters. Members of other generations, especially Gen X, who are acutely aware that life is rarely played on a level field, may describe them as entitled, but Millennials view themselves as pressured and high achieving and have grown accustomed to supportive, nurturing environments that provide them with every opportunity to succeed. During the 2000–2001 academic year, journalist David Brooks followed the first Millennial class to college at Princeton and wrote about their activities, attitudes, and aspirations. In the years of peace and prosperity before September 11, Brooks documented this academically gifted, authority minding, optimistic cohort and branded them the "meritocratic elite" (2001). Of all descriptors that pertain to the young employees now delighting, frustrating, and perplexing their supervisors, this term seems to be the most accurate.

Securing a place among the elite requires Millennials to progress through an increasingly narrow siphon. At each life stage, they have had to compete for a fixed number of highly selective and sought-after spots that have not increased quickly enough to meet record demand. As a result of the sheer size of this population of 80 million, as well as the fact that an increasing percentage of students from lower economic strata, first generation college students, and under-represented minorities are now attending college, in 2015, a record 1.5 million students took the SAT, up 13% from just seven years earlier (College Board 2015). Even before they were born, their proud, expectant helicopter parents were warned by their peers and the media to start planning for their futures, starting with pre-school. Among the more affluent, this head start was part of a trajectory to position children for admission to the best prep schools, in the hope that doing so would inevitably lead to enrollment in the nation's most highly selective colleges and universities. At the same time the oldest college-educated Millennials were beginning to enter the workforce the youngest members of the generation were entering kindergarten. According to a 2006 Nightline story, competition was so fierce among Manhattan private schools that an average of fifteen applicants competed for each available spot. One parental applicant was quoted as saying that gaining admission to the 92nd Street Y pre-school was more difficult than getting into Harvard (Bashir 2006).

In all economic strata, the higher the difficulty of access, the more pressure there is on institutions to live up to the hype that surrounds them. Parents who make sacrifices in order to move to more expensive neighborhoods located in desirable school districts, or who pay tens of thousands of dollars each year for private school education, tend to behave more like customers than like partners in the educational process. Educators over the last 20 years have faced increasing demands for better facilities, more cutting-edge technology, extended extra-curricular activities, lower student/teacher ratios, and a complete array of AP classes. In some cases, the emphasis on assuring that students achieve credentials and high grades eclipses scrutiny of actual academic content. These same parents expect their children to capitalize on every opportunity presented to them by earning the grades, varsity letters, leadership positions, debate trophies, and AP credits that the best colleges seek. Parents may coddle and protect, but they also nurture the implicit expectation that the advantages bestowed on their Millennial offspring will yield returns.

Of course, the elite, by definition, are a relatively small group. Only 66% of recent high school graduates enroll in college (National Center for Education Studies 2014) and the most competitive among them seek admission to just a small handful of schools. Although *U.S. News and World Report* annually rates more than 1,400 colleges and universities, most of the furor surrounding admission focuses on the twenty national universities that had an acceptance rate of less than 22% in 2015 ("America's Best Colleges 2016" 2016)

Among other reasons, many college-bound Millennials are anxious to attend the most prestigious school to which they are admitted because they see a strong correlation between the status of the school from which they graduate and the best job opportunities. Since 1977, only "very good academic reputation" has ranked above "graduates get good jobs" as a very important reason to attend a particular college. In addition, incoming freshmen value "prepares you for a career or profession" over any other purpose of a college education (College Board and Arts and Sciences Group 2008) and the largest number of graduate degrees are in business, with only half as many degrees awarded in the social sciences and history (National Center for Education Studies, 2012). Recruiters fuel this mentality, creating discriminating lists of 'target schools,' utilizing cut-off GPAs for job applicants, and reaching out to high performers with internship offers as well as special training and immersion programs, sometimes as early as the summer after freshman year.

It is therefore not surprising that members of this high-achieving, pressured, and sometimes privileged group of graduates are well represented among young professionals hired by thriving business organizations. As thought and opinion leaders among their peers and as role models upon whom the national media spotlight frequently shines, their attitudes and behaviors are transmitted to, as well as emulated by, others who aspire to reach the same levels of success. This suggests that even if they are not wholly representative of their generation, the elites' interactions with organizations set normative expectations—both positive and negative—and influence corporate beliefs about the best way to recruit, retain, and motivate Millennials.

Supporting Structures

Just as secondary schools and universities have alternately resisted and accommodated Millennial preferences for organizational interaction, so too do corporations seek to strike the right balance between expecting Millennials to adapt and adapting the organization to better suit them. Millennial preferences for systems and structures present one of the largest challenges for organizations. A common complaint among college professors is the degree to which current students seek clarity and detail in course assignments. Any elements of ambiguity, or any project or exam that requires Millennials to work without guidelines, templates, or examples, results in a great deal of angst, because they have not had much practice producing without explicit instructions, well defined criteria for success, and specific deadlines set by others. One result of legislation like the No Child Left Behind Act is that schools have frequently adjusted curricula and assessments to assure maximum success on standardized exams. This practice, coupled with parental demand for transparency in grading criteria, has meant that Millennials expect very clearly outlined, objective rubrics and well-defined expectations.

Universities strive to teach students to deal with uncertainty and faculty push them to follow lines of intellectual inquiry rather than adhere to outlines of class lectures. Nevertheless, it is an uphill battle. Professors who do not provide practice exams, who neglect to outline clear guidelines for successful grades, or who fail to create objective testing measures not only receive lower teaching evaluations but also may find themselves described as "arbitrary" or "unfair" on ratemyprofessors.com.

Millennial preferences for clarity and certainty do not evaporate at graduation. The Global MBA Survey of more than 5,600 students enrolled in MBA programs confirms that Millennials prefer to work in organizations with centralized decision-making, clearly defined responsibilities, and formalized procedures (Graduate Management Admission Council 2007, p. 20). Nearly three-fourths, or 72%, agreed with the statement, "I prefer a structured environment with clear rules," as compared with just 33% of Gen Xers (Epstein, n.d.).

From the perspective of the executive suite, employees who prefer stability, structure, and authority are highly desirable. Millennials naturally align themselves with the kind of objectives outlined in strategic plans: they are optimistic about the future of their companies, they value teamwork and community, they want to engage with customers, and they care about corporate missions and objectives. Seen through the right lens, they are proven change agents who are committed to enhancing the organizations and communities in which they operate. In 2000, when Zemke, Raines, and Filipczak wrote *Generations at Work*, they could barely contain their enthusiasm for the young people who were just coming of age. "At first glance, and even at second glance, Generation Next may be the ideal workforce—and ideal citizens—and generally the kind of kids you'd want dating your son or daughter," they wrote (p. 143).

However, seen through another lens, Millennials have turned out to be not quite as positive an organizational force. Some younger workers who believe in the big organizational mission are also prone to wanting to choose the specific tasks in which they will engage and the conditions under which they will engage in them. Not surprisingly, this is a source of management frustration, predicted in part by the authors of *Generations at Work*. In acknowledging what they perceived as major differences between Millennials and Gen Xers, they cautioned that the rising generation might grow up to be "a very demanding workforce" (p. 145).

Millennials and Careers: Feedback and Clarity, Work and Life, Employer Relationships, and Institutional Loyalty

Feedback and Clarity

Some managers might argue that "demanding workforce" is far too kind a phrase for Millennials. While the largely baby-boomer population ensconced in the upper echelons of companies are happy to sing Millennial praises, those involved in day-to-day management hear a different tune. Managers of Millennials frequently describe their employees as "high-maintenance" or "needy."

Interestingly, recent research has shown more workplace affinity between Boomers and Gen Y than between Gen X and either of these two generations. (Gen Y is identified in the research as starting with those born in 1979, 3 years earlier than the typical Millennial definition.) A study conducted among 50 multi-national companies by the Hidden Brain Drain Task Force looked at goals and workplace preferences among employed college graduates and "high echelon talent" across age groups and found Gen Y/Boomer commonalities with respect to work–life balance, commitment to giving back to society through work, and desire for sabbaticals and flexible working arrangements. The fact that these values are not shared to the same extent with Gen X may simply be the result of life stage, but the *Harvard Business Review* authors find the numbers compelling. They point to programs like reverse mentoring that pairs technologically proficient Millennials with senior manager Boomers, who not only learn from, but also greatly value, the connection. The feeling is mutual. More than 75% of Gen Y report that they enjoy working with Boomers and more than 58% say they turn to Boomers, instead of Xers, for mentoring and advice (Hewlett et al. 2009).

Managers of all generations may find the Millennial need for structure and reassurance draining. As trophy kids who spent their childhood receiving gold stars and shiny medals just for showing up, Millennials were indoctrinated from their earliest moment to seek approval and affirmation. In the workplace, this has led to a sometimes excessive propensity to continuously seek guidance and direction. Managers therefore often find themselves in the unenviable position of having to spend a disproportionate amount of time managing people who were presumably hired to help them. W. Stanton Smith, national director of Next Generation Initiatives at Deloitte, shares a story that illustrates this tension:

> [The CEO's] managers were complaining vehemently that they couldn't get any work done because young staff members were constantly interrupting them. The CEO listened patiently and then said, "Ladies and gentlemen, you are well paid to be interrupted. How else are they going to learn? I don't want to hear about how someone isn't developing and later find out it was because you weren't answering their questions (Smith 2008).

This anecdote highlights two factions: one represented by a senior executive, who embraces the idea of bringing young talent into the organization but does not have to directly deal with some of the more frustrating Millennial behaviors, and the other, represented by the more direct managers, on whom the burden of sharing expertise and supporting the learning process falls. It may be helpful for supervisors dealing with similar challenges to envision their Millennial charges, wearing the ubiquitous helmets of their childhood, learning to ride bicycles. Instead of letting new workers crash to the ground and emerge bruised and frightened to try again, managers who slowly but surely take off the training wheels will find that when they eventually let go, Millennials will ride on their own.

This practice works in the classroom. As educators, many of us prefer to invest initial time and energy into providing assignment guidelines and outlining expectations as a means of coaching Millennials through their first assignment. As the semester progresses, students feel comfortable riding on their own. In the same manner, those managers who have the patience to provide early guidance and appropriate feedback may find that the total expenditure of time spent supervising projects is actually less than if they continuously, and grudgingly, respond only when absolutely required.

Of course, some managers would prefer to think about swimming rather than bicycling. Their tendency is to take off the Millennial water wings, throw them in the deep end, and see if they drown. After all, that is how all previous generations were treated. However, "sink or swim" does not sit well with Millennials, who learned to float surrounded by buoyancy devices and cheering parents and coaches. For this generation. there are organizational advantages to a more structured and accommodating approach. Becki Lindley, a pre-venture capital firm principal at Cobalt Investments, recently shared how she frames assignments for her Millennial interns:

> There is no clear answer here—no correct answer. The purpose of this project is for you to identify and analyze options. Then you will make recommendations based on your research. First, conduct research using x, y, and z. Next, organize that research into compelling arguments for and against this project. Then, present this information to me in an executive summary that you will present to me verbally. (Personal communication, September, 2009)

In her experience, when she clearly framed the assignment outcomes and acknowledged the ambiguous nature of the project, her interns provided her with outstanding analysis and recommendations.

In "The Trophy Kids Grow Up," *Wall Street Journal* writer Ron Alsop relates similar ways in which companies are trying to help Millennials deal with what he calls "the gray areas of life." While all newcomers to the workforce experience transition issues, leading employers report making specific accommodations to help Millennials grapple with uncertainty and overcome aversion to risktaking. For instance, Fidelity Investments screens its interns to identify those who can think creatively and then encourages its hires to take more initiatives. Boston Consulting Group provides additional training for Millennials who have trouble dealing with the ambiguity that is inherent in client assignments. In response to recruiter comments about Millennial struggles with gray areas, many MBA programs have instituted new courses that give students practice with problem solving in less structured, more uncertain environments (Alsop 2008, pp. 125–138).

Work and Life

Millennials seek ample feedback because it provides assurance that they are continuing to move along a linear, progressive path. Almost every high school counselor's office features some sort of college preparation timeline that lets students know at a glance exactly what they should be doing at every moment to remain on track for college admission. Universities use the same kinds of graphics to outline student progress toward careers or graduate school. Millennial employees thrive in organizations that similarly create a clear path to success by identifying employees' ideal skills, creating realistic timelines for promotions, and detailing career progression (Epstein and Howes 2008, p. 3).

Chesapeake Energy, #26 in the *Fortune* "2013 100 Best Companies to Work For," is a young company in the field of natural gas. Their employees are young too: as of 2010, 50% of employees at headquarters were under 33 years old. To retain and embrace talented Millennial employees, and assure that they work well within the Chesapeake environment, the organization created several programs to ensure that members of all generations stay engaged (Martha Burger, Director of HR at Chesapeake Energy, telephone interview, July 17, 2009).

Even, or perhaps especially, in the face of falling oil prices, the company in 2016 remained focused on attracted young talent by offering a collaborative work environment, generous paid vacation, pay-for-performance incentives and a 72,000 square foot fitness center. In the geology department, Chesapeake first acknowledges and then transcends generational differences through a mentor training program. The rationale is that these relationships help managers assure their legacy and practice a more personal leadership style, while providing Millennial mentees with a supportive environment that enhances career progression, institutional knowledge, and visibility. In addition to addressing generationally specific concerns, this training addresses personality styles that transcend generations by using the Meyers-Briggs MBTI® to coach mentor and protégé based on individual preferences (Chesapeake & Performance Consulting, n.d.).

Recent trends in the energy sector led to workforce reductions at Chesapeake in 2015. In this environment, incremental compensation or accelerated career progression are unrealistic incentives to offer Millennial hires. However, as many companies learned during the recessionary period of 2007-2010, there are ample alternative means of motivating a Millennial workforce.

While employees of all generations desire work–life balance, Millennials may have the confidence and conviction to demand it from their employers

PricewatershouseCoopers reported that 71% of their millennial employees said their work interferes with their personal lives (2013a). Perhaps after observing their overworked parents, Millennials seek to adjust expectations of hours and boundaries. As students who are contemplating employment, 27% of them stated that their #1 career goal was to "balance personal and professional life" (Universum Incorporated 2008). They are more likely than previous generations to make career choices that provide a balance between security and stability and healthy work–life balance (GMAC 2007 and 50% of them want more vacation time while 61% desire more flexible schedules (Grovo 2015). In the Brain Drain study, 87% of Millennials say work–life balance matters, and significantly, 53% of those who take a work deferral or a sabbatical use the leave to "explore passions or volunteer" (Hewlett et al. 2009). This may be one factor influencing the trend toward public sector jobs, including work for the government and non-profit organizations.

The value that Millennials place on work–life balance comes from both personal observation and societal shifts toward more focus on families. Millennials observed, and often experienced, the balance sacrifices their Boomer and Xer parents made to achieve corporate success; many of them spent long days in childcare or aftercare programs while their parents put in the required "face time" at corporate jobs that lacked flexibility. As a result, even Millennials who are unmarried and have no children worry about family time when entering new jobs. In a survey that measured priority placed on work versus family, the first wave of Millennials was only 60% as likely as Boomers to describe themselves as "work-centric," and were 9% more likely to describe themselves as "family-centric" (American Business Collaboration & Families and Work Institute, 2002). In more recent times, about a third (26%) of Millennials reported finding it difficult to balance work and family life (Ernest and Young 2015). While these values may evolve over time, the overwhelming evidence is that Millennials have remained more family-oriented in terms of their relationship with their own parents than previous generations of college students.

Technology facilitates the work–life balance Millennials desire because it frees employees to work at a time and place convenient to them. In *Fortune's* list of "100 Best Companies to Work For," all of the top 10, and 22 of the top 25 companies allow employees to telecommute ("100 Best Companies," 2016). Telecommuting has the additional advantage of being an environmentally friendly approach and is consistent with Millennials' affinity for technological solutions. On the other hand, before embracing long distance work relationships, companies should think carefully about how to assure accountability, as well as how to address this population's need for frequent face-to-face interaction with peers and supervisors.

Employer Relationships

Beyond their desire to move forward in their careers and to maintain a full personal and family life outside of work, Millennials have a set of strong convictions about what the relationship with employers entails. In the fall of 2006, we assigned 150 students to conduct interviews with peers from outside their own university regarding their hopes, dreams, and aspirations. Responses to what these Millennials expected from the work environment were particularly notable in their similarity to each other. "My employer should provide me with job security, a good work environment, and a positive atmosphere," one interviewee said. "I will find a place I know is a good fit for me where I'm challenged but not overstressed." Another sought "the environment to learn, and the opportunity to better myself, both in terms of my career and my ability to help those in need" (Hershatter 2007).

The interviewed students were no less detailed with respect to how they perceived their future bosses. A young woman hoped for "a safe work environment, reasonable hours, and flexibility. If you ever need anything," she added, "you should be able to go to your employer and talk about issues you may have." Another respondent was even more specific, "He should be honest and open minded. He should be able to guide and should be a friend and co-worker". (Hershatter 2007).

While these may seem like extraordinary demands to put on a workplace, it is worth remembering that throughout their lives, Millennials have been encouraged to have, and continue to maintain, similarly close relationships with parents, teachers, mentors, and advisors. As a result, they are much more likely than Gen X to want their supervisors to take an interest in them; 66% of Millennial business students agreed with the statement, "I prefer personal relationships with my bosses," while only 52% of Gen X students agreed (Epstein, n.d.). More significantly, 58% of Millennials agreed with the statement, "When I need special treatment I feel comfortable approaching my bosses and asking for help." This is in stark contrast to the response of Gen Xers, only 31% of whom agreed with this statement (Epstein).

The difference in these preferences creates an intergenerational conflict that is further exacerbated by the fact that Millennials typically enjoy a strong and productive relationship with Boomers, who may see in them the fulfillment of their own legacies (Hewlett et al. 2009). Coupled with this natural affinity is the Millennial expectation of a flat hierarchy and access to senior leadership. It is therefore not surprising that organizational tensions may occur when new hires circumvent the system and go immediately to the top to vent their frustration, vet their ideas, and build relationships. More than one direct manager has discovered with horror that their new Millennial employee has a lunch or golf date with their boss's boss.

The challenge presented by Millennials who move freely across levels of the organization has also been faced by universities. Neither schools nor employers want to dampen the enthusiasm of those who genuinely desire to have a positive impact on the organization. On the other hand, organizational structures provide not only accountability, but also protection for more senior managers so that they are free to focus on higher-level issues. One proactive approach is to build occasional opportunities for hierarchyskipping interactions into the system. In doing so, it is possible to emphasize the chain of command, proper protocol, and the process for bringing ideas forward, while providing an approved forum for Millennials to reach up through less formal interactions like town hall meetings.

Another means of creating an appropriate vehicle for Millennials to interact with higher levels of the organization is through mentoring programs. These relationships have been shown to be effective at socializing employees, enhancing career paths, and building institutional networks for every generation, but Millennials are the first population to have been fully immersed in mentoring programs throughout their lives, starting with "big buddy" programs in elementary school. Mentor/protégé relationships can also be extremely fulfilling for members of the Baby Boom generation, who are typically at levels of the organization where they can enjoy the interest of a younger generation without feeling the conflict of potential job competition.

One organization making particularly good use of such a program to engage and develop their Millennial employees is the CIA, rated #37 by *Business Week* in their *Best Places to Launch a Career, 2008* (Gerdes 2008). General Michael V. Hayden, USAF, states, "Only if we mentor effectively—only if we teach our new recruits *and learn from them*—will we achieve the objectives of our Strategic Intent, CIA's blueprint for the future" (Hayden 2007, emphasis added). The CIA defines mentoring as, "a unique developmental relationship… built on mutual respect and trust that fosters the growth and development of all participants" (CIA, n.d.). They identify mentee benefits as increased knowledge of the culture, enhanced professional development, and an improved network with senior leadership. The CIA's three-level mentoring program—one-on-one, group, and peer-to-peer—provides Millennials with the guidance they desire and the format in which they can share ideas and lead others. This program has been incredibly effective. The CIA reports a retention rate of 94%, a particularly impressive figure because the CIA salaries are significantly lower than many of the others on the "Best Places to Launch a Career" list (Gerdes 2008).

Institutional Loyalty

Millennials who feel valued, looked after, and appreciated respond with loyalty, at least in theory. Members of the generation envision symbiotic relationships with the organizations that employ them—they are loyal to organizations that are loyal to them. In the pre-recessionary period in 2008, a PricewaterhouseCoopers survey of over 4,000 new college hires to the firm reported that 91% of Millennials agreed with the statement, "I will be loyal to the organization I work for" (PricewaterhouseCoopers 2008, p. 15). In more recent years, with more Millennials in the workforce and significant evidence of job vulnerability, loyalty has decreased. PricewaterhouseCoopers now reports that 54% of Millennials believe they will work for more than six employers. (PricewaterhouseCoopers 2013). For organizations, loyalty from Millennial employees means passionate, intelligent, and enthusiastic work. To Millennial employees, loyalty means that organizations assure that there are ample opportunities, offer professional development and training, and provide coaching and mentoring (PricewaterhouseCoopers 2013). In return, Millennials report that they will be Brooks'

"Organization kids," who place a high value on security and stability (Graduate Management Admission Council 2007), and will reject the concept of "portfolio careers" at numerous employers (PricewaterhouseCoopers, 2008, p. 13). This self-reported Millennial intention is in contrast to Gen Xers, who have shown both an entrepreneurial spirit and high job mobility.

Millennials do have the capacity to be loyal, particularly in organizations that continue to provide individual attention and a supportive, family-like environment. In the 2007 Great Places to Work Institute survey, Millennials (those under age 25) "put strong emphasis on the question, 'There is a family or team feeling here'" (Flander 2008). In 2008, Marriott International was the second largest organization among the 25 "Great Places for Millennials" ("Great Places" 2008), an achievement based in part on a consistent culture that focuses on its core values, the first of which is, "the unshakeable conviction that people are our most important asset" (Marriott, n.d.). Other Marriott core values that resonate with the desires articulated by our interviewees and in a myriad of other surveys are, "an environment that supports associate growth and personal development," and, "a performance-based reward system that recognizes the important contributions of… associates" (Marriott).

Marriott is notable because the organization has consistently and authentically embraced these values through their actions. After the 9/11 terrorist attacks, the hotel industry experienced crippling decreases in demand. Many of Marriott's competitors reneged on job offers to graduates of university hospitality programs, but Marriott did not. They honored their commitments and hired those to whom they had extended offers even though the organization did not require additional employees at the time. Marriott found creative ways to engage these new hires until the hotel industry rebounded. David Rodriguez, executive vice president of global human resources, believed that keeping their commitments created "lifelong loyalty" from many employees (Flander 2008, p. 2). In addition to happy employees, Marriott has earned multitudes of awards that recognize their values and affirm their commitment to employees, communities, sustainability, diversity, and ethics (Marriott 2016).

There are many ways an organization can model employee commitment. When Vail Resorts created a company-wide wage reduction plan in March 2009, those at the top of the organization took the largest pay cuts. CEO Robert Katz, a Gen Xer born in 1968, demonstrated his commitment to the organization's values and his employees by refusing to take any salary for a 12-month period, and then taking a 15% pay cut (Maltby and Pepitone 2009). Katz began with cuts at the top, including 10% for all executives and 20% for members of the board of directors. "If I was going to ask someone making $8 an hour to take a pay cut, they needed to know I was doing something that would really affect me" (Maltby and Pepitone 2009). In doing this, Katz reinforced the organization mission, which includes a commitment to provide an exceptional experience to employees (Vail Resorts 2007). Even under challenging conditions, Vail Resorts was able to send a very powerful message of commitment to its many Millennial employees. In response to this action, CNN chose Katz as one of its eight 2009 "Heroes of the Economy" (Maltby and Pepitone 2009).

Millennials are savvy enough to read organizational culture and they seek out this kind of alignment between an organization's values and actions. In multiple surveys, a strong majority of them report not only buying from, but also seeking employment with, companies that positively impact society or reflect values that are consistent with their own (Barton, et al. 2014; Cone Millennial CSR Study 2015; Deloitte 2014). This has far reaching implications because Millennials not only consider the level of corporate social responsibility in choosing where to earn their money, but also factors company values into deciding where they spend it.

Conclusion

Millennials care about authenticity and institutional values because they are counting on working within organizations to drive change. Unlike Gen Xers who are already making a profound mark by creating new paradigms and systems for solving complex problems, Millennials seem much more inclined to operate within existing structures. Thus far, they have been able to rely on institutions to provide them with the resources and support they need to solve the tasks set before them, and they are likely to continue to do so.

The members of this generation have a great deal to bring to the organizations within which they operate. Their comfort with technology enables them to not only access information and resources creatively and easily, but also to think and function in a world that, to them, has always been without boundaries. Although they admittedly present their fair share of management challenges, they are, as a rule, people and organization-oriented rather than alienated, thus easing the process of engaging and acculturating them.

A combination of the idealism of youth and the sheltering protection they have been afforded leads them to believe they can and should be change agents on a grand scale. Because they are collaborative, the scope of the issues they face does not seem to daunt them, but rather inspires them to pool their collective abilities to move forward. While many are impatient to realize their own aspirations, as a generation, they seem to believe that issues like environmental sustainability, ethnic persecution, and extreme poverty are best solved one can, one petition, and one dollar at a time. So too, in organizations they are equipped to work patiently to move the flywheel forward — as long as they can envision and believe in the direction in which it is turning.

Millennials want to amass the skills, knowledge, and credentials that will assist them in fulfilling both their personal and societal goals. Corporate, non-profit, and governmental entities seek driven, innovative, committed employees who will help them fulfill their organizational missions. To the extent that these two objectives are consistent with each other, there is enormous opportunity. Millennials may or may not be the next great generation, but they are certainly the next work force, and with effective management, they absolutely have the potential to be a great one.

REFERENCES

100 best companies to work for. (2016). *Fortune.* Retrieved from http://fortune.com/best-companies/.

Alsop, R. (2008). *The trophy kids grow up: How the millennial generation is shaking up the workplace.* San Francisco: Jossey-Bass.

America's best colleges 2009. (2008). *U.S. News and World Report 145*(5). Retrieved from http://colleges.usnews.rankingsandreviews. com/best-colleges.

America's best colleges 2016. (2016). *U.S. News and World Report.* Retrieved from http://colleges.usnews.rankingsandreviews.com/best-colleges/rankings/national-universities/data.

American Business Collaboration for Quality Dependent Care and the Families and Work Institute. (2002). *Generation and gender in workplace.* Retrieved August 17, 2009, from http://www. abcdependentcare.com/docs/ABC-generation-gender-workplace. pdf.

Barton, C., Beauchamp, C., & Koslow, L. (2014). *The reciprocity principle: how millennials are changing the face of marketing forever.* Boston Consulting Group. Retrieved from https://www.bcgperspectives.com/content/articles/marketing_center_consumer_customer_insight_how_millennials_changing_marketing_forever/.

Bashir, M. (2006). *Inside the cutthroat preschool wars: 'Nightline' follows three families desperate to get their kids into one of Manhattan's elite private preschools.* Retrieved July 7, 2009, from http://abcnews.go.com/Nightline/Story?id=1915973&page=1.

Bauerlein, M. (2008). *The dumbest generation: How the digital age stupefies young Americans and jeopardizes our future.* New York: Jeremy P. Tarcher/Penguin.

Brooks, D. (2001). The organization kid. *The Atlantic Monthly, 287*(4), 40–54.

Central Intelligence Agency. (n.d.). *Mentoring programs: Mentoring at the Central Intelligence Agency.* Brochure. Retrieved from https://www.cia.gov/careers/diversity/CIAmentoringbrochure. pdf.

Chesapeake Energy Corporation & Murray, R. M. (2007). *Survive and thrive in a multi-generational world: A personal guide to mastering generational diversity in the workplace.* (Internal publication). Oklahoma City: Chesapeake Energy Corporation.

Chesapeake Energy Corporation & Performance Consulting. (n.d.). *How to start your own "rock" group: A left brain guide to mentoring.* Corporation (PowerPoint slides). Oklahoma City: Chesapeake Energy.

College Board. (2015). Access & participation Retrieved from https://www.collegeboard.org/program-results/participation.

College Board. (2015). Total group profile report. Retrieved from https://secure-media.collegeboard.org/digitalServices/pdf/sat/total-group-2015.pdf.

College Board and Arts and Sciences Group. (2008). Research dispels millennial theories. *StudentPOLL 6*(2). Retrieved from http:// professionals.collegeboard.com/data-reports-research/trends/ studentpoll/millennial.

Cone, Inc. (2015). *The 2015 Cone Communication Millennial CSR Study*. Retrieved from http://www.conecomm.com/2015-cone-communications-millennial-csr-study/.

Deloitte. (2014). The Deloitte millennial survey: January 2014 executive summary. Retrieved from https://www2.deloitte.com/content/dam/Deloitte/global/Documents/About-Deloitte/gx-dttl-2014-millennial-survey-report.pdf .

Deloitte. (2014). Media consumer survey 2014: Australian media and digital preferences (Third Edition).

Epstein, M. (n.d.). *Cross-generational perceptual survey of educational norms* (Whitepaper).

Epstein, M., & Howes, P. (2008). *Recruiting, retaining and managing the millennial generation. Selected readings 2008—Management of a practice [CD ROM]*. New York: American Institute of Certified Public Accountants.

Ernst & Young. (2015). Global generations: a global study on work-life challenges across generations. Retrieved from http://www.ey.com/US/en/About-us/Our-people-and-culture/EY-study-highlights-work-life-is-harder-worldwide#.VqcmZPkrJD_.

Flander, S. (2008). Millennial magnets. *Human Resource Executive Online*. Retrieved from http://www.hrexecutive.com/HRE/story. jsp?storyId=84159035.

Fromm, J., Lindell, C. & Decker, L. (2011) *American Millennials: Deciphering the Enigma Generation*. Retrieved from https://www.barkleyus.com/millennials.

Gerdes, L. (2008). Best places to launch a career. *Business Week*. Retrieved from http://bwnt.businessweek.com/interactive_reports/ career_launch_2008/index.asp.

Graduate Management Admission Council. (2007). *Global MBA graduate survey*. Retrieved from http://www.gmac.com/community/ media/p/217.aspx.

Great places for Millennials. (2008). *Human Resource Executive Online*. Retrieved from http://www.hreonline.com/HRE/ printstory.jsp?storyId=84159054.

Grovo (2015). *The Disappearing Act: Why Millennials Leave Companies—And How L&D Can Entice Them To Stay*. Retrieved from http://resources.grovo.com/the-disappearing-act-millennials/?gref=ACQ_Referral_DisappearingMillennialsBlogContent_DisappearingMillennials_LnD_Millennials_Banner_740x390.

Hayden, M. V. *Message from the Director* (2007). Retrieved August 13, 2009, from https://www.cia.gov/careers/diversity/CIAmentoring brochure.pdf.pdf.

Hershatter, A. (2007). *Millennials on Millennials* (video produced at Emory University).

Hewlett, S. A., Sherbin, L., & Sumberg, K. (2009). How gen Y and boomers will reshape your agenda. *Harvard Business Review, 87*(7/8), 71–76.

Howe, N., & Strauss, W. (2000). *Millennials rising: The next great generation*. New York: Vintage Books.

Interview with Derek Johnson, Tatango. (2008). *Northwest Innovation*. Retrieved from http://www.nwinnovation.com/interview_ with_derek_johnson_tatango/s-0016494.html.

Lenhart, A. (2012). Teens, smartphones & texting. Retrieved from http://www.pewinternet.org/2012/03/19/teens-smartphones-texting/.

Lenhart, A., Purcell, K., Smith, A., & Zickuhr K. (2010). *Social media and young adults.* Retrieved from http://www.pewinternet.org/2010/02/03/social-media-and-young-adults/.

Lella, A., Lipsman, A., Martin, B. (2015). *The 2015 U.S. Mobile App Report* (Whitepaper). Retrieved from http://www.comscore.com/Insights/Presentations-and-Whitepapers/2015/The-2015-US-Mobile-App-Report.

Levine, P., Flanagan, C., & Gallay, L. (2008). *The millennial pendulum: A new generation of voters and the prospects for a political realignment.* Retrieved from http://www.newamerica.net/files/Millennial%20Pendulum.pdf.

Maltby, E., & Pepitone, J. (2009). *Heroes of the economy: Rob Katz.* Retrieved from http://money.cnn.com/galleries/2009/news/0903/ gallery.economy_heroes/index.html.

Marriott Corporation. (2016). *Awards & recognition.* Retrieved March 30, 2016, from http://news.marriott.com/awards-and-recognition.html.

Marriott Corporation. (n.d.). *Core values.* Retrieved March 30, 2016, from http://www.marriott.com/corporateinfo/culture/coreValues. mi.

National Center for Education Statistics (2014). *Back 2 School Stats* Retrieved from http://nces.ed.gov/programs/digest/d14/tables/dt14_302.30.asp?current=yes.

National Center for Education Statistics (2013). Fast facts Retrieved from http://nces.ed.gov/programs/digest/d14/tables/dt14_302.30.asp?current=yes.

Perrin, A. (2015) *Social Media Usage: 2005-2015* Retrieved http://www.pewinternet.org/2015/10/08/social-networking-usage-2005-2015/.

Pew Research Center for the People and the Press. (2007). *How young people view their lives, futures and politics: A portrait of 'generation next.* Retrieved from http://people-press.org/reports/ pdf/300.pdf.

PricewaterhouseCoopers. (2008). *Managing tomorrow's people: Millennials at work—perspectives from a new generation*, (Whitepaper). Retrieved from http://www.pwc.com/en_GX/gx/managing-tomorrows-people/millennials-at-work/pdf/mtp-millennialsatwork.pdf.

PricewatershouseCoopers. (2011). Millennials at work: reshaping the workplace. Retrieved from. https://www.pwc.com/gx/en/managing-tomorrows-people/future-of-work/assets/reshaping-the-workplace.pdf

PricewatershouseCoopers. (2013). PwC's nextgen: a global generational study. Retrieved from http://www.pwc.com/gx/en/hr-management-services/publications/assets/pwc-nextgen.pdf.

Pryor, J. H., Hurtado, S., DeAngelo, L., Sharkness, J., Romero, L. C., Korn, W. S., et al. (2009). *The American freshman: National norms for 2008.* (Research brief). Los Angeles: Higher Education Research Institute at University of California. Retrieved July 1, 2009, from http://www.gseis.ucla.edu/heri/PDFs/pubs/ briefs/brief-pr012208-08FreshmanNorms.pdf.

Ryan, J. E. A. (September 15, 2004) Constitutional right to preschool? Abstract. Retrieved from http://ssrn.com/abstract=605341.

Small, G., & Vorgan, G. (2008). *iBrain: Surviving the technological alteration of the modern mind*. New York: Harper Collins.

Smith, W. S. (2008). *Decoding generational differences: Fact, fiction, or should we just get back to work?* (Whitepaper). Retrieved from http://www.deloitte.com/dtt/cda/doc/content/us_Talent_ DecodingGenerationalDifferences.pdf.

Subramaniam, N., Nandhakumar, J., & Baptista (John), J. (2013). Exploring social network interactions in enterprise systems: the role of virtual co-presence. Information Systems Journal, 23(6), 475-499. doi:10.1111/isj.12019.

Tapscott, D. (2009). *Grown up digital*. New York: McGraw Hill. The National Commission on Excellence in Education. (1983). *A Nation at Risk: The Imperative for Educational Reform A Report to the Nation and the Secretary of Education United States Department of Education*. Retrieved from http://www.ed.gov/pubs/NatAtRisk/index.html.

Twenge, J. M. (2009). Generational changes and their impact in the classroom: Teaching generation me. *Medical Education, 43*, 398–405.

Universum, Incorporated. (2008). *Universum Student Survey, 2008* (Whitepaper). Retrieved from http://www.dur.ac.uk/resources/ careers-advice/durhamuniversitystaff/UniversumStudentSurvey 08_v1.pdf.

Vail Resorts. (2007). *What We Believe*. Retrieved August 17, 2009, from http://www.vailresorts.com/Corp/info/values.aspx.

Zemke, R., Raines, C., & Filipczak, B. (2000). *Generations at work: Managing the clash of veterans, Boomers, Xers, and Nexters in your workplace*. New York: Amacom/American Management Association.

Zickuhr K. & Smith, A (2012). Digital differences. Retrieved from http://www.pewinternet.org/2012/04/13/digital-differences/.

Why have these changes occurred in workplace values? Sociological approaches view attitudes and values as complex outcomes that are shaped by personal orientations *and* social experiences (e.g., Johnson & Monserud 2010; Csikszentmihalhi & Schneider 2000). As one of the employers in Konstam's interviews states: "The previous generation were great doctors, but they did it at the expense of their family life. You have far more two career families, and that has changed. That puts a new slant on family life" (2015, p. 173). Another of the reasons corporate structure is less relevant to younger generations is the declining opportunity to stay employed long-term by a single company. What is more common than a corporate ladder today, is a jungle gym of job surfing. Thus, rather than look for a long-term workplace mutual commitment, Millennials tend to value jobs that provide meaningful experiences and relationships.

LABOR MARKET REALITIES

As has been hinted at already, the current labor market climate has a great deal to do with the ways Millennials approach work. While occupational stratification has long existed across the life course (e.g., Mare et al. 1984; Warren et al. 2002), intra-occupational inequality has been on the rise (e.g., Kim & Sakamoto 2008), with threat of midlife job loss (e.g., Mendenall et al. 2008) contributing to increased job mobility to keep skills fresh and marketable (e.g., Fuller 2008).

Given the high degree of occupational uncertainty, exploration, and aimlessness (e.g., Staff et al. 2010), what explains who does well in their work trajectories and who fares less well? As in the prior chapters, the answer to that question is multiplicative (e.g., Lyons et al. 2014). Advantaged contexts contribute to upward mobility, especially for white males (e.g., Stuber 2005). Internet use is also predictive of differences in income earnings (e.g., DiMaggio & Bonikowski 2008).

Gender remains a major factor in labor market realities for emerging adults (e.g., Cech et al. 2011; Polavieja & Platt 2014; Brand et al. 2014), largely because of the interconnections between establishing work and forming long-term romantic relationships (e.g., Branje 2014; Ranta et al. 2014). Single mothers in particular face vulnerabilities in job opportunities due to ongoing role conflicts (e.g., Brand et al. 2014). Social background and personality characteristics also play a role (e.g., Gelissen & de Graaf 2006), and prior chapters showed how those are shaped over time in more or less advantaged social contexts.

In the second and final reading of this chapter, Maxwell (2006) sheds the light of reality on popular perceptions of low-skilled jobs, describing their economic environment and working conditions.

READING 6.2

Low-Skilled Jobs: The Reality Behind the Popular Perceptions

By Nan L. Maxwell

My first job, I was 17 years old. I start[ed] working as a nurse's assistant in a hospital. Under my care I had 12 patients. Their lives were in my hands.

—A low-wage worker

Individuals that work full time spend about 20 percent of their year—and nearly one-third of their waking hours—at work. Individuals have some control over this time, in that they can invest in skills that help shape their work life. Hate working in an office? Build construction skills. Want to help people? Build social interaction skills.

Unfortunately, investing in the skills necessary to get your job of choice is not foolproof, as the market for skills is governed by the laws of supply and demand. These economic forces shape an individual's work life by determining employment probabilities, wages, and potential for career progression.

Most individuals toiling in the labor market focus heavily on the outcomes of labor demand and supply forces. They see their wages as being too low, leaving them without the ability to achieve the life to which they aspire. While virtually all

Nan L. Maxwell, "Low-Skilled Jobs: The Reality Behind the Popular Perceptions," The Working Life: The Labor Market for Workers in Low-Skilled Job, pp. 1-15, 22. Copyright © 2006 by W.E. Upjohn Institute for Employment Research. Reprinted with permission.

workers voice such complaints, workers in jobs requiring relatively few skills have special concerns, for their wages frequently will not keep their family out of poverty. Perhaps because full-time work may not afford a middle-class lifestyle for workers in low-skilled jobs, questions arise as to whether or not demand and supply forces are fair. How fair is it that some workers must face a life of struggle as they precariously balance full-time work, home responsibilities, and subsistence-level economic needs (DeParle 2004; Munger 2002)?

This book tells the story of the low-skilled jobs available to workers with little formal education or work experience. In the process of telling the story, we debunk several popular perceptions about how the labor market for workers in low-skilled jobs operates. Frequently, this labor market is portrayed as one in which an excess supply of job seekers competes for relatively few jobs (Newman 1999), and in which employers maintain unrealistic employment criteria even when faced with labor shortages (Jasinowski 2001). Because employers (supposedly) can easily find workers, low-skilled jobs are thought to turn into lowwage, dead-end positions.

When we surveyed employers and asked them about their lowskilled positions, they provided a dramatically different description of the labor market and led us to very different conclusions about its operation. Most importantly, employers told us that the labor market for workers in low-skilled jobs is a market for skills. Specifically, they made the following points:

Low-skilled jobs require skills. Low-skilled jobs are not the same as no-skilled jobs, they said. Most jobs require English, math, problemsolving, and communication skills, the so-called new basic skills. More than three-fourths of low-skilled jobs require oral and written comprehension of English, more than half require oral and written expression and deductive reasoning, and at least half require math, reading com prehension, active listening, writing, and speaking. Workers in lowskilled jobs are expected to act appropriately at work and to perceive cues from others correctly. Many low-skilled jobs also require physical abilities and mechanical skills. In fact, low-skilled jobs require physical and mechanical skills at higher levels than other jobs.

Shortages of appropriately skilled workers in low-skilled jobs exist, even when labor markets are slack. Close to 60 percent of the firms in the local labor market in this study had difficulty—one-fourth of them had extreme difficulty—finding qualified workers for lowskilled jobs when unemployment rates exceeded 7.0 percent.

Skills are rewarded in the labor market for workers in lowskilled jobs. Firms increase wages in low-skilled jobs that require skills the firms have difficulty obtaining. Specifically, low-skilled jobs requiring skills with a high relative demand in the local labor market (i.e., skills in short supply) carry increased occupational wages.

Low-skilled jobs offer promotional opportunities. Over 90 percent of entry-level, low-skilled jobs have promotional opportunities. Firms structure promotional opportunities for workers in the entry-level, low-skilled job by requiring workers to expand their abilities to encompass the skill sets used in the job above entry level. The modal title of the position above entry level is lead, supervisor, or manager. Even though entry-level jobs require English and problem-solving skills, jobs above entry-level require higher-level skills in each of these areas.

Hiring requirements in low-skilled jobs are relaxed in tight labor markets. Firms match recruiting and screening methods to the skills needed in the low-skilled job. As labor markets loosen, firms use less extensive recruiting methods—as might be expected with greater numbers of applicants—but adopt more intensive screening methods. The increased screening during loose labor markets suggests that firms sift through the greater number of applicants in order to uncover workers with the skill sets needed in the job.

What are Low-Skilled Jobs?

We define low-skilled jobs as those requiring workers to have no more than a high school education and no more than one year of work experience. We posit that such jobs are low-skilled by virtue of their limited entrance requirements. Indeed, when we asked firms about education and work requirements for such jobs, about 25 percent stated that there were no educational requirements, and just over 40 percent required no work experience. Only about 30 percent of the positions required that the worker speak, understand, and read English "extremely well."

We characterize low-skilled jobs using both national and local databases.[1] One clear characterization that emerges from the data is that low-skilled jobs are concentrated in a few industries and occupations (Table 6.1). Under the Industry category, the service sector houses nearly 40 percent of low-skilled jobs (and about 37 percent of all jobs). Services, retail trade, and manufacturing together house 75 percent of the low-skilled jobs but only 68 percent of all jobs nationwide. Services (other than business services and education and medical services), trade (both retail and wholesale), and public administration all contain a disproportionately large number of low-skilled jobs.

Under the Occupation category, six types of jobs—office and administrative support, production, food preparation and serving, sales, building and grounds maintenance, and transportation and material moving—account for 84.5 percent of low-skilled jobs in the San Francisco Bay Area (results not shown) and 75.5 percent of low-skilled jobs nationwide, but only 34.6 percent of all positions nationwide. Office

---

1   We use the U.S. Department of Labor's (USDOL) Occupational Information Network (O*NET) database (USDOL 2006) to describe the knowledges, skills, and attitudes needed to perform a wide variety of jobs throughout the economy. We use the Bay Area Longitudinal Surveys (BALS) to describe specific tasks of low-skilled jobs.

Table 6.1 Industrial and Occupational Distribution of Low-Skilled Jobs

	All jobs	Low-skilled jobs
Industry		
Services	36.7	39.8
Education	16.4	14.2
Business	10.6	11.0
Other	9.8	14.6
Retail trade	16.6	22.0
Manufacturing	14.7	13.2
Wholesale trade	4.0	6.5
Finance, insurance, and real estate	6.5	5.8
Public administration	4.4	5.2
Transportation, communication, public utilities	7.2	4.1
Construction	7.0	2.7
Agriculture/mining	2.8	0.8
Occupation		
Office and administrative support	7.3	41.3
Production	14.5	11.1
Food preparation and serving	2.1	9.8
Sales and related	2.7	8.5
Building and grounds cleaning/maintenance	1.2	7.6
Transportation and material moving	6.8	7.1
Personal care and service	4.3	2.8
Installation, maintenance, and repair	6.9	2.1
Education, training, and library	7.5	1.9
Protective service	2.6	1.7
Construction and extraction	7.5	1.2
Health-care support	1.9	1.1
Health-care practitioner/technical	6.0	0.6
Business and financial	3.6	0.5

Farming, fishing, and forestry	1.7	0.5
Computer and mathematical	2.1	0.4
Community and social services	1.8	0.4
Art, design, entertainment, sports, and media	4.8	0.4
Management	3.9	0.3
Architecture and engineering	4.5	0.1
Military	0.0	0.1
Life, physical, and social science	5.1	0.0
Legal	1.2	0.0
N	—	2,052

Note: Numbers represent the percentage in each category. N varies slightly with item-specific missing data. Data on the distribution of occupations are establishment data and are based on the number of occupations, not employment, within a firm, as is consistent with the BALS data.

Source: Bay Area Longitudinal Surveys (BALS) Phone Survey (HIRE 2006) Bureau of Labor Statistics (2002a); U.S. Census Bureau (2003a).

and administrative support account for over 40 percent of low-skilled positions but under 8 percent of all positions nationwide. Food preparation/serving and sales jobs each make up a little less than 10 percent of low-skilled positions but a little more than 2 percent of all positions nationwide.

Low-skilled jobs require relatively fewer skills than other jobs in many areas, which may explain their low educational and work experience requirements. Indeed, when we compare low-skilled jobs to other jobs in the U.S. economy, we see that the knowledge, skill, and ability requirements in low-skilled jobs are modest (Table 6.2). Low-skilled jobs have lower requirements in 21 of the 33 measures of knowledge, 27 of the 35 measures of skills, and 15 of the 51 measures of abilities.[2] The relatively lower requirements in low-skilled jobs all fall into areas that would be classified as new basic skills (academic, problem-solving, and communication skills).

Despite the relatively low educational and work experience requirements of low-skilled jobs, workers must use a relatively large number of skills on the job (Table 6.2). Most notably, physical and mechanical skills are required at higher levels in low-skilled jobs than in other jobs. Sixty percent of low-skilled jobs require mechanical knowledge, about 75 percent require operation and control skills, and over 80 percent

---

[2] Table 6.2 does not present the complete list of O*NET's knowledges, skills, and abilities. It presents only those that are used in 50 percent or more of Job Zone 1 jobs.

Table 6.2 Knowledge, Skills, and Abilities Used in Low-Skilled Jobs

	All jobs	Low-skilled jobs
Knowledge		
Mechanical	52.0	60.0
Mathematics	74.1**	59.3
Skills		
Operation and control	66.6**	74.8
Equipment selection	78.7	71.9
Mathematics	80.0**	67.4
Reading comprehension	87.1**	66.7
Monitoring	83.4**	60.7
Active listening	75.9**	59.3
Writing	70.4**	57.0
Operation monitoring	50.3	53.3
Quality control analysis	70.7**	52.6
Equipment maintenance	40.6**	51.9
Speaking	71.2**	48.9
Low-skilled tasks		
Interact to accomplish a task		90.8
Exhibit appropriate behavior at work		85.3
Perceive cues from others		81.5
Read written instructions, safety warnings, labels, etc.		78.3
Write simple sentences, short notes, and simple memos		77.6
Fill out forms, record data, time		74.1
Read manuals, computer printouts, contracts, and agreements		73.8
Identify work-related problems		70.3
Prioritize tasks		68.8
Read forms, memos, and letters		67.6
Deal with customers		64.6
Use telephone systems		63.6
Problem-solve collaboratively		63.3
Gather information		62.6
Identify potential solutions to problems		52.9

Abilities

Near vision	97.6**	91.1
Information ordering	94.1	89.6
Manual dexterity	69.6**	84.4
Problem sensitivity	88.9**	81.5
Wrist/finger speed	69.4**	80.7
Written comprehension	86.7**	76.3
Oral comprehension	81.9	75.6
Extent of flexibility	53.9**	74.8
Arm/hand steadiness	63.3**	74.1
Static strength	49.1**	74.1
Control precision	59.9**	70.4
Multilimb coordination	53.0**	70.4
Number facility	72.0	69.6
Trunk strength	56.5**	68.9
Finger dexterity	64.4	67.4
Selective attention	69.0	66.7
Oral expression	74.4**	61.5
Visualization	65.2	57.0
Written expression	68.7**	54.8
Deductive reasoning	82.3**	54.8
Time sharing	56.9	52.6
Perceptual speed	52.2	51.9
Reaction time	36.6**	51.9
Speed of limb movement	32.9**	51.1
Stamina	25.8**	51.1

Note: Information is only listed for skills required by at least half of the low-skilled jobs, defined as Job Zone 1 jobs. Data on knowledge, skills, and abilities (KSA) are from the O*NET database at www.onetcenter.org. A listing of all KSA in O*NET is available from the author. Numbers for knowledge, skills, and abilities represent the percentage of occupations that report that that particular knowledge, skill, or ability is important in the job. Importance is defined as a 3 or above on a 5-point scale in which 1 = not important and 5 = extremely important. ** indicates that significant (p ≤ 0.05) differences exist between Job Zone 1 and all jobs, as determined by a t-test. Numbers for low-skilled tasks are from BALS data, described in Chapter 2, with information reported only for those tasks used in 50 percent or more of the BALS jobs. Numbers represent the percentage of jobs that report using the skill.

Blank = not applicable.

Source: Occupational Information Network (O*NET) Resource Center (USDOL 2006); Bay Area Longitudinal Surveys (BALS) data (HIRE 2006).

require manual dexterity and wrist or finger speed. Physical abilities include manual dexterity, wrist/finger speed, extent of flexibility, arm/hand steadiness, static strength, control precision, multilimb coordination, trunk strength, reaction time, speed of limb movement, and stamina.[3] Mechanical knowledge and skills include quality control analysis, operation and control, and equipment maintenance.

Most low-skilled jobs require workers to possess the new basics of academics (English and math), communication, and problem-solving. Communication skills are the most used: over 90 percent of low-skilled jobs require workers to interact with coworkers to accomplish a task, over 80 percent require workers to act appropriately at work and to perceive cues from others correctly, and over 60 percent require workers to deal with customers or work in teams. Academic skills also are heavily used in low-skilled jobs: over three-fourths require oral and written comprehension of English, including such skills as reading written instructions, safety warnings, labels, invoices, work orders, logs, or journals. Low-skilled workers are also required to write simple sentences, to fill out forms and logs, and to read manuals, computer printouts, contracts, agreements, forms, memos, and letters. Nearly 70 percent of the positions require workers to add and subtract. Over half of low-skilled jobs require oral and written expression. Workers in low-skilled positions are also expected to problem-solve: over 54 percent of the positions require deductive reasoning, and most of the jobs require workers to problem-solve, identify work-related problems, prioritize tasks, deal with customers, work in teams, or gather information.

Who Fills Low-Skilled Positions?

Workers in low-skilled positions are often thought to be at the bottom of the workplace totem pole. They fill the positions that many of us held as youths or that we relegate to others for execution. Two distinct groups generally hold low-skilled jobs: youth and the economically disadvantaged. Youth, who by definition have little education or work experience, constitute as many as half of the workers in low-skilled jobs. Some youth are transitory participants in the low-skilled labor market, occupying those positions only until they complete their education or gain work skills on the job and advance beyond the entry-level, lowskilled positions. The other group, the economically disadvantaged, have a truncated education and intermittent work experience, and they frequently struggle in low-skilled employment throughout much of their life. For this group, low-skilled jobs are a way of life.

These two groups approach the labor market with vastly different expectations. Youth, especially youth that do not continue their education past high school, frequently flounder between jobs as they attempt to match their budding interests and skills with the appropriate job (Osterman 1980). In some cases, short-term youth joblessness (Becker and Hills 1980, 1983) and initial employment in minimum wage

---

3 Because Table 6.2 lists only knowledges, skills, and abilities required in 50 percent or more of low-skilled jobs, some physical and mechanical skills are left out. Among the physical abilities not listed are dynamic strength, spatial orientation, dynamic flexibility, response orientation, explosive strength, and overall body coordination.

jobs (Carrington and Fallick 2001) eventually yield to long-term opportunities for advancement. In other cases, floundering creates long-term unemployment and harms career development because of a lack of work experience during the years of career formation, reducing subsequent wages (D'Amico and Maxwell 1994; Ellwood 1982; Lynch 1989; Meyer and Wise 1982). Youth that, for whatever reason, never fully integrate into the labor market and do not continue their education past high school can become mired in low-skilled jobs and enter the realm of the economically disadvantaged.

Both national and local databases make it easy to paint a statistical portrait of workers that potentially hold low-skilled jobs.[4] In 2000, about 44 percent of the U.S. population aged 25–64 could be considered to be in the labor market for low-skilled jobs, because these people had a high school education or less (U.S. Census Bureau 2003c). An additional 30 percent had some college, but, because these people did not have a college degree, they may have found themselves in low-skilled jobs. Individuals with only a high school education were disproportionately African American or from households in which English was not spoken (Table 6.3), and those disproportions increased in the older age groupings. In 1979, about 69 percent of a sample of youth aged 14–22 with a high school education or less were white, and about 78 percent spoke English in the home as an adolescent. Twenty-one years later, only 60.6 percent of members of the same group were white and 75.8 percent were from English-speaking families. This suggests that whites and individuals from English-speaking households have a greater tendency to continue their education beyond high school and, perhaps, move from low-skilled jobs at a more rapid rate than nonwhites and individuals from non-English-speaking households.

Individuals with only a high school education and little work experience—characteristics that roughly correspond to our definition of low-skilled job requirements—are more likely than individuals with more than a high school education and extensive work experience to have low wages and household income and to face labor market barriers (Table 6.4). Low-skilled individuals have hourly wages that are about half those of high-skilled individuals; such individuals are one-third as likely to receive tips or bonuses, and are four times as likely to live in a household with an income of less than $20,000.

The labor market challenges facing low-skilled individuals could prevent their becoming full participants in the labor market (Table 6.4). Potential challenges include youth (45 percent of low-skilled individuals are under 30, compared to only 20 percent of high-skilled individuals), greater child care responsibilities (over 80 percent

---

4 We use the Census Public Use Microdata Sample [PUMS] (U.S. Census Bureau 2003c) to describe a cross-section of the population aged 25–64 in 2000 with no more than a high school education; we use the National Longitudinal Surveys youth sample [NLSY79] (BLS 2002b) to describe how the composition of individuals with no more than a high school degree changes as it ages; and we use the Bay Area Longitudinal Surveys [BALS] (HIRE 2006) to describe the characteristics of and challenges facing low-skilled individuals as compared to individuals with higher levels of skills.

Table 6.3 Demographics and Cohort Aging of Workers in Low-Skilled Jobs (% of population)

	U.S. population in 2000 (Age 25–64)	High school education or less			
		Age 14–22 in 1979	Age 18–26 in 1983	Age 28–36 in 1993	Age 35–43 in 2000
Race					
White	76.3	69.3	68.0	60.9	60.6
Black	11.6	25.1	26.0	32.3	32.9
Other	12.1	5.6	6.0	6.8	6.5
N	1,472,037	12,610	8,545	5,281	4,512
Foreign language at home at age 14					
Yes	18.1	22.0	22.2	24.9	24.2
No	81.9	78.0	77.8	75.1	75.8
N	1,472,037	12,681	8,593	5,316	4,541

Note: 2000 U.S. population data are from the (weighted) 1 percent sample of the Public Use Microdata Samples (PUMS). Statistics in columns 2 through 5 are taken from the 1979 National Longitudinal Surveys and represent the percentage of the population in each category.

Source: U.S. Census Bureau (2003c); Bureau of Labor Statistics (2002b).

of low-skilled individuals have children under 18), and less access to reliable transportation (low-skilled individuals are less likely to have a driver's license, insurance, regular access to a car, or own a car; and are more likely to use public transportation, walk, or use a friend or neighbor's car for their primary mode of transportation). Low-skilled individuals may be more likely to have health problems that inhibit them from working, as fewer are covered by health insurance and more of them have (or had) a substance abuse problem or a physical disability.

The Economic Environment Facing Workers in Low-Skilled Positions

Throughout most of the twentieth century, the wage structure in the United States became more compressed (Goldin and Margo 1992). Although education levels were generally rising, a strong demand for unskilled labor supported wages at the bottom end of the earnings distribution. Sometime during the 1970s this trend reversed, and by the late 1980s the wage dispersion was back to what it was in the 1950s. Workers at the bottom of the distribution began losing ground. Between 1963 and 1989, real

Table 6.4 Income and Labor Market Challenges for Workers with Low, Medium, and High Skill (% of population)

	Total	Low skill	Medium skill	High skill
Income				
Labor market				
Hourly rate of pay ($)	18.18	11.64	15.76**	20.78**
Tips or bonuses	27.1	22.6	18.9	33.2**
Household income				
Less than $20,000	16.1	31.9	17.4**	7.1**
$20,000–$49,999	33.8	23.7	37.7**	29.0
$50,000–$74,999	19.5	15.6	17.4	25.3**
$75,000–$99,999	11.2	6.7	12.6**	15.2**
$100,000–$249,999	7.4	2.2	4.9	13.4**
$250,000–$499,999	3.0	0.0	2.8**	5.2**
$500,000 or greater	0.4	0.0	0.4	0.7
Don't know	8.5	20.0	6.9**	4.1**
Labor market challenges				
Age				
18–25	16.3	31.9	23.0	7.9**
26–30	11.0	14.9	10.7	12.9
31–45	39.2	38.3	44.8	47.3
46–55	15.4	10.6	14.3	22.6**
56–64	7.7	1.4	4.0	8.6**
65 or older	10.3	2.8	3.2	0.7
Children				
Have children (under18)	64.4	81.3	73.0	65.6**

Continued

	Total	Low skill	Medium skill	High skill
Have children living in household	61.6	79.4	70.2**	61.6**
If yes, number of children	1.4	2.0	1.5**	1.3**
Taking care of children last week	40.1	56.7	42.1**	41.6**
Total number of children	1.5	2.2	1.7**	1.5**
Transportation				
Have valid driver's license	77.5	47.5	76.6**	93.5**
Have regular access to car	83.9	59.6	83.7**	96.4**
If yes, have car insurance	94.3	86.6	93.8**	97.0**
Typical mode of transportation				
Own car	79.2	50.4	78.6**	92.4**
Public	16.6	37.6	16.3**	7.6**
Walk	13.1	27.7	11.9**	6.5**
Friend or relative's car	6.7	14.9	5.6**	3.6**
Medical				
Respondent covered by health insurance	81.7	62.9	76.6**	91.0**
Medical problem prevents employment	9.0	12.1	9.2	7.2
Mental health issues/depression	8.2	11.4	6.4	8.2
Substance abuse	6.6	11.3	5.6	5.0**
Physical abuse	6.8	10.6	6.0	5.7
Physical disability	7.8	12.3	8.3	5.7**
N	766	141	252	279

Note: Numbers represent the percentage of the population in each category. Total includes retired individuals. "Low skill" applies to individuals with only a high school education and no more than one year of work experience. "Medium skill" applies to individuals either having only a high school education or no more than one year of work experience. "High skill" applies to individuals with more than a high school education and more than one year of work experience. ** indicates a statistically significant ($p \leq 0.05$) difference, compared to low skill, as determined by a t-test.

Source: Bay Area Longitudinal Surveys (BALS) Household Survey (HIRE 2006).

average weekly wages for the least skilled workers declined by about five percent, while wages for the most skilled rose by about 40 percent (Juhn, Murphy, and Pierce 1993).[5]

The reasons for the increasing wage inequality are both varied and integrated; nonetheless, all agree that the economic changes underlying the growing gap have been great. Product market shifts from manufacturing to services (Murphy and Welch 1993) and the adding of skills to production and clerical jobs—traditional sources of employment for low-skilled workers (Cappelli 1993)—favored the more skilled workers in the labor market (Katz and Murphy 1992). These economic changes moved workers' jobs away from routine cognitive and manual tasks and toward non-routine analytic and interactive tasks (Autor, Katz, and Krueger 1998; Autor, Levy, and Murnane 2003), which increased the demand for skills in our economy. As a consequence, skills became increasingly important in determining wages (Murnane, Willett, and Levy 1995), wage differentials (Teulings 1995), employment (Pryor and Schaffer 1999), and wage inequality (Juhn, Murphy, and Pierce 1993); and labor force participation declined among the less skilled (Juhn 1992). Declines in unionization (Freeman 1993) and in school quality (Card and Krueger 1992a), increases in competition (Revenga 1992) and in the use of technology (Autor, Katz, and Krueger 1998), and changes in federal policies (Sawicky 1999) also contributed to the shrinking economic opportunities for the low-skilled. As a result, individuals with below-average skills often remain unemployed or part of the working poor (Handel 2003), and they face increased spells and durations of nonemployment and job instability (Farber 1999) and higher job turnover (Holzer and LaLonde 2000) than more-skilled individuals.

The increased demand for skills also explains the deteriorating labor market for less-educated individuals (Autor, Katz, and Krueger 1998; Murnane, Willett, and Levy 1995), as the less-educated enter the labor market with few skills needed in the workplace (Card and Lemieux 2001). As a result, hiring has moved away from the less-educated and toward the more-educated (Murphy and Welch 1993), and the wage premium for college graduates has increased (Katz and Murphy 1992), which has decreased earnings (Levy and Murnane 1992) and employment (Murphy and Topel 1997; Juhn, Murphy, and Pierce 1993) among less-educated workers. Downturns in the business cycle have exacerbated the plight of less-skilled workers (Hoynes 2000), as college-educated or highly skilled individuals take jobs normally filled by high school–educated or lesser-skilled individuals (Devereux 2002).

---

5   The growing gap between economic outcomes for the haves and the have-nots is impervious to the definition of have-nots. "Have-nots" can be defined as individuals with low levels of education (Blackburn, Bloom, and Freeman 1990), individuals with low skills (Autor, Levy, and Murnane 2003), children in poverty (Iceland et al. 2001), or members of racial or ethnic minorities (Bound and Holzer 1993). Definitions of economic outcomes also seem not to matter. Earnings (Levy and Murnane 1992), employment (Murphy and Topel 1997; Juhn 1992), wealth (Levy and Michel 1991), and income (Levy 1987) eroded for the have-nots, while the wage premium for education for high-ability workers (Cawley et al. 2000; Blackburn and Neumark 1993) and inequality (Karoly 1993) increased.

The Argument for Skills

These trends present a powerful argument for building skills in individuals with low levels of education to enhance their employment opportunities and wages. But which skills should be built? In a review of five studies on workforce readiness, the National Center for Research on Evaluation, Standards, and Student Testing identified three major categories of basic skills needed by lesser-skilled individuals in jobs: academic skills, higher order thinking skills (problem-solving), and interpersonal and teamwork (communication) skills (O'Neil, Allred, and Baker 1997).[6] These basic skills—academic, problem-solving, and communication skills—frequently serve as a foundation for vocational skills used in the workplace. In fact, policies and programs designed to make individuals workforce-ready (e.g., the Workforce Investment Act, Welfare-to-Work, School-to-Work) begin by building these basic skills and, if the individual is still not employed, continue training to provide more specific workplace skills.

Research also supports the need for building a strong foundation in these basic skills. Academic skills increase employment (Johnson and Corcoran 2003) and job stability (Holzer and LaLonde 2000) for lowwage workers and determine their wages (Murnane, Willett, and Levy 1995), most probably because employers of low-wage workers require these skills. Over half of the employers in the Multi-City Study of Urban Inequality required daily reading of at least a paragraph, about half required the use of computers and arithmetic, and nearly half required writing—all academic skills. These same employers also value basic communication skills, particularly in retail firms (Moss and Tilly 2001). Specific workplace skills, which are often acquired on the job, were required by under half of the low-wage Multi-City employers (Holzer 1996). The only specific workplace skill required by at least half of the employers was computers (Autor, Katz, and Krueger 1998; Bartel and Lichtenberg 1987), which some consider to be the fifth component of the new basic skills (Murnane and Levy 1996).

---

6 A fourth category exists in the framework that is not skill-based: personal characteristics and attitudes.

In sum, navigating to long-term, stable, and enjoyable work is challenging, perhaps even more so for today's generation of young people (e.g., Bozick et al. 2011; Purtell & McLoyd 2013). Though each generation expects to perform better than the generation of their parents, the data do not support that this is likely to be the fate of the majority of emerging adults today. Instead, the previous chapters, along with this chapter, highlight the importance of gaining versatile skills to stay afloat in a rapidly changing market. In fact, it is the kinds of *soft skills* that the social sciences and humanities teach that most managers desire in their employees, given that specific and technology-based skills are quickly out of date.

REFERENCES

Bozick, Robert and Stefanie DeLuca. 2011. "Not Making the Transition to College: School, Work, and Opportunities in the Lives of American Youth." *Social Science Research* 40(4):1249–62.

Brand, Jennie E. and Juli Simon Thomas. 2014. "Job Displacement among Single Mothers: Effects on Children's Outcomes in Young Adulthood." *American Journal of Sociology* 119(4):955–1001.

Branje, Susan, Lydia Laninga-Wijnen, Rongqin Yu, and Wim Meeus. 2014. "Associations among School and Friendship Identity in Adolescence and Romantic Relationships and Work in Emerging Adulthood." *Emerging Adulthood* 2(1):6–16.

Cech, Erin, Brian Rubineau, Susan Silbey, and Caroll Seron. 2011. "Professional Role Confidence and Gendered Persistence in Engineering." *American Sociological Review* 76(5):641–66.

Clydesdale, Tim. 2015. *The Purposeful Graduate: Why Colleges Must Talk to Students about Vocation*. University of Chicago Press.

Csikszentmihalhi, Mihaly and Barbara Schneider. 2000. *Becoming Adult: How Teenagers Prepare for the World of Work*. Basic Books.

DiMaggio, Paul and Bart Bonikowski. 2008. "Make Money Surfing the Web? The Impact of Internet Use on the Earnings of U.S. Workers." *American Sociological Review* 73(2):227–50.

Fuller, Sylvia. 2008. "Job Mobility and Wage Trajectories for Men and Women in the United States." *American Sociological Review* 73(1):158–83.

Gelissen, John and Paul M. de Graaf. 2006. "Personality, Social Background, and Occupational Career Success." *Social Science Research* 35(3):702–26.

Gerson, Kathleen. 2009. "Changing Lives, Resistant Institutions: A New Generation Negotiates Gender, Work, and Family Change." *Sociological Forum* 24:735–53.

Grant, Don, Alfonso Morales, and Jeffrey J. Sallaz. 2009. "Pathways to Meaning: A New Approach to Studying Emotions at Work." *American Journal of Sociology* 115(2):327–64.

Hershatter, Andrea and Molly Epstein. 2010. "Millennials and the World of Work: An Organization and Management Perspective." *Journal of Business Psychology* 25:211–23.

Husted, Bryan W. and David B. Allen. 2008. "Toward a Model of Cross-Cultural Business Ethics: The Impact of Individualism and Collectivism on the Ethical Decision-Making Process." *Journal of Business Ethics* 82:293–305.

Johnson, Monica Kirkpatrick and Jeylan T. Mortimer. 2011. "Origins and Outcomes of Judgments about Work." *Social Forces* 89(4):1239–60.

Johnson, Monica Kirkpatrick and Maria Monserud. 2010. "Judgments about Work and the Features of Young Adults' Jobs." *Work and Occupations* 37(2):194–224.

Johnson, Monica Kirkpatrick. 2002. "Social Origins, Adolescent Experiences, and Work Value Trajectories during the Transition to Adulthood." *Social Forces* 80(4):1307–40.

Kalleberg, Arne L. 1977. "Work Values and Job Rewards: A Theory of Job Satisfaction." *American Sociological Review* 42(1):124–43.

Kim, ChangHwan and Arthur Sakamoto. 2008. "The Rise of Intra-Occupational Wage Inequality in the United States, 1983 to 2002." *American Sociological Review* 73:129–57.

Konstam, Varda. 2015. "Voices of Employers: Overlapping and Disparate Views." In *Emerging and Young Adulthood, Advancing Responsible Adolescent Development*, 161–82. Springer International Publishing.

Krahn, Harvey J., Andrea L. Howard, and Nancy L. Galambos. 2014. "Exploring or Floundering? The Meaning of Employment and Educational Fluctuations in Emerging Adulthood." *Youth & Society* 47(2):245–66.

Lyons, Sean T., Eddy S. Ng, and Linda Schweitzer. 2014. "Changing Demographics and the Shifting Nature of Careers: Implications for Research and Human Resource Development." *Human Resource Development Review* 13(2):181–206.

Mare, Robert D., Christopher Winship, and Warren N. Kubitschek. 1984. "The Transition from Youth to Adult: Understanding the Age Pattern of Employment." *American Journal of Sociology* 90(2):326–58.

Maxwell, Nan L. 2006. "Low-Skilled Jobs: The Reality behind the Popular Perceptions." In *The Working Life: The Labor Market for Workers in Low-Skilled Jobs*, 1–23. W.E. Upjohn Institute.

Mayseless, Ofra and Einat Keren. 2014. "Finding a Meaningful Life as a Developmental Task in Emerging Adulthood: The Domains of Love and Work Across Cultures." *Emerging Adulthood* 2(1):63–73.

Mendenhall, Ruby. 2008. "Job Loss at Mid-Life: Managers and Executives Face the 'New Risk Economy.'" *Social Forces* 87(1):185–209.

Murphy, Kerri A., David L. Blustein, Amanda J. Bohlig, and Melissa G. Platt. 2010. "The College-to-Career Transition: An Exploration of Emerging Adulthood." *Journal of Counseling and Development* 88(2):174–81.

Polavieja, Javier G. and Lucinda Platt. 2014. "Nurse or Mechanic? The Role of Parental Socialization and Children's Personality in the Formation of Sex-Typed Occupational Aspirations." *Social Forces* 93(1):31–61.

Purtell, Kelly M. and Vonnie C. McLoyd. 2013. "A Longitudinal Investigation of Employment Among Low-Income Youth: Patterns, Predictors, and Correlates." *Youth & Society* 45(2):243–64.

Ranta, Mette, Julia Dietrich, and Katariina Salmela-Aro. 2014. "Career and Romantic Relationship Goals and Concerns during Emerging Adulthood." *Emerging Adulthood* 2(1):17–26.

Rindfuss, Ronald R., Elizabeth C. Cooksey, and Rebecca L. Sutterlin. 1999. "Young Adult Occupational Achievement: Early Expectations versus Behavioral Reality." *Work and Occupations* 26(2):220–63.

Schullery, Nancy M. 2013. "Workplace Engagement and Generational Differences in Values." *Business Communication Quarterly* 76(2):252–65.

Staff, Jeremy, Angel Harris, Ricardo Sabates, and Laine Briddell. 2010. "Uncertainty in Early Occupational Aspirations: Role Exploration or Aimlessness?" *Social Forces* 89(2):659–83.

Stuber, Jenny M. 2005. "Asset and Liability? The Importance of Context in the Occupational Experiences of Upwardly Mobile White Adults." *Sociological Forum* 20:139–66.

Twenge, Jean M. and Tim Kasser. 2013. "Generational Changes in Materialism and Work Centrality, 1976–2007: Associations with Temporal Changes in Societal Insecurity and Materialistic Role Modeling." *Personality and Social Psychology Bulletin* 39(7):883–97.

Twenge, Jean M., Stacy M. Campbell, Brian J. Hoffman, and Charles E. Lance. 2010. "Generational Differences in Work Values: Leisure and Extrinsic Values Increasing, Social and Intrinsic Values Decreasing." *Journal of Management* 36(5):1117–42.

Verschoor, Curtis C. 2013 "Ethical Behavior Differs among Generations." *Strategic Finance* 95(2):11–4.

Warren, John Robert, Jennifer T. Sheridan, and Robert M. Hauser. 2002. "Occupational Stratification across the Life Course: Evidence from the Wisconsin Longitudinal Study." *American Sociological Review* 67(3):432–55.

Wray-Lake, Laura, Amy K. Syvertsen, Laine Briddell, D. Wayne Osgood, and Constance A. Flanagan. 2011. "Exploring the Changing Meaning of Work for American High School Seniors from 1976 to 2005." *Youth & Society* 43(3):1110–35.

Zimmer-Gembeck, Melanie J. and Jeylan T. Mortimer. 2006. "Adolescent Work, Vocational Development, and Education." *Review of Educational Research* 76(4):537–66.

CHAPTER 7

Family Formations & Romantic Partnerships

The previous chapters have summarized the longer duration that most young people in America spend emerging into adulthood. The expectations for advanced education have risen, requiring years of investment before establishing careers, and it has become more challenging to be hired into a long-term, well-paying position. Thus, emerging adults often spend much of their 20s, and beyond, fluctuating between semi-permanent or temporary statuses, attempting to settle down. What does all this mean then for finding romantic partners and forming families? This chapter describes changes to romantic relationships and contextualizes them within the marital discords of previous generations and changing meanings of marriage. The chapter then shifts to understanding changing family patterns as adult children boomerang back home for periods of time—expanding and contracting family households like an accordion. The end of the chapter connects these trends back to the technological changes described in Chapter 2 and discusses modern conceptualizations of high-speed families.

MEN, WOMEN, BABIES

Shulman and Connolly (2013) find that romantic relationships have undergone changes from previous stage theories. In the past it was thought—at least for men—that identity was formed first, during adolescence. Then intimacy, via forming long-term romantic partnerships, was the primary task of young adulthood. However, scholars find that instead identity and intimacy are today often worked on simultaneously, then one for a while, then the other, then the reverse, and so on (e.g., Arnett 2015; Settersten & Ray 2010). Emerging adults are attempting to resolve both these developmental tasks simultaneously while trying to figure out how to integrate career paths, life plans, and romantic partners into something that works for each and the other.

Some youth, with a high degree of focus on academic achievement, tend to bracket serious romantic partnerships for later on in their developmental process (e.g., Giordano et al. 2008). Conversely, lower-income emerging adults who take on adult employment roles early due to the need to work to support themselves are more likely to become parents at a younger age than their more-resourced peers (e.g., Rauscher 2011). There are also differences in dating and relationship patterns among African American youth as compared to the majority white trends that are often depicted in national averages, which do not differentiate trends by race and ethnicity (e.g., Raley & Sullivan 2009; Hall et al. 2014; Wallace et al. 2014). In sum, the question "How do emerging adults fall in love and form families?" has a million answers. There is no one, singular path.

The result is a period of life that is often relatively unclear in terms of how it is that dating or sexual partners become long-term romantic partners, or if that is even desirable. Settersten and Ray (2010) called their chapter on family formation "First Comes Love, Then Comes … ?" (p. 77), and Arnett (2015) describes the process as "meandering toward marriage" (p. 114). Sawhill (2014) describes young people as "drifting" into sex and parenthood without marriage, sometimes at all, and often not before having sex and perhaps not before becoming a parent. Despite diversity in pathways to marriage, long-term partnership, or family formation, scholars agree that identity found in romantic relationships, work, and the combination of the two remain important in transitioning to adulthood (e.g., Branje et al. 2014).

MARITAL DISCORDS

How did we get to this point at which it seems nearly "anything goes," when just a few short decades ago people would be scorned for having a baby out of "wedlock" or having sex before marriage? It all started with changes to marriage, skyrocketing divorce rates, increasing cohabitation, and changes to normative expectations regarding marriage and family formation.

As described in previous chapters, the social changes resulting from deindustrialization make it more challenging for people from working-class backgrounds to find long-term and stable employment (e.g., Cherlin 2014). But many cannot afford the kind of long-term investment needed for advanced levels of education that are required to participate in the upper echelons of the knowledge-based economy. However, industrial labor no longer provides a large working-class base of Americans with the ability to earn a decent living without advanced degrees—as in times past.

This culminates in something Silva (2013) refers to as a *risk society*—describing a social-level insecurity in the kind of economic instability and unknown futures that many emerging adults face in the years ahead, especially if they do not have large social and economic resources to drawn upon in adulthood transitions. Increasingly, Americans have to be willing to be physically mobile in order to be socially mobile. They often have to move multiple times for new jobs and educational opportunities, forming a rootlessness—or disconnection to locations and institutions (Cherlin 2014). Meeting people and having families is not easy when multiple moves are involved. Since for many forming a stable life is thought to be best after stable employment trajectories are established, the difficulties of establishing employment roles affect family formation—patterns of establishing long-term partnerships and having children.

As a result, the timing of entering into marriage began to push backward, with the median ages of marriage increasing for men and women (e.g., Modell et al. 1978). These structural changes led to rising forms and instances of marital disruptions (e.g., Morgan & Rindfuss 1985; Schwartz & Han 2014). Scholars looking backward at historical changes from the 1970s to 1990s refer to the processes of social and cultural changes in the United States, at least, as the deinstitutionalization of marriage—meaning changes in the normative structure of how most people view the social institution of marriage—changing from marriage as obligation to marriage as companionship (Cherlin 2004).

With this new understanding of marriage for companionship and personal fulfillment, Americans became more likely to end their marriages when disagreements arose. Rather than staying committed to the relationship, conflicts indicate declines in marital companionship and become cause to end the marriage (Cherlin 2004). As previous generations increasingly dissolved their marriages in often-painful breakups of families and households, young people grew up more tentative about seeing marriage as a desired and ideal adulthood marker (e.g., Manning et al. 2007). Furstenberg (2007) describes this reluctance to marry by stating:

> The young adults provided a host of explanations for their skittishness about marriage, at least during their early and middle twenties. Most drew on direct observations of members of their family and community. Virtually all watched their parents go through divorce or never even make it to marriage, and they also witnessed numerous kin and friends go through painful separations. Many referred back to their childhood to explain why they were in no rush to settle down with a partner.... Their commentary about marriage was sobering, to say the least. Looming large in the background was the apprehension on the part of both men and women that marriages were risky undertakings (p. 111).

The most marked retreat from marriage as a regularly pursued adulthood pathway occurred among low-income populations (e.g., Gibson-Davis et al. 2005). The reading for this chapter is a section of a book by Edin and colleagues (2011), *Promises I Can Keep: Why Poor Women Put Motherhood before Marriage*. They describe a breakdown of trust in the institution of marriage. Given rising divorce rates, and the high costs involved in merging and later dissolving family units, many of the low-income women in this study describe turning away from marriage as a viable option, at least for now.

READING 7.1

What Marriage Means

By Katherine Edin, Maria J. Kefalas, and Frank Furstenberg

"I'm not Making any Promises I'm not Gonna be able to Keep."

When we ask Mahkiya Washington where she thinks her relationship with Mike will be in five years, she responds, "I don't know if we will be together [but] I hope that we will be together and married by [then]." She continues, "I hope that we are married, …. [I] went to school, graduated, … got a good job,… he went to school and graduated [too], so my daughter can have two parents as role models.… I don't want to have to be [in the situation where] he got another girlfriend, and I got another boyfriend. I don't want that. I don't want her to be around that 'cause I been around that. I want it to be two parents, so she will have a good role model and she knows how to bring up her family being married … not having different people." She concludes, "Mikey is all right, but he got a lot of maturing to do. … I am trying to stick in there because I want it to work."

When we discuss marriage with Antonia Rodriguez, she tells us she's "not going to get married now, but maybe in the future." Antonia has a lot she'd like to accomplish before she

Kathryn Edin, Maria J. Kefalas, and Frank Furstenberg, "What Marriage Means," Promises I Can Keep: Why Poor Women Put Motherhood Before Marriage, pp. 133–137. Copyright © 2011 by University of California Press. Reprinted with permission.

marries Emilio. "[First], my dream for me is to have a secure job I can count on, [with] retirement, everything else." "A lot of people are getting married [that shouldn't]," she continues. "They just love each other and they're just doing it [without thinking it through]. Just doing it for them." Antonia's strong condemnation of marrying merely for love stems from her belief that people should not marry unless they are sure they can live up to their vows.

When we interview her the first time, Jen Burke has been thinking a lot about marriage, as Rick has just proposed. She too says that both she and her boyfriend Rick have a lot of obstacles to overcome before they should embark upon marriage. Of him, she demands, "If he doesn't have a job, I want him to go get a job.... I think he should stay home with me and take care of [the baby], not go out and party all the time with his friends. He's gonna have to show me … do all that stuff before I marry him." Of herself, she demands the following: "I wanna have a real job.... I wanna have a nice-sized house." She clarifies, "Not a big house, just a [comfortable] one for us. I would want it to be up in the northeast [part of the city], where it's real nice at." Furthermore, as noted above, Jen wants to hold tide to the house herself. She reflects, "I think about all that stuff first. I wanna have everything ready in case something goes wrong." Deena Vallas beautifully sums up these sentiments when she tells us, "I'm not gonna do nothing, like make any promises that I'm not gonna be able to keep."

While many assume that the high rate of nonmarital childbearing among residents living in high poverty areas of America's inner cities means the marriage norm is dead, our mothers say this is far from true. Despite living in a social world in which parents, siblings, and friends seldom marry, most mothers hold to the dream of marriage, and many have it as an explicit life goal. Furthermore, a substantial minority of mothers say they're now in a relationship with a man whom they think they will marry in time, though most feel that they are not ready to take that step yet. The failed past relationships of those young women living in impoverished communities, along with the pervasive distrust of men, make marriage seem risky. They mitigate this risk by holding marriage to a high standard both in economic and in relational terms—so high that many will never marry at all.

Much has been written about the retreat from marriage in recent years. Some have argued that the decline of marriage, which is most pronounced among the poor, can be traced to declining male wages. Indeed, men with a high school education or less have seen large losses in hourly wages over the last thirty years, and far fewer are able to find full-time, year-round employment. But it is clear from these stories that even if the employment and wage rates in these neighborhoods returned to their 1950s levels, in the heyday of Philadelphia's economy, the marriage rate probably wouldn't increase much. Though male wages for unskilled workers were higher in those days and jobs more plentiful, unskilled male laborers were not paid that well, and the nature of Philadelphia's system of small craft production meant that even jobholders in the 1950s still faced a highly unstable job market.

Most studies suggest that at best, declining male employment and earnings can only account for about 20 percent of the sharp downturn in marriage.[1] Our stories suggest that many of the men who would have been considered marriageable in the 1950s would not be so today, for few 1950s marriages waited on the acquisition of a home mortgage, a car, some furniture, and two solid jobs. Even fewer 1950s brides insisted on monitoring their mates' behavior over four, five, or six years' time before they believed they could trust them enough to wed.

In the 1950s, marriage equaled social personhood. Being unmarried meant being a square peg in a round hole, not able to fit into the social milieu of the community. And if marriage was deemed necessary to take one's place as a normal adult, it was even more imperative to be married in order to bear and raise children. Today, a wedding ring is no longer the passport to personhood that it once was. In a society where the middle class waits longer and longer to marry, more and more of a person's early adult years are spent single, making singleness an acceptable state. In fact, early marriage is now frowned upon as unwise in virtually all sectors of our society. Poor women clearly believe that they can be perfectly adequate adults and parents outside of marriage, though the middle class might disagree. While they recognize that marrying first and having children second is the ideal way of doing things, they don't see how they can meet that goal in their circumstances. While poor women believe strongly that a child needs two parents, they don't see why they need marriage to accomplish that goal. Couples who live together can parent as easily as those who are married. And just because a man and a woman find they can't stay together doesn't mean a man cannot still play the role of father to his child.

This does not mean that marriage has lost its significance, either for the culture as a whole or for the poor. The most fundamental truth these stories reveal is that the meaning of marriage has changed. It is no longer primarily about childbearing and childrearing. Now, marriage is primarily about adult fulfillment, it is something poor women do for themselves, and their dreams about marriage are a guilty pleasure compared to the hard tasks of raising a family. Though women living in disadvantaged social contexts often wish they could indulge in a marriage at the same time that they're raising their children, it is simply not practical for most. If a marriage is to be lasting, it must have a strong economic foundation that both partners help to build, in which the woman maintains some level of economic independence. The couple relationship must also be strong enough to overcome the problems that so frequently lead to divorce, because marriage, which most still say is sacred, involves making promises—promises to be faithful and stay together for a lifetime. And as Deena Vallas puts it, most are not willing to make promises they are not sure they can keep.

Readers may wonder why so many of these women continue to hope for marriage when the men in their lives seem to be such bad risks. As we've said earlier, these

---

1   See Ellwood and Jencks (2002), Moffitt (2000), and Oppenheimer (2000).

couples live in a world where the better-off men go to the better-off women. Thus, unless poor women can improve their own positions through education and work, they have no choice but to abandon the dream of marriage altogether or attempt to change the available men. For most, giving up on the possibility of marriage means abandoning the hope that their difficult economic and social situations will get better in time.

Marriage is the prize at the end of the race. Because these women live in circumstances that are often too bleak to endure without hope that someday, in some way, they can make it, they still hope for marriage. But "getting themselves together" while also trying to redeem the fathers of their children is hard work, and failure is more common than success. Yet the fact that some succeed is enough cause for hope.

Instead, many low-income women opt to trust in themselves as solo caretakers of their children and often avoid getting married before having children. This does not mean that they no longer desire to be married. In fact, it is something more significant than that, as this study and others like it reveal that the meaning of marriage has altered (Edin, Kefalas, & Furstenberg 2013; Cherlin 2004). Even, or perhaps especially, disadvantaged Americans view marriage as not primarily about co-childrearing or sharing economic expenses. They can do both of those tasks together today without being married. Instead, marriage is viewed to be a form of personal fulfillment that comes with a set of promises for long-term faithfulness and constructing a life together that many low-income emerging adults do not feel equipped to offer.

In this context, marriage becomes an advantaged status, with those entering into it later typically having longer-term marital success (e.g., Glenn et al. 2010). Marriage is a luxury that many low-income women hope to someday be able to afford:

> For most, giving up on the possibility of marriage means abandoning the hope that their difficult economic and social situations will get better in time. Marriage is the prize at the end of the race. Because these women live in circumstances that are often too bleak to endure without hope that someday, in some way, they can make it, they still hope for marriage (Edin & Kefelas 2013, 136–137).

Marriage still holds symbolic meaning and, for many, results in personal, social, and economic benefits. But, with social changes and bifurcating inequalities, marriage is something that many think they cannot economically, socially, and personally afford.

Many emerging adults profess the desire to marry someday, but their beliefs about marriage were more "fluid and changing" (Willoughby & Hall 2014). As emerging adults age, they place more emphasis on getting married but also decreasingly emphasize the centrality of being married in their identity and view of their adulthood roles, creating a marriage paradox:

> They begin to place more importance on getting married yet less importance on their future spousal role compared to other obligations in life. Other scholars have noted that current cohorts of emerging adults may experience internal conflict as they attempt to balance educational, career, and relational goals (Willoughby et al. 2015, 226).

Though two-thirds of young people view marriage as important and expect to marry, they are concerned about divorce rates of previous generations (Manning et al. 2007).

The result is a stabilization of the divorce rate, but not because Americans today are less likely to dissolve relationships. Instead, there has been a decline and delay in entrance into marriage (e.g., Cherlin 2014). In other words, to have divorce there first has to be marriage. However, emerging adults are less likely to get married and have higher rates of *cohabitation*—living with a romantic partner without being married. Many scholars find that young people tend to view cohabitation as a strategy to defend against the patterns they watched the previous generation undergo and to manage the turbulence of their uncertain situations, while still participating in desirable intimacies with romantic partners. They "perceive cohabitation as a future union choice in a context of high uncertainty" and see it as "a way to move a relationship forward without making a strong interpersonal commitment" resulting in a "flexibility that is not possible in marriage" (Manning et al. 2007, 560)

In some cases, couples share a home as a response to economic hardships, more akin to roommates than long-term partners (e.g., Seltzer et al. 2012). But what appears to be more often the case is that emerging adults view cohabitation as a means of "trying on" potential partners in a progressive move across the life course toward more serious and long-term relationships (e.g., Sassler & Joyner 2011), a process called serial cohabitation—meaning living in romantic partnership with one partner, then ending that relationship and later moving in with another romantic partner, and then another (Lichter et al. 2010, 2014). The rate of participating in serial cohabitation has increased by nearly 40 percent in the last two decades, and this process is disproportionately concentrated among disadvantaged young people (Lichter et al. 2014). Carbone and Cahn (2014) call this the remaking of the American family. Rather than being able to form forever-like bonds, many emerging adults adapt to their unknown futures—and the need to be physically mobile in order to be socially mobile—by instead forming relational bonds that are tentative and potentially shorter term. The authors report:

> The identification of marriage with interdependence and sharing not only fails to express the implicit terms of working-class relationships; it ties it to a script that assumes two adults making comparable, if not always equal, investments in the relationship. For those who can manage neither parity of contribution nor unqualified trust, it makes marriage an impossible bargain (p. 118).

With declines and delays in entry to marriage, and less opportunity for long-term and stable positions for the majority of Americans, there has been a decline in intact families, parent-married families living with in-house biological children. This is a status now held by the minority of American families (Cherlin 2004). Instead, many get married after having children; years, money, and children are invested in these post-conception unions only to often dissolve them and start again (Cohen & Manning 2010).

Studies find that the well-being of children growing up in less cohesive and more disrupted homes is worse than those growing up in stable homes with two biological parents (Mitchell et al. 2015; Fomby & Cherlin 2007). Yet, the trends described above highlight that it is not that younger generations want to get married any less, or intend to provide less stable homes to their children. The fact is, cohabitation is a rising response to an unstable and unknown future, with marriage increasingly becoming an advantage that many only dream off. Disadvantage is particularly marked by the timing of childbearing, with more unintentional pregnancies resulting for people from low-income backgrounds (Furstenberg 2007). All of which is not to say that advantaged families do not also have struggles. In fact, delays in marriage to first pursue elongating educational and career trajectories means that many run up against biological clock issues by the time adulthood gets more firmly established. Infertility is a troubling result for emerging adults at the other end of the socioeconomic spectrum, often resulting in feeling like a failure with this life course transition (Loftus & Andriot 2012).

The point is not simply that one group benefits at the expense of the other group; the point is that marriage and family formation patterns have become disrupted, complex, and challenging for all involved, in distinct ways. Cherlin (2014) refers to these processes of establishment, dissolution, and re-establishment as the "churning of households" and the *marriage-go-round*. He and others find the fallout of this system is particularly acute for those from disadvantaged backgrounds, because they have fewer resources to invest in making the long haul to emerging adulthood that all young people in America are facing today. He states: "The patterns have significant social costs: Children face instability and complexity in their home lives, and adults drift away from the institutions that historically have anchored social life" (p. 195).

BOOMERANGS & ACCORDIONS

To make matters even more complex, parenting today typically involves a greater duration of in-house parenting than for the generations of recent history. Emerging adults often have to return home for periods of time to save money, regroup, and launch again. This is a process that people have labeled "boomerang kids"—referring to emerging adults moving out of their parents' home, then moving back in, back out again, and so on (e.g., Goldscheider 2012).

Recognizing that it is harder to afford independent residences without the jobs to support it, coupled with higher costs of longer time spent pursuing education, many parents of emerging adults challenge the "old-fashioned" notion that turning 18 years old necessarily equates with living on their own. Instead, middle-class families today often become "accordion families"—these are families with multiple generations in the same household who accept adult, or emerging adult, children back home for intermittent periods of time, expanding to accommodate them in times of need and contracting again when able to afford residences of their own (Newman 2012).

Less informed about the broader trends—including the formation of the new life stage of emerging adulthood and rising challenges with establishing adulthood roles in the normative traditions of times past—the mass media outlets of mainstream society have attached negative connotations to this parenting style. Labels such has "helicopter parenting"—referring to parents who hover over their children and are deeply involved in watching and navigating their choices—are meant to chastise parents for what is considered an inappropriate parenting strategy. However, scholars studying emerging adulthood warn that the use of such labels misses the mark tremendously. For example, Settersten and Ray (2013) point out that it is really the emerging adults who have no one involved in helping them navigate their lives who are the most vulnerable. They do not receive adequate information and guidance about the complexities of adulthood trajectories and wind up shouldering the burden of mistakes on their own.

When an entire generation of parents undergoes a marked shift in its understanding of parenthood, the individual-level explanations embedded in the chastisement of helicopter parent fall short of recognizing parenting patterns as a response to changing social experiences. While parents all make mistakes and misunderstand what is the best advice to give children and how to deliver it, the majority of parents mean well and have good intentions to guide children to successful adulthood. The trouble is that launching into adulthood has changed. More educated parents have greater access to updated knowledge about these changes and respond by increasing involvement in children's' lives (Settersten & Ray 2010; Newman 2013).

Likewise, many parents today enjoy the changes to parenting that mirror changes to marriage, namely the shift from obligation to companionship across the life course, resulting in parents of emerging adults often being considered good friends (Arnett 2015; Settersten & Ray 2010). In fact, most conflict that occurs in families during emerging adulthood results from parents not making this transition to a companionship relationship at the same time that their emerging adult children begin to desire it. Therefore, the other aspect that the helicopter parent label misses is that repeated contact with parents during emerging adulthood is less about social control—in most cases of companion-based, middle-class parenting styles—and more about relational support, with emerging adults willingly calling to talk life with their parents.

However, as with all the trends discussed in this chapter and throughout the book, there is not a single family configuration today. A minority of emerging adults still follow the traditional model of leaving home at 18 years of age and never returning to live under their parents' roof. Others make a pit stop after graduating college and head out again. Still others return and return again throughout their adulthood transitions. In some of these cases, emerging adults reenter dependency status, relying on their parents to cover living expenses and have primary responsibility over their day-to-day lives. In other cases, emerging adults and their parents negotiate a new arrangement, even in the case of living together again, with new responsibilities and expectations, including at times chipping in on or fully paying for their share of the rent or mortgage. There is a greater degree of variety and apparent choice involved in parenting.

At the same time, the kind of family structure children and emerging adults have translates to marked differences in their outcomes. How families handle financial transfers across generations (e.g., Clark & Kenney 2010), what happens to parent–child relationships when parents finish their education after having children versus completing it before or not at all (e.g., Domina & Roksa 2012), the way interpersonal closeness is felt by parents and children (e.g., Arnett 2015), and a range of other outcomes are affected by family configurations (e.g., Schumm 2012; Brand & Thomas 2014). Embedded in these multiplicative choices is a number of real constraints, and greater and lesser degrees of knowledge about, preparation for, and resources to respond to the changing role of parents in the lives of their emerging adult children.

HIGH-SPEED FAMILIES

Also changing is the way that technology mediates family relationships. Today's high-speed families navigate the complexities of work and love with technology-mediated communications. Dating, long-distance relationships, and even multicity partner locations happen through the social intermediary of the Internet and often via social media applications (e.g., Rosenfeld & Thomas 2012). Some families bemoan and reject the use of technology to mediate their relationships, while others adopt technologies such as family circle messaging, virtual visitation for traveling or divorced family members, child friendship activities at a distance through virtual and multiplayer video games, or synchronous communication vehicles that allow messages left for one another over time on digital spaces that mimic family white boards (e.g., Neustaedter et al. 2012). Does technology mediate, moderate, diminish, or enhance relationships? The answer is that families have to figure out what role technology will have in their relationships. As Neustaedter and colleagues (2012) explain:

> The idea of "family" can no more be defined by a network of blood relations than the concept of "home" can be described as a physical building. At some level, we may think of family as a collective of partners, parents, children, grandparents, and various other relations. But to stop here would be to gloss over what we really mean when we talk about being part of a family, spending time with family, or making a family home. These richer, everyday concepts point to a much more nuanced and profound idea of what a family is. When seen in these terms, it is clear that the notion of family is to some extent an aspiration—something we strive to achieve and a goal that we aim toward. Furthermore, moving toward this goal requires effort—and sometimes a great deal of effort—to maintain family, to nurture it, and to adapt domestic life to its changing needs and unfolding circumstances. In short, family is something that we do, not something that simply is. More than this, the doing of family is never complete. It is always a "work in progress" (p. 2).

However, middle-class families today typically spend little time together in shared physical space and engaged in dialog with or attention to one another, often too busy keeping up with their busy schedules, a state that Ochs and Kremer-Sadlik (2013) call *fast-forward families*. Yet families of all types still strive for a balance of all else with family life, and emerging adults all crave the love and support of family, friends, and romantic partners (e.g., Smith et al. 2011).

The challenge is that what it means to be a family; how one becomes a family; where families are located; how they will be supported; and when, how, and in what ways they will raise children are all less specified than they were in times past. There are changes in the timing of marriages—including enthusiasts, delayers, and the ambiguous middle marital paradigms (Willoughby & Hall 2014). Plus, many cohabitate with romantic partners that may or may not eventually become marital spouses, and there are many changes to—but also certain stabilities in—household divisions of labor (e.g., Miller & Sassler 2010). Even attitudes towards relationships and their desirability differ across emerging adults (e.g., Poortman & Liefbroer 2010).

This all amounts on the one hand to opportunities for diverse configurations of love and families, and on the other hand internalizes the normative structure of family and love life from a dominant societal mode to one that must be negotiated within each micro family (or semi-family) unit. Work and partner conflicts are more likely and take more ongoing discussion, investment, and reconfiguration if they are to remain durable in the midst of economic and locational flexibility (e.g., Seiffge-Krenke & Luyckx 2014; Seiffge-Krenke et al. 2014; van Dulmen et al. 2014). In the vast array of options for family configurations, Streib (2015) finds cultural differences in family of origin often appear *within* families via conflicting understandings and taken-for-granted assumptions regarding what it means to be parents, how to raise children, who does what around the house, and general *family sensibilities* to "go with the flow" versus "order, prioritize, and manage" the happenings of family life.

In summary, emerging adults are "moving in different directions.... It's not just that they have different expectations about their relationships, though they do. It is that their emerging norms, the scripts that allow them to make sense of their lives, are moving further apart" (Carbone & Cahn 2014, 104). The pathways to adulthood are complex and in a rapid state of flux, but social institutions, law, and policy have not yet caught up and responded accordingly. Some families are aware of and embrace these changes, others resist them, still others are less aware of some or the other of these changes and their meaning for love and family life.

REFERENCES

Arnett, Jeffrey Jensen. 2015. *Emerging Adulthood: The Winding Road from the Late Teens through the Twenties.* 2nd edition. Oxford University Press

Branje, Susan, Lydia Laninga-Wijnen, Rongqin Yu, and Wim Meeus. 2014. "Associations among School and Friendship Identity in Adolescence and Romantic Relationships and Work in Emerging Adulthood." *Emerging Adulthood* 2(1):6–16.

Brand, Jennie E. and Juli Simon Thomas. 2014. "Job Displacement among Single Mothers: Effects on Children's Outcomes in Young Adulthood." *American Journal of Sociology* 119(4):955–1001.

Carbone, June and Naomi Cahn. 2014. *Marriage Markets: How Inequality Is Remaking the American Family.* Oxford: Oxford University Press.

Cherlin, Andrew J. 2004. "The Deinstitutionalization of American Marriage." *Journal of Marriage and Family* 66(4):848–61.

Cherlin, Andrew J. 2014. *Labor's Love Lost: The Rise and Fall of the Working-Class Family in America.* New York: Russell Sage Foundation Publications.

Clark, Shelley and Catherine Kenney. 2010. "Is the United States Experiencing a 'Matrilineal Tilt?': Gender, Family Structures and Financial Transfers to Adult Children." *Social Forces* 88(4):1753–76.

Cohen, Jessica and Wendy Manning. 2010. "The Relationship Context of Premarital Serial Cohabitation." *Social Science Research* 39(5):766–76.

Domina, Thurston and Josipa Roksa. 2012. "Should Mom Go Back to School? Post-Natal Educational Attainment and Parenting Practices." *Social Science Research* 41(3):695–708.

Edin, Kathryn and Maria J. Kefalas. 2011. "What Marriage Means." In *Promises I Can Keep: Why Poor Women Put Motherhood before Marriage*, 104–37. Berkeley: University of California Press.

Fomby, Paula and Andrew J. Cherlin. 2007. "Family Instability and Child Well-Being." *American Sociological Review* 72(2):181–204.

Furstenberg, Frank F. 2007. *Destinies of the Disadvantaged: The Politics of Teen Childbearing.* Russell Sage Foundation.

Gibson-Davis, Christina M., Kathryn Edin, and Sara McLanahan. 2005. "High Hopes but Even Higher Expectations: The Retreat from Marriage among Low-Income Couples." *Journal of Marriage and Family* 67(5):1301–12.

Giordano, Peggy C., Kenyatta D. Phelps, Wendy D. Manning, and Monica A. Longmore. 2008. "Adolescent Academic Achievement and Romantic Relationships." *Social Science Research* 37(1):37–54.

Glenn, Norval D., Jeremy E. Uecker, and Robert W. B. Love. 2010. "Later First Marriage and Marital Success." *Social Science Research* 39(5):787–800.

Goldscheider, Frances K. 2012. "The Accordion Family: Boomerang Kids, Anxious Parents, and the Private Toll of Global Competition by Katherine Newman." *American Journal of Sociology* 118(3):821–22.

Hall, Naomi M., Anna K. Lee, and Daphne D. Witherspoon. 2014. "Factors Influencing Dating Experiences among African American Emerging Adults." *Emerging Adulthood* 2(3):184–94.

Lichter, Daniel T., Richard N. Turner, and Sharon Sassler. 2010. "National Estimates of the Rise in Serial Cohabitation." *Social Science Research* 39(5):754–65.

Lichter, Daniel T., Sharon Sassler, and Richard N. Turner. 2014. "Cohabitation, Post-Conception Unions, and the Rise in Nonmarital Fertility." *Social Science Research* 47:134–47.

Loftus, Jeni and Angie L. Andriot. 2012. "'That's What Makes a Woman': Infertility and Coping with a Failed Life Course Transition." *Sociological Spectrum* 32(3):226–43.

Manning, Wendy D., Monica A. Longmore, and Peggy C. Giordano. 2007. "The Changing Institution of Marriage: Adolescents' Expectations to Cohabit and to Marry." *Journal of Marriage and Family* 69(3):559–75.

Miller, Amanda and Sharon Sassler. 2010. "Stability and Change in the Division of Labor among Cohabiting Couples." *Sociological Forum* 25:677–702.

Mitchell, Colter, Sara McLanahan, Daniel Notterman, John Hobcraft, Jeanne Brooks-Gunn, and Irwin Garfinkel. 2015. "Family Structure Instability, Genetic Sensitivity, and Child Well-Being." *American Journal of Sociology* 120(4):1195–225.

Modell, John, Frank F. Furstenberg Jr., and Douglas Strong. 1978. "The Timing of Marriage in the Transition to Adulthood: Continuity and Change, 1860–1975." *American Journal of Sociology* 84:S120–50.

Morgan, S. Philip and Ronald R. Rindfuss. 1985. "Marital Disruption: Structural and Temporal Dimensions." *American Journal of Sociology* 90(5):1055–77.

Neustaedter, Carman, Steve Harrison, and Abigail Sellen. 2012. *Connecting Families: The Impact of New Communication Technologies on Domestic Life*. Springer Science & Business Media.

Newman, Katherine S. 2013. *The Accordion Family: Boomerang Kids, Anxious Parents, and the Private Toll of Global Competition*. Boston: Beacon Press.

Ochs, Elinor, and Tamar Kremer-Sadlik, eds. 2013. *Fast-Forward Family: Home, Work, and Relationships in Middle-Class America*. University of California Press.

Poortman, Anne-Rigt and Aart C. Liefbroer. 2010. "Singles' Relational Attitudes in a Time of Individualization." *Social Science Research* 39(6):938–49.

Raley, R. Kelly and M. Kate Sullivan. 2009. "Social-Contextual Influences on Adolescent Romantic Involvement: The Constraints of Being a Numerical Minority." *Sociological Spectrum* 30(1):65–89.

Rauscher, Emily. 2011. "Producing Adulthood: Adolescent Employment, Fertility, and the Life Course." *Social Science Research* 40(2):552–71.

Rosenfeld, Michael J. and Reuben J. Thomas. 2012. "Searching for a Mate: The Rise of the Internet as a Social Intermediary." *American Sociological Review* 77(4):523–47.

Sassler, Sharon and Kara Joyner. 2011. "Social Exchange and the Progression of Sexual Relationships in Emerging Adulthood." *Social Forces* 90(1):223–45.

Sawhill, Isabel V. 2014. *Generation Unbound: Drifting into Sex and Parenthood without Marriage*. Washington, DC: Brookings Institution Press.

Schumm, Walter R. 2012. "Methodological Decisions and the Evaluation of Possible Effects of Different Family Structures on Children: The New Family Structures Survey (NFSS)." *Social Science Research* 41(6):1357–66.

Schwartz, Christine R. and Hongyun Han. 2014. "The Reversal of the Gender Gap in Education and Trends in Marital Dissolution." *American Sociological Review* 79(4):605–29.

Seiffge-Krenke, Inge and Koen Luyckx. 2014. "Competent in Work and Love? Emerging Adults' Trajectories in Dealing With Work–Partnership Conflicts and Links to Health Functioning." *Emerging Adulthood* 2(1):48–58.

Seiffge-Krenke, Inge, Koen Luyckx, and Katariina Salmela-Aro. 2014. "Work and Love during Emerging Adulthood: Introduction to the Special Issue." *Emerging Adulthood* 2(1):3–5.

Seltzer, Judith A., Charles Q. Lau, and Suzanne M. Bianchi. 2012. "Doubling up When Times Are Tough: A Study of Obligations to Share a Home in Response to Economic Hardship." *Social Science Research* 41(5):1307–19.

Settersten, Richard and Barbara E. Ray. 2010. *Not Quite Adults: Why 20-Somethings Are Choosing a Slower Path to Adulthood, and Why It's Good for Everyone*. New York: Bantam.

Shulman, Shmuel and Jennifer Connolly. 2013. "The Challenge of Romantic Relationships in Emerging Adulthood: Reconceptualization of the Field." *Emerging Adulthood* 1(1):27–39.

Silva, Jennifer M. 2013. *Coming Up Short: Working-Class Adulthood in an Age of Uncertainty*. New York: Oxford University Press.

Smith, Christian, Kari Christoffersen, Hilary Davidson, and Patricia Snell Herzog. 2011. *Lost in Transition: The Dark Side of Emerging Adulthood*. New York: Oxford University Press.

Streib, Jessi. 2015. *The Power of the Past: Understanding Cross-Class Marriages*. Oxford University Press.

van Dulmen, Manfred H. M., Shannon E. Claxton, W. Andrew Collins, and Jeffry A. Simpson. 2014. "Work and Love among Emerging Adults: Current Status and Future Directions." *Emerging Adulthood* 2(1):59–62.

Wallace, Scyatta A., Lisa M. Hooper, and Malini Persad. 2014. "Brothers, Sisters and Fictive Kin Communication about Sex among Urban Black Siblings." *Youth & Society* 46(5):688–705.

Willoughby, Brian J. and Scott S. Hall. 2014. "Enthusiasts, Delayers, and the Ambiguous Middle Marital Paradigms among Emerging Adults." *Emerging Adulthood* 3(2):123–35.

CHAPTER 8

Connective Friendships & Supportive Communities

Previous chapters highlighted how macro-structural changes have differentiated society into multiple subgroups. Pockets of diverse social arrangements characterize the myriad social groups forming a complex cultural mosaic that is the U.S. social milieu. This chapter focuses on the ways those changes work their way through connectivity, belonging, communities, and forms of contact. It describes the contours of emerging adult friendships and social supports as social changes occur in the meanings of friendship and the kinds of connectivity enabled by new forms of social media.

CONNECTIVITY

Connectivity is an important aspect of a concept in social sciences called *social capital*—the relationships that people have and how relationships more or less provide social and economic support (e.g., Portes 1998). Christakis and Fowler (2011) studied the connections among people and summarize their findings in *Connected: The Surprising Power of Our Social Networks and How They Shape Our Lives.* They find that our *social networks*—the collection of social ties that we have to others, a.k.a. our social relationships—relate to many social outcomes, often without our consciously recognizing that.

One thing that emerging adults and all Americans share in common is living in a hyper-connected society. In *Linked: How Everything Is Connected to Everything Else and What It Means for Business, Science, and Everyday Life,* Barabasi (2003) describes the interconnections that exist between people, social settings, and all aspects of social life. Brown (2008) describes emerging adults as existing within a *media-saturated world*:

> Young people today use a wide range of different kinds of media, including music, movies, magazines, newspapers, and the Internet for entertainment and information—and have since they were very young (p. 279).

This affects everything from how identity gets formed and repeatedly shaped in online spaces, to how people choose who they are friends with and who gets access to what information about them online, to how people experience and manage emotions online, to the many and varied sorts of interactions that can be had online (Brown 2008).

Scholars are curious about the ways these massive changes to connectivity affect social life. Some studies point to changing values due to emerging adults having grown up using distinct social connection technologies. For example, Madden et al. (2010) find that younger generations are not nearly as concerned about privacy as are previous generations, and Twenge et al. (2010) find that younger generations place a higher emphasis on leisure activities. Both of these changes could well be due to changes in technology-mediated connections. Since people are less able to mediate the kinds of information available about them on the web, they grow up more accepting of that as the way it is. In addition, with gaming and relationships ever-accessible, young people may be able to make leisure a greater part of their lives than previous generations.

The outcome with the most attention, in terms of changes brought about by connectivity, is social isolation—the extent to which people are cut off from others. A landmark book by Riesman (1950) raised concerns as to whether Americans were becoming more lonely, pointing to the counterintuitive phenomenon of crowd loneliness—that the loneliest place to be is in the middle of a large number of people who are personally unknown.

Related to this concern, McPherson and colleagues (2006) published a study that has received considerable attention; they found that social isolation was increasing in the United States over time. They found that though Americans were increasingly connected technologically, their interpersonal connectivity was declining. They measured this through a construct called core discussion networks. They asked people to list who they speak with about important social and political matters. What the authors found was that the number of people listed for this measure had declined in recent decades, meaning today people are more connected, technically, but less interpersonally connected that in times past.

However, this finding has been challenged from a number of different directions, investigating changes to social network sizes (e.g., Wang & Wellman 2010). Direct challenges have pointed out the ways in which the measure is faulty or how changes to the measure over time could indicate more about the savvy of people taking surveys than a change in the phenomenon itself (e.g., Fischer 2009; 2011; Paik & Sanchagrin 2013). For example, scholars pointed out that survey respondents have become aware of this core discussion measure and know that if they list more people in their network, then they have to answer more questions in the follow-up grid—they will be asked questions for each person listed. They defend against this respondent fatigue by listing fewer people. This means the change detected could not be an actual decline in the number of people with whom important matters are discussed.

The broader point made by Fischer (2011) in *Still Connected: Family and Friends in America Since 1970*, is that changes have occurred over time in the ways families and friends are connected. However, the evidence is not unilateral one way or the other. "It depends" is the most accurate way to describe this state of affairs, as it is not the case that all measures have declined—some have stayed stable and others have increased. What is clear is that the ways people connect have changed, and the meaning of those changes may have too.

Easley and Kleinberg (2010) summarize findings from a study about Facebook connections and find that while the overall average of connections is high, around 500 people on average, the number of people that Facebook users actually directly communicate with is in the average range of ten to 20, meaning the rest are people they follow more passively. Thus, it may be the case that emerging adults today are more able to passively follow people that are more like acquaintances than friends, despite receiving the same Facebook label as the friends who they actually know more deeply and talk with more regularly. This may have a range of implications for social life.

For example, Granovetter (1973) labeled a phenomenon called the "strength of weak ties"—which refers to the fact that it is often the acquaintances that people have, rather than their stronger and primary ties, which aid them in getting jobs. Applied to the Facebook study, this could mean that emerging adults are on the whole more connected to the kind of weak ties that can get them jobs, which may be more necessary today given the employment situation described in Chapter 6. However, a study on that alone does not indicate anything, necessarily, about the extent to which emerging adults feel emotionally and socially supported by the ties they have.

Instead it is important to keep in mind what Parigi and Henson (2014) find, which is that there are simultaneously structural and subjective experiences embedded in social network connections. Structural connections refer to the number of people known and the ways those connections are organized, and examples of these include:

- Network closure—the extent to which everyone in the network knows all others.
- Structural holes—pockets of network tie absences, spaces where no one is connected.
- Embeddedness—how deeply integrated a person is within a network.
- Overlap—how much people of one network know people in another network.

These features tell social scientists about important features of network connectivity, *and* subjective experiences are equally crucial to understand.

BELONGING

Studies focused on belonging in youth and emerging adulthood find peers are as important as ever, if not even more important, to adulthood transitions (e.g., Young et al. 2015). In fact, in the reading for this chapter, Milner (2006) finds that experiences of belonging with peers are crucial in structuring development trajectories. This is in part because the education system is structured such that teens spend more time with peers than interacting with adults. This reading also highlights how the social inequalities in Chapter 3 affect youths' belonging patterns through the ways that peer interaction sites, such as high schools, are stratified by *social esteem*—young people separate into distinct social groups and gain identity through participation in those groups.

READING 8.1

Why Do They Behave Like That/Fitting In, Standing Out, and Keeping Up

By Murray Milner

Status Groups: Adolescence as A Caste System

Status groups: The German sociologist Max Weber used the term *status group*, which he contrasted with notions of class and political party, to refer to social formations that were based on differences in status and lifestyle.[1] According to Weber, the most extreme form of status group was Hindu castes. In traditional India, members of one caste did not usually marry or eat with members of another caste. The higher status castes tended to minimize their contact with lower castes and expected to be treated with deference by those from lower castes. These patterns are common for teenagers. Other status groups such as the Boston Brahmans, the New York Social Register, or a local country club set are less intense forms of this pattern. Still other status groups may be even more amorphous with indistinct boundaries, as much a subculture as a concrete group. Examples include Latinos, Italian-Americans, and wine connoisseurs. Instead of sharing simply a common economic or political location, members of a status group share a common lifestyle, that is, common

---

1 Weber (1968), *Economy and Society*, Chap. IV, IX.

Murray Milner, "Why Do They Behave Like That/Fitting In, Standing Out, and Keeping UP," Freaks, Geeks, and Cool Kids, pp. 22–25, 40–45, 244–245, 247–248. Copyright © 2006 by Taylor & Francis Group. Reprinted with permission.

patterns of consumption and use of common symbols and rituals. Wealth or political power may be a prerequisite, but they are not sufficient. The new multimillionaire who smokes big cigars and brags loudly about his wealth is not likely to be accepted into exclusive upper-class social circles. A teenager may be rich, handsome, and knowledgeable about punk bands, and still be shunned by local punks if he wears khakis, button-down dress shirts, and a "Just Say No" button.[2] Both the new millionaire and the preppy teenager are rejected because they have not adopted the appropriate lifestyle.

Crowds and cliques: I will argue that teenage *crowds* are another example of status groups. Because they are a status group and a subculture, they show an enormous concern with lifestyle and acceptance by peers.[3] Often they engage in behaviors that are highly reminiscent of castes. Crowds are often composed of multiple overlapping cliques. In contrast to crowds, *cliques* are relatively small numbers of individuals who interact with one another regularly.[4] Crowds are a social category, a type of subculture, a reference group, and a status group; cliques are small groups that embody, transmit, and transform such subcultures. Categories that have become broadly established in the wider society are *societal categories*. They are often widely discussed and portrayed in the media. For example, most high schools have few if any skinheads, but most high school students will know that skinheads are stereotypically associated with adolescence, shaved heads, racist attitudes, and aggressive behavior.[5] Sometimes these societal categories are borrowed or adopted to create local social categories and cliques.

When people talk about these matters they sometimes say "crowd" when they mean "clique" and vice versa, but usually the context indicates whether they are referring to a clique or a more amorphous crowd or societal category.[6] For teenagers, acceptance or rejection by peer cliques and crowds—preps, jocks, nerds, etc.—is

---

2 "Just Say No" was a phrase made familiar during Ronald Reagan's presidency by his wife, Nancy, when she advised young people about drug use.

3 Brown, Mory, and Kinney (1994), "Casting Adolescent Crowds in a Relational Perspective," have suggested a "relational perspective" of crowds that considers the significance of crowds for social identities, as channels for creating interpersonal ties, and as contexts that shape behavior and attitudes. I do not disagree with this, but partly because of my particular theoretical interests and partly because of the nature of the data I am using, I will not try to systematically deal with all of these aspects. I will primarily focus on status processes, which is not to deny that other factors shape the social organization of crowds.

4 In a five-school network study Ennett and Bauman (1996), "Adolescent Social Networks," found that cliques ranged in size from 3 to 10 members with an average membership of 5. Schools varied in the degree to which students were clearly members of a clique versus being isolates or "liaisons," but their study does not include a sufficient number of schools to show the sources of such variations.

5 Like many stereotypes this is probably generally true, but often exaggerated and misleading in specific cases. See for example Finnegan (1998), *Cold New World,* "book four" for a description of non-racist skinheads; and Soeffner (1997), *The Order of Rituals,* for an account of the emergence of punks and skinheads.

6 Even in the scholarly literature the use of such terms as status group, subculture, crowd, and clique varies. See Dunphy (1963), "The Social Structure of Urban Adolescent Peer Groups," for a seminal use of this distinction applied to Australian youth. See Steinberg (1993), *Adolescence,* for a standard discussion in a textbook on adolescents. Both types of units play important and somewhat distinctive roles. As Brown (1990), "Peer Groups and Peer

often perceived to be much more important than academic success. Some become virtually obsessed with social distinctions made by their peers.

In addition to clarifying the nature of the teenage crowds and cliques, let me summarize some of the characteristics and variations in teenage behavior that need to be explained:

1. Why do contemporary teenagers behave in the various ways mentioned in the introduction, including their intense concern with appearance, clothing, music, privacy, gossip, peer relationships (especially who they eat with in the lunchroom and who "goes out with" whom), partying, athletic events, television, etc.?
2. Why do teenagers' behavioral patterns seem quite different from patterns of earlier or later stages of life?
3. Why are contemporary teenagers in many respects quite different from those of earlier historical periods and other societies?
4. Why is this pattern spreading to other societies?
5. Why is the American pattern changing toward greater diversity?
6. Why is the pattern being extended to both younger and older age groups?[7]

Learning from the caste system: As strange as it may seem, I believe that I have found the answers to some of the above questions by studying the Indian caste system.[8] The results of this earlier study are reported in my book *Status and Sacredness*.[9] The classic Indian caste system is characterized by (1) avoidance of intimate associations with those of lower status, (2) conformity to the norms characteristic of one's particular caste, (3) elaborate rituals and symbols to mark social boundaries, and (4) prohibitions against cross-caste mobility, marriage, and dining.[10] Both Indian castes and adolescent subcultures are systems in which status is the key resource. My argument is not that there is some vague parallel between Indian castes and high school stratification systems. Rather, I am claiming that what I have learned about how status systems operate from studying castes, significantly clarifies what goes on in our high schools. The pre-modern Indian caste system is arguably the most elaborate status system in

---

Cultures," 184, notes, "clique affiliation indicates merely who an adolescent's close friends are; crowd affiliation indicates who an adolescent is—at least in the eyes of his peers."

7 These questions emphasize the relative uniqueness of American teenagers at the beginning of the twenty-first century. This is not to deny that the antecedent social processes of childhood are important or that there are no similarities between contemporary youth and earlier societies. But the reason teenagers in contemporary society are perceived to be a social problem is not because of the "eternal problems" of youth, but rather because of the particular characteristics at the beginning of the twenty-first century.

8 Ogbu (1978), *Minority Educations and Caste*, also draws on the notion of caste to analyze American high schools, but he primarily uses the term to describe discrimination against minorities. I will take up the issue of racial and ethnic segregation later. Here I am focusing on the distinctions that students create even when schools are racially and ethnically homogeneous.

9 Milner (1994), *Status and Sacredness*.

10 This is a very concise and oversimplified description of the Indian caste system. For a more elaborate characterization and analysis, see Milner (1994), *Status and Sacredness*, especially Chaps. 4–6.

human history. The intensity of status concerns in the Indian context makes it easier to see social processes that shape the status system. My argument is that these same processes are present, but more obscure in other historical situations. Therefore a key to understanding American high schools is to understand why status systems operate the way they do. This means seeing that there are similar social processes that are relevant to both Indian castes and American high schools—as well as other social systems. Of course, the precise ways these processes operate are shaped by the specific historical and cultural contexts in which they occur.

Are Indian castes and teenage crowds important? The Indian caste system is rapidly changing and in important respects disappearing even in village India. Other historic social structures in which ascribed statuses were central have largely disappeared. Except for a few faint cultural echoes, European feudalism is long gone. Even the apartheid of South Africa and the racism of the American South were dramatically transformed in the last quarter of the twentieth century. The feminist movement has significantly reduced gender inequality. If rigid status systems are disappearing as a central mechanism for organizing whole societies, they are nonetheless present in important pockets within twenty-first-century societies. The fact that these are limited enclaves does not mean that they are not important to the larger society. In the nineteenth century both the British aristocracy and the racially segregated American South were bounded enclaves, but they had enormous importance for the societies in which they were located. Both shaped the national culture of which they were a part in ways that still profoundly affect these societies.[11] High schools are places where status is very important and, as we shall see, this has important implications for the broader society. Thus our next task is to understand what it is about the social situation of teenagers that produces such an intense concern with peer status. I touched on this in the introductory chapter, but now we need to elaborate the story.

Why is Status So Important to Teenagers?

If peers are so influential, how do they exercise this influence? A primary means is through creating status differences. Of course, all social systems create some kinds of status differences. So why are these so important for teenagers? In all societies, as individuals mature they develop some level of independence from their parents; their autonomy increases. Schoolchildren in modern societies, in effect, go off to work" and spend most of their day away from their parents. Teachers and administrators supervise them, but the scope of these adults' authority is much narrower than that of

---

11   The intense racism of the American South allowed the milder forms of discrimination in the rest of the nation to be largely ignored for nearly a century. The residues of this history continue to be a central feature of the United States. The elitism of the British aristocracy and the patterns of privilege and deference associated with it still shape patterns of social interaction in Britain, even though they have had little formal political power for a century. This is not to say that these status patterns in the U.S. and Britain have not been significantly weakened even within their core enclaves. Nonetheless the crucial point here is that these status systems, which were primarily restricted to a limited segment of the society, had reverberations for the entire society.

parents. The ratio of supervisors to subordinates also decreases significantly. This new autonomy and reduced control by adults usually means that the influence of peers is amplified dramatically.[12] All of these processes are further intensified when students reach high school. They move to larger, more complex schools, gain increased mobility (often by driving cars), and greater communication facilities (via the telephone, e-mail, and the Internet). Not only school time, but most leisure time is spent in the presence of peers or in communication with them. "In a typical week, even discounting time spent in classroom instruction (23% of an average student's waking hours), high school students spend twice as much of their time with peers (29%) as with parents or other adults (15%)."[13] The separation of school and peers from family, the increased mobility, and the independent communication networks mean that the actions of students are less visible to adults, and hence less subject to supervision and control.

As noted in the introduction, adolescents have more autonomy, but little economic or political power. They cannot change the curriculum, hire or fire the teachers, decide who will be admitted to their school, or move to another school without the permission of adults.[14] At the time of life when the biological sources of sexuality are probably strongest, in a social environment saturated with sexual imagery and language, they are exhorted to avoid sex. In many situations they are treated as inferior citizens who are looked upon as at best a nuisance. They are denied the right to buy alcohol or see "adult" movies and are subject to the control not only of parents, teachers, and police, but numerous petty clerks in stores, movies, and nightclubs who "check their IDs."

In one realm, however, their power is supreme; they control their evaluations of one another. That is, the kind of power they do have is status power: the power to create their own status systems based on their own criteria. Predictably, the creation and distribution of this kind of power is often central to their lives. Therefore, what is needed to understand the patterns of behavior that emerge in such social systems is a theory of status relations. ...

---

12 I have already outlined the debate about how much influence peers have. But there is also debate over how peers influence one another. Are members of cliques and crowds similar to one another because they pressure each other to behave in a certain way, or did those who had similar dispositions and inclinations simply come together? Studies seem to indicate that the latter process is stronger than the first, but this is certainly conditioned by the type of behavior that is involved. The extent to which peer influence is positive or negative—from the point of view of parents and other adults—is also unclear. See Brown (1990), "Peer Groups and Peer Cultures," 190-195, for an overview of these matters. See also Toison and Urberg (1993), "Similarities Between Adolescent Best Friends." Despite these qualifications, as I have already indicated, I believe that in many areas of their lives adolescents are strongly influenced by peers and peer culture. For example, when fashions in clothing, music, and language change—sometimes relatively quickly and dramatically—and are almost universally adopted within a given clique or crowd, this change is due to mutual influence, not self-selection or parental influence.
13 Brown (1990), "Peer Groups and Peer Cultures," 179.
14 Younger children also see adults as controlling their lives and often resist this and increase their autonomy in various ways. See Corsaro (1997), *Sociology of Childhood*. Adolescents, however, are increasingly able to escape the supervision and control of adults and hence these processes are significantly accentuated. This growing autonomy is probably rooted both in changing cultural expectations—it is recognized that adolescents have a right of more privacy—and because their lives are more physically segregated from adults.

Some Crowds and Their Rankings

In the majority of the schools analyzed, students were stratified by status, and most had variations on a common structure. A female student from the Tacoma, Washington, area provides a typical description:

> The ideal of a social status was clear to all incoming sophomores ... [T]here were six primary groups on campus which followed a specific hierarchy: the "Preps" (image-conscious types), the "Jocks" (highly athletic-oriented; usually involved in at least two sports), the "Rockers" (alternative grunge, skateboard types; Pacific Northwest version of the California "surfer" stereotype), the "Nerds" (academic-oriented; studious), the Punks/Weirdos (seen by the other groups as nonconformists; apathetic to [the school's] social hierarchy), and the "G's" (gangsters, "wannabe" gangsters)
>
> ... [Everyone agreed that two groups in particular distinguished themselves from the rest—the "Preps" and the "Jocks" ... [Our] high school had a deeply-embedded tradition of school spirit and sports— especially football. The closer associated one was with this tradition, the more popular one became. Therefore, members of the sports teams, the cheerleading squad, and the dance team were considered the "royalty"...[15]

In other schools there were fewer distinctions—for example, everyone who was not a prep, a jock, or a nerd might be labeled "alternative."

As the above quote indicates the "popular crowd"—those who were "cool"—were usually composed of a combination of male preps and athletes and the most attractive females in the school. Usually most of the female cheerleaders were core members of "the royalty." One young man from a small Texas town provides a stereotypical description:

> All cheerleaders have a nice golden, crispy tan and it is so obvious during the winter that they have unlimited tanning at the local tanning salon. If a guy got up the nerve to ask a cheerleader out then that was the talk of the week for their clique ... The cheerleaders are very snobbish and feel too good to

---

[15] SP54. Eder and Kinney (1995), "The Effect of Extracurricular Activities on Adolescents' Popularity," found that in middle school cheerleading could raise your visibility but also increase people's hostility toward you. While I have no systematic data on this issue, this tendency seems to be less the case in "traditional" high schools. As we shall see, in pluralistic high schools, the status of cheerleaders is often much lower. For a study of the relative prestige of different sports and extracurricular activities based on the opinions of college students taking an introductory psychology course, see Holland and Andre (1995), "Prestige Ratings of High School Extracurricular Activities." Suitor and Reavis (1995), "Football, Fast Cars, and Cheerleading," found that in the period 1979–89 the prestige of cheerleading had declined, but they did not have a nationally representative sample and it is likely that this varies by region and school. It appears that as cheerleaders have lost their traditional prestige as the "cool" and "hot" girls, there have been efforts to transform this activity into a sport or performance activity. Hence, in many schools cheerleaders execute rather complicated gymnastic and dance routines and are selected not only for good looks and "personality," but for skill in these activities.

talk to anyone but themselves and people on a high economic level. Since the cheerleaders did a lot of jazz /dance, they listened to pretty much anything that had a fast beat so they could shake any body part they got a chance to.[16]

In some schools female members of the drill team were less exalted members of the popular crowd.[17] Star athletes were well known not only in the school but were community celebrities.

The dominance of a popular crowd is not a West Coast or Southern or a small town phenomenon. A boy from a high status and very historic Boston suburb reports:

> The social scene ... was split broadly into two extreme groups commonly called the "jocks" and the "freaks" ... The jocks were not necessarily all athletes ... rather they were the "cooler" and more popular students ... Although the different cliques ... were not openly ranked, most people would agree that the jocks were the more prestigious, popular, and "cooler" students by the traditional high school standards ... A "cooler" or more popular student rarely formed a friendship ... with a less popular student ... The strict barriers around different cliques made it very hard for students to get to know students well from other social groups.[18]

If there is a "top," there is also a "bottom." Toward the bottom were the "geeks" or "nerds." Sometimes a distinction was made between "nerds" who were openly preoccupied with academic success and an even lower strata referred to variously as "dorks," "trash," or "geeks." These students were considered hopelessly inept when it came to social events, dress and style. Often they also had low grades and were poor athletes. In academically oriented schools a distinction was made between "brains," who were moderately high in status, and "nerds," who were simply socially inept or too publicly studious.

In all but the smallest schools, there was usually an "alternative" group. The name or names used for this group included "freaks," "weirdos," "druggies," "hippies," "deadheads," "punks," "goths," and "the chain gang." (The last term refers to the practice of attaching their billfolds to their belts with a silver chain or wearing such chains in connection with items of clothing.) It should be noted that some of these terms are what groups call themselves; other labels are created by outsiders. In various ways these groups rejected many conventional middle- class values. They tended to be especially critical of what they saw as the hypocrisy of the preps, who were often sexually active and used alcohol and drugs, but were careful to keep this behavior hidden from adults. The more alienated of these alternative groups often flaunted their deviance.[19] Contrary to popular stereotypes, such groups were not limited to California or the

---

16 SP235.
17 See Merten (1996b), "Burnout as Cheerleader," for an account of the role of cheerleaders and pep squads in a Midwestern junior high school and what happens when a low status burnout becomes a cheerleader.
18 SP98.
19 See Merten (1996b), "Burnout as Cheerleader," 56-58.

East Coast. A male from Alaska reports: "[The radical group] would wear black combat boots, bell bottomed pants, and ragged tee-shirts with sarcastic messages such as 'I love Cops.' These students were more likely to have pierced ears, eyebrows, noses, and belly buttons. One of the main ideals which the radical group wanted to be associated with was individuality."[20] Even elite Catholic girls' schools have such groups: "The 'freaky' girls danced to a beat different than the rest of the cliques at St. Mary's.[21] They wore pale makeup with dark lipstick. They seemed to all have dyed hair colors and wore knee-high socks. Most of them wore Dr. Seuss or windsock hats to school. They were quiet and usually kept to themselves."[22]

Often there were important internal distinctions within the alternative category. Skaters sometimes formed a distinct subgroup. This group in turn could be divided between those who specialized in "boards" (skateboards) and those who used "blades" (straight-bladed roller skates attached to boots). In many schools, skaters were associated with drug use. In at least one school, cigarette smokers were seen as a nonconforming semi-hippy group.[23] Hippies were often considered as quite distinct from groups that had more aggressive styles such as punks, goths, and metalheads.[24] Often these subdivisions were based on a preferred style of music: hard rock, punk, ska, blues, etc. Alternative groups may or may not have actually used drugs, but they were characterized by what others considered bizarre dress, hairstyle, and body ornamentation such as nose rings. These symbolized their rejection of both adult authority and the cultural dominance and superior status of the popular crowd. The status of alternatives—or at least the less extreme versions of it— was frequently characterized as neutral—that is neither high nor low, but for the most part outside of the system. In some respects, they seem to be analogous to monks or ascetics in pre-modern societies. (In more hierarchical schools, these groups represent latent or embryonic pluralism.) In situations where such styles were associated with poor academic performance or openly defiant and aggressive behavior, these groups were seen as low-status "losers."[25] One of the most cohesive of these alternative groups is the "straight-edgers." Their distinctive characteristic is that they eschew drugs, alcohol, or promiscuous sex. Many of them are vegetarian or even vegans, who also avoid the use of all animal products such as wool clothes or leather shoes."[26]

---

20 SP37.
21 Less information will be provided about the geographical location of Catholic and private schools since this might make it possible to identify the specific school being described.
22 SP230.
23 SP175.
24 See Kinney (1999), "'Headbangers' to 'Hippies.'"
25 As we shall see, there are both continuities and differences between schools in the particular mix and prevalence of various crowds. For studies of the prevalence, characteristics, and overlap of various crowds, see Youniss, McClellan, and Strouse (1994), "We're Popular, but We're Not Snobs," and Brown, Mory, and Kinney (1994), "Adolescent Crowds in a Relational Perspective."
26 The common noun referring to "a straight tool for measuring or drawing" is usually spelled "straightedge," but the Websites and other references to these groups usually use "straight-edge." The name "straight-edge" and the original inspiration for the movement come from the song by that name recorded by the "hardcore" punk

In many non-metropolitan schools there is a contingent identified as "country," "cowboys," "rednecks," or "kickers" (which is short for "shit kickers"). They are usually from families of working class or rural backgrounds. Country music and various forms of "Western" dress, such as cowboy boots, are preferred. Large pickup trucks are their key status symbol. Where these groups are present they tend to be looked down upon by others—though they do not necessarily accept their lower status. Many of these students are alienated from academic endeavors.

A number of schools identified groups known as "hoodlums,"[27] "dirt-bags,"[28] "hoods," "gangstas," "thugs," etc. They were identified with gangs who were willing to threaten and use force. In the schools for which we have data they have low status, though they may be feared.[29] In many schools, especially those with significant numbers of racial or ethnic minorities, there were often "pretend hoodlums." These were students who might dress and walk like those associated with gangs, but who were in fact reasonably well-behaved students concerned about their academic performance.

Most students modeled themselves to a significant degree after the popular crowd, but were not members of the core clique or cliques; they were respectable members of the community who have not been banished to "nerd-dom," but they were neither social stars nor members of the other groups mentioned. Frequently they were referred to as "normals," "regulars," or "average students." Most schools also had "drifters" or "floaters." These students manage to participate in more than one group. There is some evidence that as students mature more of them focus on particular friendships and liaisons rather than clique membership.[30] Floaters are probably an example of this tendency. Usually floaters were not the highest-status individuals in a group, but they were accepted members. Ordinarily they had a

---

band Minor Threat in the early 1980s. The movement was originally associated with this type of music, though many now prefer other types of music as well. Sometimes there are disputes over whether being a straight-edge is primarily a matter of loyalty to a particular kind of music or whether it is primarily a commitment to particular ethical norms. (This is reminiscent of debates within religious groups over the relative importance of proper ritual and moral rules.) The symbol of straight-edgers is usually a black X, which they mark on various things, including their bodies. A common variation on this symbol is sXe. Another symbol is some version of XdrugXfreeX. The symbol probably comes from the X that is often stamped on the hand of someone too young to buy liquor when they go to dance clubs or bars (FW26). Straight-edgers are often relatively identifiable because of this symbolism and their strong sense of group solidarity. At the same time they claim to value individual thought, and in many respects do. This personal innovativeness must, however, be within the context of their broad world-view. They look with great disdain upon those who copy their style without embracing their values. Some students didn't like the straight-edge group because they were perceived to have a "holier-than-thou" mentality (FW33). In some areas they have a reputation for getting into fights with other groups.

27 SP304.
28 SP75.
29 It is possible that in some urban schools some of these gangs may have relatively high status, but these schools are underrepresented in our data. See Horowitz (1983), *Honor and the American Dream*, and Rathbone (1998), *On the Outside looking In*.
30 Shrum and Cheek (1987), "Social Structure During the School Years."

primary group, but significant associations with other groups as well.[31] A suburban Dallas student remarks:

> At my high school, people normally had to choose a group that would be the most important to them ... Even if a person was a member of multiple groups, they almost always had one that they were the most loyal to. Race was often the most important [characteristic]. After all there was no way to get around what race you were but you could always drop out of other clubs and groups.[32]

Someone from a small Gulf coast city agrees, "any member of any group could be a member of a certain club, academic achievement group, or team, but they usually classified themselves as members of the group that contained most of their colleagues or friends."[33]

As is the case in most stratification systems, the top and the bottom groups are usually more clearly defined than those who rank in the middle.[34] Those at the top must avoid classmates of only modest status if they are to maintain their superiority; students of modest rank must shun those of even lower status to avoid becoming outcasts themselves. As we shall see, where there are significant numbers of African Americans or other distinctive ethnic groups, the structure becomes even more complicated. This will be discussed below. In sum, most high school students are organized into sets of crowds and cliques with distinguishable identities and most students are associated with one of these particular identities.[35] The details of these groups and their styles can vary from school to school and year to year, but the basic structure is common to most hierarchical high schools.

Of course, these identities and groups do not have the same relevance in every situation. Just as the occupation of an adult does not shape all interaction with other people, neither does the participation of an adolescent in an identifiable crowd shape everything else teenagers do. Moreover, the boundaries of both occupation and crowd are often fuzzy. Some people have more than one occupation and some teenagers associate with more than one crowd. Nonetheless, occupation powerfully shapes the experience of most adults, and crowd membership is central to the experience of most teenagers. In the next chapter I will say more about when and why the boundaries of these crowds are more rigid and salient in some contexts than others.

---

31 SP206, SP166.
32 SP51.
33 SP106.
34 SP45.
35 My research is primarily interested in the role of adolescent status structures in schools and the broader society, not in how to get particular students to avoid one group or join another. Hence, I do not address the question of why particular students join particular crowds or groups. Past research suggests that there is both self-selection and mutual influence operating. That is, students with certain characteristics tend to seek each other out and then tend to reinforce and accentuate their common attributes. For example, why a group regularly uses drugs is partly a function of the students who are inclined in that direction joining together in a group and partly a function of mutual influence. See, for example, Kandel (1978), "On Variations in Adolescent Subcultures." See Brown (1990), "Peer Groups and Peer Cultures," for a discussion of the limits of our knowledge about this matter.

Aspects of Conformity and Elaboration

First, we will examine some of the obvious norms of teenagers and how they are important in shaping the student status structures in schools. These include norms about beauty, athletic ability, clothes and style, athletic uniforms and letter jackets, speech, body language, collective memories, humor, ritual, popular music, dancing and singing, and space and territory. It is not news to point out that these concerns are often important to adolescents. The important thing to see is how they are all variations on the same themes: seeking status through conformity in order to fit in, that is, to gain a sense of acceptance and belonging. The paradox is that in order to be successful in the "conformity game" students must constantly change, elaborate, and complicate the norms in order to gain a competitive advantage. This is not the case for most traditional status systems and, as we will see, even a few aspects of high school life.

Beauty and Athletic Ability

Let's begin with the obvious. In many schools the most important factors influencing a teenager's status are largely inherited: athletic ability for men and good looks for women.[36] A male from a suburb east of Oakland, California, says, "Social rank was determined largely by physical attractiveness, and to a lesser extent by cheerfulness, [and] a willingness to 'party' (with alcohol and marijuana) … "[37] A woman who attended a Catholic school said, "Females received high status if they were pretty. In fact, all the 'cool' girls had to be at least reasonably attractive."[38] A young man from the Washington, DC, area observed, 'The best looking girls were always invited [to parties] first."[39] He elaborates: "For females, appearance was the single most important factor… Girls who were considered attractive dated the popular males and were invited to the cool parties, and therefore gained high status"[40] Of course, beauty is not simply determined by biology. Norms concerning makeup, hairstyles, body weight, and clothes affect the definition of what is attractive. Often significant amounts of time are spent applying makeup and styling hair.

---

36 This is not to say that the importance of these factors is the same in all social settings, age groups, or periods. Tedesco and Gaier (1988), "Friendship Bonds in Adolescence," found that in choosing friends the importance of physical characteristics and achievement declined relative to interpersonal qualities as the students matured. Suitor and Reavis (1995), "Football, Fast Cars, and Cheerleading," comparing college students who had graduated between 1979 and 1982 with those who had graduated in 1988-89 found that there had been very little change in the significance of these factors in determining peer status. They did, however, find that in the later time period women received more respect for athletic achievement. We will consider these factors again when we look at pluralistic high schools in Chapters five and six.
37 SP246.
38 SP253.
39 SP215.
40 SP215. The relationship between appearance and status begins in childhood. See Kennedy (1990), "Determinants of Peer Social Status," for an interesting analysis of the link between appearance and status for children in grades 2 through 8.

I n this reading, Milner (2006) is applying the social theories of Max Weber to high school social status systems:

> The German sociologist Max Weber used the term status group, which he contrasted with notions of class and political party, to refer to social formations that were based on differences in status and lifestyle.... Teenage crowds are another example of status groups. Because they are a status group and a subculture, they show an enormous concern with lifestyle and acceptance by peers (p. 22).

What Milner helps elucidate is that teenagers spend twice as much of their time, 29 percent, with peers as they do with parents and other adults combined, 15 percent, forming a social group.

The reason these high school patterns are important for social life is that, as Milner (2006) states: "typically, individuals and groups attempt to influence and control their environment by the type of power that is most readily available to them" (p. 29). As youth try out friendships and fitting into different groups, they are attempting to find a sense of belonging, which bolsters a sense of self-esteem and mastery (e.g., Falci 2011). Over time, experiences belonging in some groups and not others bundles into friend identity, which often lasts into emerging adulthood (e.g., Branje et al. 2014).

What happens in the high school sorting process is that social groups are typically formed around the implicit, "invisible," social class dynamics reported in Chapter 3. Embedded in those dynamics are also issues of race and gender (e.g., Mouzon 2014; Falci 2011). Some groups form their status around activities that are expensive—such as shopping for fashionable clothes or having athletic hobbies that require gear—and thus fitting in within those groups requires monetary investment. Youth who do not have the money to participate will either not attempt to fit into those groups, or they will make an attempt but have negative experiences that can diminish self-esteem.

These patterns can have long-lasting effects that play a role even in whether emerging adults will view themselves as "college material," and if so who they will think they fit in with on college campus. As reported in Chapter 5, there are patterns to college experiences which can be grouped into college pathways predicated on who emerging adults desire to fit in with and be accepted by. Participating in one or the other of these groups has long-term ramifications for socioeconomic access that are even further patterned by the degree to which the groups they desire to fit in with accept them (Armstrong & Hamilton 2013).

As Young and colleagues find (2015), transitions to adulthood are a "peer project"—meaning that friendships play a crucial role in the adulthood construction process. Close friendships are an important social setting in which emerging adults work out their identity exploration. Through co-processing everything from school studies to romantic relationships to major and project career paths, emerging adults facilitate each other in talking through how to reach their various goals. Emerging adults often rely upon close friendships to process relationships with others:

> *Friendships appeared as a meaningful, secure context participants used to help them negotiate other significant relationships in their lives. Friendships allowed peers to connect over a shared understanding of how relationships with significant others in their lives should be or progress. Also, their friends' experiences often helped them to better understand or find solutions for the situation they found themselves in, thus seeking each others' support on issues such as relationship with romantic partners, family members, other friends, and roommates (p. 173).*

In the process, emerging adults work out a "contextual conceptualization of identity" (p. 175) involving perception of selves and life goals in iterative relationships with their friends. Perhaps in more significant ways than parents, friends play an important role in emerging into adulthood.

COMMUNITY

In addition to friendships, communities are another important social setting for emerging adults. Since the social theories of Tönnies (2011), sociologists have been concerned about the decline of social community within physical space. Likewise, Kai Erikson, son of Erik Erikson—the famous psychologist who developed one of the most accepted and known theories of life course development—in a book entitled *Everything In Its Path: Destruction of Community in the Buffalo Creek Flood* (1978), called community "the most sociological of all concepts" (p. 13). What Erikson was referring to in the concept of *community* was a sense of belonging among people living in a locally bounded geographic area, social belonging within physical space.

In *The Vanishing Neighbor: The Transformation of American Community*, Dunkelman (2014) explains that what was of crucial importance in the kinds of locally based communities of times past is what he refers to as "middle-ring social connections"—those ties between the inner-ring of primary family and close friendships ties and the outer-ring of acquaintances and work or other loosely connected social ties, namely ties to neighbors. The author summarizes numerous community studies and describes that the historical change in community over time has not necessarily been a loss of community so much as a change in its construction. Americans have decreased their investment in connections with middle-ring neighbor ties and increased their investment in both inner-ring and outer-ring connections (see also Swartz 2009 on increased investment in primary ties).

Thus, the shrinking core discussion networks discussed toward the beginning of the chapter may be tapping this phenomenon. Perhaps people do not discuss important social and political matters with their closest friends and family members, preferring instead to affiliate with them based on emotional support and deeper understanding. On the other end, Americans may associate with acquaintances and looser connected ties based on finding common ground, such as discussing the weather, sports, or other sorts of affiliation bonds that reaffirm the relationship.

Dunkelman (2014) describes middle-ring connections with neighbors as key for bridging the gap between close family-like relationships and far compatriot connections. He agrees with Wellman and colleagues (1996) that rather than a net decline in connections, Americans have moved their experiences of community to their online social network, termed virtual communities. Yet Dunkelman draws attention to this involving more than simply a shift in the medium of communication. He cites a study finding that "for every minute an individual spends on the Internet, the time he or she spends with friends is reduced by seven seconds, and time spent with colleagues by eleven ... for every e-mail sent or received, an individual lost a minute of time with his or her family" (p. 125). He continues by stating: "Our newfound capacity to reinvest our social capital in our most and least intimate relationships has impelled us to abandon those in between" (p. 239). The significance of this is best articulated when he states:

> The sorts of interactions that were once typical between Americans who were friendly but not intimate were a medium through which the norms in one pocket of society became accessible to those who lived nearby. Inner- and outer-ring relationships are generally centered on similarities: you're a member of the same family; you share the same love of vintage baseball cards. But relationships formed in the middle are not. And so, given the winnowing of the American township, the sort of mutual ignorance ... now exists, in many circumstances, among those who live next door to one another (p. 137).

Thus, it is not a decline in community but a change to it that can affect emerging adults.

Since the rise of Internet use, Americans have been increasingly able to connect across physical distance, and Internet use resulted in decreased levels of local, community participation (Stern & Dillman 2006). Likewise, even the construct of "community attachment"—sense of feeling at home, not wanting to leave, and being interested in happenings in local areas—varies at the individual-level more significantly than it does the community-level, indicating that the physical area is less consequential even in a measure of community (Flaherty & Brown 2010). All of this means people are more able to pick their non-primary ties based on voluntary associations, creating affiliations of interest, rather than ties bounded within physical proximity.

However, this does not negate the role of community context. First, many Americans still live in rural areas where attachment to local community is stronger, which affects adulthood transition patterns (Cox et al. 2014). Second, local communities still provide the most viable employment opportunities to recent graduates and especially to those without a college degree. When coupled with community attachment (Ulrich-Schad et al. 2013), employment opportunities predict degrees of outmigration from the local area and the state (Stroope et al. 2014).

Based on these changes to community support, an important aspect of emerging adulthood is then to understand the role of various sorts of social support systems. It is not the case that social support for emerging adults, and Americans more generally, has ubiquitously declined. Rather emerging adults have a greater degree of variation in their social support systems, since they are less likely to communicate with and be supported by neighbors who helped moderate the differences in more extreme variations between affiliational and primary ties.

In terms of the types of social supports that matter in emerging adulthood, besides friends, parents are found to be important partners in emerging adult identity formation processes (e.g., Schachter & Ventura 2008). Likewise, intergenerational communication remains important to emerging adults (e.g., Swartz 2009), if not becoming even more important in working to maintain given the decline of middle-ring communications (Dunkelman 2014). Perhaps most importantly for developing ties with social supports who bridge across social class backgrounds are ties to nonifamilial adults typically known through participation in formal organizations such as schools (e.g., Chhuon & Wallace 2014) and after-school programs (e.g., Jones & Deutsch 2011).

CONTACT

Another aspect to consider with regard to friendships and communities supporting emerging adulthood is the role of face-to-face contact versus technology-mediated contact. Though some aspects of that are expressed above, a remaining dimension is whether connecting through online mediums changes the meaning of contact. In a book entitled *The Village Effect: How Face-to-Face Contact Can Make Us Healthier, Happier, and Smarter*, Pinker (2014) summarizes numerous studies finding that face-to-face contact is crucial for a range of positive outcomes. Despite how this book is often interpreted, the studies do not specifically address whether technology-based communications supplant face-to-face contact or are merely in addition to it.

However, other studies raise causes for concern. For example, Ljepava and colleagues (2013) find marked differences in the personalities of Facebook users and nonusers, and self-esteem is lower, on average, for social network site users (Steinfield et al. 2008). Studies find evidence that social network site usage does not lead to closeness offline (Pollet et al. 2011) or the same levels of offline connectedness online (Grieve et al. 2013). Some innovative approaches to using technology to maintain close connections were summarized in the previous chapter (Neustaedter et al. 2012), and the trends show that technology-mediated communication, such as cell phone use, does correlate with increased closeness and relational satisfaction with parents (Miller-Ott et al. 2014). Additionally, studies find that some modes of communication work for one family type versus another, specifically that texting worked well for less traditional families than did calling (Rudi et al. 2015).

Reinecke and Trepte (2014) find an overall positivity bias in the kinds of personal information shared on social media, creating less authenticity. Likewise, Turkle (2012, 2015) finds that technology can give a false sense of connection, labeled feeling *alone together*. What particularly concerns Turkle is that the meaning of connection has changed due to decreased time spent in face-to-face contact. Specifically, Turkle is concerned that people today rarely feel that they can truly count on others to be fully present and connected with them. For example, studies find that people react positively to caretaking provided by robots because they find them to be comforting in their reliable and predictable provision of care without requiring reciprocation.

Turkle (2015) is also concerned that technology gives people too much of a sense of control: "These days, we want to be with each other but also elsewhere, connected to wherever else we want to be, because what we value most is control over where we put our attention" (p. 19). People cannot assume undivided attention in the presence of others because the opportunity (or threat) of contact with others is always available, even if the phone is silent for the moment. This is concerning to Turkle because "human relationships are rich, messy, and demanding. When we clean them up with technology, we move from conversation to the efficiencies of mere connection. I fear we forget the difference" (p. 21). Turkle urges society generally, and especially parents of the younger generation, to rekindle face-to-face interactions:

> This is our nick of time and our line to toe: to acknowledge the unintended consequences of technologies to which we are vulnerable, to respect the resilience that has always been ours. We have time to make the corrections. And to remember who we are—creatures of history, of deep psychology, of complex relationships. Of conversations artless, risky, and face-to-face (p. 362).

That is the urge, and here is a call to action—invite a neighbor that you do not know that well out for a coffee or a lunch. This could be someone living down the hall from you in your dorm or apartment. They must be someone within a ten-mile radius of you and a person that you have never considered to be one of your close friends. Take this book with you and ask them to read your favorite passage from it. It could be a passage that you particularly like, or one that gets particularly under your skin. After they read it, ask them what they think about it and why. Then do something perhaps even a bit more out of the ordinary—truly listen, listen for deep understanding.

REFERENCES

Armstrong, Elizabeth A. and Laura T. Hamilton. 2013. *Paying for the Party: How College Maintains Inequality.* Cambridge, MA: Harvard University Press.

Barabasi, Albert-Laszlo. 2003. *Linked: How Everything Is Connected to Everything Else and What It Means for Business, Science, and Everyday Life.* New York: Plume.

Branje, Susan, Lydia Laninga-Wijnen, Rongqin Yu, and Wim Meeus. 2014. "Associations among School and Friendship Identity in Adolescence and Romantic Relationships and Work in Emerging Adulthood." *Emerging Adulthood* 2(1):6–16.

Brown, Jane D. 2008. "Emerging Adults in a Media-Saturated World." In *Emerging Adults in America: Coming of Age in the 21st Century*, edited by Jeffrey J. Arnett and Jennifer L. Tanner, 279–99. American Psychological Association.

Chhuon, Vichet and Tanner LeBaron Wallace. 2014. "Creating Connectedness through Being Known: Fulfilling the Need to Belong in U.S. High Schools." *Youth & Society* 46(3):379–401.

Christakis, Nicholas A. and James H. Fowler. 2011. *Connected: The Surprising Power of Our Social Networks and How They Shape Our Lives.* Little, Brown, and Company.

Cox, Genevieve R., Corinna Jenkins Tucker, Erin Hiley Sharp, Karen T. Van Gundy, and Cesar J. Rebellon. 2014. "Practical Considerations: Community Context in a Declining Rural Economy and Emerging Adults' Educational and Occupational Aspirations." *Emerging Adulthood* 2(3):173–83.

Dunkelman, Marc J. 2014. *The Vanishing Neighbor: The Transformation of American Community.* New York: W. W. Norton & Company.

Easley, David and Jon Kleinberg. 2010. "Strong and Weak Ties." In *Networks, Crowds, and Markets: Reasoning about a Highly Connected World*, 47–84. Cambridge University Press.

Erikson, Kai T. 1978. *Everything in Its Path: Destruction of Community in the Buffalo Creek Flood.* Simon & Schuster.

Falci, Christina D. 2011. "Self-Esteem and Mastery Trajectories in High School by Social Class and Gender." *Social Science Research* 40(2):586–601.

Fischer, Claude S. 2009. "The 2004 GSS Finding of Shrunken Social Networks: An Artifact?" *American Sociological Review* 74(4):657–69.

Fischer, Claude S. 2011. *Still Connected: Family and Friends in America Since 1970.* New York: Russell Sage Foundation.

Flaherty, Jeremy and Ralph B. Brown. 2010. "A Multilevel Systemic Model of Community Attachment: Assessing the Relative Importance of the Community and Individual Levels." *American Journal of Sociology* 116(2):503–42.

Granovetter, Mark S. 1973. "The Strength of Weak Ties." *American Journal of Sociology* 78(6):1360–80.

Grieve, Rachel, Michaelle Indian, Kate Witteveen, G. Anne Tolan, and Jessica Marrington. 2013. "Face-to-Face or Facebook: Can Social Connectedness Be Derived Online?" *Computers in Human Behavior* 29(3):604–9.

Jones, Jeffrey N. and Nancy L. Deutsch. 2011. "Relational Strategies in After-School Settings: How Staff–Youth Relationships Support Positive Development." *Youth & Society* 43(4):1381–406.

Ljepava, Nikolina, R. Robert Orr, Sean Locke, and Craig Ross. 2013. "Personality and Social Characteristics of Facebook Non-Users and Frequent Users." *Computers in Human Behavior* 29(4):1602–7.

Madden, Mary, Amanda Lenhart, Sandra Cortesi, Urs Gasser, Maeve Duggan, Aaron Smith, and Meredith Beaton. 2010. "Teens, Social Media, and Privacy." Pew Research Center.

McPherson, Miller, Lynn Smith-Lovin, and Matthew E. Brashears. 2006. "Social Isolation in America: Changes in Core Discussion Networks over Two Decades." *American Sociological Review* 71(3):353–75.

Miller-Ott, Aimee E., Lynne Kelly, and Robert L. Duran. 2014. "Cell Phone Usage Expectations, Closeness, and Relationship Satisfaction between Parents and Their Emerging Adults in College." *Emerging Adulthood* 2(4):313–23.

Milner, Murray. 2006. *Freaks, Geeks, and Cool Kids.* New York: Routledge.

Mouzon, Dawne M. 2014. "Relationships of Choice: Can Friendships or Fictive Kinships Explain the Race Paradox in Mental Health?" *Social Science Research* 44:32–43.

Neustaedter, Carman, Steve Harrison, and Abigail Sellen. 2012. *Connecting Families: The Impact of New Communication Technologies on Domestic Life.* Springer Science & Business Media.

Paik, Anthony and Kenneth Sanchagrin. 2013. "Social Isolation in America: An Artifact." *American Sociological Review* 78(3):339–60.

Parigi, Paolo and Warner Henson. 2014. "Social Isolation in America." *Annual Review of Sociology* 40(1):153–71.

Pinker, Susan. 2014. *The Village Effect: How Face-to-Face Contact Can Make Us Healthier, Happier, and Smarter*. New York: Spiegel & Grau.

Pollet, Thomas V., Sam G. B. Roberts, and Robin I. M. Dunbar. 2011. "Use of Social Network Sites and Instant Messaging Does Not Lead to Increased Offline Social Network Size, or to Emotionally Closer Relationships with Offline Network Members." *Cyberpsychology, Behavior, and Social Networking* 14(4):253–8.

Portes, Alejandro. 1998. "Social Capital: Its Origins and Applications in Modern Sociology." *Annual Review of Sociology* 24:1–24.

Reinecke, Leonard and Sabine Trepte. 2014. "Authenticity and Well-Being on Social Network Sites: A Two-Wave Longitudinal Study on the Effects of Online Authenticity and the Positivity Bias in SNS Communication." *Computers in Human Behavior* 30:95–102.

Riesman, David. 1950. *The Lonely Crowd: A Study of the Changing American Character*. Yale University Press.

Rudi, Jessie H., Amy Walkner, and Jodi Dworkin. 2015. "Adolescent–Parent Communication in a Digital World: Differences by Family Communication Patterns." *Youth & Society* 47(6):811–28.

Schachter, Elli P. and Jonathan J. Ventura. 2008. "Identity Agents: Parents as Active and Reflective Participants in Their Children's Identity Formation." *Journal of Research on Adolescence* 18(3):449–76.

Steinfield, Charles, Nicole B. Ellison, Cliff Lampe. 2008. "Social Capital, Self-Esteem, and Use of Online Social Network Sites: A Longitudinal Analysis." *Journal of Applied Developmental Psychology* 29:434–45.

Stern, Michael J. and Don A. Dillman. 2006. "Community Participation, Social Ties, and Use of the Internet." *City & Community* 5(4):409–24.

Stroope, Samuel, Aaron B. Franzen, Charles M. Tolbert, and F. Carson Mencken. 2014. "College Graduates, Local Retailers, and Community Belonging in the United States." *Sociological Spectrum* 34(2):143–62.

Swartz, Teresa Toguchi. 2009. "Intergenerational Family Relations in Adulthood: Patterns, Variations, and Implications in the Contemporary United States." *Annual Review of Sociology* 35:191–212.

Tönnies, Ferdinand. 2011. *Community and Society*. Dover Publications.

Turkle, Sherry. 2012. *Alone Together: Why We Expect More from Technology and Less from Each Other*. Basic Books.

Turkle, Sherry. 2015. *Reclaiming Conversation: The Power of Talk in a Digital Age*. Penguin Press.

Twenge, Jean M., Stacy M. Campbell, Brian J. Hoffman, and Charles E. Lance. 2010. "Generational Differences in Work Values: Leisure and Extrinsic Values Increasing, Social and Intrinsic Values Decreasing." *Journal of Management* 36(5):1117–42.

Ulrich-Schad, Jessica D., Megan Henly, and Thomas G. Safford. 2013. "The Role of Community Assessments, Place, and the Great Recession in the Migration Intentions of Rural Americans." *Rural Sociology* 78(3):371–98.

Wang, Hua and Barry Wellman. 2010. "Social Connectivity in America: Changes in Adult Friendship Network Size From 2002 to 2007." *American Behavioral Scientist* 53(8):1148–69.

Wellman, Barry, Janet Salaff, Dimitrina Dimitrova, Laura Garton, Milena Gulia, and Caroline Haythornthwaite. 1996. "Computer Networks as Social Networks: Collaborative Work, Telework, and Virtual Community." *Annual Review of Sociology* 22:213–38.

Young, Richard A., Sheila K. Marshall, Leah J. Wilson, Amy R. Green, Laura Klubben, Filomena Parada, Emily L. Polak, Krista Socholotiuk, and Ma Zhu. 2015. "Transition to Adulthood as a Peer Project." *Emerging Adulthood* 3(3):166–78.

CHAPTER 9

Faith, Meaning-Making, & Religion

Unlike the word count figures displayed in prior chapters, the word counts of popular press descriptions for books about Millennials and religion, as well as for political engagement in the next chapter, evidence a more collective-oriented curiosity. The prior word counts all had us and them among the top words, but these final two have *we* and *our* among the top. This chapter reviews trends in changing religiosity and spirituality among young people, resulting in fewer emerging adults being socially religious while maintaining a high degree of personal, individualized spirituality.

PRIVATE FAITH, PUBLIC WORSHIP

What does youth and emerging adult religiosity, faith, or spirituality look like today? It turns out this is not an easy question to answer. Defining religiosity and spirituality is like trying to explain what differentiates a tree from a bush—we tend to know both when we see them, but the minute we start trying to put boundaries around where one category ends and the other begins, specificity evades us. Being a social scientist may actually be predicated upon a willingness to tolerate ambiguity and being compelled to continually pursue greater knowledge about phenomena, which may never be fully known. Perhaps the same is true of any scientist.

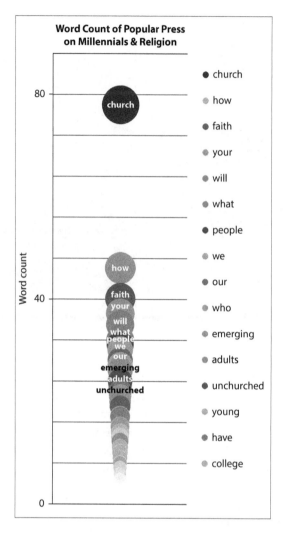

FIGURE 9.1 Millennial Popular Press Word Count

The most typical measures of religiosity are frequency of religious service attendance; religious tradition affiliation; importance of faith in everyday life; and frequency of personal religious behaviors, such as personal prayer. The first two of these measures assess forms of religiosity that are more public and socially connected, while the latter two assess more personal forms. Numerous studies investigating what predicts youth religiosity find that parents, other family members, and friends are tremendously influential (e.g., Copen & Silverstein 2008; Ellison et al. 2011; Cheadle & Schwadel 2012; Brimeyer & Smith 2012; Smith et al. 2014; Hoffmann 2014).

Stability and change in these and other measures of religiosity during youth and emerging adulthood is another common topic (e.g., Uecker et al. 2007; Koenig et al. 2008; Smith & Snell 2009; Petts 2009; Wuthnow 2010; Dean 2010; Layton et al. 2011; Hayward & Krause 2013; Hardie et al. 2013; Chan et al. 2014; Glass et al. 2015). Overall, the trend generally in America, the UK, and many other industrialized countries has been what Davie (1994) calls "believing without belonging"—referring to the persistence of high personal forms of religiosity paired with declines in most forms of public or social forms of religiosity. The same is true of the overall trend across transitions from youth to emerging adulthood (e.g., Smith & Snell 2009). In the reading for this chapter, Levenson and colleagues (2013) summarize findings on religious development, recounting that interest in religion and religious identity remain high, while attendance declines.

READING 9.1

Spiritual Well-Being, Spiritual Intelligence, and Healthy Workplace Policy

By Michael R. Leveson, Carolyn M. Aldwin, and Heidi Igarashi

Changes in Religiousness in Young Adults in the United States

Studies of changes in religiousness and spirituality among young adults yield a complex picture. Findings on change and stability in religiousness vary as a function of method—more precisely, of how questions are asked. People's self-attributions of religiousness show different trends than participation in formal religious ceremonies, which in turn show often different trends froim private religious practice. Further completing the picture is the often ill-defined difference between religiousness and spirituality (see Oman, Chapter 2, for an in-depth discussion). We first address changes in religiousness, defined loosely as the affirmation of affiliation with one specific religion—more specifically, attendance at religious services or observations—both in the United States and then in other countries. Following this, we address changes in spirituality, or religious experience.

Overall religious attendance has declined in the United States among young adults. Analyses of the GSS found that

Michael R. Leveson, Carolyn M. Aldwin, and Heidi Igarashi, "Religious Development from Adolescence to Middle Adulthood," Handbook of Psychology of Religion & Spirituality, ed. Raymond F. Paloutzian and Crystal L. Park, pp. 186–188. Copyright © 2011 by Guilford Press. Reprinted with permission.

those 21–45 years of age who report never attending, religious services has increased from 14 to 20% in the 25 years ending in 2002 (Wuthnow, 2007). Further, analyses of the longitudinal National Survey of Youth and Religion (NSYR) found that, in 2007–2008, 35% of those in the United States between ages 18 and 23 never attend services, an increase of 18% in 5 years (Smith & Snell, 2009). Over that period, there was a decline in every index of religious practice in the NSYR with the exception of meditation practice (excluding prayer), which increased from 11 to 16%.

However, there may be individual differences in those secular trends. Wuthnow (2007) reported an increase in weekly attendance among those 18–25 years between 1990 and 2000, perhaps reflecting an increase in evangelical religion among the young. Further, religious attendance in the United States increased as a function of age, at least in the GSS data collected from 1998–2002. In part, this may result from the tendency to increase religious attendance after having children. The number of children in the family is also associated with greater parental attendance (although this may be due to the more religious having more children). However, the analyses of the GSS also reported a decline in attendance for parents after the children have left home.

Beyond attendance of religious services, Smith et al. (2009) endeavored to assess strength of religious commitment and change in commitment using a composite measure of data collected from a U.S. representative sample surveyed at three times: 2003, 2005, and 2007–2008. At first measurement, participants were between 13 and 17 years old; at the third wave, they were 18–23 years old. Besides frequency of attendance, the measure included reported importance of faith and the frequency with which respondents prayed on their own. These indices were then combined to form a measure of religious strength ranging from lowest through minimal and moderate to highest. This measure was then compared across Waves 1 and 3.

The basic result was that all "levels of religiousness" declined between Waves 1 and 3, except the lowest, which increased. For example, those who scored highest at Wave 1 decreased 12% by Wave 3. This was the overall pattern for all levels, with "moderate" also declining, except for "minimal" and "lowest," which increased by 11%, regardless of religious denomination.

Simple zero-order correlations suggested that religious commitment was related to attendance at services, attributing high importance to faith, frequency of solitary prayer, frequency of religious experiences, and having very religious parents. Frequency of scripture reading was most strongly associated with retention of a belief in the importance of faith from Waves 1 to 3. Logistic regression showed that strong parental religious involvement, frequency of individual prayer, high importance attributed to religious faith, and frequency of reading scripture at Wave 1 were the strongest influences on religious strength at Wave 3.

There was stability in some subgroups. The religiously "devoted" at Wave 1 were by far the most likely to be at the highest level of religious strength at Wave 3. Other categories ranged from the regular" at Time 1, who were somewhat religious at Wave 3, through the sporadic" and the "disengaged," who were not at all likely to be at the highest level at Wave 3. However, Smith and Snell (2009) noted that *within* each group at Wave 1, there were some mavericks who did exhibit different trajectories.

Qualitative analyses traced six pathways to the higher levels of religiousness. Four of these pathways included strong parental involvement and one involved the strong involvement of other adults. The sixth was more independent, emphasizing the individual's faith and personal religious experiences. In all six, the teenager at Wave 1 had no doubt about their religious faith. Four pathways to lower religiousness over 5 years all began with low parental religious service attendance. It is regrettable that quantitative pathways to sustained or diminished religiousness were not computed.

The Pew Forum report, *Religion among the Millennials* (2010), documented a steady decline in the most widely used indices of religiousness over the past 40 years in each of the five generations that emerged into adulthood in the 20th century, as assessed most recently near the end of the first decade of the 21st. For example, religion was important to 75% of the oldest of the generations (the "Greatest") at the most recent assessment but to only 40% of the Millennials. However, 53% of the Millennials expressed certainty in their belief in God compared to 61% of Generation X and 65% of Boomers. Interestingly, in the late 1990's, 59% of Generation X expressed certainty of God's existence. In the late 1980s, 59% of Boomers were certain. Perhaps not too much should be made of this, but there is a hint of an increase in certainty with age and a suggestion that not everyone perceives the importance of religious institutions as equivalent to a certain belief in God.

Looking at the apparently declining religiousness among young adults, Wuthnow (2007, p. 214) remarked that if he were a religious leader, he would be troubled by the data describing the religious lives of young Americans. Although most data for older young adults point to a story of decline in religiousness, the GSS revealed some interesting exceptions. First, there has been an increase in belief in life after death among those ages 21-45 years. Moreover, the percentages are very high, reaching 87% of women who were 40-45 years of age in 1998-2002 (Wuthnow, 2007). There is also a strong belief in the United States in the existence of angels. Fifty-six percent of the U.S. longitudinal sample believed in the existence of angels, including 36% of those who considered themselves to be nonreligious. Twenty-five percent of this group aslo believed in demons and evil spirits, 37% in miracles from God, 24% in life after death, and 36% in God's judgment on judgment day (Smith & Snell, 2009, p. 124). Although a larger percentage of the religious affiliates believed in these things, the fact that a quarter to a third of *nonreligious* emerging adults did as well as in not trival. It at least makes one wonder what "nonreligious" means among these people. Could nonreligious mean "Spritual" but not attracted to a specific religion among some of them? Or could there be a loss of connection between specific beliefs on the one hand and knowledge of the contexts in which they developed on the other? In other word, is religious belief increasingly disconnected from religious eduction?

Changes in Religiousness among Young Adults in Other Countries

Looking around the world, there is remarkable diversity in religiousness. This is especially striking in the former Soviet Bloc, where, for example, 75% of Poles but only 12% of Czechs were found to pray daily (Smith, 2009). Sorting through the ocean of data provided by Smith's report for the Templeton Foundation, derived from the World Values Survey and the International Social Survey Program, we found that the percentage of those younger than 30 who considered themselves to be religious persons generally was somewhat smaller than among those who were 30-39 years of age. However, the differences between countries eclipsed age and period effects.

Argentina and Brazil provide interesting examples of cross-national differences. In Argentina in 1984, 59% of those younger than 30 considered themselves to be religious compared with about 61% of those 30-39 years old. In 1999, 79% of those younger than 30 reported being religious compared with 86.7% of those aged 30-39. In contrast, in neighboring Brazil, in 1991 82.5% of those younger than 30 considered themselves to be religious compared to 81.3% in 1997. In Bulgaria, adults under 30 were much more religious in 1999 (43%) than in 1990 (29%), but there is a similar relationship with age, with 42% of 30- to 39-year-olds regarding themselves as religious in 1999 as compared to 31% in 1990.

The message is quite clear that religion is not in decline in all places and among all peoples. In some countries, such as (East) Germany and Estonia, religiousness appears to be at a low ebb. In China, on the other hand, religiousness is steadily increasing (Chau, 2001, 2011; Dillon, 1994; Lee, 2007). Moreover, as these authors documented, religious participation is increasing in Christianity and Islam, as well as more traditional religions of China.

The national differences reported by Smith (2009) were certainly large and dramatic. They also reflected ongoing change. Smith addressed secularization theory, which hold that economically more developed societies are increasingly secular and that more educated people are less religious. There is some evidence for secularization theory, but the evidece is mixed and shows wide variability. Scandinavian countries and Japan are increasingly secular, but China, the United States, and Argentina are not. It will be interesting to observe the effects of rapid economic development in Brazil and India, especially among adolescents and young adults. Some formerly communist countries remain nonreligious while others have experienced a reemergence of religion.

In *After the Baby Boomers: How Twenty- and Thirty-Somethings are Shaping the Future of American Religion*, famous sociologist of religion Robert Wuthnow describes generational changes in the contours of religiosity in the United States. Wuthnow (2007) calls Millennials a generation of "tinkerers"—by which he means this:

> A tinkerer puts together a life from whatever skills, ideas, and resources that are readily at hand.... They do not rely on only one way of doing things. Their approach to life is practical. They get things done, and usually this happens by improvising, by piecing together an idea from here, a skill from there, and a contact from somewhere else (pp. 13–14).

Wuthnow explains that tinkering is more common when a great deal of varied information is available, and this is certainly the case for Millennials growing up in the "information age"—the time period since the rapid expansion of the Internet made information available at the click of a button. Applied to religiosity, Wuthnow describes younger generations as melding various religious traditions together. Though theologically there are distinctions between these religious traditions, many Millennials seek to find the commonalities among them and reduce to the common denominator. Not only does this help respond to a great deal of information available on different religious traditions, it also can be a way to downplay or avoid conflicts among them.

Something along these lines has been found in other studies as well (e.g., Smith et al. 2011; Dean 2010). Dean (2010) explains that "21 is the new 16 and refers to Millennials as becoming "Christian-ish," and has having a "loveless faith"—belief in a supernatural being continues without feelings of personal connection. In describing the importance of understanding youth religiosity, Dean (2010) states:

> In the midst of these swirling currents, teenagers—like centuries of young people before them—find themselves in search of a faith, religious or otherwise, that they can call their own. In fact, the faith teenagers develop during adolescence serves as a kind of barometer of the religious inclinations of the culture that surrounds them, giving parents, pastors, teachers, campus ministers, youth pastors, and anyone else who works closely with teenagers fifty-yard-line seats from which to watch American's religious future take shape (p. 9).

In summary, personal religiosity remains high for American youth and emerging adults while public-social forms of religiosity decline across generations and within cohorts.

THE MEANING-MAKING CRISIS

Many scholars have highlighted the importance of establishing a sense of meaning during developmental processes, especially by establishing a relatively clear sense of identity (e.g., Côté

2002; Barry & Nelson 2005; 2008; Good & Willoughby 2008; Wink 2009; Kimball et al. 2013; Mayseless & Keren 2014; Barry & Abo-Zena 2014; Arnett 2015). Religious and faith identity matter for a host of emerging adult outcomes. For example, Madge and colleagues (2014) find that faith identity impacts non-faith identity, and a sense of divine involvement can give meaning to life (Jung 2015) and fill experiences of voids in the purpose of it all (Barkin et al. 2015).

James Fowler (1981, 1991) described "faith as a universal, dynamic quality of human meaning making" (1991, p. 27). Fowler differentiated faith from religion, viewing the former as the process of meaning-making and the latter as the inheritance of specific religious traditions and theologies. He further delineated belief as the expression of faith. To Fowler, faith was about trusting in a "master story"—a cohesive script that provides an orienting perspective and guides life decisions:

> Faith is an existential orientation formed in our relations with others that links us, in shared trusts and loyalties, to each other, to shared values, and to a transcendent framework of meaning and power (Fowler 1991, 33).

Fowler defined six stages in the developmental process, each of which was thought to be a stair-like progression from the one before it. This and other ideas along these lines came to be known as FDT—faith development theory.

While the theory gained a great deal of traction and continues to resonate with people as a useful way to describe faith and meaning-making, it also has a great deal of critique—studies finding counterevidence or in other ways challenging the claims. For example, Streib (2005) reviews studies finding that "development, thus also faith development, may not proceed in a coherent and invariant series of stages, but that there may be domain-specific progress" (p. 103). Likewise, Parker (2010) finds that, in decades of research, FDT has had little empirical validation—meaning evidence that supports the theory. Though inconclusive, there has been some support for age and/or sequence patterns occurring in the development of some of the process FDT predicted. However, they are marginal and nonexistent once beyond adolescence. Thus, while Fowler's faith development theory has been helpful for describing processes involved in meaning-making, it also misses the mark in providing a universal and stepwise progression, which likely does not exist in the same way for all emerging adults today.

Perhaps the reason this set of theories lacks adequate explanation of meaning-making processes during the transition to adulthood is that life today is too complex and full of a great deal of diversity to be explained by a singular trajectory (Cook et al. 2014; Schafer 2011). Moral frameworks and values are developed in context (Longest et al. 2013), and different groups are socialized to hold diverse values (Pratt et al. 2003; Cottone et al. 2007). Plus, values can and do change during the transition, especially in response to learning during college and other formative experiences during transitions to adulthood (Gutierrez & Park 2014; Stoppa & Lefkowitz 2010; Hill 2011; Mayrl & Uecker 2011; Longest & Smith 2011; Schwadel 2014).

In fact, what is more universally true of emerging adults today is nearly the opposite of Fowler's theory. Rather than developing meaning-making into a coherent set of beliefs—known as a moral framework—most youth and emerging adults instead express inconsistent and often incoherent morality. This state of affairs has been described as morality adrift with relatively low moral reasoning skills—the ability to think through complex moral dilemmas (Smith & Snell 2009).

These findings are based on the books *Souls in Transition: The Religious Lives of Emerging Adults in America* (Smith & Snell 2009) and *Lost in Transition: The Dark Side of Emerging Adulthood* (Smith et al. 2011), which are the result of cumulative investigations on the National Study of Youth and Religion, in which we tracked the same group of people from their teenage years in 2001 (13–17 years old during the first wave) through emerging adulthood (24–28 years old in the fourth wave) in 2013. This is a nationally representative survey with more than two thousand people having participated in all four waves of data collection. In addition, we collected face-to-face, in-depth interviews with a subsample of the survey respondents during each wave, with 300 interviewees in the fourth wave.

Perhaps as a defense mechanism against a societal milieu that requires repeated moves and a vague sense of where one will be living in six months, let alone six years, many emerging adults do not prioritize regular, sustained, or deep affiliation with and participation in formal organizations (Smith & Snell 2009; Smith et al. 2011). This lack of participation in formal organizations occurs at the same time that emerging adults are often retracting from social support from parents. Moreover, many young people have not yet settled into adulthood support systems, including forming friendships with people that they think they may remain in touch with in the future. They are in limbo. The friends they do have are often held-over from childhood, or are coworkers whom they are not certain they will remain in touch with a few years from now. The organizations they are involved in feel temporary at best, and constraining at worst.

Thus, in many ways, emerging adults are on their own to sort out their personal sense of how to make meaning in a pluralistic and disjointed set of pathways to adulthood (Smith & Snell 2009; Smith et al. 2011). Many of them are unsure what makes something right or wrong, or who they can trust to help them figure that out. We found that one-third of our survey sample had no idea what it is that makes something morally right or wrong, and the remainder said they have some sense but then struggled to articulate it. Emerging adults tend on the whole to have a fairly individualistic sense of morality. That is, 60 percent of emerging adults think morality is a personal choice, a matter of individual decision. They tend to think moral rights and wrongs are essentially opinions, which everyone is entitled to have. In response to the diverse and often conflicting points of view which they can easily find in the information superhighway, they say, "Who am I to say?" and "To each his own."

Arnett and Jensen (2002) call this having a "*congregation* of one"—referring to the cultural trend for emerging adults to have make-your-own religions that encompass a wide array of religious beliefs formed together in a unique and non-dogmatic way. Beliefs are self-chosen and highly individualized. The famous moral philosopher Charles Taylor (2002) reports that in response to the varieties of religion today, people tend to make sense of the diversity through looking inward to an individualized pursuit of happiness (p. 88). This amounts to something called "individualism"—a focus on personhood as abstract concepts of self that tend to be based on psychological traits, such as "I am intelligent." It is generally considered to be the opposite of collectivism—a focus on personhood as a social entity that has personal meaning through interactions in social roles, such as "I am a student, son/daughter" (e.g., Farias & Lalljee 2008).

Since the social theories of Max Weber and Emile Durkheim, religion has been a central part of sociology due to the ways it provided a cohesive, universalizing meaning to social life, forming a rootedness in a shared sense of what was good to be and do in social life (e.g., Robertson 1977). Religion has often been thought to be a "gateway" to participation in other forms of engagement in social life by providing a shared sense of meaning (e.g., Oh & Sarkisian 2011). Because of this, many sociologists—including Robert Bellah and colleagues (1985), the authors of the reading in the next chapter—have been concerned about trends toward decreased participation in social forms of religion and increasing individualistic moral frames.

Scholars find that the "archipelago of faith" that is the diverse American cultural milieu (e.g., Madsen 2009) forms a tapestry of "moral tribes"—groups who band together over like-minded orientations to social life (e.g., Greene 2013). This moral landscape was what pervaded the previous generation's formation into adulthood, and thus the Baby Boom generation tends to have a moral rootedness in at least diffused religious traditions, while also having a moderate degree of awareness of the existence of other moral frames (e.g., Wuthnow 2010). While that may have been true in the past, what the studies summarized here are finding is that emerging adults today are increasingly less likely to have been exposed to and raised within these coherent moral frames. Rather than being part of one and looking out from within it to see the existence of the others, emerging adults are often outside all the moral frames, looking across rather than in. In attempting to abstract out moral truths and ethical orientations from these diverse frames, what is often constructed is a "watered down" sense of spiritualism without much substance to compel individuals to be involved collectively for the good of any whole (Oh & Sarkisian 2011).

This rising individualistic moral frame is what has led many psychologists and cultural critics to label the Millennial generation as increasingly narcissistic—focused primarily on self-benefit and self-aggrandizement rather than self as vehicle toward contributing to collective good (Wink et al. 2005). However, the popular press (e.g., Barone 2015) and numerous scholars (e.g., Arnett 2015) are quick to point out that Millennials are not entirely selfish and do hold a number of altruistic values, especially when it comes to issues of environmental sustainability. At the same time, the continual bombardment of options (e.g., Schwartz 2005) often leaves Millennials with a less-than-coherent logical system to guide their behaviors into actions (e.g., Taggart 2012).

Given the importance of ethical orientations, moral convictions, and spiritual well-being for collective enterprises, such as workplaces (e.g., Johnson 2002; Husted & Allen 2008; Paloutzian et al. 2011), it seems this generation of emerging adults is facing a crisis of meaning—lacking meaningful constellations of invisible moral frameworks for social life (Seidman 1985). In the absence of collective orientations, the question arises as to who will focus on civic changes directed at the bifurcating inequalities reported in Chapter 3. If each person becomes increasingly out for themselves, then what compels us to work together on forming a cohesive and just society?

RELIGION & CIVIC LIFE

Studies have long found a link between religious participation and civic engagement (e.g., Youniss et al. 1999; Chaves 2011; Putnam & Campbell 2010). This link has been especially strong in social forms of religiosity such as religious service attendance, which have been declining across generations (Putnam & Campbell 2010). Yet, the religiosity–civic link is also apparent in more personal forms of religiosity. For example, having a salient religious identity can be a motivation to do community service (Youniss et al. 1999), and private prayer and other forms of intrinsic religious connections to civic involvement (Loveland et al. 2005; Johnson et al. 2013). Religious congregations, as a social group, have also played important roles in shaping civic life (Chaves 2011).

In fact, religious effects—positive social and life outcomes associated with increased religiosity—likely result primarily through the social and organizational ties and learned competencies gained through participating in religious groups (Smith 2003). In particular for youth involvement, social support from non-familial adults is an important outcome of participating in religious youth activities which mediates the relationship between religious involvement and positive social outcomes (Snell 2009).

The network bonds formed in religious participation have been found to be so consistently important for an array of social outcomes (e.g., Muller & Ellison 2001; Lim & Putnam 2010) that some have coined a separate social capital term called religious capital. Likewise, having a moral orientation relates to more general involvement in economic, civic, and political life (e.g., Polletta & Tufail 2014; Snell 2010). Cumulatively, these forms of engaged spirituality (Stanczak 2006) are central to the generalized social trust that undergirds social life. In the words of Ecklund and colleagues (2013): "Religion provides Americans who participate in religious communities with *motivations* and *resources* for civic engagement outside their religious organizations" (p. 375). This—civic engagement—is the topic of the next chapter.

REFERENCES

Arnett, Jeffrey Jensen. 2015. *Emerging Adulthood: The Winding Road from the Late Teens through the Twenties*, 2nd edition. Oxford University Press.

Arnett, Jeffrey J. and Lene A. Jensen. 2002. "A Congregation of One: Individualized Religious Beliefs among Emerging Adults." *Journal of Adolescent Research* 17(5):451–67.

Barkin, Samuel H., Lisa Miller, and Suniya S. Luthar. 2015. "Filling the Void: Spiritual Development among Adolescents of the Affluent." *Journal of Religion and Health* 54(3):844–61.

Barone, Michael. 2015. "Meet the New Victorians: By Almost Any Standard of Behavior, Millennials are More Virtuous than the Previous Generation." *National Review Online* January 27, 2015. www.nationalreview.com

Barry, Carolyn McNamara and Larry J. Nelson. 2005. "The Role of Religion in the Transition to Adulthood for Young Emerging Adults." *Journal of Youth and Adolescence* 34(3):245–55.

Barry, Carolyn McNamara and Larry J. Nelson. 2008. "The Role of Religious Beliefs and Practices on Emerging Adults' Perceived Competencies, Perceived Importance Ratings, and Global Self-Worth." *International Journal of Behavioral Development* 32(6):509–21.

Barry, Carolyn McNamara and Mona M. Abo-Zena. 2014. *Emerging Adults' Religiousness and Spirituality: Meaning-Making in an Age of Transition*. Oxford University Press.

Bellah, Robert N., Richard Madsen, William M. Sullivan, Ann Swidler, and Steven M. Tipton. 1985. *Habits of the Heart: Individualism and Commitment in American Life*. University of California Press.

Brimeyer, Ted M. and William L. Smith. 2012. "Religion, Race, Social Class, and Gender Differences in Dating and Hooking Up among College Students." *Sociological Spectrum* 32(5):462–73.

Chan, Melissa, Kim M. Tsai, and Andrew J. Fuligni. 2014. "Changes in Religiosity across the Transition to Young Adulthood." *Journal of Youth and Adolescence* 1–12.

Chaves, Mark. 2011. *American Religion: Contemporary Trends*. Princeton University Press.

Cheadle, Jacob E. and Philip Schwadel. 2012. "The 'Friendship Dynamics of Religion,' or the 'Religious Dynamics of Friendship'? A Social Network Analysis of Adolescents Who Attend Small Schools." *Social Science Research* 41(5):1198–212.

Cook, Kaye V., Cynthia N. Kimball, Kathleen C. Leonard, and Chris J. Boyatzis. 2014. "The Complexity of Quest in Emerging Adults' Religiosity, Well-Being, and Identity." *Journal for the Scientific Study of Religion* 53(1):73–89.

Copen, Casey E. and Merril Silverstein. 2008. "The Transmission of Religious Beliefs across Generations: Do Grandparents Matter?" *Journal of Comparative Family Studies* 39(1):59–71.

Côté, James E. 2002. "The Role of Identity Capital in the Transition to Adulthood: The Individualization Thesis Examined." *Journal of Youth Studies* 5(2):117–34.

Cottone, John, Philip Drucker, and Rafael A. Javier. 2007. "Predictors of Moral Reasoning: Components of Executive Functioning and Aspects of Religiosity." *Journal for the Scientific Study of Religion* 46(1):37–53.

Davie, Grace. 1994. *Religion in Britain Since 1945: Believing without Belonging*. Wiley-Blackwell.

Dean, Kenda Creasy. 2010. *Almost Christian: What the Faith of Our Teenagers Is Telling the American Church*. New York: Oxford University Press.

Ecklund, Elaine Howard, Celina Davila, Michael O. Emerson, Samuel Kye, and Esther Chan. 2013. "Motivating Civic Engagement: In-Group versus Out-Group Service Orientations among Mexican Americans in Religious and Nonreligious Organizations." *Sociology of Religion* 74(3):370–91.

Ellison, Christopher G., Anthony B. Walker, Norval D. Glenn, and Elizabeth Marquardt. 2011. "The Effects of Parental Marital Discord and Divorce on the Religious and Spiritual Lives of Young Adults." *Social Science Research* 40(2):538–51.

Farias, Miguel and Mansur Lalljee. 2008. "Holistic Individualism in the Age of Aquarius: Measuring Individualism/Collectivism in New Age, Catholic, and Atheist/Agnostic Groups." *Journal for the Scientific Study of Religion* 47(2):277–89.

Fowler, James W. 1981. *Stages of Faith: The Psychology of Human Development and the Quest for Meaning*. Harper & Row.

Fowler, James W. 1991. "Stages in Faith Consciousness." *New Directions for Child Development* 52:27–45.

Glass, Jennifer L., April Sutton, and Scott T. Fitzgerald. 2015. "Leaving the Faith: How Religious Switching Changes Pathways to Adulthood among Conservative Protestant Youth." *Social Currents* 2(2):126–43.

Good, Marie and Teena Willoughby. 2008. "Adolescence as a Sensitive Period for Spiritual Development." *Child Development Perspectives* 2(1):32–7.

Greene, Joshua. 2013. *Moral Tribes: Emotion, Reason, and the Gap Between Us and Them.* Penguin.

Gutierrez, Ian A. and Crystal L. Park. 2014. "Emerging Adulthood, Evolving Worldviews: How Life Events Impact College Students' Developing Belief Systems." *Emerging Adulthood* 3(2):85–97.

Hardie, Jessica Halliday, Lisa D. Pearce, and Melinda Lundquist Denton. 2013. "The Dynamics and Correlates of Religious Service Attendance in Adolescence." *Youth & Society*. doi: 10.1177/0044118X13483777.

Hayward, R. David and Neal Krause. 2013. "Patterns of Change in Religious Service Attendance across the Life Course: Evidence from a 34-Year Longitudinal Study." *Social Science Research* 42(6):1480–89.

Hill, Jonathan P. 2011. "Faith and Understanding: Specifying the Impact of Higher Education on Religious Belief." *Journal for the Scientific Study of Religion* 50(3):533–51.

Hoffmann, John P. 2014. "Religiousness, Social Networks, Moral Schemas, and Marijuana Use: A Dynamic Dual-Process Model of Culture and Behavior." *Social Forces* 93(1):181–208.

Husted, Bryan W. and David B. Allen. 2008. "Toward a Model of Cross-Cultural Business Ethics: The Impact of Individualism and Collectivism on the Ethical Decision-Making Process." *Journal of Business Ethics* 82:293–305.

Johnson, Monica Kirkpatrick. 2002. "Social Origins, Adolescent Experiences, and Work Value Trajectories during the Transition to Adulthood." *Social Forces* 80(4):1307–40.

Johnson, Kathryn A., Adam B. Cohen, and Morris A. Okun. 2013. "Intrinsic Religiosity and Volunteering during Emerging Adulthood: A Comparison of Mormons with Catholics and Non-Catholic Christians." *Journal for the Scientific Study of Religion* 52(4):842–51.

Jung, Jong Hyun. 2015. "Sense of Divine Involvement and Sense of Meaning in Life: Religious Tradition as a Contingency." *Journal for the Scientific Study of Religion* 54(1):119–33.

Kimball, Cynthia, Kaye Cook, Chris Boyatzis, and Kathleen Leonard. 2013. "Meaning Making in Emerging Adults' Faith Narratives: Identity, Attachment, and Religious Orientation." *Journal of Psychology and Christianity* 221–33.

Koenig, Laura B., Matt McGue, and William G. Iacono. 2008. "Stability and Change in Religiousness during Emerging Adulthood." *Developmental Psychology* 44(2):532–43.

Layton, Emily, David C. Dollahite, and Sam A. Hardy. 2011. "Anchors of Religious Commitment in Adolescents." *Journal of Adolescent Research* 26(3):381–413.

Levenson, Michael R., Carolyn M. Aldwin, and Heidi Igarashi. 2013. "Religious Development from Adolescence to Middle Adulthood." In *Handbook of the Psychology of Religion and Spirituality, 2nd Edition*, edited by Raymond F. Paloutzian and Crystal L. Park, 183–98. Guilford Press.

Lim, Chaeyoon and Robert D. Putnam. 2010. "Religion, Social Networks, and Life Satisfaction." *American Sociological Review* 75(6):914–33.

Longest, Kyle C. and Christian Smith. 2011. "Conflicting or Compatible: Beliefs about Religion and Science among Emerging Adults in the United States." *Sociological Forum* 26:846–69.

Longest, Kyle C., Steven Hitlin, and Stephen Vaisey. 2013. "Position and Disposition: The Contextual Development of Human Values." *Social Forces* 91(4):1499–528.

Loveland, Matthew T., David Sikkink, Daniel J. Myers, and Benjamin Radcliff. 2005. "Private Prayer and Civic Involvement." *Journal for the Scientific Study of Religion* 44(1):1–14.

Madge, Nicola, Peter Hemming, and Kevin Stenson. 2014. *Youth On Religion: The Development, Negotiation and Impact of Faith and Non-Faith Identity*. New York: Routledge.

Madsen, Richard. 2009. "The Archipelago of Faith: Religious Individualism and Faith Community in America Today." *American Journal of Sociology* 114(5):1263–1301.

Mayseless, Ofra and Einat Keren. 2013. "Finding a Meaningful Life as a Developmental Task in Emerging Adulthood: The Domains of Love and Work across Cultures." *Emerging Adulthood* 2(1): 63–73.

Mayrl, Damon and Jeremy E. Uecker. 2011. "Higher Education and Religious Liberalization among Young Adults." *Social Forces* 90(1):181–208.

Muller, Chandra and Christopher G. Ellison. 2001. "Religious Involvement, Social Capital, and Adolescents' Academic Progress: Evidence from the National Education Longitudinal Study of 1988." *Sociological Focus* 34(2):155–83.

Oh, Seil and Natalia Sarkisian. 2012. "Spiritual Individualism or Engaged Spirituality? Social Implications of Holistic Spirituality among Mind-Body-Spirit Practitioners." *Sociology of Religion* 73(3):299–322.

Paloutzian, Raymond F., Robert A. Emmons, and Susan G. Keortge. 2011. "Spiritual Well-Being, Spiritual Intelligence, and Healthy Workplace Policy." In *Handbook of Workplace Spirituality and Organizational Performance*, Robert A. Giacalone and Carole L. Jurkiewicz, 73–86. Routledge.

Parker, Stephen. 2010. "Research in Fowler's Faith Development Theory: A Review Article." *Review of Religious Research* 51(3): 233–52.

Petts, Richard J. 2009. "Trajectories of Religious Participation from Adolescence to Young Adulthood." *Journal for the Scientific Study of Religion* 48(3):552–71.

Polletta, Francesca and Zaibu Tufail. 2014. "The Moral Obligations of Some Debts." *Sociological Forum* 29(1):1–28.

Pratt, M. W., B. Hunsberger, S. M. Pancer, and S. Alisat. 2003. "A Longitudinal Analysis of Personal Values Socialization: Correlates of a Moral Self-Ideal in Late Adolescence." *Social Development* 12(4):563–85.

Putnam, Robert D. and David E. Campbell. 2012. *American Grace: How Religion Divides and Unites Us*. Simon & Schuster.

Robertson, Roland. 1977. "Individualism, Societalism, Worldliness, Universalism: Thematizing Theoretical Sociology of Religion." *Sociological Analysis* 38(4):281–308.

Schafer, Markus H. 2011. "Ambiguity, Religion, and Relational Context: Competing Influences on Moral Attitudes?" *Sociological Perspectives* 54(1):59–82.

Schwadel, Philip. 2014. "Birth Cohort Changes in the Association between College Education and Religious Non-Affiliation." *Social Forces* 93(2):719–46.

Schwartz, Barry. 2005. *The Paradox of Choice: Why More Is Less*. Harper Perennial.

Seidman, Steven. 1985. "Modernity and the Problem of Meaning: The Durkheimian Tradition." *Sociological Analysis* 46(2):109–30.

Smith, Christian and Patricia Snell. 2009. *Souls in Transition: The Religious and Spiritual Lives of Emerging Adults*. New York: Oxford University Press.

Smith, Christian, Kari Christoffersen, Hilary Davidson, and Patricia Snell Herzog. 2011. *Lost in Transition: The Dark Side of Emerging Adulthood*. NY: Oxford University Press.

Smith, Jeffrey A., Miller McPherson, and Lynn Smith-Lovin. 2014. "Social Distance in the United States: Sex, Race, Religion, Age, and Education Homophily among Confidants, 1985 to 2004." *American Sociological Review* 79(3):432–56.

Snell, Patricia. 2009. "What Difference Does Youth Group Make? A Longitudinal Analysis of Religious Youth Group Participation and Religious and Life Outcomes." *Journal for the Scientific Study of Religion* 48(3):572–87.

Stanczak, Gregory C. 2006. *Engaged Spirituality: Social Change and American Religion*. Rutgers University Press.

Stoppa, Tara M. and Eva S. Lefkowitz. 2010. "Longitudinal Changes in Religiosity among Emerging Adult College Students." *J. of Research on Adolescence* 20(1):23–38.

Streib, Heinz. 2005. "Faith Development Research Revisited: Accounting for Diversity in Structure, Content, and Narrativity of Faith." *International Journal for the Psychology of Religion* 15(2):99–121.

Taggart, Andrew. 2012. "On the Need for Speculative Philosophy Today." *Cosmos & History: The Journal of Natural and Social Philosophy* 8(1):47–61.

Taylor, Charles. 2002. *Varieties of Religion Today*. Harvard University Press.

Uecker, Jeremy E., Mark D. Regnerus, and Margaret L. Vaaler. 2007. "Losing My Religion: The Social Sources of Religious Decline in Early Adulthood." *Social Forces* 85(4):1667–92.

Wink, Paul, Michele Dillon, and Kristen Fay. 2005. "Spiritual Seeking, Narcissism, and Psychotherapy: How Are They Related?" *Journal for Scientific Study of Religion* 44(2):143–58.

Wink, Paul. 2009. "Religious and Spiritual Development in Adulthood." In *Handbook of Research on Adult Learning and Development*, edited by M. Cecil Smith and Nancy Defrates-Densch, 436–59. Routledge.

Wuthnow, Robert. 2010. *After the Baby Boomers: How Twenty- and Thirty-Somethings Are Shaping the Future of American Religion*. Princeton, NJ: Princeton University Press.

Youniss, James, Jeffrey A. McLellan, and Miranda Yates. 1999. "Religion, Community Service, and Identity in American Youth." *Journal of Adolescence* 22(2):243–53.

CHAPTER 10

Civic Engagement & Collective Voices

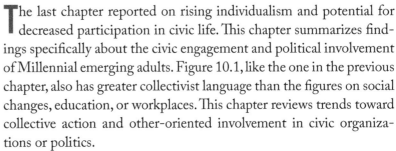

The last chapter reported on rising individualism and potential for decreased participation in civic life. This chapter summarizes findings specifically about the civic engagement and political involvement of Millennial emerging adults. Figure 10.1, like the one in the previous chapter, also has greater collectivist language than the figures on social changes, education, or workplaces. This chapter reviews trends toward collective action and other-oriented involvement in civic organizations or politics.

This is especially important given that findings of previous chapters show a rising disconnection of younger generations from mainstream social institutions. What then is to be made of the bifurcating inequalities patterning extended durations to launch into adulthood? Will the emerging leaders of tomorrow engage in changing these patterns?

GENERATION ME OR GENERATION WE?

According to an article published in *Time Magazine*, Millennials are "generation me." The article was titled "Millennials: The Me, Me, Me Generation" (Stein 2013) and it caused quite a stir. Millennials were labeled as a self-centered generation, and a group that was unlikely to be up to much for the collective good. A counterargument was published a few months later in the *USA Today* in an article titled "Millennials: The Giving Generation?" (Newlon, 2013). One of the charitable organization representatives interviewed for the article said that they should rather be called the "misunderstood generation." So, which is it?

It turns out that scholars have not come to a consensus on what to make of the Millennial generation either. Twenge (2006, 2013a, 2013b) finds that all things collective, including civic engagement and empathy for others, are declining as a result of rising narcissism—inflated and positive view of the self coupled with attention-seeking behavior and desirability for uniqueness. However, Arnett and colleagues (2013) rebutted by calling these claims "generational myth-making"—creating impressionistic implications from misconstrued data. Arnett (2013) also directly countered Twenge by showing narcissism trends from a different study were stable. Additionally, he pointed out that some of the indicators employed in the typical narcissism scale are the same qualities we value in leaders and cautioned against use of indexes that lump all these factors together. Twenge (2013b) replied by stating:

Like any generation, today's emerging adults have strengths and weaknesses. I agree that we should praise their strengths. However, ignoring their weaknesses will not make the negative cultural trends go away. Instead, we could start by challenging the American cultural message that thinking you are great is the key to success, when it is not" (p. 24).

Twenge continues by stating: "Or we could try to discover why one out of nine Americans takes an antidepressant.... Denial, however, will get us nowhere" (p. 24).

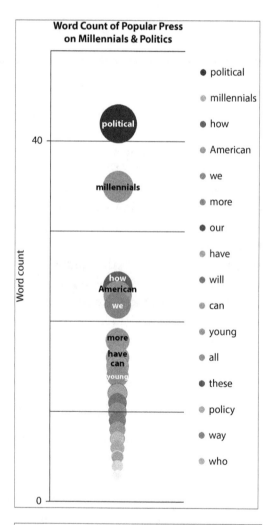

FIGURE 10.1 Millennial Popular Press Word Count

A NATION OF INDIVIDUALS

Concern over rising disconnection from social institutions is what led Bellah et al. (1985) to theorize a rise in American individualism. As opposed to the traditional psychological take that individualization is a primary task of adulthood (e.g., Schwartz et al. 2005), sociologists tend to be wary of the typical American perspective that individuals are freely able to be and choose as they please (e.g., Hartmann & Swartz 2006). Instead, Bellah and colleagues critique this view and highlight the troubling trends for society brought about by individuals decreasingly recognizing social forces.

READING 10.1

Individualism

By Robert N. Bellah, Richard Madsen, William M. Sullivan, Ann Swidler, and Steven M. Tipton

The Social Sources of Ambivalence

As we saw [previously], individualism is deeply rooted in America's social history. Here the bondservant became free, the tenant became a small landowner, and what Benjamin Franklin called the self-respecting "middling" condition of men became the norm. Yet the incipient "independent citizen" of colonial times found himself in a cohesive community, the "peaceable kingdoms" that were colonial towns, where ties to family and church and respect for the "natural leaders" of the community were still strong.[1] Individualism was so embedded in the civic and religious structures of colonial life that it had not yet found a name, even though John Locke's ideas about individual autonomy were well known. It took the geographical and economic expansion of the new nation, especially in the years after 1800, to produce the restless quest for material betterment that led Tocqueville to use the word

---

[1] See, particularly, Michael Zuckerman, *Peaceable Kingdoms: New England Towns in the Eighteenth Century* (New York: Random House, 1970). The phrase "peaceable kingdom" is, of course, eschatological in its reference. It is what the New Englanders aspired to be, not what they claimed they were.

Robert N. Bellah, Richard Madsen, William M. Sullivan, Ann Swidler, and Steven M. Tipton, "Individualism," Habits of the Heart: Individualism and Commitment in American Life, pp. 147–152, 320. Copyright © 1985 by University of California Press. Reprinted with permission.

"individualism" to describe what he saw.[2] The new social and economic conditions did not create the ideology of modern individualism, most of whose elements are considerably older than the nineteenth century, but those conditions did make it possible for what we have called utilitarian and, later, expressive individualism to develop their own inherent tendencies in relative independence from civic and religious forms of life, important though those still were.

Tocqueville was quick to point out one of the central ambiguities in the new individualism—that it was strangely compatible with conformism. He described the American insistence that one always rely on one's own judgment, rather than on received authority, in forming one's opinions and that one stand by one's own opinions. We have already heard many examples of this attitude in the conversations recorded in earlier chapters—in the assertion, for example, that compromise with others is desirable, but not if you sacrifice your own "values." But, as Tocqueville observed, when one can no longer rely on tradition or authority, one inevitably looks to others for confirmation of one's judgments. Refusal to accept established opinion and anxious conformity to the opinions of one's peers turn out to be two sides of the same coin.[3]

There has been a long-standing anxiety that the American individualist, who flees from home and family leaving the values of community and tradition behind, is secretly a conformist. Mark Twain depicted the stultifying conformity of the mid-nineteenth-century town of his youth in recounting the adventures of boys who tried to break free of it and never quite succeeded. As late as the 1920s, Sinclair Lewis identified a classic American type in his portrait of *Babbitt*, the small town businessman too afraid of censure from neighbors and family to develop his political convictions or pursue his own happiness in love. The advice Babbit gives his son not to make the mistake he has made is typical: "Don't be scared of the family. No, nor all of Zenith. Nor of yourself, the way I've been."

In the past hundred years, individualism and its ambiguities have been closely linked to middle-class status. As pointed out [previously], the "middle class" that began to emerge in the later part of the nineteenth century differed from the old "middling condition." In the true sense of the term, the middle class is defined not merely by the desire for material betterment but by a conscious, calculating effort to move up the ladder of success. David Schneider and Raymond Smith usefully define the middle class as a "broad but not undifferentiated category which includes those who have certain attitudes, aspirations, and expectations toward status mobility, and who shape their actions accordingly." Status mobility has increasingly depended on advanced education and competence in managerial and professional occupations that

---

2 On the introduction of the term individualism by Tocqueville and the American response see Yehoshua Arieli, *Individualism and Nationalism in American Ideology* (Cambridge, Mass.: Harvard University Press, 1964), pp. 183-210, 246–76. On the emergence of the term in the European context see Koenraad W. Swart, "Individualism in the Mid-Nineteenth Century," *Journal of the History of Ideas* 23 (1962): 77–90.
3 Alexis de Tocqueville, *Democracy in America*, trans. George Lawrence, ed. J. P. Mayer (New York: Doubleday, Anchor Books, 1969), vol. 2, part 1, chapters 1 and 2.

require specialized knowledge. For middle-class Americans, a calculating attitude toward educational and occupational choice has been essential and has often spilled over into determining criteria for the choice of spouse, friends, and voluntary associations. From the point of view of lower-class Americans, these preoccupations do not necessarily seem natural. As one of Schneider and Smith's informants put it, "To be a square dude is hard work, man."[4]

For those oriented primarily to upward mobility, to "success," major features of American society appear to be "the normal outcome of the operation of individual achievement." In this conception, individuals, unfettered by family or other group affiliation, are given the chance to make the best of themselves, and, though equality of opportunity is essential, inequality of result is natural. But the ambiguities of individualism for the middle-class person arise precisely from lack of certainty about what the "best" we are supposed to make of ourselves is. Schneider and Smith note that "there are no fixed standards of behavior which serve to mark status. The only clearly defined cultural standards against which status can be measured are the gross standards of income, consumption, and conformity to rational procedures for attaining ends." Middle-class individuals are thus motivated to enter a highly autonomous and demanding quest for achievement and then left with no standard against which achievement is to be measured except the income and consumption levels of their neighbors, exhibiting anew the clash between autonomy and conformity that seems to be the fate of American individualism.[5]

But perhaps Schneider and Smith's third cultural standard, "rational procedures for attaining ends," offers a way of asserting individual autonomy without the anxious glance at the neighbor. In the case of middle-class professionals whose occupation involves the application of technical rationality to the solution of new problems, the correct solution of a problem or, even more, an innovative solution to a problem, provides evidence of "success" that has intrinsic validity. And where such competence operates in the service of the public good—as, for example, in medical practice at its best—it expresses an individualism that has social value without being conformist.[6]

But to the extent that technical competence is enclosed in the life pattern that we have designated "career," concern for rational problem solving (not to speak of social contribution) becomes subordinated to standards of success measured only by income and consumption. When this happens, as it often does to doctors, lawyers, and other professionals, it raises doubts about the intrinsic value of the work itself. These doubts become all the more insistent when, as is often the case, the professional must operate in the context of a large public or private bureaucracy where much ingenuity must be spent, not on solving external problems, but on manipulating the bureaucratic rules and roles, both in order to get anything done and in order to move ahead in one's

---

4   David M. Schneider and Raymond T. Smith, *Class Differences and Sex Roles in American Kinship and Family Structure* (Englewood Cliffs, N.J.: Prentice-Hall, 1973), pp. 19, 20.
5   Ibid., p. 24.
6   Ibid., p. 46.

career. Anxieties about whether an "organization man" can be a genuine individual long predate William H. Whyte's famous book *The Organization Man*.[7] The cowboy and the detective began to appear as popular heroes when business corporations emerged as the focal institutions of American life. The fantasy of a lonely, but morally impeccable, hero corresponds to doubts about the integrity of the self in the context of modern bureaucratic organization.

The irony of present-day middle-class American individualism derives from the fact that while a high degree of personal initiative, competence, and rationality are still demanded from individuals, the autonomy of the successful individual and even the meaning of "success" are increasingly in doubt. It is as though the stress on the rationality of means and on the importance of individual wants, the primary emphases of utilitarian and expressive individualism, have come loose from an understanding of the ends and purposes of life, in the past largely derived from the biblical and republican traditions. One response to this situation is to make occupational achievement, for so long the dominating focus of middle-class individualism, no longer an end in itself, but merely an instrument for the attainment of a private lifestyle lived, perhaps, in a lifestyle enclave. Yet this solution, as we saw [previously], is subject to doubt. The same inner contradictions that undermined occupational success as a life goal also threaten to deprive private life of meaning when there is no longer any purpose to involvement with others except individual satisfaction.

The ambiguity and ambivalence of American individualism derive from both cultural and social contradictions. We insist, perhaps more than ever before, on finding our true selves independent of any cultural or social influence, being responsible to that self alone, and making its fulfillment the very meaning of our lives. Yet we spend much of our time navigating through immense bureaucratic structures—multiversities, corporations, government agencies—manipulating and being manipulated by others. In describing this situation, Alasdair MacIntyre has spoken of "bureaucratic individualism," the form of life exemplified by the manager and the therapist.[8] In bureaucratic individualism, the ambiguities and contradictions of individualism are frighteningly revealed, as freedom to make private decisions is bought at the cost of turning over most public decisions to bureaucratic managers and experts. A bureaucratic individualism in which the consent of the governed, the first demand of modern enlightened individualism, has been abandoned in all but form, illustrates the tendency of individualism to destroy its own conditions.

But in our interviews, though we saw tendencies toward bureaucratic individualism, we cannot say that it has yet become dominant. Rather we found all the classic polarities of American individualism still operating: the deep desire for autonomy and self-reliance combined with an equally deep conviction that life has no meaning unless shared with others in the context of community; a commitment to the equal right to dignity of every

---

7 William H. Whyte, *The Organization Man* (New York: Simon and Schuster, 1956).
8 Alasdair MacIntyre, *After Virtue* (South Bend, Ind.: University of Notre Dame Press, 1981), p. 33.

individual combined with an effort to justify inequality of reward, which, when extreme, may deprive people of dignity; an insistence that life requires practical effectiveness and "realism" combined with the feeling that compromise is ethically fatal. The inner tensions of American individualism add up to a classic case of ambivalence. We strongly assert the value of our self-reliance and autonomy. We deeply feel the emptiness of a life without sustaining social commitments. Yet we are hesitant to articulate our sense that we need one another as much as we need to stand alone, for fear that if we did we would lose our independence altogether. The tensions of our lives would be even greater if we did not, in fact, engage in practices that constantly limit the effects of an isolating individualism, even though we cannot articulate those practices nearly as well as we can the quest for autonomy.

The Limits of Individualism

We have pointed out the peculiar resonance between middle-class life and individualism in America. We have also stressed the special nature of the middle class, the fact that it is not simply a "layer" in a "system of stratification" but rather a group that seeks to embody in its own continuous progress and advancement the very meaning of the American project. To a large extent, it has succeeded in this aspiration. It so dominates our culture that, as Schneider and Smith put it, "middle-class values can be said to encompass both lower- and upper-class values." This is true for the lower class in that not only are middle-class values understood and respected but "lower-class people explain their inferior position in terms of circumstances that have prevented them from behaving in a middle-class fashion." The upper class sometimes takes comfort in its special sense of family and tradition, but it does not try to substitute its values for the dominant ones. On the contrary, its members praise middle-class rationality and achievement as the values on which our society is based, even when they do not choose to follow them.[9]

The nature of middle-class individualism becomes even clearer when we contrast it to lower-class and upper-class culture. Schneider and Smith describe the contrast very suggestively when they say that the middle class sees "individual and social behavior as predominantly determined by the application of technical rules to any situation that arises," whereas the lower class (and, interestingly enough, the upper class) have a more "dramaturgical view of social action." By "dramaturgical" they mean action that takes on meaning because of a particular history of relationships. Abstract rules are less important than the examples set by individuals. Schneider and Smith argue, for example, that it is in the lower class that ethnicity, as a specific pattern of cultural life, survives in America, and that as individuals enter the middle class, ethnicity loses distinctive social content even when it is symbolically emphasized.[10] The point is not

---

9 Schneider and Smith, *Class Differences*, p. 27.
10 Ibid., pp. 107, 39. "The direct experience of our field research was that, while consciousness of ethnic identity persists at all levels of society, it is of rapidly decreasing significance as a factor affecting the behavior of those

that lower- and upper-class Americans are not individualistic, but rather that their individualism is embedded in specific patterns of relationship and solidarity that mitigate the tendency toward an empty self and empty relationships in middle-class life. The contrast is expressed by middle-class Americans themselves when they entertain envious fantasies about more "meaningful community" among lower-class racial and ethnic groups or among (usually European) aristocracies.

Important though the distinctions we have been drawing are, we should not over-emphasize the degree to which rationality and technical rules govern middle-class life. Children do not grow up through abstract injunctions. They identify with their parents, they learn through role modeling, and they are influenced by the historic specificity of their family, church, and local community. It is the middle-class orientation toward technical education, bureaucratic occupational hierarchies, and the market economy that encourages the greater emphasis on universal rules and technical rationality. The upper and lower classes can maintain greater cultural specificity (though in the United States that specificity is only relative) because they are less oriented to these rationalizing institutions.

Since middle-class people, too, are embedded in families, churches, and local communities, they also experience conflict between the more rational and the more dramaturgic spheres of life. The tensions that divide middle-class Americans from other Americans also exist within the middle class itself. Much is said about the cultural diversity and pluralism of American life. But perhaps what divides us most is not that diversity, but the conflict between the monoculture of technical and bureaucratic rationality and the specificity of our concrete commitments.[11]

---

who are middle class. In fact, one aspect of becoming middle class is the abandonment of most of the behavioral characteristics of ethnicity, a process considerably aided by orientation toward individual achievement, the rational control of events and things, and looking to the future rather than to the past" (pp. 35–36).

11 Richard M. Mcrelman in *Making Something of Ourselves: On Culture and Politics in the United States* (Berkeley and Los Angeles: University of California Press, 1984) defines this conflict as between loose-boundedness and tight-boundedness. He sees it as the major conflict in American life today.

Thomson (1989) provided historical context to these trends by reviewing rising individualism in the 1920s, as compared to the variety emerging in the 1970s which Bellah and colleagues wrote about. Thomson finds that in the 1920s the social context was one of heavy social control and pressures for conformity, in which tendencies toward individualism were about self-expression in the midst of a still cohesive society. This contrasts markedly with the cultural and structural changes between the 1920s and 1970s. Breakdown in societal cohesion and social control across those decades meant the individualism of the 1970s resulted instead in self-absorption and the need to develop oneself personally, with less focus on contributions to societal good. Thomson describes this as the societal shift from a focus on development of character, giving way to a focus on personality, and later transitioning to ongoing discovery of fluid identity. In a contemporary version of the same sentiments, Putnam (2015) states:

> We Americans like to think of ourselves as "rugged individualists"—in the image of the lone cowboy riding toward the setting sun, opening the frontier. But at least as accurate a symbol of our national story is the wagon train, with its mutual aid among a community of pioneers. Throughout our history, a pendulum has slowly swung between the poles of individualism and community, both in our public philosophy and in our daily lives. In the past half century we have witnessed, for better or worse, a giant swing toward the individualist (or libertarian) pole in our culture, society, and politics. At the same time, researchers have steadily piled up evidence of how important social context, social institutions, and social networks—in short, our communities—remain for our well-being and our kids' opportunities (p. 206).

While not all scholars agree on whether an overarching theory of individualism explains social changes (e.g., Hart 2001), it is clear that a precursor to getting involved in civic life is having moral evaluations of a good society and one's role within it (e.g., Perrucci & Perrucci 2014).

TAKING COLLECTIVE ACTIONS

Despite all the hype in recent elections regarding massive turnouts in the *youth vote*, voting by emerging adults has only marginally increased, and only in national-level elections (Settersten & Ray 2010). As with all the average trends reported at the national level, the trouble is the important subgroup differences that averages obscure. It is important to know the general trend, but it is also critical to investigate differences from that trend by drilling into the diversity. When digging beneath the surface, it is clear that participation in civic life is unequal, even further bifurcated than many trends reported in Chapter 3. It is especially divided along the college-degreed fault line (e.g., Putnam 2015, 2000; Settersten & Ray 2010; Rosenstone & Hansen 2003).

What motivates emerging adults to get involved in civic and political life? There are several how-to books on this question (e.g., Davis 2012; Saratovsky & Felmann 2013), yet social science research lags behind in answering this question well. It is clear, however, that we need to learn more about the youth civic engagement processes of today (Youniss 2009; Youniss et al. 2002) and how these processes are changing given the ability to connect more directly in democracy without as much need for physical "brick and mortar" buildings to organize it (Settersten & Ray 2010).

Scholars studying emerging adult engagement find that younger generations are more motivated by interest in particular causes than loyalty to certain organizations. They also value transparency in the intentions of organizations and do not necessarily trust that organizations are explicit in their values (e.g., Quéniart 2008). As Settersten and Ray (2010) describe, Millennials have sensitive "sniffers" for overly managed and marketed messages, having grown up with bombardments of consumer-driven marketing campaigns surrounding them.

Beginning already in adolescence, youths are motivated to participate in causes that support their identity within their social circles (Youniss et al. 2001). With Milner's (2006) findings on high schools in the reading of Chapter 8, it should come as no surprise that peer groups and esteem within them are an important factor in civic engagement patterns. This is likely why the most successful youth activism activities today are those that employ social media.

Paralleling friendship groups, religious participation is also important for engendering underlying civic orientations and prosocial behaviors (Crystal & DeBell 2002) and for fostering close network ties with whom youth and emerging adults can be engaged (Schafer 2015). Experiences with discrimination and marginalization can also foster participation in civic life, including examples of participation from racial and ethnic minorities (Kelly 2008), young immigrant civic engagement (Mollenkopf et al. 2012), and community participation by Muslim youth who felt marginalized as a religious group in post-9/11 American society (Sirin & Katsiaficas 2011).

GAINING CIVIC EXPERIENCES

Studies show the importance of youth gaining access to civic experiences early in their development trajectories in order to ward off later becoming disconnected from civic and political life due to lack of information or little concern about a distant and abstract system (Snell 2010). Studies find a growing bifurcation in who has political voice, which is largely patterned by the same social class dynamics and access to social and economic resources that pattern all the other aspects of emerging adult lives covered in this text (e.g., Rosenstone & Hansen 2002; Verba et al. 1995). For example, full-time work early in life course transitions hinders participation in politics, while attending school facilitates participation (Oesterle et al. 2004).

At the same time, people from lower social class backgrounds are more inclined to give interpersonally through more informal means of helping out people in their families and communities (e.g., Piff et al. 2010). When youths in low-income communities were engaged in processes of decision-making for community development grants, the youth and broader community benefited from their participation, and this study reveals the importance of finding ways to broaden the spectrum of participation in civic experiences (Blanchet-Cohen et al. 2012). A number of studies find that participating in civic processes, especially early in the life course, is important for engendering long-term commitment to be engaged (e.g., Metz et al. 2003; Seider 2007), including to be a giving alumni on college campus (Freeland et al. 2015).

What is abundantly clear then is that there is no one-size-fits-all approach to emerging adult civic engagement. There are numerous varieties of civic experience (e.g., Schudson 2009), and giving voice to the wide diversity that the demographics of Millennial emerging adults represent means being open to a variety of approaches to civic and political engagement. Settersten and Ray (2010) highlight the importance of political and charitable causes catering to the Internet attention of the "iDecide" generation, though they also caution against engagement that ends with a simple click of a button. Engagement is at the fingertips of emerging adults, and supportive adults with invitations to longer-term engagement need to be on the other end.

REFERENCES

Arnett, Jeffrey Jensen, Kali H. Trzesniewski, and M. Brent Donnellan. 2013. "The Dangers of Generational Myth-Making: Rejoinder to Twenge." *Emerging Adulthood* 1(1):17–20.

Arnett, Jeffrey Jensen. 2013. "The Evidence for Generation We and Against Generation Me." *Emerging Adulthood* 1(1):5–10.

Bellah, Robert N., Richard Madsen, William M. Sullivan, Ann Swidler, and Steven M. Tipton. 1985. *Habits of the Heart: Individualism and Commitment in American Life*. University of California Press.

Blanchet-Cohen, Natasha, Sarah Manolson, and Katie Shaw. 2014. "Youth-Led Decision Making in Community Development Grants." *Youth & Society* 46(6):819–34.

Crystal, David S. and Matthew DeBell. 2002. "Sources of Civic Orientation among American Youth: Trust, Religious Valuation, and Attributions of Responsibility." *Political Psychology* 23(1):113–32.

Davis, Emily. 2012. *Fundraising and the Next Generation: Tools for Engaging the Next Generation of Philanthropists*. John Wiley & Sons, Inc.

Freeland, Robert E., Kenneth I. Spenner, and Grace McCalmon. 2015. "I Gave at the Campus: Exploring Student Giving and Its Link to Young Alumni Donations After Graduation." *Nonprofit and Voluntary Sector Quarterly* 44(4):755–74.

Hart, Stephen. 2001. "Individualism and Its Discontents." In *Cultural Dilemmas of Progressive Politics: Styles of Engagement among Grassroots Activists*, 189–211. University of Chicago Press.

Hartmann, Douglas and Teresa Toguchi Swartz. 2006. "The New Adulthood? The Transition to Adulthood from the Perspective of Transitioning Young Adults." *Advances in Life Course Research* 11:253–86.

Kelly, Diann Cameron. 2008. "In Preparation for Adulthood: Exploring Civic Participation and Social Trust among Young Minorities." *Youth & Society* 40(4):526–40.

Metz, Edward, Jeffrey McLellan, and James Youniss. 2003. "Types of Voluntary Service and Adolescents' Civic Development." *Journal of Adolescent Research* 18(2):188–203.

Milner, Murray. 2006. *Freaks, Geeks, and Cool Kids*. New York: Routledge.

Mollenkopf, John, Jennifer Holdaway, Philip Kasinitz, and Mary Waters. 2012. "Politics among Young Adults in New York: The Immigrant Second Generation." In *Transforming Politics, Transforming America: The Political and Civic Incorporation of Immigrants in the United States*, edited by Lee Taeku, S. Karthick Ramakrishnan, and Ricardo Ramirez, 175–93. University of Virginia Press.

Newlon, Cara. 2013. "Millennials: The Giving Generation?" *USA Today*.

Oesterle, Sabrina, Monica Kirkpatrick Johnson, and Jeylan T. Mortimer. 2004. "Volunteerism during the Transition to Adulthood: A Life Course Perspective." *Social Forces* 82(3):1123–49.

Perrucci, Robert and Carolyn C. Perrucci. 2014. "The Good Society: Core Social Values, Social Norms, and Public Policy." *Sociological Forum* 29(1):245–58.

Piff, Paul K., Michael W. Kraus, Stéphane Côté, Bonnie Hayden Cheng, and Dacher Keltner. 2010. "Having Less, Giving More: The Influence of Social Class on Prosocial Behavior." *Journal of Personality and Social Psychology* 99(5):771–84.

Putnam, Robert D. 2000. *Bowling Alone: The Collapse and Revival of American Community*. Simon & Schuster.

Putnam, Robert D. 2015. *Our Kids: The American Dream in Crisis*. NY: Simon & Schuster.

Quéniart, Anne. 2008. "The Form and Meaning of Young People's Involvement in Community and Political Work." *Youth & Society* 40(2):203–23.

Rosenstone, Steven J. and John Mark Hansen. 2003. *Mobilization, Participation, and Democracy in America*. Longman.

Saratovsky, Kari Dunn and Derrick Feldmann. 2013. *Cause for Change: The Why and How of Nonprofit Millennial Engagement*. Jossey-Bass.

Schafer, Markus H. 2015. "Religiously Traditional, Unusually Supportive? Examining Who Gives, Helps, and Advises in Americans' Close Networks." *Social Currents* 2(1):81–104.

Schudson, Michael. 2009. "The Varieties of Civic Experience." In *The Civic Life of American Religion*, edited by Paul Lichterman and C. Brady Potts, 23–47. Stanford University Press.

Schwartz, Seth J., James E. Côté, and Jeffrey Jensen Arnett. 2005. "Identity and Agency in Emerging Adulthood: Two Developmental Routes in the Individualization Process." *Youth & Society* 37(2):201–29.

Seider, Scott. 2007. "Catalyzing a Commitment to Community Service in Emerging Adults." *Journal of Adolescent Research* 22(6):612–39.

Settersten, Richard and Barbara E. Ray. 2010. *Not Quite Adults: Why 20-Somethings Are Choosing a Slower Path to Adulthood, and Why It's Good for Everyone*. New York: Bantam.

Sirin, Selcuk R. and Dalal Katsiaficas. 2011. "Religiosity, Discrimination, and Community Engagement: Gendered Pathways of Muslim American Emerging Adults." *Youth & Society* 43(4):1528–46.

Snell, Patricia. 2010. "Emerging Adult Civic and Political Disengagement: A Longitudinal Analysis of Lack of Involvement with Politics." *Journal of Adolescent Research* 25(2):258–87.

Stein, Joel. 2013. "The Me, Me, Me Generation: Millennials Are Lazy, Entitled Narcissists Who Still Live with Their Parents." *Time Magazine*.

Thomson, Irene Taviss. 1989. "The Transformation of the Social Bond: Images of Individualism in the 1920s versus the 1970s." *Social Forces* 67(4):851–70.

Twenge, Jean M. 2006. *Generation Me: Why Today's Young Americans Are More Confident, Assertive, Entitled—and More Miserable Than Ever Before*. Atria Books.

Twenge, Jean M. 2013a. "The Evidence for Generation Me and against Generation We." *Emerging Adulthood* 1(1):11–16.

Twenge, Jean M. 2013b. "Overwhelming Evidence for Generation Me: A Reply to Arnett." *Emerging Adulthood* 1(1):21–26.

Verba, Sidney, Kay Lehman Scholozman, and Henry E. Brady. 1995. *Voice & Equality: Civic Voluntarism in American Politics*. Harvard University Press.

Youniss, James, Susan Bales, Verona Christmas-Best, Marcelo Diversi, Milbrey McLaughlin, and Rainer Silbereisen. 2002. "Youth Civic Engagement in the Twenty-First Century." *Journal of Research on Adolescence* 12(1):121–48.

Youniss, James, Jeffrey A. Mclellan, and Barbara Mazer. 2001. "Voluntary Service, Peer Group Orientation, and Civic Engagement." *Journal of Adolescent Research* 16(5):456–68.

Youniss, James. 2009. "Why We Need to Learn More about Youth Civic Engagement." *Social Forces* 88(2):971–75.

CONCLUSION

Social Changes & Pathways to Adulthood

The final figure is a word cloud of all the prior chapters, showing the most common words. As the word cloud shows, this book summarizes trends regarding young people and the life course by contextualizing them within social changes. In particular, diversity of family formation, elongated education, and social class dynamics are important for understanding emerging adult organizational participation and its implications on adulthood trajectories. The key takeaway of this book is that rising complexity resulting from historical social differentiation means growing up is a more complicated process than it used to be. Emerging adults have a range of options available to them. But hidden behind these new choices are remaining social inequalities. Young people establish adulthood patterns via a combination of individual preferences and social structures that pattern the options most available to them.

TROUBLING PASTS

Taking stock of the historical trends, there is a great deal to appreciate in this wonderful day and country, and at the same time there have been some troubling trends occurring over time: bifurcating inequalities, divorce and cohabitation, economic reconfiguration, disconnection.

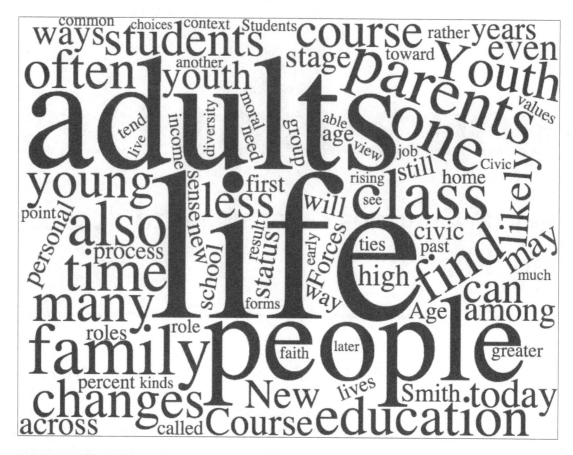

FIGURE C.1 Word Cloud

COMPLEX PATHS

While adulthood trajectories are diverse and non-normative, what is ubiquitously the case is that there is not one simple path into adulthood. Understanding emerging adults means recognizing multiplicity.

OPTIMISTIC POTENTIALS

The upside is that millennial emerging adults are best equipped to navigate this complexity. With reflection on themselves in social context, they can lead us all to a better tomorrow.

ACKNOWLEDGMENTS

Social science is a social process. Many people contributed to the existence of this text, and the thoughts preceding it. I am indebted to the insights and data produced by scholars studying emerging adults, the life course, and social change more generally. While I retain responsibility for anything unclear in this text, the knowledge it contains would literally not be possible were it not for the broad "shoulders of giants" upon which I stand in summarizing their great works.

Most notably, I owe a special thanks to Jeffrey Arnett for journeying to the University of Arkansas and asking me the wonderful question: "What would a sociologist have to say about this?" We decided, in the midst of the engaging discussion that followed, that Arnett is what I would call a "sociologically friendly psychologist," and I a "psychologically friendly sociologist." At the intersection between our two disciplines lies a burgeoning body of scholarship that has yet remained unincorporated in most traditional sociology textbooks. The realization of how little was available out there to summarize what many sociologists would and already have said about emerging adulthood spurred this text's creation. For that, I thank Jeffrey. There are a myriad of responses to his question, and I contribute one version of summarizing their answers.

I am also thankful to the publisher for providing a streamlined format to publication that draws from the best of contemporary technology, and to Adam Pope for editing and spurring needed clarifications.

Through this rather unique platform, we are able to offer an accessible way for emerging adults and others to have updated information without paying dearly for it. Support for the structural time to read and write portions of this text were graciously provided by the IUPUI Lilly School of Philanthropy Lake Institute and the colleague I have found there in David King. Thanks to Chris Smith for contributing in countless ways to this, and to me. Mil gracias.

For numerous forms of reinforcement, I am incredibly grateful to the support of my Department Chair, Anna Zajicek. It is with her unending support, cheer, and inspiration that I pursued this project, and enjoyed it. I am also most grateful to Shauna Morimoto, Heather Price, and Jared Peifer for being conversation partners in sorting through the complexities, while seeking balance between nuance and synthesis. Whatever faults remain in that regard are my own, as the result is already considerably improved from their input. I am also thankful to colleagues who have generously given their time and attention to discussing emerging adulthood or social change topics, sharing insights and opportunities for thought-provoking discussions. There are too many to name, but those in most recent years include Yvette Murphy-Erby, Casey Harris, Brandon Jackson, Bill Schwab, Song Yang, Juan Bustamante, Steven Worden, Lori Holyfield, Kevin Fitzpatrick, Brent Smith, Shaun Thomas, Mindy Bradley, Rod Engen, Doug Adams, Marcella Thompson, Natalia Karnes, Barbara Fitzpatrick, Hilary Davidson, Nicolette Manglos-Weber, Melinda Denton, and Lisa Pearce.

Umpteen emerging adults have participated in ways they are acutely aware of and in so many ways they may never know in the formation of this text. I am most grateful for collaborations with students along the way, including Christina Williams, DeAndre' Terrell Beadle, Stephanie Collier, Tatianna Balis, Tiffany Hood, Grant King, Connor Thompson, Sanjana Venugopal, and other students at the University of Arkansas for prompting me to share my research curiosities and to distill the mosaic of contemporary scholarship in forms other than journal articles. To Ashley Snell: Thank you for sharing your authenticity and for holding up a humbling mirror reflecting an image of the society we are passing on to coming generations. It is the bumps in your road that willed my hands to type into the wee hours, and most surely which set me on this journey in the first place.

Through all the moments of this process, I owe everything to my parents and family. We are not immune to the social changes surrounding families, and the troubles they sometimes bring, but we have managed to keep a sense of togetherness across the many miles, moves, and cities between us. Thank you for continuing to find creative means to stay bonded across space and time, and for being my first teachers. I especially am grateful for the loving support of my husband, who even in the midst of our independent work lives reminds me daily that we can carve a new path together. To my kids, I write this book for you, in the hopes that the years between it and your own emerging adulthood relegate this to a work of history in a considerably brighter future.

GLOSSARY

Achievement Gap: Disparities in a number of educational measures between the performance levels of subgroups of students, often evidencing marked differences based on income or wealth, race and ethnicity, and gender.

Achievement Attitude: An attitude that is oriented toward achievement, typically in academics but also in life. Believing that it is important to achieve educational goals.

Adolescence: A life stage corresponding to the years popularly known as the teens. Adolescents are teenagers.

Adulthood Roles: Traditional markers demarcating someone as an adult, typically including completing education, establishing long-term employment, getting married, and having children, and usually thought to happen in that order.

Adulthood Transitions: Understood sociologically to be an intersection of structure and agency, meaning they reflect individual choices made in reference to changing social contexts, available social and economic resources, and different social experiences.

Age of Identity: A name for emerging adulthood that highlights the inward, self-focus of this stage in the life course when people typically rely upon themselves as the source of authority for what they should be and do.

Agrarian Societies: Societies whose primary economy is agricultural. In sociology, this is often referred to historically, as a societal mode that existed in the period prior to industrialized societies.

Anomie: A state of normlessness when an individual is detached from mainstream social institutions.

Aptitude: Cognitive ability, as typically measured by standardized tests.

Baby Boomers: Generational term referring to people born roughly between 1946 and 1964.

Churning: Rapid turnover in employment and educational statuses.

Civil Society: Activities in public sector and the economy and which form the basis of democratic societies.: Cohabitation: A living situation that involves two people who are romantically involved and not married.

Collective Action: Social behaviors with the intention of benefiting large numbers of people and which are undertaken by large groups of people or by people acting through organized channels of social interaction to cause change.

Congregations: A term referring to a religious organization that is primarily involved in worship services, and which is more inclusive than the term churches, which refers only to Christian worship sites.

Culture / Cultural Knowledge: The values, norms, and material goods that characterize a society, a time period, or a subgroup of people. Information on the rules of engagement for social roles, statuses, and positions.

Denomination: A religious sect that is institutionalized and organizes the theology, rituals, and other characteristics of many religious congregations.

Deviance: Behaviors which do not conform to dominate social norms and which are considered to be unusual and often undesirable by the majority of a given society during a specific historical period.

Disconnected Youth: Young people who are disconnected from all mainstream social roles associated with adulthood. While most emerging adults have not acquired all the social roles associated with adulthood—such as completing education, establishing long-term careers, and forming families—some emerging adults are in the vulnerable position of not having transitioned into any adulthood roles.

Disordered Adulthood: Process of transitioning to adulthood that describes contemporary emerging adulthood in which variation is the norm, and people become adults through a wide array of pathways in terms of when, how, and in what order they establish adult roles—such as completing education, obtaining a job, and forming families.

Emerging Adulthood: A relatively new life stage that begins after adolescence and before young adulthood, roughly corresponding to the ages eighteen to thirty or perhaps up to thirty-five.

Emerging Adults: Individuals who are not as dependent upon their parents as when teenagers and who have not yet fully settled into adulthood roles, which generally is the case for people in their 20s.

Extra-Familial Adults: Supportive adults outside of immediate families, especially support gained from leaders in business, educational, religious, philanthropic, or civic organizations.

Gen Xers: Generational term referring to people born roughly between 1965 and 1980.

Generational Disconnects: Conflicts that can be experienced interpersonally between generations interacting in the same social setting or that can be displayed in public representations of different generations. Changes over time mean that different generations can hold distinct cultural viewpoints. Different generational perspectives can lead to confusions and misrepresentations. As with other forms of cultural diversity, social conflicts can occur when people presume similar cultural perspectives when groups can and do have different social norms, goals, or values.

Heterogeneous: Groups with different experiences; diverse groups.

Homogeneous: Groups with similar experiences; groups without noticeable diversity.

Industrial Revolution: Historical time period beginning toward the end of the 1800s that shifted the primary economy of Western societies from farming to manufacturing.

Industrialization: The process of societies becoming further based on manufacturing, machine-based modes of production.

Industrialized Societies: Societies whose primary economy is manufacturing, production lines, factories. In sociology, this term often refers to a societal configuration existing in time after agrarian societies.

Life Course / Life Course Capital: The progression of stages that people transition into and out of as they age. Knowledge about how to minimize exposure to risks, navigate challenges, and receive best social outcomes.

Macro Sociology: Studying large-scale social groups, such as social institutions or social systems.

Meso Sociology: Studying intermediary, medium-scale social groups, such as social organizations.

Micro Sociology: Studying small-scale, interpersonal social groups or dynamics, such as relationships or personal experiences.: Millennials: Generational term referring to people born after or around 1980 who represent the first generation to grow up entirely since the widespread availability of the Internet and, in formative years, the widespread availability of smart phones and Wi-Fi enabling constant connection.

Modal Path for Adult Transitions: The pathway to adulthood with the largest single majority of young people; refers to the sequencing of acquiring adulthood roles that composes the mode.

Mode of Production: The primary economic system, such as agriculture or manufacturing.

Modern: Historical time period associated with industrialized, manufacturing societies.

Norm (Social): An expectation for socially acceptable behavior.

Normative Pathway into Adulthood: An expected sequence for assuming adulthood roles that is thought to characterize how most young people become adults, which has typically been thought to be complete education, establish long-term work, get married, and have a baby.

Postmodern: A historical time period associated with service economies that developed after societies were first industrialized.

Premodern: Historical time period associated with agrarian societies.

Psychological Approach: A social science approach that focuses on the personal, neurobiological, and individual elements explaining outcomes, behaviors, and intentions.

Recentering: A life course process typically engaged during emerging adulthood when people reevaluate the social norms they took for granted during their childhood. They may experience conflict with their parents or other important socializers from their childhood as they consider alternative perspectives.

Self-Focus: A central characteristic of emerging adulthood that involves young people turning inward and focusing most of their energy on trying to establish who they are and what they want, constructing and reconstructing their self-identity.

Self-Perceived Adulthood: Perceiving oneself to be an adult, perhaps regardless of age, adulthood markers, or whether or not others perceive one to be an adult.

Service- or Knowledge-Based Societies: Societies with economies based mostly in providing services or producing knowledge. In sociology, this term often refers to societal configurations that occurred in time after industrialized societies.

Silent Generation: Generational term referring to people born roughly between 1928 and 1945.

Social Class: A group of people who share similar economic circumstances, lifestyles, and consumptive patterns.

Social Differentiation: Rise in smaller social groups marking distinctions among people. Postindustrial society is characterized by many more social groups and various options for social life, less commonality.

Social Process of Science: Social changes in knowledge as interpretive paradigms shift and new data are collected; often characterized by a new idea that is not widely accepted, then mounting evidence in support of the new idea, and then more widespread adoption of the new paradigm until it eventually becomes more commonplace knowledge.

Social Structure: Organized patterns of relationships that are built collectively by people and which then become taken for granted as normal, patterning social actions without conscious attention.

Socialization / Socializing Institutions: The process of being taught and internalizing social norms into personal expectations and behaviors. Examples of later-life socializing institutions are marriage and parenthood.

Socioeconomic Status (SES): Social and economic position people hold within the social stratification system.

Sociological Imagination: Connection of personal troubles and public issues; seeing individuals within social contexts.

Sociological Approach: A social science approach that focuses on the social, relational, and structural factors explaining outcomes, behaviors, and intentions.

Value (Social): An ideal, something that people want, that is considered socially desirable.:

CPSIA information can be obtained
at www.ICGtesting.com
Printed in the USA
LVHW03s2059170818
587305LV00011B/77/P